Preventing and Reducing

JUVENILE DELINQUENCY

SECOND EDITION

To my dear mom, Ethel Howell, the sweetest mother on Earth

Preventing and Reducing

JUVENILE DELINQUENCY

A Comprehensive Framework

SECOND EDITION

James C. Howell

⑤SAGE

Los Angeles • London • New Delhi • Singapore • Washington DC

For information:

SAGE Publications, Inc.
2455 Teller Road
Thousand Oaks, California 91320
E-mail: order@sagepub.com

SAGE Publications Ltd.
 1 Oliver's Yard
55 City Road
London EC1Y 1SP
United Kingdom

SAGE Publications India Pvt. Ltd.
B 1/I 1 Mohan Cooperative Industrial Area
Mathura Road, New Delhi 110 044
India

SAGE Publications Asia-Pacific Pte Ltd
33 Pekin Street #02-01
Far East Square
Singapore 048763

Printed in the United States of America

Library of Congress Cataloging-in-Publication Data

Howell, James C.
Preventing and reducing juvenile delinquency : a comprehensive framework/
James C. Howell.—2nd ed.
    p. cm.
Includes bibliographical references and index.
ISBN 978-1-4129-5638-3 (pbk.)
1. Juvenile delinquency—United States—Prevention. 2. Youth and violence—United States—Prevention. 3. Violent crimes—United States—Prevention. 4. Juvenile delinquents—Rehabilitation—United States.
I. Title.

HV9104.H76 2009
364.36—dc22   2008010388

This book is printed on acid-free paper.

08   09   10   11   12   10   9   8   7   6   5   4   3   2   1

Acquisitions Editor:	Jerry Westby
Editorial Assistant:	Eve Oettinger
Production Editor:	Catherine M. Chilton
Copy Editor:	Carol Anne Peschke
Typesetter:	C&M Digitals (P) Ltd.
Proofreader:	Doris Hus
Indexer:	Diggs Publication Services
Cover Designer:	Bryan Fishman
Marketing Manager:	Christy Guilbault

Brief Contents

Contents

Preface

I t is useful for readers to know the historical context of this book. The United States is currently approaching the 40th year of a general emphasis on punishment as the main instrument of criminal justice policy. The main impact of this trend on the criminal justice system can be viewed in the imprisonment trend line (Chapter 11, Figure 11.3). Of course, the "get tough on crime" movement worked insofar as increased imprisonment was the immediate objective. A prison-building binge naturally followed (Schlosser, 1998). Unfortunately, parole was largely abolished at the same time. Predictably, the current crisis is the return of adult inmates to society in droves and unrehabilitated—as many as 700,000 of them each year (Sabol, Minton, & Harrison, 2007).

Juvenile justice policies were influenced significantly by the punishment trend in the criminal justice system (Mears, 2006) but not to the extent of the criminal justice apparatus. A major factor is a "habit of the heart" that continues to guide juvenile justice (Cullen, Bose, Jonson, & Unnever, 2007), meaning that most adults are unwavering in their belief that juveniles can be rehabilitated—from personal experience if nothing else. Yet the juvenile justice system was severely affected by the punishment trend in the adult system, because it is joined at the hip to the criminal justice system (by police and prosecutors on the front end), and by ill-informed outsiders who concocted an imaginary forthcoming horde of juvenile "superpredators" and a "wave" of violence, creating a "bloodbath." This prospect was scary (see Chapter 1).

The federal Office of Juvenile Justice and Delinquency Prevention, where I worked at the time of the punishment surge, became concerned about the knee-jerk reactions to juvenile delinquency that were growing in the late 1980s and early 1990s. New punitive policies clearly were bringing more and more young offenders into the juvenile justice system, yet the new offenders did not seem to be more dangerous. A colleague (John J. Wilson) and I set out to formulate a balanced approach for the juvenile justice system that might appease conservatives (with graduated sanctions) and at the same time draw support from liberals for delinquency prevention and rehabilitation of juvenile offenders. We called it the Comprehensive Strategy for Serious, Violent, and Chronic Juvenile Offenders (Wilson & Howell, 1993).

This framework was developed at the height of moral panic over delinquency. U.S. Department of Justice policy at the time called for harsh sanctions for first-time juvenile offenders, a position stated in a policy paper issued by U.S. Attorney General William Barr. The policy paper contended that the best way to prevent juvenile offenders from becoming adult career criminals is

> by imposing tough, smart sanctions that are carefully tailored for the first-time juvenile offender. . . . Such punishment actually benefits the juvenile more than lenient sanctions, or no sanctions at all. Excessive leniency can result in additional transgressions, culminating in a life of crime. . . . A juvenile justice system that is too lenient can become, in effect, a conveyor belt for career criminals. (McBride, Scott, Schlesinger, Dillingham, & Buckman, 1992, p. 26)

The policy paper recommended that states "establish a range of tough juvenile sanctions that emphasize discipline and responsibility to deter nonviolent first-time offenders from further crimes. . . . These sanctions should include the option of institutional settings. . . . One possibility is boot camps" (McBride et al., 1992, p. 27). In addition, the policy paper recommended that those making up the small group of chronic violent juvenile offenders should be treated as adults, contending that they "are as hardened as any adult offender" (p. 28).

The Comprehensive Strategy shifted the U.S. Department of Justice's orientation to include prevention and its intervention policy to give priority to juvenile offenders who have histories of serious or violent offenses. This position was based on self-report studies showing that only a fraction of all juvenile offenders are serious chronic offenders (Elliott, Huizinga, & Morse, 1986) or violent offenders (Hamparian, Schuster, Dinitz, & Conrad, 1978). The attorney general's policy paper ignored the issue of prevention; in contrast, the Comprehensive Strategy placed top priority on prevention, especially through the strengthening of social institutions, beginning with families.

Needless to say, the Comprehensive Strategy was not released from the U.S. Department of Justice until the value of a balanced approach was seen. It was then implemented, at least in part, in more than 50 localities in 20 states across the country.

This book contains information that students of juvenile justice, laypersons, lawmakers, policy makers, and practitioners should find useful in designing strategic plans that address juvenile delinquency. Part I begins with an examination of the myths about juvenile delinquency and the juvenile justice system (Chapter 1) and the ensuing moral panic these myths stimulated (Chapter 2). Both of these phenomena are contrasted with empirical data on juvenile delinquency trends (Chapter 3), demonstrating that neither the myths nor panic was justified.

The chapters in Part II feature the research base on juvenile delinquency and gang activity. I present a research-based theory of delinquency and gang involvement in Chapter 4. It is followed by reviews of the research on juvenile offender careers (Chapter 5) and youth gangs (Chapter 6). This section concludes with a review of research-based programs for addressing gang problems (Chapter 7).

Part III features the Comprehensive Strategy framework (Chapter 10), which can be used to design and reform juvenile justice systems. It is important to recognize that the Comprehensive Strategy is not a prescriptive program; rather, it is a self-empowering framework that guides states, cities, and communities in assessing their own delinquency and gang problems and selecting their own solutions from the array of evidence-based programs and strategies.

My presentation of the Comprehensive Strategy is preceded by an overview of the latest research on principles and characteristics of evidence-based programs (Chapter 8), followed by the most effective services (Chapter 9). The Comprehensive Strategy continuum from prevention to reentry is then illustrated with programs and strategies. The book concludes with current information on what doesn't work in preventing and reducing juvenile delinquency and gang problems (Chapter 11). The final chapter examines in detail the worst practice in the "get tough on juveniles" movement: the transfer of juveniles to the criminal justice system.

A personal disclaimer is in order: To pretend that I am a dispassionate observer of the juvenile justice system would be misleading. The juvenile court system in the United States was founded on the recognition that children are not little adults and, in all justice and fairness, should not be treated as such (Tanenhaus, 2004). Because of their diminished capacity, deviant children and adolescents should be given room to reform, to keep their life chances intact. Thus the juvenile justice system was created as an alternative to the harsh, punishment-oriented criminal justice system, whose prisons serve as schools for crime and whose failure to rehabilitate criminal offenders disqualifies it as a model that should be used for juvenile offenders. The juvenile court is a unique American invention in the late 19th century that has since been replicated around the world. As Zimring (2002) notes, "No developed nation tries its youngest offenders in its regular criminal courts.... No legal institution in Anglo-American legal history has achieved such universal acceptance among the diverse legal systems of the industrialized democracies" (p. 142). How a society treats its young is an important measure of its claim to civilization. Juvenile courts are a cornerstone of our society.

Acknowledgments

I would be remiss if I did not personally express a debt of appreciation to several colleagues who contributed directly or indirectly to this book. John J. Wilson, former head of the OJJDP, earned my respect for several things. His steadfast support of the principles and legal requirements of the Juvenile Justice and Delinquency Prevention Act of 1974 is admirable. He remains the strongest advocate of juvenile justice that I have had the pleasure of knowing. His example inspired me during my tenure at OJJDP and made my collegial work with him all the more rewarding. As I explain in the preface to this book, we collaborated in developing the Comprehensive Strategy for Serious, Violent, and Chronic Juvenile Offenders. We regularly communicate on important developments in juvenile justice and continue to collaborate whenever the opportunity presents itself.

Mark Lipsey helped me understand meta-analysis and the strengths and weaknesses of various approaches to moving research into practice. He recently created the Standardized Program Evaluation Protocol for this purpose. It is an evidence-based tool that scores current programs against research-based guidelines with uncanny precision, which I never even imagined would be possible. This brilliant creation of his has the potential to advance evidence-based programming in juvenile justice by leaps and bounds because it can be applied on a statewide basis using automated client tracking data. This unique system permits program evaluations at will. I'm thrilled to be a partner in his pioneering work. In all fairness, he should be credited as co-author of Chapters 8 and 9 of this book.

John P. Moore, director of the National Youth Gang Center, has created an environment at the center that gives me many opportunities for rewarding gang research, on both the underlying causes of gang involvement and practical solutions to gang problems. Col. Moore (I address him thus out of respect for his distinguished career of public service in military intelligence) ingenuously led skilled technicians at our parent organization (the Institute for Intergovernmental Research) in creating a prototype Internet-based application for communities to use in strategic planning to address gang and delinquency problems (the Strategic Planning Tool: http://www.iir.com/nygc/tool/). Led by the White House, nine federal agencies collaborated in expanding our prototype into the tool that is now available, the *Helping America's Youth Community Guide* (http://guide.helping americasyouth.gov/). I have provided guidance to students in using it in conjunction with material in Chapters 7–10. First Lady Laura Bush has introduced the *Community Guide* across the United States in regional gatherings. For the first time in history, a user-friendly yet evidence-based tool is accessible on the Internet that any community can use, free of charge, to guide an assessment of their own delinquency and gang problems and build a continuum of research-based programs.

My presentation of gang research in this book has benefited enormously from work with other colleagues at the National Youth Gang Center, Arlen Egley and Christina O'Donnell, and also David Curry at the University of Missouri, St. Louis, and Deborah Weisel at North Carolina State University. I also owe a special debt of gratitude to Marcus Felson, who kindly assisted me in presentations of his brilliant insights into youth gangs.

The entire juvenile justice field is indebted to Rolf Loeber (Pittsburgh), Terry Thornberry (Rochester), and David Huizinga (Denver) as the directors of the three major U.S. longitudinal studies of the causes and correlates of delinquency (see "In Focus" Box 5.1 in Chapter 5). These studies were launched 20 years ago by the OJJDP, in its Program of Research on the Causes and Correlates of Delinquency. These three landmark studies are the most comprehensive prospective studies of the causes and correlates of juvenile delinquency in the world. More than 200 published reports have emanated from them, and I draw on a number of them in this book. In this connection, I am honored to serve as special advisor to the Life History Research Program at the University of Pittsburgh that Rolf and Magda Stouthamer-Loeber expertly direct. They recently began the third longitudinal project in their Life History Research Program, the Pittsburgh Girls Study (http://www.wpic .pitt.edu/research/famhist/index.htm). All four of these great scholars have generously assisted me in my research for this book.

Many others have kindly facilitated my research for this book. David Farrington ("Sir David," I prefer to call him) thoughtfully provides me copies of his outstanding scholarly works. Among his many criminology hats, Prof. Farrington is past president of the American Society of Criminology. He and his co-author in systematic reviews to identify evidence-based programs, Brandon Welsh, have generously supplied me with their valuable and numerous publications.

Dan Oates, library director, and Suzanne Sinclair, librarian, Health Sciences Library, First Health of the Carolinas, in Pinehurst, North Carolina, assisted my research greatly by obtaining publications from other libraries and various sources.

I also thank the outside reviewers for valuable feedback on the first edition of this book. These thoughtful people included Kelly Asmussen, Lee Ellen Ayers, Colleen Clarke, Dorinda Dowis, Price Foster, Denise Herz, David Kotajarvi, Alfred Montalvo, and Sean Varano. In addition, Russell Smandych volunteered some particularly helpful suggestions.

I owe a special debt of gratitude to Secretary George Sweat, North Carolina Department of Juvenile Justice; Rob Lubitz, Director, Juvenile Justice Services Division, Arizona Administrative Office of the Courts; and Steven Hornsby, Deputy Commissioner for Juvenile Justice, Tennessee Department of Children's Services. These visionary gentlemen gave me and Mark Lipsey the opportunity to work with them in developing and pilot testing his Standardized Program Evaluation Protocol. Because of their unwavering commitment to effective juvenile justice programs and to a comprehensive system, the experience of working with them gave vitality to this book.

I am indebted to my wife and life-course partner, Karen, for her steadfast support of my work and for her genuine interest in it. I also continually benefit professionally from a close, collegial relationship with our daughter, Megan, a research assistant and data analyst in the North Carolina Department of

Juvenile Justice and Delinquency Prevention, particularly from her keen eye for important developments in the field.

As is the case with any researcher's book, this one draws on other research that I have published since the first edition, in particular the following works:

Howell, J. C. (2003). Diffusing research into practice using the Comprehensive Strategy for Serious, Violent, and Chronic Juvenile Offenders. *Youth Violence and Juvenile Justice, 1,* 219–245.

Howell, J. C. (2006). *The impact of gangs on communities.* NYGC Bulletin No. 2. Tallahassee, FL: National Youth Gang Center.

Howell, J. C. (2007). Menacing or mimicking? Realities of youth gangs. *The Juvenile and Family Court Journal, 58,* 9–20.

Howell, J. C., & Egley, A. Jr. (2005). *Gangs in small towns and rural counties.* NYGC Bulletin No. 1. Tallahassee, FL: National Youth Gang Center.

Howell, J. C., & Egley, A. Jr. (2005). Moving risk factors into developmental theories of gang membership. *Youth Violence and Juvenile Justice, 3,* 334–354.

Howell, J. C., & Howell, M. Q. (2007). Violent juvenile delinquency: Changes, consequences, and implications. In D. Flannery, A. Vazonsyi, & I. Waldman (Eds.), *Cambridge handbook of violent behavior* (pp. 501–518). Cambridge, MA: Cambridge University Press.

Weisel, D. L., & Howell, J. C. (2007). *Comprehensive gang assessment: A report to the Durham Police Department and Durham County Sheriff's Office.* Durham, NC: Durham Police Department.

I gratefully acknowledge these publishers for my use of material in this book.

James C. (Buddy) Howell
Pinehurst, North Carolina

PART I

The Historical Context of Current Juvenile Justice System Policies and Practices

This first section provides some historical context for an understanding of current juvenile justice system policies and practices. The chapters in Part I present an overview of juvenile delinquency from three perspectives. Chapter 1 considers several key myths about juvenile violence and the ability of the juvenile justice system to handle modern day juvenile delinquents. The "superpredator" myth—that a new breed of juvenile offenders emerged in the late 1980s and the 1990s—is a predominant one examined in the chapter. Chapter 2 examines the current moral panic over juvenile delinquency and the consequences of this so-called crisis for both juvenile offenders and juvenile justice system operations. The chapter shows that this moral panic has created a crisis in juvenile justice system policies and practices. Chapter 3 examines serious and violent juvenile delinquency trends from 1980 to the present and addresses the distinguishing features of serious and violent juvenile delinquency to help put these forms into proper perspective. This chapter presents an analysis of delinquency trends as indicated by three main data sources: official records, victimization reports, and self-reports of delinquency involvement. Technical terms are defined in the Glossary (beginning on p. 333).

CHAPTER 1

Superpredators and Other Myths About Juvenile Delinquency

The juvenile justice field is littered with myths, for no apparent reason. This chapter explores key myths that have been promoted recently. First, what is a myth? Bernard (1992) describes myths as "beliefs about the past that are strongly held and convenient to believe but are based on little actual information. Myths are not necessarily false—people generally just don't know or care whether they are true or false. They hold the belief because it is convenient to do so" (p. 11) ("In Focus" Box 1.1). We begin this chapter by focusing on the most bizarre myth ever perpetrated about juvenile delinquency—the "superpredator"—after which other popular myths are discussed.

IN FOCUS 1.1

Myths About Juvenile Delinquency

The following are some common myths about juvenile delinquency (Bernard, 1992, p. 12):

- **The myth of progress:** *Delinquency in the past was much more serious than it is today.* Few people believe this myth; rather, they fear that if they let their guard down, delinquency will get worse.

(Continued)

> (Continued)
>
> - **The myth that nothing changes:** *Delinquency in the past was about the same as it is today.* More people believe this myth than believe the first one. It is supported by the view that delinquency is part and parcel of human nature—"boys will be boys."
> - **The myth of the good old days:** *Delinquency in the past was much less serious than it is today.* More people probably believe this myth than believe the first and second ones combined. This myth is true some of the time and false at other times. The view that delinquency was better controlled at one time implies that simple solutions (quick fixes) should solve the problems associated with juvenile delinquency today.

The Juvenile Superpredator Myth

A professor of politics and public affairs on the political science faculty at Princeton University, John DiIulio, created and popularized the super-predator concept. He coined the term *superpredator* (1995b) to call public attention to what he characterized as a "new breed" of offenders, "kids that have absolutely no respect for human life and no sense of the future. . . . These are stone-cold predators!" (p. 23). Elsewhere, DiIulio and co-authors have described these young people as "fatherless, Godless, and jobless" and as "radically impulsive, brutally remorseless youngsters, including ever more teenage boys, who murder, assault, rob, burglarize, deal deadly drugs, join gun-toting gangs, and create serious [linked] disorders" (Bennett, DiIulio, & Walters, 1996, p. 27).

The superpredator myth gained further popularity when it was linked to forecasts by James Q. Wilson and John DiIulio of increased levels of juvenile violence. Wilson (1995) asserted that "by the end of [the past] decade [i.e., by 2000] there will be a million more people between the ages of 14 and 17 than there are now. . . . Six percent of them will become high rate, repeat offenders—thirty thousand more young muggers, killers and thieves than we have now. Get ready" (p. 507). DiIulio (1995a, p. 15) made the same prediction. Media portrayals of juvenile superpredators have created the impression that juveniles are most likely to be armed—heavily armed—and to use guns in attacks.

A year later, DiIulio (1996a) pushed the horizon back 10 years and raised the ante, projecting that "by the year 2010, there will be approximately 270,000 more juvenile super-predators on the streets than there were in 1990" (p. 1). DiIulio based his projection of 270,000 on two factors. First, he assumed that the 6% figure that the Philadelphia Birth Cohort Study found in relation to Philadelphia boys who were chronic offenders in the 1960s would remain constant. Second, he factored this figure in with projections of the growth of the juvenile population made by the U.S. Bureau of the Census. According to these projections, the ages 0–17 population group in the United States was expected to grow by 14% (4.5 million) between 1996 and 2010 (Box 1.2).

DiIulio (1996b) warned that juvenile superpredators would be "flooding the nation's streets," coming "at us in waves over the next 20 years. . . . Time is running out" (p. 25). He also used inflammatory language, warning, "We must therefore be prepared to contain the ['crime bomb'] explosion's force and limit its damage" (DiIulio, 1995a, p. 15). However, he expressed hopelessness, saying, "This crime bomb probably cannot be defused," and asserting that the superpredators would be here within 5 years (i.e., by the year 2000) (p. 15). They never arrived.

Two other criminologists contributed to DiIulio's exaggeration. Speaking at a meeting of the American Association for the Advancement of Science, Fox warned of a "bloodbath" of teen violence (quoted in Associated Press, 1996). He also warned elsewhere of a juvenile "crime wave storm" (Fox, 1996a). In a report to the U.S. attorney general, Fox (1996b) said, "Our nation faces a future juvenile violence problem that may make today's epidemic pale in comparison" (p. 3). He called attention in particular to the projected growth in the black teenage population (ages 14–17), which would increase 26% by 2005. He also issued a warning: "There is, however, still time to stem the tide, and to avert the coming wave of teen violence. But time is of the essence" (p. i).

Blumstein's (1995a, 1995b, 1996) analysis showed that the homicide rates among juveniles, the numbers of gun homicides, and the arrest rates of nonwhite juveniles for drug offenses all doubled in the late 1980s and early 1990s, and he tied these three findings together around the "crack cocaine epidemic" of that era (Campbell & Reeves, 1994; Hartman & Golub, 1999). Blumstein contended that youngsters who joined the illicit drug industry felt it necessary to carry guns for self-protection from other armed juvenile drug sellers, and that the spread of guns among adolescents and young adults led to violent crimes and growth in the homicide rate among these age groups. It is interesting to note that in Canada, juvenile homicide rates increased sharply in the mid- to late 1980s without the presence of any crack cocaine epidemic (Hagan & Foster, 2000). Blumstein also feared that the youth violence epidemic would continue with the growth of the young population and warned that "children who are now younger (about ages 5 to 15) represent the future problem" (Blumstein, 1996, p. 2; see also Blumstein & Rosenfeld, 1999, pp. 161–162).

Where Did the Superpredators Go?

The short answer is that the large cadre of superpredators that DiIulio described never existed, and the growth of this mythical group never happened. Several researchers have debunked the superpredator myth and doomsday projections (Howell, 1998c; Males, 1996; Snyder, 1998; Snyder & Sickmund, 2000; Zimring, 1998a). The illogical nature of DiIulio's projection is readily apparent. He assumed that 6% of babies and children as well as juveniles would be chronic offenders (see Zimring, 1996). If we were to apply the 6% figure to the 1996 population under age 18, according to DiIulio's analysis, there already were 1.9 million superpredator juvenile offenders in the United States. This number is larger than the total number of children and adolescents referred to juvenile courts each year. Wilson and DiIulio were guilty of other errors in logic (see Zimring, 1998a, pp. 61–65).

In addition, DiIulio and Wilson apparently were not aware that the majority of the 6% "chronic" offenders in the Philadelphia Birth Cohort Study were never arrested for a serious violent crime (Weitekamp, Kerner, Schindler, & Schubert, 1995). The 6% figure was based on police contacts, not actual arrests. In fact, only one-third of the police contacts resulted in an arrest, and only half of this group's police contacts resulted in a court adjudication of delinquency (Bernard & Ritti, 1991). This oversight exaggerated further the potential dangerousness of future juvenile offenders.

DiIulio, Fox, and Wilson also made the mistake of assuming a direct correlation between population size and crime rates. As Cook and Laub (1998) have shown, the size of the juvenile population "is of little help in predicting violence rates" (p. 59). In fact, they found a negative relationship between the size of the juvenile population and the number of homicides in the late 1980s and early 1990s. That is, the high juvenile homicide rates of this period occurred when the size of the adolescent population was low. Juvenile homicides and other violent crimes are decreasing, while the size of the juvenile population is increasing. In fact, the end of the period covered in the doomsday projections (1995–2010) of waves of juvenile violence is near, and juvenile violence decreased from 1994 to 2005 (Butts & Snyder, 2006; Snyder & Sickmund, 2006). For a decade (through 2004), juvenile Violent Crime Index offenses decreased, proving that DiIulio, Wilson, and Fox were seriously wrong in their forecasts (Butts & Snyder, 2006; Butts & Travis, 2002). Specifically, between 1994 and 2004, the juvenile arrest rate for Violent Crime Index offenses fell 49% (Snyder, 2006). As a result, the juvenile Violent Crime Index arrest rate in 2004 was at its lowest level since at least 1980. From its peak in 1993 to 2004, the juvenile arrest rate for murder fell 77% (Snyder, 2006).

Forecasting juvenile delinquency rates—and adult crime rates, for that matter—is risky business. As McCord, Widom, and Crowell (2001) note, criminologists' capacity to forecast crime rates is very limited, and "errors in forecasts over even relatively short periods of two to three years, let alone for a decade or more, are very large" (p. 65). When observers attempt to make such forecasts, they should be careful to include both warnings about the inherent inaccuracy of projected estimates in this area and cautions about the limited appropriate use of such estimates. In addition, juvenile justice policy makers should guard against giving much credence to forecasts made by reputed "experts" from outside the field of juvenile justice who are unfamiliar with the implications of using arrest data to measure juvenile delinquency. Uncritical acceptance of juvenile arrest data is a common problem in the juvenile justice field (Elliott, 1995, 2000).

Despite these problems with DiIulio's, Wilson's, Blumstein's, and Fox's doomsday forecasts, they were taken seriously for a number of years. Some research was even sponsored to interview young people to see how they were managing in everyday life to cope with the presumed pervasive violence (Irwin, 2004). Not surprisingly, they were managing just fine. The two images foremost in these forecasts, of "superpredators" and a growing "crime bomb," were powerful, and they played well in the broadcast media and with politicians who wanted to appear tough on juvenile crime. Several popular magazines featured stories on the predicted crime wave, and many depicted on their covers young black thugs—often gang members—holding handguns. Stories that played to readers' fears were common (e.g., Gest & Pope, 1996). Articles spoke of "baby-faced criminals" (Lyons, 1997). Fear of young people grew in the public's mind (Soler, 2001). In a national survey of parents conducted in 2000, one-third of those responding said that the threat of violence affecting their own children was a major concern (Villalva, 2000).

Studies gradually discredited the doomsday forecasts of growing numbers of superpredators, and research on juvenile offender careers proved pivotal. Snyder (1998) conducted an analysis of juvenile court referrals in Maricopa County, Arizona (the county that includes Phoenix and other, smaller cities), that produced the first empirical description of the parameters that distinguish serious, violent, and chronic juvenile offenders. There is a standing policy in Maricopa County that all youth arrested must be referred to juvenile court for screening. Therefore, the court records in that county provide complete histories of all youthful offenders' official contacts with the juvenile justice system (Snyder & Sickmund, 1999, p. 80).

Figure 1.1 illustrates the overlap of the three delinquent offender subgroups. The entire circle in the figure represents all individuals in 16 birth cohorts who were referred to juvenile courts from ages 10 through 17. Snyder (1998) found that almost two-thirds (64%) of juvenile court careers were nonchronic (fewer than four referrals) and did not include any serious or violent offenses. These offender careers are shown in the clear outer circle of Figure 1.1. Conversely, just over one-third (36%) of the delinquent careers contained serious, violent, or chronic offense histories. Nearly 18% of all careers contained serious nonviolent referrals and were nonchronic, 8% of all careers contained violent referrals but were not chronic, and slightly more than 3% of all offender careers were chronic and included serious and violent offenses. (Note that it is inappropriate to total these percentages because an individual offender can be represented in more than one career.)

In sum, about 18% of all careers included serious (but nonviolent) offenses, just 8% included violent offenses, and only 3% of the careers were serious, violent, *and* chronic. These are far smaller proportions among all delinquents than DiIulio imagined. Even given the overlap of the career types, less than a

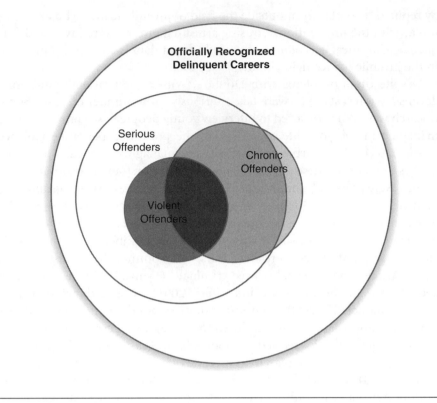

Figure 1.1 Overlap of Serious, Violent, and Chronic Offender Careers

third (29%) of the chronic offenders were also violent offenders, only about a third (35%) of the serious offenders were also chronic offenders, and about half (53%) of the violent offenders were also chronic offenders.

Other Myths About Juvenile Delinquency

Myth 1: A juvenile violence epidemic occurred in the late 1980s and early 1990s.

This is a questionable assertion. Public health scientists use the word *epidemic* to refer to particular health problems that affect numbers of the population above expected levels, but they do not specify what constitutes an "epidemic level." The evidence does not necessarily support the conclusion that there was an epidemic of overall juvenile violence in the late 1980s and early 1990s; only the increase in homicides might be considered to have reached such a level. At the height of the so-called "juvenile violence epidemic" (in 1993), "only about 6% of all juvenile arrests were for violent crimes and less than one-tenth of one percent of their arrests were for homicides" (McCord et al., 2001, p. 33).

It can properly be said that a gun homicide epidemic occurred in the late 1980s and early 1990s, and juveniles were a part of this. From 1984 through

1993, the number of juveniles killed with firearms tripled, and the number of nonfirearm homicides remained nearly constant. However, the gun homicide epidemic was by no means limited to juveniles; the biggest absolute change was for young adults (Butts et al., 2002; Cook & Laub, 1998, p. 60).

The availability of guns was the predominant factor. From 1973 through 1994, the number of guns in private ownership in the United States rose by 87 million (Malcolm, 2002), to an estimated 200 million (Reich, Culross, & Behrman, 2002). The growing number of privately owned guns continued into the new millennium, and the latest estimate is 258 million privately owned firearms, of which 93 million are handguns (Wellford, Pepper, & Petrie, 2005). Approximately 4.5 million new (i.e., not previously owned) firearms are sold each year in the United States, including 2 million handguns (Hahn et al., 2005). The estimated total number of firearms transactions ranges from 7 to 9.5 million per year, of which between 47% and 64% are new firearms.

It can also be said that a gun suicide epidemic occurred in the 1980s and early 1990s. Just as gun homicides increased, so did gun suicides. Surprisingly, for each young person murdered, another commits suicide (Snyder & Sickmund, 1999). The rate of adolescent suicides involving firearms increased 39% from 1980 through 1994, whereas the rate of suicides not involving firearms remained nearly unchanged during this period (Snyder & Sickmund, 1999). More than 20,000 juveniles committed suicide between 1981 and 1998, almost as many as were victims of homicide during the same period (Snyder & Swahn, 2004). During this period, white juveniles ages 13–17 were more likely to kill themselves than to be killed by others. Thus it would be accurate to say that an adolescent gun suicide epidemic occurred at the same time as the adolescent gun homicide epidemic, particularly among young black males. Any explanation for the increase in adolescent gun homicides in the late 1980s and early 1990s must also account for the increase in adolescent gun suicides during that period. The emergence of "superpredators" is not a plausible explanation for both phenomena. Rather, the increased availability of guns and gang growth both occurred then (see Chapter 6).

Myth 2: Juveniles frequently carry guns and traffic in them.

The increase in juvenile and young adult homicides from the mid-1980s through the mid-1990s prompted the U.S. Department of the Treasury to launch the Youth Crime Gun Interdiction Initiative (YCGII), which gathered valuable information on the ages of illegal gun carriers. Under the YCGII, the Bureau of Alcohol, Tobacco and Firearms in the Department of the Treasury supported 27 cities in developing systems that would allow them to trace all recovered crime guns. Surprisingly, nearly 9 out of 10 of the illegal guns recovered by police in the 27 cities in 1997–1998 were in the hands of adults (ages 18 and older); only 11% were recovered from juveniles (Bureau of Alcohol, Tobacco and Firearms, 1999). Nearly three times more recovered guns (32%) were in the hands of young adults, ages 18–24, than were in the hands of juveniles. Since then, federal gun interdiction initiatives have focused mainly on young adults.

Myth 3: Juvenile violence is the top crime problem in the United States.

Actually, adult violence is our nation's top crime problem. FBI data show that juveniles accounted for only 5% of the murders and only 12% of all serious violent crimes in the United States cleared by arrests in 2004 (Snyder, 2006). These figures are far below juveniles' proportional representation (19%) in the age range of the total population that commits most crime (ages 10–49) (Snyder & Sickmund, 1999). Young adult offenders ages 18–24 have the highest violent crime arrest rates (Cook & Laub, 1998), and the overwhelming majority of gun homicides and gun assaults in the United States involve adult perpetrators and victims (Cook & Ludwig, 2001).

Myth 4: Juveniles were the driving force behind the increase in violence in the United States from the mid-1980s through the early 1990s.

In reality, studies conducted by researchers at the National Center for Juvenile Justice have shown that adults, not juveniles, accounted for two-thirds of the increase in murders in the late 1980s and early 1990s, and those adults were responsible for nearly three-fourths of the increase in violent crime arrests during this period (Snyder, Sickmund, & Poe-Yamagata, 1996). Murders increased 23% from 1985 through 1994 (Snyder et al., 1996, p. 20). If murders by juveniles had remained constant over this period, murders in the United States would have increased by 15%.

Myth 5: School shootings represent a second wave of the juvenile violence that doomsday forecasters Fox and DiIulio prophesied.

School shooters do not fit the profile of mythical superpredators—or any other high-risk youth profile, for that matter. It is important to recognize that student school shooters represent only a fraction of all mass killers, a group that is overwhelmingly made up of adults (Fessenden, 2000). All types of rampage shootings increased in the 1980s and 1990s, corresponding with increased production of semiautomatic pistols (Fessenden, 2000). The extent of the panic over school shootings (see Chapter 2) is evident when one contrasts the reality of this form of violence with public perceptions of the problem. School crime did not increase in the early 1990s and has dropped since then (Brooks, Schiraldi, & Ziedenberg, 2001; Snyder & Sickmund, 1999). In fact, school-associated violent deaths dropped 40% at the end of the 1990s, and the chance that a school-aged child would die in a school was 1 in 2 million (Brooks et al., 2001). Yet 71% of people responding to a public poll in 1998 said that they thought a school shooting was likely to happen in their community. Actually, violent events in schools have declined significantly for more than a decade, at least up to 2005 (National Center for Education Statistics, 2007).

Myth 6: Juvenile offenders are committing more and more violent crimes at younger ages.

The federal Office of Juvenile Justice and Delinquency Prevention (OJJDP) Study Group on Very Young Offenders concluded that there is no empirical evidence to support this claim (Loeber & Farrington, 2001a; see also Butts & Snyder, 1997; Snyder, 1998). The proportion of all juvenile violent arrests involving children ages 10–12 remained essentially constant in the 1980s and 1990s (Snyder & Sickmund, 1999, p. 121). Just 1% of all juvenile arrests involved youth under age 10 in 2004 (Snyder, 2001, 2006).

A comparison of national self-report studies showed that the proportion of child delinquents involved in serious and violent delinquency did not change from 1976 through 1999 (Espiritu, Huizinga, Crawford, & Loeber, 2001). Yet the number of arrested child delinquents increased from 1980 through 1996 (Snyder, 2001), and law enforcement agencies referred a larger percentage of the child delinquents they arrested to the juvenile courts in 1997 than in 1988. Thus child delinquents came to constitute a large proportion (10%) of all juvenile cases by the late 1990s (Butts & Snyder, 1997; Snyder, 2001).

To resolve the "superpredator" issue, the OJJDP, in the U.S. Department of Justice, undertook a program of research to determine the size and characteristics of the worst juvenile offenders, which was spearheaded by Snyder's 1998 Maricopa County study described in Chapter 5. Snyder used that database to examine three key claims about juvenile violence that had been tied to the superpredator myth:

- That the relative proportion of serious and violent offenders among all juvenile delinquents is growing
- That juvenile offenders are becoming younger
- That juveniles are committing more and more violent crimes

None of these assumptions proved to be correct. An Arizona study (Snyder, 1998) showed that the proportion of chronic offender careers increased by only 4% from the 1980s to the 1990s. Moreover, the worst offenders in the latter period were not significantly more active, more serious, or more violent. Second, there was no evidence that the juveniles in his study were beginning their court careers at younger ages. Third, no increase was found in the numbers of crimes for which serious and violent offenders were charged. Rather, Snyder found that the juvenile justice system may be spreading its net wider, bringing in more juveniles, not more serious juvenile offenders. Other research shows that the proportion of children under 13 involved in delinquency has not changed much over the past two decades (Espiritu et al., 2001).

Myth 7: The juvenile justice system in the United States is a failure; it is collapsing because it cannot handle today's more serious offenders.

In the midst of the moral panic over delinquency, such unusually critical statements were made about the juvenile courts—including charges that they are "kiddie courts," too lenient, and quaint, and that probation is a farce (Butterfield, 1997)—that some critics proposed scrapping them altogether (see Chapter 12). The notion that the juvenile justice system has become ineffective is based on the following three assumptions (Tracy & Kempf-Leonard, 1998):

- Sanctions in juvenile courts are neither certain enough nor severe enough to deter serious delinquents from continually committing serious crimes.
- The rehabilitative techniques used by juvenile courts have not sufficiently reduced recidivism (i.e., returning to criminal activity).
- The preponderance of noncustodial sanctions (such as probation) and the very short institutional sanctions that are applied allow delinquents to pose a continued and severe risk to public safety.

These and other related myths about the juvenile justice system are discussed next.

DiIulio's preposterous claims left no plausible role for the juvenile justice system in stemming the coming tide of superpredators. The juveniles who achieved this mythical status were said to be beyond redemption; jailing and imprisonment was the presumed answer. Just desert advocates promoted the use of punitive laws, policies, and practices in the juvenile justice system, including three-strike laws, determinate sentences, longer sentences, sentencing to boot camps, electronic monitoring, drug testing, shock incarceration, and other punitive measures (Howell, 2003b). Such policies and practices, which deemphasize prevention of juvenile crime and rehabilitation of juvenile offenders, became common in the juvenile justice system through new state legislation. Together, DiIulio's superpredator concept and just desert principles spawned a major myth that the juvenile justice system could not be effective with the new breed of juvenile offenders and was no longer relevant in modern-day crime control (Box 1.2).

IN FOCUS 1.2

The Logic of DiIulio's Superpredator Prediction

- The Philadelphia Birth Cohort Study found that 6% of the boys in the study sample were chronic offenders (Wolfgang, Figlio, & Sellin, 1972).
- From 1996 through 2010, the number of boys under age 18 would increase by a total of 4.5 million (from 32 million to 36.5 million).
- Therefore, by 2010, the United States would have 270,000 (.06 × 4.5 million) more superpredators (chronic offenders) who would perpetrate a "coming wave of teen violence."

SOURCE: DiIulio (1995b).

Myths About the Juvenile Justice System (JJS)

JJS Myth 1: Rehabilitation is no longer a priority in the juvenile justice system; punishment is now favored.

Declarations that the rehabilitative mission of the juvenile justice system is in serious decline, if not dead, are common (Box 1.3). Many state legislatures did indeed rewrite their juvenile codes to endorse punitive objectives (Torbet & Szymanski, 1998); however, 45 of them maintained an allegiance to the juvenile justice system's traditional benevolent mission (Bishop, 2006). In fact, Bishop noticed in her review of the past 3 years (2003–2005) of legislative actions that "efforts are underway to mitigate or even abandon punitive features [of juvenile laws enacted in the past decade and] to address the treatment needs of most juvenile offenders" (p. 660).

IN FOCUS 1.3
Claims That the Juvenile Justice System Fails to Meet Expectations

"Politicians and the public have repudiated the [juvenile] court's original rehabilitative premises" (Feld, 1993).

"[The system is] unable to stem the tide of declining public support" (Bazemore & Umbreit, 1997, p. 5).

"In many jurisdictions [the juvenile justice system] does not consistently serve the public safety, hold juveniles accountable, or meet the treatment and rehabilitation needs of each juvenile offender" (Bilchik, 1998, p. 1).

"The voices calling for the abolition of the juvenile court are no longer falling on deaf ears, but are beginning to capture the attention of state and nationally elected public officials, the media, and other opinion leaders" (Schwartz, Weiner, & Enosh, 1998, p. 534).

"Demands for an overhaul of the juvenile justice system continue to be commonplace at the national, State, and local levels" (Hsia & Beyer, 2000, p. 1).

"The original purpose of the juvenile court has systematically unraveled" (Garascia, 2005, p. 489).

JJS Myth 2: The public no longer supports rehabilitation of juvenile offenders.

Others say that the efforts of "child savers" are all for naught anyway because of a lack of public support for rehabilitation of juvenile offenders (Box 1.4). These observers assume that the impact of the just desert movement on the adult criminal justice system—in greatly diminishing the use of treatment programs—has filtered down to the juvenile justice system. Is this a matter of fact? Decidedly not. "The notion that the American public is opposed to the treatment of juvenile offenders is a myth" (Cullen, 2006, p. 665). Cullen notes that a 2001 national survey found that 80% of the sample of adults thought that rehabilitation should be the goal of juvenile correctional facilities and that more than 9 in 10 favored a variety of early intervention programs, including parent training, Head Start, and after-school programs. "The legitimacy of the rehabilitative ideal—especially as applied to youthful offenders—appears to be deeply woven into the fabric of American culture" (p. 666). Therefore, it is not surprising that state and local juvenile justice officials have taken steps to soften the impact of punitive reforms (Bishop, 2006; Mears, 2002).

IN FOCUS 1.4
Key Myths About Juvenile Delinquency

- A juvenile violence "epidemic" occurred in the late 1980s and early 1990s.
- Juvenile violence is the top crime problem in the United States.
- Juveniles were the driving force behind the increase in violence in the United States from the mid-1980s through the early 1990s.
- Juvenile offenders are committing more and more violent crimes at younger ages.
- School shootings represent a second wave of the juvenile violence that doomsday forecasters Fox and DiIulio prophesied.
- The juvenile justice system in the United States is a failure; it is collapsing because it cannot handle today's more serious offenders.
- The public no longer supports rehabilitation of juvenile offenders.
- Rehabilitation is no longer a priority in the juvenile justice system; punishment is now favored.
- Transferring juveniles to the criminal justice system is the way to reduce juvenile delinquency.

JJS Myth 3: Juvenile correctional systems are a dismal failure.

Whether confinement in juvenile reformatories halts or accelerates juvenile criminal behavior is a question that has been debated since the mid-19th century (Krisberg & Howell, 1998). For the first time, reasonably good data are available that provide a rough approximation of recidivism rates among offenders released from state juvenile correctional facilities (Virginia Department of Juvenile Justice, 2005). The gathered state reports were not uniform. Some measured recidivism by rearrests (9 states), others used reconvictions (12 states), and the final group used reincarceration (12 states). A total of 33 states provided data, so there is overlap in the formats in which data were reported (but only 4 states reported recidivism data using all three measures). The average recidivism rates were as follows: rearrests (57%), reconvictions (33%), and reincarceration (20%).

These averages appear to be far better than juvenile justice system critics have assumed and also much better than comparable measures for the criminal justice system: Two-thirds (67%) of released prisoners are rearrested within 3 years, and more than half of released inmates are returned to prison (Langan & Levin, 2002). Actually, the adult recidivism rates should be lower than those for juveniles because adolescents are on the upward side of the age–crime curve and adults are on the downward side, already in a desistance mode.

JJS Myth 4: Transferring juveniles to the criminal justice system is the way to reduce juvenile delinquency.

DiIulio said "by my estimate, we will probably need to incarcerate at least 150,000 juvenile criminals in the years just ahead" (DiIulio, 1995b, p. 28). In one fell swoop, DiIulio dismissed the relevance of the juvenile justice system. But it already had been dealt a serious blow from the just desert movement (specific and extreme punishments for crimes), which I will discuss in more detail in the next chapter.

However, as we shall see in Chapter 12, studies have shown that juveniles who are transferred to criminal court and placed in adult prisons are actually more likely to recidivate than juveniles retained in the juvenile justice system, and their recidivism rates, offense rates, and offense severity appear to increase after they are released from prison. Nevertheless, many research questions about transfers remain to be answered (Mears, 2003). Equally important, the business of transferring juveniles to another system not designed for them presents myriad complex matters that rarely are considered (Mears, 2000).

The unifying theme in these four myths is the notion that punishment is now predominant in juvenile justice policies and practices, driven by shifting public opinion. However, Bishop (2006) astutely observes that "to the public, the idea of punishment versus rehabilitation is a false dichotomy" (p. 656) and that "we have sold the public short for a long time regarding the degree to which it supports the rehabilitation of juvenile offenders" (p. 656). The reality, she says, is that the public endorses both strategies simultaneously. Indeed, Bishop sees that the public embraces a balanced approach of punishment for offenses while also providing the necessary treatment to help offending youth move on into adulthood with their life chances intact. This is the essence of effective juvenile justice system philosophy, a concept that politicians and legislators appear to have difficulty grasping.

Recap

The most damaging and erroneous myth propagated in the 100-year history of the juvenile justice system in the United States is that concerning the emergence of a new breed of juvenile offenders called "superpredators." Observers have linked this mythical image with forecast increases in the size of the juvenile population. DiIulio reportedly now regrets using the term, and Wilson has acknowledged that he was wrong in making the erroneous forecast. But their misgivings came too late. Frightening images of "waves of violent adolescents coming at us over the next decade," producing a "bloodbath," had already been presented over and over by the broadcast media.

Other myths about juvenile violence fit well with the superpredator myth and the myth of an epidemic of juvenile violence, such as the myth that juvenile offenders are committing more and more violent crimes at younger ages and the myth that the juvenile justice system lacks the capacity to deal effectively with the new breed of superpredators and the coming juvenile violence epidemic. Such myths have led to a perception of juvenile delinquency as equivalent to adult crime, and some observers have come to believe that turning juvenile offenders over to the criminal justice system is a solution. This has proved to be a flawed policy, however.

The current state of juvenile justice has nothing to do with superpredators or new waves of violent juvenile offenders, as DiIulio, Fox, and Wilson have suggested. Rather, the erroneous perceptions of these observers have contributed to a moral panic over juvenile delinquency that has led to a problem of overload in the juvenile justice system; I turn to this topic in Chapter 2.

Discussion Topics

1. Why are myths about juvenile delinquency developed?

2. What are the essential ingredients for sustaining them?

3. What is the most believable myth? Most unbelievable?

4. Try to come up with your own myth about juvenile delinquency and develop a plan for promoting it.

5. How can such myths be stopped?

CHAPTER 2

Moral Panic Over Juvenile Delinquency

This chapter addresses the origins and history of the current moral panic over delinquency in the United States. What is this phenomenon? The term *moral panic* (Cohen, 1980) refers to circumstances in which the perceived threat from some group or situation is greatly exaggerated compared with the actual threat. Thus, in a state moral panic, political and social leaders suddenly define a specific group of people as a major threat to our values and behavioral standards. Put simply, moral crusaders in a society create moral panics to stigmatize as evil the people or actions they find offensive.

I begin this chapter with a brief discussion of the history and development of the current moral panic and then address the consequences of this panic for today's juvenile offenders and for the juvenile justice system. The present moral panic over juvenile delinquency is the seventh one in America. Curiously, juveniles are the targets of moral panics in the United States about every 10–15 years. The previous six moral panics occurred in the 1920s and around 1932, 1946, 1954, 1964, and 1977 (Bernard, 1992). In each of these eras, the current cohort of delinquents was described as "worse than ever before." This characterization of juvenile delinquents is not unusual. "From antiquity every generation has entertained the opinion that many if not most of its youth are the most vicious in the history of the race" (Hamparian, Schuster, Dinitz, & Conrad, 1978, p. 11).

Origins of the Current Moral Panic

The current moral panic over juvenile delinquency has its origins in two main factors. The first is often called the *cycle of juvenile justice*, a strangely unique feature of American juvenile justice. Bernard (1992) explains the cycle as follows: Americans have strongly held and conflicting views about juvenile delinquency policies and the philosophy of juvenile justice historically applied in the United States. One group in our society believes that the juvenile justice system is too lenient. They contend that the leniency of the system encourages delinquency. They call for harsher treatment of juveniles. After these policies are put into effect, another group begins to oppose harsh punishments, pointing out that they do not appear to reduce juvenile crime. These arguments lead to the return of more lenient treatment of juvenile offenders, beginning the cycle all over again.

It's difficult to pinpoint the exact times at which philosophical shifts occur because the process typically is gradual. The most recent philosophical shift from rehabilitation to punishment began in the 1970s, and it started in the criminal justice system. At about that point, the main purpose of criminal justice intervention became punishment. Attacks on criminal justice policies in the 1970s and 1980s came from both liberal and conservative ends of the political spectrum (Travis & Petersilia, 2001). Liberals viewed indeterminate sentences and disparate sentences for the same offenses as unjust. They wanted to see more consistency in criminal justice policies. Conservatives viewed the criminal justice system as too lenient; they wanted to see more punishment elements in criminal justice policies. They advocated the just desert principle, a retributive philosophy that holds that offenders should suffer the infliction of deserved pain, commensurate with the severity of the offense. An Office of Juvenile Justice and Delinquency Prevention administrator (a just desert advocate) put it thus: "The only way to deal with [chronic juvenile offenders] is to let them feel the sting of the [criminal] justice system" (Regnery, 1986, p. 44).

The second contributing factor is the superpredator myth and the mistaken belief that waves of predatory youth were to come at us over the next decade, producing a bloodbath, which engendered enormous fear of juvenile offenders. It is difficult to capture in words the depth of the emotion that was part of the moral panic that began in the 1990s. The demonization of juveniles and catchy phrases about the dangers they posed were repeated over and over in the media and by politicians in the early 1990s. As Torbet and Szymanski (1998) explain, "Extensive media coverage of violent crimes by juveniles—especially homicides with firearms—fueled perceptions of a juvenile violence epidemic. This, in turn, led to a response by governors and legislators to 'get tough' on juvenile crime" (p. 1).

The two compelling images, of superpredators and an imminent crime bomb (when new waves of the superpredators would arrive), were powerful, and they played well in the broadcast media and with politicians who wanted to draw public support by appearing tough on juvenile crime. Stories that played to readers' fears were common (Zimring, 1998a). Fear of young people grew in the public's mind, and the majority of U.S. adults believed that the projected violent crime increases were coming (Dorfman & Schiraldi, 2001).

Legislators were quick to insert the pejorative images of the "new breed" of juvenile offenders and the potential juvenile crime explosion into their draconian proposals. The inflammatory rhetoric fueled the seventh U.S. moral panic over juvenile delinquency (Howell, 2003b), which was in full bloom by the late 1990s. The conditions of a moral panic (Goode & Ben-Yehuda, 1994) had been met: a consensus that the threat is real and serious, a heightened level of concern, concern that is disproportionate to the objective threat posed by the identified group, hostility directed at those engaged in the deviant behavior, and volatile reactions.

Aphorisms such as "If you're old enough to do the crime, you're old enough to do the time" became the mantras of the leaders of the moral panic. Variations on this theme were "Do adult crime, do adult time," "Do the crime, do the time," and "If they are going to act like adults, treat them as adults" (Hunzeker, 1995). *Accountability* became a euphemism for deserved punishment (i.e., just desert). But much of this posturing was part of an effort by prosecutors and other politicians to shift public policy toward harsher, more repressive solutions to youth crime (Beckett & Sasson, 2003). Some observers argue that the exceptional performance of juvenile courts in the 1970s and 1980s rendered them vulnerable to attacks by those who had succeeded in radically altering punishments in the criminal justice system; they saw a "punishment gap" between the two systems (Zimring, 2002). In this sense, juvenile offenders became a battleground for a get-tough orientation that had permeated the adult criminal justice system.

The convergence of these factors produced the most pronounced of the moral panics over juvenile delinquency in the 100-year history of the American juvenile justice system. Moved by rhetoric, legislators lined up to introduce or support legislation aimed at stopping the coming wave of youth violence (Logan, 1998). Whenever an adolescent offender picked up one of the 200 million guns in circulation at that time inside this country, legislators were quick to lower the age of transfer to the criminal justice system and even to introduce the possibility of capital punishment. The states of Washington and Vermont enacted legislation allowing sentences of life without the possibility of parole for juveniles as young as ages 8 and 10, respectively (Logan, 1998). By the end of the decade, every state had enacted laws that made their juvenile justice systems more punitive or made it easier to transfer juveniles to the criminal justice system.

Consequences of the Moral Panic in the Juvenile Justice System

One comparison illustrates the overall direction of changes in the juvenile justice system's handling of delinquents as a consequence of the most recent moral panic. From 1990 through 1999, the total number of juvenile arrests for violent offenses *decreased* by 55%, and juvenile arrests for serious property offenses *decreased* by 23% (Snyder, 2000). However, during approximately the same period, the total number of referrals to juvenile court *increased* by 44% (Stahl, 2001), creating burgeoning juvenile court intake and probation caseloads. Punitive legislative changes designated larger proportions of juveniles as serious and violent offenders, resulting in the incarceration of more nondangerous juveniles and extended periods of confinement in juvenile correctional facilities (Howell, 2003b). Detention centers and juvenile reformatories became and remain overcrowded, particularly with nonserious offenders (Snyder & Sickmund, 2006, pp. 198, 200). The number of delinquents held in public facilities rose 36% from 1991 to 1999 and then dropped 13% by 2003 (Snyder & Sickmund, 2006, p. 199). Conditions of confinement also worsened, partly as a result of the overcrowding (Puritz & Scali, 1998). Rehabilitation programs often were abandoned, whereas boot camps, "Scared Straight" programs, more detention centers, and more juvenile reformatories increasingly populated the nation's landscape (Howell, 2003b; Males, 1996; Roush & McMillen, 2000).

The more punitive provisions added to many states' juvenile codes (laws governing juvenile delinquency) had the following effects:

- They brought more children into the juvenile justice system.
- They designated larger proportions of juveniles as serious and violent offenders, resulting in the incarceration of more juveniles in detention centers, juvenile correctional facilities, and adult jails and prisons.
- They extended periods of confinement in juvenile correctional facilities.
- They lowered the ages at which juvenile offenders could be transferred to the criminal justice system.
- They excluded more juvenile offenders from juvenile court jurisdiction.
- They expanded the lists of crimes for which juveniles can be transferred to the criminal justice system.

In short, a "war on juveniles" was launched. Lawmakers and policy makers in the United States tend to "declare war" on social problems, leading them to apply policies and other strategies that are characterized by aggression (Zimring, 1998a). Feelings of stress, anger, and even rage on the part of policy makers are evident in the juvenile justice policies that have ensued from the seventh juvenile delinquency panic, in which punishment is a central theme. Legislators, prosecutors, and other politicians seemingly have been unable to control their urges to add more punishments and punishments of greater severity.

For example, in 1999 a few congressmen proposed the Violent and Repeat Juvenile Offender Accountability and Rehabilitation Act. It would have transferred some 10-year-olds accused of particular crimes to criminal court. Some 200 criminologists signed a joint letter to the U.S. Senate in 1999 opposing this legislation. The letter urged the senators to cease using outdated juvenile crime trend data and called their attention the fact that, at that point, the juvenile homicide arrest rate had dropped again for the fourth straight year. The letter also urged the senators to reject the super-predator myth and the false prediction of a coming bloodbath. In this context, the letter advised the senators to resist the temptation to replace sound data and rational review with sound bites and rhetoric.

In addition, growing numbers of juveniles were removed from the juvenile justice system altogether and transferred to the criminal justice system. I focus on this extreme result of the most recent moral panic over delinquency in Chapter 12. I next consider how the moral panic played out in America's public schools.

Hysteria in Public Schools and the Birth of "Zero Tolerance"

The term *zero tolerance* (ZT) means that certain behaviors will not be tolerated. These policies specify predetermined mandatory consequences or punishments for specific offenses. In the school setting, ZT is a disciplinary policy that sends this message by punishing all offenses severely, no matter how minor, and suspension from school is the most common punishment. There is no room for discretion. ZT policies are also called "one strike and you're out" policies.

The Origins of ZT

Interestingly, ZT policies had already permeated public schools before the spate of school shootings occurred. ZT policies grew out of state and federal drug enforcement policies in the late 1980s (Skiba & Noam, 2001; Skiba & Peterson, 1999). The Reagan administration promoted aggressive enforcement of antidrug laws. The first use of the ZT term was in 1983, when the Navy reassigned 40 submarine crew members for suspected drug abuse (Skiba & Peterson, 1999). In 1986, ZT was used as the title of a policy developed by a U.S. attorney in San Diego to justify impounding seacraft that were caught carrying any amount of drugs, no matter how small.

By February 1988, the program had received national attention, and U.S. Attorney General Edwin Meese authorized customs officials to seize the boats, automobiles, and passports of anyone crossing the border with even trace amounts of drugs and to charge those people in federal court.

In late 1989, school districts in Orange County, California, and Louisville, Kentucky, promulgated ZT policies that called for expulsion for possession of drugs or participation in gang-related activity.

In New York, a school superintendent proposed a sweeping ZT program as a way of taking action against students who caused school disruption. With its restricted school access, ban on hats, immediate suspension for any school disruption, and increased use of law enforcement, the program contained many of the elements that have come to characterize ZT approaches in the past decade.

By 1993, ZT policies were adopted by school boards across the country, often broadened to include not only drugs and weapons but also tobacco use and school disruption. Originally intended to restrict drug use, gang involvement, and gun possession, ZT had evolved into an instrument to punish minor student misconduct.

In 1994, the federal government stepped in to mandate a ZT policy in schools nationwide when President Clinton signed the Gun-Free Schools Act into law (part of the Goals 2000: Educate America Act, Public Law 103-227). This law mandates an expulsion of one calendar year for possession of a weapon and referral of students who violate the law to the criminal or juvenile justice system. It also provides that the 1-year expulsions may be modified by the "chief administrative officer" of each local school district on a case-by-case basis (Skiba & Noam, 2001).

By the late 1990s, at least three-fourths of all schools reporting to the National Center for Education Statistics (1997) said that they had ZT policies in place for various student offenses, including bringing firearms or other weapons to school; gang activity; alcohol, drug, and tobacco offenses; and physical attacks or fighting.

Not surprisingly, inconsistencies in the application of ZT policies are reported. Truly dangerous behavior occurs infrequently in schools, and the most common disciplinary events are minor disruptive behaviors such as tardiness, class absence, disrespect, and noncompliance (Skiba & Knesting, 2001). Therefore, targeting both forms of behavior equally (which ZT policies encourage) will result in the punishment of a small number of serious infractions and a much larger number of minor misbehaviors. Because expulsion from school appears to be reserved for the few moderate- to high-severity offenses, suspension is among the most widely used disciplinary techniques, and it is used as a punishment for a broad range of behaviors (Skiba & Knesting, 2001). Indeed, students are suspended for the most serious offenses (drugs, weapons, vandalism, and assaults) infrequently; fights or other forms of physical aggression among students are consistently found to be among the most common reasons for suspension. Suspension is also commonly used for a number of minor offenses, such as disobedience and disrespect, attendance problems, and general classroom disruption (pp. 28–29). But the strongest predictors of high school suspension rates are not the bad behavior or attitudes of students; rather, school characteristics are strongest, including teacher attitudes, administrative centralization, quality of school governance, teacher perception of student achievement, and racial makeup of the school (Skiba & Knesting, 2001).

During the 1997–1998 school year, the American public was riveted by print and broadcast media images of school shootings in Pearl, Mississippi; West Paducah, Kentucky; Jonesboro, Arkansas; Edinboro, Pennsylvania; Richmond, Virginia; and Springfield, Oregon (Donohue, Schiraldi, & Ziedenberg, 1999).

Then the 1999 shootings at Columbine High School in Littleton, Colorado, dramatized further the horrifying vulnerability of schools to gun attacks by mass killers. As Brooks, Schiraldi, and Ziedenberg (2001) observe, responses across the nation to the killing of 12 children and a teacher at Columbine included panic and desperate fear for the safety of children in schools. American society started questioning why these incidents occurred in schools and demanded that strategies be put into place to prevent them from happening again. Yet no cries rang out to reduce juveniles' access to firearms (Lawrence & Mueller, 2003).

Instead, the panic over school shootings led to hysteria, which contributed significantly to the growth of ZT school disciplinary policies, a trend that had already begun as a result of the general panic over youth violence and fear that an adolescent bloodbath was around the corner, to be ushered in by a wave of superpredators. A reported resurgence in cocaine use among high school students in the late 1990s (Johnston, O'Malley, Bachman, & Schulenberg, 2006) also fueled the flames of hysteria. ZT would be the easy answer: Just stop kids from all things that might lead to mass shootings at school, bringing firearms to school, drug use, and gang activities in particular. However, even strong school security measures in and of themselves do not appear to be solutions to student victimization at school (Howell & Lynch, 2000). Yet this is typically the option first chosen.

Once control of school safety is returned to school administrators, a more deliberate threat assessment procedure can be put in place to handle these episodes. A threat assessment approach gives school authorities flexibility in choosing the disciplinary consequences for students who make threats. Under a ZT policy, many students would have been expelled for making threats to kill or injure someone. Using threat assessment guidelines (Box 2.9), in Virginia schools only 3 of the 188 threat cases resulted in expulsion: a 6th grader who picked up a pair of scissors and threatened to stab a classmate, an 8th grader who threatened to shoot a classmate, and a 9th grader who threatened to stab another student and was found to have a knife in her locker. In each case, the student had 10 or more disciplinary violations before the threat, and the decision to expel was based on a broader consideration of the student's ability to function in school (Osher, Dwyer, & Jackson, 2004).

Threat assessment should be considered a component of a comprehensive approach toward maintaining a safe school (Osher et al., 2004). Threat assessment identifies students who may need additional services as well as more general problems in the school environment, such as bullying, that merit broader attention. Wilson, Lipsey, and Derzon (2003) reviewed 221 studies of school-based interventions for aggressive or disruptive behavior by students and found that well-implemented demonstration programs are highly effective.

More broadly, the foundation for a safe school rests on the creation of a healthy school climate, a caring community where students feel safe and secure (Gottfredson, Gottfredson, Payne, & Gottfredson, 2005). Safety and security derive from two conditions: an orderly, predictable environment where school staff provide consistent, reliable supervision and discipline; and a school climate where students feel connected to the school and supported by their teachers and other school staff. A balance of structure and support is essential and requires an organized, school-wide approach that is practiced by all school personnel. The good news is that there are effective programs and approaches, and threat assessment can help school authorities to use them effectively and efficiently by identifying student conflicts and problems before they lead to violence.

The Center for the Prevention of School Violence has developed a systematic process by which schools can address the challenge that high suspension rates present. It's called Project ReSET (Response to Suspension and Expulsion Trends). The center has created a toolkit that gives school districts step-by-step instructions on how to create an alternative program for suspended kids. I describe it in more detail below.

The Immediate Effects of ZT Policies

Surprisingly, national data on school suspensions and expulsions are scant and not very current. The most recent nationwide data on the total number of suspensions published by the U.S. Department of Education are almost a decade old. That source indicates that more than 3 million suspensions or expulsions were made from public elementary and secondary schools in 2000 (U.S. Department of Education, 2003). That number is probably an underestimate, and it appears certain that the total number of suspensions and expulsions is much higher. I compared the reported total for North Carolina in the 2000–2001 school year (120,520 suspensions and expulsions in the U.S. Department of Education, 2003, report) with the actual number reported by the North Carolina Department of Public Instruction (217,683) (North Carolina Child Advocacy Institute, 2005, p. 3). This comparison shows a serious undercount (by 45%) in the federally reported number and suggests that if just one state reported almost one-quarter million suspensions and expulsions then it is extremely likely that the national figure of 3 million students is a gross underestimate. In the National Longitudinal Survey of Youth, 33% of the youngsters reported having been suspended from school between ages 12 and 17 (Table 2.1) (Snyder & Sickmund, 2006, p. 70).

To put the problem in perspective, the 1-year rate of suspensions and expulsions in North Carolina schools in 2004–2005 was 1 in 10 (North Carolina Child Advocacy Institute, 2005). The proposition that 1 in 10 public school students in North Carolina could present such serious behavioral problems *each year* that they should be suspended is highly unlikely. North Carolina ranked sixth among all states in 2000—behind number 1 California, followed by Florida, Texas, Ohio, and Michigan (U.S. Department of Education, 2003). Similarly, it is extremely unlikely that one in three students nationwide should be suspended before graduating.

Table 2.1   Youths Suspended From School or Involved in Other Problem Behavior

Behavior	Proportion of youth reporting ever engaging in the behavior by age 17					
	All youth	Male	Female	White	Black	Hispanic
Suspended from school	33%	42%	24%	28%	56%	38%
Ran away from home	18	17	20	18	21	17
Belonged to a gang	8	11	6	7	12	12
Vandalized	37	47	27	39	33	34
Theft less than $50	43	47	38	44	38	41
Theft more than $50	13	16	10	12	15	14
Assaulted with intent to seriously hurt	27	33	21	25	36	28
Sold drugs	16	19	12	17	13	16
Carried a handgun	16	25	6	16	15	15

Equally incredible, an estimated 5,117 children ages 3 to 4 years old are expelled from state-funded pre-kindergarten school systems each year across the country (Gilliam, 2005). The pre-kindergarten expulsion rate in the 2003–2004 school year was more than three times the national rate for K–12 grades. This finding astounded Yale University researcher Walter Gilliam. There is no obvious explanation for the incredibly high pre-kindergarten expulsion rate except an insidious spread of a ZT mentality throughout all types of organized schooling.

This epidemic level of school suspension rates begs this question: When were public schools excused from educating all our children and teaching them how to act? Schools are a core socializing institution in our society, and even toddlers must be socialized (Tremblay, 2003). Pre-kindergarten "schools" exist for the specific purpose of early childhood training to control natural disruptive tendencies in children.

The Long-Term Effects of ZT: The School-to-Prison Pipeline

The "school-to-prison pipeline" (Wald & Losen, 2003) begins with students in high-poverty, high-minority schools that are routinely provided fewer resources than their more affluent white peers. "In fact, the racial disparities within the two systems are so similar—and so glaring—that it becomes impossible not to connect them" to separate pathways of success and failure (p. 11). Such phrases as *schoolhouse-to-jailhouse* and *school-to-prison pipeline* describe these dual trends. Many travelers along this path "will be taught by unqualified teachers, tested on material they never reviewed, held back in grade, placed in restrictive special education programs, repeatedly suspended, and banished to alternative outplacements before dropping or getting pushed out of school altogether" (p. 11). Without a safety net, the likelihood that these young travelers will wind up arrested and incarcerated increases sharply.

Many public schools "have turned into feeder schools for the juvenile and criminal justice systems" (Advancement Project, 2005, p. 11). Youths are finding themselves increasingly at risk of falling into the school-to-prison pipeline through school policies that have the effect of pushing more and more students—particularly minority youths—out of school. These policies are tantamount to systematic exclusion through suspensions, expulsions, discouragement, and high-stakes testing.

The long-lasting effects of ZT policies are obvious: increased suspension and expulsion rates, referrals to inadequate alternative schools, lower test scores, higher dropout rates, and racial profiling of students (Advancement Project, 2005, p. 12). The criminalization of children by their schools leaves more scars, including the emotional trauma, embarrassment, and stigma of being handcuffed and taken away from school (Figure 2.1). More and more police are stationed in schools, generally called "School Resource Officers." Their dual role involves handling minor disciplinary matters formerly handled by school officials and making growing numbers of arrests of students, typically for minor offenses, many of which cannot be classified in police reports. Prosecutors are often happy to adjudicate the minor charges, which enhances their "get tough" image (Advancement Project, 2005). The American Bar Association (2001) laments that

> public policy towards children has moved towards treating them more like adults and in ways that increasingly mimic the adult criminal justice system. The most recent version of this movement is so-called "ZT" in schools, where theories of punishment that were once directed to adult criminals are now applied to first graders. (p. 1)

> In the name of school safety, schools have implemented unforgiving, overly harsh ZT discipline practices that turn kids into criminals for acts that rarely constitute a crime when committed by an adult. . . . Schools have teamed up with law enforcement to make this happen by imposing a "double dose" of punishment: suspension or expulsion and a trip to the juvenile justice system. (Advancement Project, 2005, p. 11)

In the 1980s, extensive investigations of the causes and correlates of dropping out of school consistently found that school suspension is a moderate to strong predictor (Skiba & Peterson, 1999). Once they are no longer attending school, dropouts are likely to increase their delinquency involvement. A nationwide survey of young people by the Centers for Disease Control (1994) found that out-of-school youth of school age are

Figure 2.1   The Dark Side of Zero Tolerance

significantly more likely to become involved in physical fights; carry a weapon; smoke; use alcohol, marijuana, and cocaine; engage in sexual intercourse; and have four or more sexual partners than in-school youth.

The remaining steps to prison from the intermediate step of referral to the juvenile justice system are clear. School exclusion increases the likelihood of detention, followed by a greater probability of secure confinement in a state juvenile correctional facility, and next a greater risk of imprisonment (Christle, Jolivette, & Nelson, 2005; Miller, Ross, & Sturgis, 2005; Richart, Brooks, & Soler, 2003). Approximately two-thirds of prisoners are high school dropouts (Thornburgh, 2006).

ZT Makes Zero Sense

The growing problem of school suspensions is a product of "zero tolerance" of student misbehaviors (Boxes 2.1 and 2.2). Unfortunately, current national data are not available. The most recent data, for the year 2000, indicated that the national average was 6.6% (U.S. Department of Education, 2003). Some states have much higher rates. North Carolina is a good example, with a 9.6% rate in the federal report, or almost one out of every 10 students (Weisel & Howell, 2007).

IN FOCUS 2.1
Zero Tolerance Victims

- A 17-year-old in Richmond, Illinois, shot a paper clip with a rubber band, missing his target but hitting a cafeteria worker instead. He was expelled (Crowley, 2007).

(Continued)

(Continued)

- A 12-year-old in Ponchatoula, Louisiana, diagnosed with a hyperactivity disorder told others in a lunch line not to eat all the potatoes, or "I'm going to get you." He was charged with making "terroristic threats" and spent several weeks in a juvenile detention center (Crowley, 2007).
- A 13-year-old in Denton County, Texas, was assigned in class to write a "scary" Halloween story. He concocted one that involved shooting up a school, which got him a visit from police and 6 days in jail before the courts confirmed that no crime had been committed (Crowley, 2007).
- A 7-year-old African American boy in Monticello, Florida, who has attention deficit disorder was arrested and hauled off to the county jail for hitting a classmate, a teacher, and a principal and scratching a school resource officer. The second grader was fingerprinted and eventually cried himself to sleep in his jail cell (Advancement Project, 2005, p. 12).
- A kindergarten boy in Newport News, Virginia, was suspended for bringing a beeper on a class trip (Richart et al., 2003).
- A 6-year-old boy from Madison, North Carolina, who kissed a girl on the cheek was given a 1-day suspension. (Richart et al., 2003).
- An 11-year-old girl from Columbia, South Carolina, was arrested and suspended for having a steak knife in her lunchbox to cut chicken she had brought to school to eat (Richart et al., 2003).
- An 8-year-old girl from Alexandria, Louisiana, was expelled for bringing to school a 1-inch pocketknife that was attached to her grandfather's pocket watch chain (Richart et al., 2003).

IN FOCUS 2.2

Law Enforcement Goes to School

The morning of November 5, 2003, seemed like a typical school day at Stratford High School in Goose Creek, South Carolina. Students mingled in the crowded hallways as they prepared for their next class. Then a police Special Weapons and Tactics (SWAT) team entered the school. With guns drawn, the SWAT team with dogs stormed the hallways, screaming at the teens, shoving them to the ground, and holding some of them down with guns pointed at their heads. Students who did not respond in a split second to the orders barked at them were handcuffed.

"They hit that school like it was a crack house, like they knew there were crack dealers in there with guns," stated Elijah Simpson, parent of a 14-year-old student caught in the raid and a deputy sheriff and SWAT team member. "A school drug raid is not a SWAT team situation." Simpson's son was held at gunpoint and detained on his knees facing the wall during the raid.

> The horrifying raid at Stratford High School has left an indelible mark on the minds of the students whose rights and self-esteem were attacked that day, but it also left an imprint on the minds of many Americans who saw the videotape of the raid on television. Innocent youths treated like hardened criminals in the one place that is supposed to be safe, secure, and sheltered from the problems of the streets: their school. The school allegedly requested law enforcement assistance to address a suspected drug problem. Law enforcement excused its commando-style raid by stating that where drugs are found, weapons are also typically found.
>
> The raid turned up no drugs and no weapons at Stratford High School.

Voices of reason have called attention to the urgent need to reform ZT policies. Education experts were the first to recognize the devastating effects of ZT on students (e.g., Hyman & Perone, 1998; Skiba & Peterson, 1999). Another leader, the American Bar Association (2001), voted to oppose ZT policies that have a discriminatory effect or that mandate either expulsion or referral of students to juvenile or criminal court without regard to the circumstances or nature of the offense or the student's history. Others have spoken forcefully, equating ZT with zero sense (Henry, 2007) and urging policy makers, school administrators, and lawmakers to "get a grip" (Herbert, 2007a, 2007b). Another widely respected and influential organization, the American Psychological Association, has become concerned about the lasting effects of ZT on students. It has exercised national leadership through the formation of a ZT Task Force, which is considered next.

American Psychological Association Response to ZT

The American Psychological Association created a ZT Task Force (Skiba et al., 2006) to examine research bearing on the effects of ZT policies on child development, the relationship between education and the juvenile justice system, and students, families, and communities. The task force was also charged with formulating recommendations on the improvement of ZT policies and identifying promising alternatives to ZT. The following are key findings of the ZT Task Force.

The Task Force considered a general question: Have ZT policies made schools safer and more effective in handling disciplinary problems? To organize available information, the Task Force examined five key assumptions of ZT policies in this area. In general, data tended to contradict the presumptions made in applying a ZT approach to maintaining school discipline and order (Skiba et al., 2006, pp. 3–5):

Assumption 1: School violence is at a serious level and increasing, necessitating forceful, no-nonsense strategies for violence prevention.

Although violence and disruption are unacceptable in schools and this is a key concern that must be continually addressed in education, the evidence does not support an assumption that violence in schools is out of control. Serious and deadly violence remain a small proportion of school disruptions, and the data consistently indicate that school violence and disruption have remained stable, or even decreased somewhat, since approximately 1985.

Assumption 2: Through the provision of mandated punishment for certain offenses, ZT increases the consistency of school discipline and thereby the clarity of the disciplinary message to students. The evidence strongly suggests that ZT has not increased the consistency of school discipline. Rather, rates of suspension and expulsion vary widely across schools and school districts. Moreover, this variation appears to be due as much to characteristics of schools and school personnel as to the behavior or attitudes of students.

Assumption 3: Removal of students who violate school rules will create a school climate more conducive to learning for those who remain. A key assumption of ZT policy is that the removal of disruptive students will result in a safer climate for others. Although the assumption is strongly intuitive, data on a number of indicators of school climate have shown the opposite effect, that is, that schools with higher rates of school suspension and expulsion appear to have less satisfactory ratings of school climate and less satisfactory school governance structures and to spend a disproportionate amount of time on disciplinary matters.

Assumption 4: The swift and certain punishments of ZT have a deterrent effect on students, thus improving overall student behavior and discipline. The notion of deterring future misbehavior is central to the philosophy of ZT, and the impact of any consequence on future behavior is the defining characteristic of effective punishment. Rather than reducing the likelihood of disruption, however, school suspension in general appears to predict higher future rates of misbehavior and suspension among those who are suspended. In the long term, school suspension and expulsion are moderately associated with a higher likelihood of school dropout and failure to graduate on time.

Assumption 5: Parents overwhelmingly support the implementation of ZT policies to ensure the safety of schools, and students feel safer knowing that transgressions will be dealt with in no uncertain terms. The data regarding this assumption are mixed and inconclusive.

The task force also examined the impact of ZT policies on the nexus between the educational system and the juvenile justice system (Skiba et al., 2006, pp. 8–9). The key question that guided this inquiry was this: How has ZT affected the relationship between education and the juvenile justice system? ZT policies appear to have increased the use and reliance in schools on strategies such as security technology, security personnel, and profiling;

however, there are almost no empirical data examining the extent to which such programs result in safer schools or a more satisfactory school climate. To be sure, ZT policies have resulted in an increase of referrals to the juvenile justice system for infractions that were once handled in school. The study of this phenomenon has been called the school-to-prison pipeline. Research indicates that many schools appear to be using the juvenile justice system to a greater extent and, in a large percentage of cases, the school-based infractions for which juvenile justice is called on are not those that would generally be considered dangerous or threatening. To the extent that school infractions lead to increased contact with the juvenile justice system, the cost of treatment appears to escalate dramatically.

The task force also explored the availability and effectiveness of other options for maintaining school safety and reducing suspensions (Skiba et al., 2006, pp. 10–11). The specific guiding question was this: Are there other disciplinary alternatives that could make a stronger contribution toward maintaining school safety or the integrity of the learning environment while keeping a greater number of students in school? The task force concluded that abundant research and a number of government panels have been highly consistent in identifying a host of strategies that have demonstrated efficacy in promoting school safety and reducing the potential for youth violence. The most effective schools tend to implement a three-level continuum from low to high intensity, described as follows (Dwyer & Osher, 2000):

Level 1: Build a school-wide foundation that targets all students. Research at the University of Oregon's Institute on Violent and Destructive Behavior suggests that most schools with effective school-wide systems that focus on learning and behavior can prevent at least 80% of problematic student behaviors.

Level II: Provide early intervention strategies that target students who may be at risk for violence or disruption—approximately 10–15% of students who continue to experience behavioral problems even when school-wide interventions are in place. Youth served at this level should meet several of the early warning criteria (Box 2.3). Of course, immediate attention would be given to youth who have made serious threats of violence.

IN FOCUS 2.3

Early Warning Signs That a Child May Need Assistance

- Social withdrawal
- Excessive feelings of isolation or being alone
- Excessive feelings of rejection

(Continued)

(Continued)

- Being a victim of violence
- Feelings of being picked on and persecuted
- Low school interest and poor academic performance
- Expression of violence in writing and drawings
- Uncontrolled anger
- Patterns of impulsive and chronic hitting, intimidating, and bullying behaviors
- History of discipline problems
- History of violent and aggressive behavior
- Intolerance for differences and prejudicial attitudes
- Drug and alcohol use
- Affiliation with gangs
- Inappropriate access to, possession of, and use of firearms
- Serious threats of violence (also an imminent warning sign)

Level III: Provide intensive intervention that targets students who have already engaged in disruptive or violent behavior. This is the remaining 5–10% of children who experience significant emotional and behavioral problems. Specific interventions and their intensity depend on the nature, severity, and frequency of each child's emotional and behavioral problems. Students who meet any of the imminent warning signs (Box 2.4) should receive help or control measures immediately, although cautions should be exercised to avoid an overreaction (Box 2.5).

IN FOCUS 2.4
Imminent Warning Signs

- Serious physical fighting with peers or family members
- Severe destruction of property
- Severe rage for seemingly minor reasons
- Detailed threats of lethal violence
- Possession or use of firearms and other weapons
- Other self-injurious behaviors or threats of suicide

IN FOCUS 2.5

Principles for Using the Early Warning Signs of Violence

- Do no harm.
- Understand violence and aggression in context.
- Avoid stereotypes.
- View warning signs in a developmental context.
- Understand that children typically exhibit multiple warning signs.

The U.S. Office of Special Education Programs has developed a framework that integrates these three levels of intervention, called Positive Behavioral Interventions and Supports (PBIS). The main goal is to create a positive social culture in schools in which prosocial behaviors are explicitly taught and reinforced for all students at all three levels. Although a growing number of schools across the United States are beginning to implement PBIS, many of these schools are still in the beginning stages of designing effective systems for students with the most challenging behaviors (Freeman et al., 2006). The goal in Level III is to develop individualized behavior support plans that are derived from functional assessment, include multicomponent interventions, and are tied together in a wraparound or system of care framework. But it has been "a continuing challenge . . . to develop and apply research-based strategies to move individual behavior support toward practice on a larger scale in schools and communities" (Freeman et al., 2006, p. 3).

The Office of Special Education Programs Center on Positive Behavioral Interventions and Supports (2004) acknowledges that successful integration of the three-part PBIS strategy has not yet been empirically validated. In short, the resources, people, and time to implement multidisciplinary and integrated treatment plans may not be available in a school-wide context, and practitioners in the field note that even when schools implement PBIS, students with the most significant disabilities often continue to be placed in segregated settings (Freeman et al., 2006). In addition, it may be unrealistic to implement strength-based school interventions for students with emotional behavioral disorders if teachers and school staff are frustrated by a high incidence of antisocial behaviors across the student body as a whole (Eber, Sugai, Smith, & Scott, 2002). Existing youth gang problems in schools are likely to elevate antisocial behaviors even more (Peterson, Taylor, & Esbensen, 2004).

These realities suggest that troubled schools with elevated antisocial behaviors, gang problems, high school suspension rates, and ZT policies need to consider taking action immediately on three fronts. First, excessive school suspensions must be reduced (Box 2.6). Direct and immediate actions are needed in any schools that are experiencing epidemic levels of suspensions (e.g., where about 1 in 10 students is suspended) and where few in-school suspension alternatives are provided. The Center for the Prevention of School Violence has developed a systematic process by which the schools can address the challenge that high suspension rates present. A toolkit is available that will give school districts step-by-step instructions for creating an alternative program for suspended kids (Box 2.7). This is the top priority: reduce unwarranted school suspensions immediately.

IN FOCUS 2.6

Concerns About the Widespread and Increasing Use of Suspensions

- Suspensions have a detrimental effect on achievement and are used most often with students who can least afford to be out of the classroom.
- Suspensions may reinforce rather than deter negative behavior.
- Students of ethnic or racial minorities are overrepresented relative to their enrollments among the students suspended. They have been reported to receive disciplinary referrals for less serious and more subjective reasons than majority students and to be given more serious consequences for infractions.
- It has been suggested that by removing students from a supervised environment, suspensions increase opportunities for disruption, delinquency, and involvement with the police.
- Suspensions are often used for minor infractions that might be addressed in other ways that would have fewer negative academic consequences for students.
- In some schools suspensions are not used as a disciplinary (i.e., teaching) strategy but are part of a highly punitive environment.

IN FOCUS 2.7

A Toolkit for Establishing Alternative-to-Suspension Programs

Phase I—A Survey: Assessing the Need for the Program

Phase II—The Building Plan: Planning the Program

Phase III—Securing Financing: Finding Funding for the Program

Phase IV—The Construction: Implementing the Program

Phase V—The Inspection: Evaluating the Impact and Success of the Program

Phase VI—Upkeep and Maintenance: Sustaining the Program

Second, school districts should consider establishing a school-based assessment center to provide community-based mental health services for school-age children and youth. Indeed, such a model has been described in detail (Kutash, Duchnowski, & Lynn, 2006). Kutash and her colleagues specify the main steps that any community must take to implement such school-based mental health services. This need not be a complex structure. The Norfolk, Virginia, Community Services Board (a mental health agency) created the school-based Norfolk Assessment Center to identify and assess children and youth at risk for delinquent behavior, especially associated drug use and mental health problems (Pindur & Elliker, 1999). The center is staffed by several agencies, including the Community Services Board, public schools, the court services unit, the Department of Human Services, and the Boys and Girls Club. Each of these agencies makes referrals of at-risk youths—youths who are experiencing mild to moderate emotional or behavioral difficulties—to the center. Each referred youth first receives a comprehensive mental health assessment, after which center personnel develop an individual service plan for the youth to address his or her needs in the areas of mental health, substance abuse, medical attention, education, human services, court services, recreation, and employment. The center also provides follow-up and case management services for the youth and family. The case managers facilitate interagency service delivery, empower clients, offer emotional support, arrange appointments, monitor compliance, make home and school visits, and perform other needed services. Such a center would simplify the pursuit of important twin goals: helping students in the early stages of problem behaviors (Level II candidates in the PBIS model) and the most troubled students (Level III students). Special attention must be paid to students with numerous short-term suspensions. The odds are very high that these students are experiencing problems in other life domains—especially in their families and communities—that are contributing to school problems.

Third, school districts that are implementing the PBIS system should continue Level I programming (school-wide climate improvements). Universal programs can be effective (see Chapter 9 for recommended programs). Other specific objectives should be established as part of the overall school improvement plan (Box 2.8).

IN FOCUS 2.8
Keys to Reforming Zero Tolerance Policies

Change Practices

- Apply ZT policies with greater flexibility, taking context and the expertise of teachers and school administrators into account. Define all infractions, whether major or minor, carefully and train all staff in appropriate means of handling each infraction.
- Evaluate all school discipline or school violence prevention strategies to ensure that all disciplinary interventions, programs, or strategies are truly improving student behavior and school safety.

Change Policies

- Reserve zero tolerance disciplinary removals for the most serious and severe disruptive behaviors.
- Replace one-size-fits-all disciplinary strategies with graduated systems of discipline, wherein consequences are matched to the seriousness of the infraction.
- Require school police officers who work in schools to have training in adolescent development.
- Increase training for teachers in classroom behavior management and culturally sensitive pedagogy.
- Increase training for teachers, administrators, and other school personnel to address sensitivity related to issues of race.

Develop Alternatives to Zero Tolerance

- Implement preventive measures that can improve school climate and improve the sense of school community and belongingness.
- Seek to reconnect alienated youth and reestablish the school bond for students at risk of discipline problems or violence. Use threat assessment procedures to identify the level of risk posed by student words.
- Develop a planned continuum of effective alternatives for students whose behavior threatens the discipline or safety of the school.
- Improve collaboration and communication between schools, parents, law enforcement, juvenile justice, and mental health professionals to develop an array of alternatives for challenging youth.

IN FOCUS 2.9
The Virginia Model for Student Threat Assessment

1. The leader of the threat assessment team interviews the student who made the threat, using a standard set of questions. The principal also interviews the

recipient of the threat and any witnesses. The principal is concerned not only with what the student said or did but with the context in which the threat was made and what the student intended by making the threat.

2. The principal must make an important distinction between *transient* threats, which are easily resolved because they are not serious threats, and *substantive* threats, which are serious in the sense that they pose a continuing risk or danger to others. Transient threats can be readily identified as expressions of anger or frustration (or perhaps inappropriate attempts at humor) that dissipate quickly when the student reflects on the meaning of what he or she has said. In contrast, substantive threats represent a sustained intent to harm someone beyond the immediate incident. If there is doubt whether a threat is transient or substantive, the threat is regarded as substantive. One way to identify a threat as substantive is to look for certain characteristics that suggest that the threat is likely to be serious:

   • The threat includes plausible details, such as a specific victim, time, place, and method of assault.
   • The threat has been repeated over time or communicated to multiple people.
   • The threat is reported as a plan, or planning has taken place.
   • The student has accomplices or has attempted to recruit accomplices.
   • The student has invited an audience of peers to watch the threatened event.
   • There is physical evidence of intent to carry out the threat, such as a weapon or bomb materials.

3. A transient threat can be resolved quickly without engaging the full team in a comprehensive threat assessment. The principal may require the student to apologize or explain to those affected by threat, or take other action to make amends for the student's behavior. The principal may also respond with a reprimand or other disciplinary consequence if the behavior was disruptive or violated the school's discipline code. If a transient threat was sparked by an argument or conflict, the principal can involve other team members in helping to address or resolve the problem.

4. If the threat is substantive, the principal skips step 3, and the substantive threat is determined to be *serious* or *very serious*. The distinction between serious and very serious threats is based on the intended severity of injury. A *serious* threat is a threat to assault, strike, or beat up someone. A *very serious* threat is a threat to kill, sexually assault, or severely injure someone. A threat involving the use of a weapon is generally considered a threat to severely injure someone.

5. In the case of a serious substantive threat, the team takes action to protect potential victims. Protective actions depend on the circumstances of the threat and how soon and where the threat might be carried out. Immediate protective actions include cautioning the student about the consequences of

(Continued)

(Continued)

carrying out the threat and contacting the student's parents. The team also has the responsibility for notifying the intended victim of the threat.

6. Very serious threats require the most extensive action by the team. The team skips step 5. Again the team takes immediate action to ensure that the threat is not carried out, but also the student should be suspended from school, pending a complete assessment of the threat and determination of the most appropriate school placement. The team conducts a more comprehensive safety evaluation that includes both mental health and law enforcement components. The mental health assessment is conducted by the school psychologist or another suitably trained mental health professional, and the law enforcement investigation is conducted by the school resource officer.

7. The team integrates findings from the safety evaluation into a written safety plan. The safety plan is designed both to protect potential victims and to address the student's educational needs. At this point, the principal decides whether the student can return to school or should be placed in an alternative setting. If the student is permitted to return to school, the plan describes the conditions that must be met and the procedures in place to monitor the student when he or she returns.

This was field tested over the course of one school year in 35 Virginia schools (K–12). It worked very well. Officials dealt with 188 student threats. The majority (70%) of threats were easily resolved as transient threats. Of the remaining 30% that were substantive threats, 22% (42 cases) were *serious* substantive threats that involved a threat to fight or assault someone, and 8% (15 cases) were *very serious* substantive threats to kill or severely injure someone. Each of these was resolved at step 7 with individual safety plans.

Discussion Topics

1. What causes a moral panic?

2. How does moral panic turn into mean-spirited behaviors by adults?

3. Why have zero tolerance policies been a popular response to perceptions of increased violence?

4. How can school authorities' use of ZT policies be reduced?

5. What are the necessary steps toward returning schools to their essential role as a core institution in our society for socializing as well as educating our children?

CHAPTER 3

Juvenile Delinquency Trends

An unprecedented youth violence epidemic is said to have occurred in the late 1980s and early 1990s (Blumstein, 1995a, 1995b; Cook & Laub, 1998; Fox, 1996b). In this chapter I examine the so-called epidemic, focusing on serious and violent juvenile delinquency trends in two time periods: from 1980 to the present and from the late 1980s through the early 1990s. The longer time frame puts in proper perspective the increases in violent juvenile delinquency reported for the late 1980s and early 1990s. In the first section of the chapter, I examine in detail the rates of serious and violent delinquency in both of the time periods; I then provide information on the claims that a new juvenile crime wave actually occurred.

Serious and Violent Juvenile Delinquency Trends

Three different kinds of measures are used to gauge changes in the levels of serious and violent delinquency: police arrests, victimization surveys, and delinquency self-report surveys. Observers can draw different conclusions regarding juvenile violence trends in the late 1980s and early 1990s, depending on the data sources they use to measure changes. The patterns of delinquency suggested by victimization reports, arrest data, and self-report measurements are distinctly different from one another for this period.

Arrest Data

Violent juvenile delinquency arrests increased in the late 1980s and early 1990s. Arrest data reported in the Federal Bureau of Investigation's (FBI's) annual compilation of data reported by localities across the country (*Uniform Crime Reports,* Box 3.1) are the most widely recognized juvenile delinquency trend data. State and federal legislators, the broadcast and print news media, and state and local policy makers most commonly refer to these FBI data in tracking juvenile delinquency trends and making policy changes. However, it is important to note that arrest data indicate society's *response* to juvenile delinquency, not the actual level of delinquency. Police choose to make arrests depending on local policies, and arrest rates vary from community to community for the same kinds of offenses (Shannon, 1968, 1988).

IN FOCUS 3.1
Uniform Crime Reports

UCR data document the number of crimes reported to police, not the number committed (Snyder & Sickmund, 2006, p. 122). Although this information is useful in identifying trends in the volume of reported crime, it is important to recognize that not all crimes are brought to the attention of law enforcement.

Crimes are more likely to be reported if they involve a serious injury or a large economic loss and if the victim wants law enforcement involved in the matter. Therefore, some crimes are more likely to come to the attention of law enforcement than are others. For example, the National Crime Victimization Survey for 2003 found that victims reported 77% of motor vehicle thefts to police, 61% of robberies, 59% of aggravated assaults, 54% of burglaries, 42% of simple assaults, 39% of sexual assaults, and 32% of thefts. Overall, victims reported to law enforcement only 48% of violent crimes and 38% of property crimes.

The UCR Crime Index is divided into two components: the Violent Crime Index and the Property Crime Index. The Violent Crime Index includes murder and nonnegligent manslaughter, forcible rape, robbery, and aggravated assault. The Property Crime Index includes burglary, larceny–theft, motor vehicle theft, and arson. Although the Violent Crime Index excludes some violent crimes, such as kidnapping and extortion, it contains most of the crimes generally considered to be violent. In contrast, a substantial proportion of the crimes in the Property Crime Index are generally considered less serious crimes, such as shoplifting, theft from motor vehicles, and bicycle theft, all of which are included in the larceny–theft category. Otherwise, the Property Crime Index contains what are generally considered to be serious crimes.

Data are collected from jurisdictions containing a majority of the U.S. population, typically between 60% and 90% of residents nationwide (Butts & Snyder, 2006, p. 2). The primary publication of UCR data, *Crime in the United States,* is based on data from police agencies able to participate fully in the UCR program each year. Full participation requires that agencies submit their data to the FBI on time and their data cover all arrests for a minimum number of months during the year. For 2005, the jurisdictions that participated fully represented 73% of the U.S. population. Nearly all the arrest statistics generated by the UCR program are based on this sample. They are not national estimates.

There are several other drawbacks to using national arrest data published in the UCR as a measure of delinquency (McCord et al., 2001, pp. 26–28). Most important, as noted earlier, arrest data indicate society's responses to crime, not the actual level of crime. Police choose to make both adult and juvenile arrests depending on local policies, and arrest rates vary from community to community for the same kinds of offenses. For a number of crimes, no arrests are made because many crimes are not reported to law enforcement. On the other hand, multiple people are often arrested for the same crime. Importantly, not everyone who is arrested actually committed the offense for which he or she was arrested. Equally important, arrest data exaggerate juveniles' criminal involvement because they tend to be arrested in groups, giving the appearance that several crimes were committed when there was only one.

UCR data also capture the proportion of crimes that were "cleared" (solved) by an arrest. Assessments of the juvenile contribution to the U.S. crime problem are often based on this proportion. Arrest and clearance statistics give a very different picture of the juvenile contribution to crime. A crime is considered cleared if someone is formally charged with the crime. To use the UCR data properly, one must understand this difference (for an excellent illustration, see Snyder & Sickmund, 2006, p. 123). For all the reasons enumerated here, victimization and self-reported data are considered to be more reliable and valid as a measure of crime than official records.

Arrest data show that, after years of stability, the violent juvenile delinquency arrest rate began to increase in the late 1980s (Figure 3.1). This focused national attention on the juvenile violence problem. In 1989, the violent juvenile arrest rate increased to its highest level since the 1960s (Snyder & Sickmund, 1999, p. 120). This rate continued to climb each year thereafter, until it reached a peak in 1994. In the period 1988 through 1994, the violent juvenile arrest rate increased 62% (Snyder & Sickmund, 1999, p. 120). From 1984 through 1994, the *number* of arrested juvenile homicide offenders tripled (Snyder & Sickmund, 1995, p. 56; Snyder, Sickmund, & Poe-Yamagata, 1996). This development grabbed headline attention, and it was repeatedly cited as evidence that juvenile delinquency was out of control in the United States. However, the juvenile murder arrest *rate* barely doubled, from just under 6 to 14 per 100,000 juveniles ages 10–17 (Snyder & Sickmund, 1999, p. 122). The murder rate for young adults (ages 18-24) was much higher: 25 in 1994, having increased from 15 in 1984 (Fox, 1996b, p. 4).

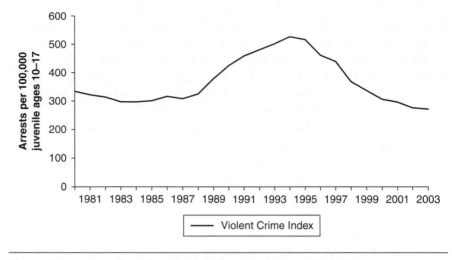

Figure 3.1   Juvenile Violent Crime Index Arrest Rates: 1981–2003

It is interesting to note that juvenile arrest rates for Property Crime Index offenses (larceny–theft, burglary, motor vehicle theft, and arson) changed little from the late 1980s to the early 1990s (Snyder & Sickmund, 1999, p. 126). Because juvenile violence arrest rates increased and juvenile serious property arrests did not increase noticeably, the delinquency increase was characterized as a juvenile violence epidemic, not an epidemic of overall juvenile delinquency. The possible occurrence of an epidemic of juvenile violence without a similar increase in nonviolent delinquency suggests that juvenile offenses deemed violent were specifically targeted for arrest and prosecution (Zimring, 1998a).

Violent juvenile arrests have been in a sharp downturn since 1994 (Snyder & Sickmund, 2006). In 2004, the United States experienced its 10th consecutive year of an unprecedented drop in the rate of juvenile arrests for violent offenses (Snyder, 2006). By 2003, it already had fallen below the levels of the early 1980s (Snyder & Sickmund, 2006, p. 132). A similar pattern was seen for the juvenile arrest rate for murder. From its peak in 1993 to 2004, the juvenile arrest rate for murder fell 77%, to a level below the rate in the early 1980s (Snyder, 2006). In 2004, juveniles were involved in only 12% of all cleared violent crimes—specifically, 5% of murders, 12% of forcible rapes, 14% of robberies, and 12% of aggravated assaults (Snyder, 2006, p. 1).

For several reasons, arrest data are not as reliable as either victimization data or self-report survey data as a measure of actual crimes for juvenile offenders. First, juveniles are more likely than adults to be arrested in groups, and they may be more easily apprehended because of their group offending and lack of criminal stealth (Reiss, 1988). Second, juveniles are more likely than adults to be arrested for certain crimes that are reported to police. Finally, it appears that many minor juvenile offenses were upgraded to more serious charges in the 1988–1992 period (Zimring, 1998a) because of the lower degree of tolerance of juvenile delinquency that followed the publicized increases in serious and violent delinquency. The lower tolerance is attributable, in particular, to the "wars" on crime, drugs, juveniles, and gangs that I discuss elsewhere in this book.

Victimization Trends

Victimization data collected in the National Crime Victimization Survey (NCVS, Box 3.2), conducted by the Bureau of Justice Statistics, show that violent juvenile victimizations increased in the late 1980s and early 1990s (Figure 3.2). In an analysis of NCVS data covering the period 1987–1992, Moone (1994) found that the juvenile violent victimization rate increased 23%. However, two-thirds of the violent juvenile victimizations (rape, robbery, aggravated assault, and simple assault) during this period were simple assaults that did not involve weapons and resulted in nothing more than minor injuries. Juvenile serious violent victimizations (rape, robbery, aggravated assault) did not increase significantly in this period. In fact, the proportion of violent juvenile victimizations that resulted in serious injury declined from 11% to 7% between 1987 and 1992, and the percentage of serious violent incidents resulting in injury and hospital stays and that involved the use of weapons remained essentially the same (Snyder & Sickmund, 1999). Thus national victimization data suggest that the increase in assaults reported in the late 1980s and early 1990s was accounted for mainly by simple assaults that did not result in serious injury.

IN FOCUS 3.2

National Crime Victimization Survey

Since 1972, the NCVS has collected data on nonfatal crimes against people age 12 or older, reported and not reported to the police, from a nationally representative sample of U.S. households. The NCVS provides information about the following:

- Victims (age, gender, race, ethnicity, marital status, income, and education level)
- Offenders (gender, race, approximate age, and victim–offender relationship)
- Criminal offenses (time and place of occurrence, use of weapons, nature of injury, and economic consequences)

(Continued)

(Continued)

With all its strengths, the NCVS has two significant limitations in describing the extent of juvenile victimizations. First, the NCVS does not collect information from or about victims below age 12 (because designers of the survey believed that younger respondents are not able to provide the requested information). Thus juvenile victimizations reported by the NCVS cover only those involving juveniles ages 12–17. It should also be noted that the information on victims' perceptions about offenders may not be very precise (Butts & Snyder, 2007).

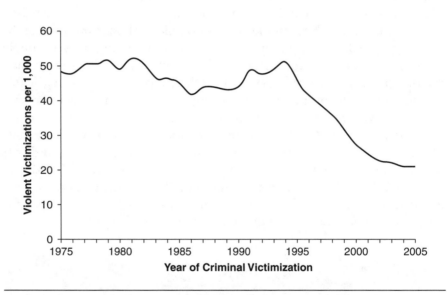

Figure 3.2   Violent Victimizations, 1975–2005

The 23% increase in reported violent victimizations from 1987 to 1992 shown in Moone's (1994) analysis is only about one-third as large as the increase (62%) in juvenile arrests for violent crimes between 1988 and 1994 (Snyder & Sickmund, 1999, p. 120). These sources would not show such a large discrepancy if both of them were valid measures of delinquent activity. Because of the limitations of national arrest data (see Box 3.1), victims' reports are more valid than arrest rates as a measure of delinquency (see Box 3.2).

Violent juvenile victimizations began dropping before the mid-1990s. From 1993 through 1997, the number of serious violent victimizations with at least one juvenile offender dropped 33%; the drop in such victimizations in which all offenders were adults was lower, 25% (Snyder & Sickmund, 1999, pp. 62–63). Thus serious violent victimizations involving juvenile offenders dropped at a much faster rate than those for adults.

The rate of violent crimes dropped steeply after 1994 and has not increased in recent years (Butts & Snyder, 2006). In fact, juvenile victimization data reported in *Indicators of School Crime and Safety, 2006* (Dinkes, Cataldi, Kena, & Baum, 2006) shows that the percentage of students ages 12–18 who were victimized at school in the previous 6 months decreased between 1995 and 2005 from 10% to 4%. However, there was an increase in the number of violent crimes in which the victim believed the offender was younger than age 18 (Dinkes et al., 2006, p. 5). The number of these incidents grew 57% between 2002 and 2005. Nevertheless, the number of under-18 crimes in 2005 was still 60% lower than the 1.1 million reported in 1993. Therefore, trends based on victimization data are somewhat mixed.

Self-Reported Delinquency Trends

In self-reports obtained through surveys of juvenile populations, respondents give information on their own delinquent acts. Although any survey data have limitations, self-report measures have long been considered to be the most reliable and valid measure of crime (Blumstein, Cohen, Roth, & Visher, 1986; Dunford & Elliott, 1984; Hindelang, Hirschi, & Weis, 1981; Huizinga, Esbensen, & Weiher, 1996; Thornberry & Krohn, 2000). Self-report data from a matched sample of respondents in the National Youth Survey (NYS) and the Denver Youth Survey showed no substantial changes in the prevalence of delinquency over the 1979–1991 period except for prevalence of gang fights (Huizinga, Weiher, Espiritu, & Esbensen, 2003). In addition, the level of injury from violent offenses had increased substantially.

Data from two national self-report studies show that there was no sharp increase in juvenile violence in the 1980s and early 1990s (Box 3.3). In an examination of trends in the Monitoring the Future (MTF) survey over the 1982–1994 period, Johnston, Bachman, and O'Malley (1995) found that high school seniors did not report more significant involvement in any of the 15 behaviors (except theft over $50) over the course of the 13 years of the survey; in fact, they reported modest *decreases* in involvement in most of the behaviors measured by the survey (Maguire & Pastore, 1995, pp. 258–259). The percentage of U.S. students who use illicit drugs or drink alcohol continued a decade-long drop in 2006, according to the annual MTF survey (Johnston et al., 2006).

IN FOCUS 3.3
National Self-Reported Delinquency Surveys

The NYS is the most cited and analyzed self-report survey. It was a prospective longitudinal study of a national probability sample of 1,725 youths ages 11–17 in 1976. The researchers designed the survey to measure delinquent behavior and drug use, and they selected youths from a national probability sample of U.S. households. The panel was interviewed annually from 1976 to 1980 and every 3 years thereafter. At the time of the last interview, in 1993, the members of the panel were ages 27–33. Official arrest record data are available for all respondents. Now that the panel members are adults, this excellent survey no longer provides data on juveniles.

The MTF study continues to measure illicit drug use and delinquency among a national sample of high school seniors (eighth and tenth graders were added in 1991). Beginning in 1982, students have been asked to report their involvement during the preceding 12 months in 15 behavioral areas. The survey includes six questions covering violent acts (called the MTF Violence Index): arguing or fighting with parents, hitting an instructor or supervisor, getting into a serious fight at school or work, group fighting, hurting someone so seriously they needed medical attention, and using a weapon to take something. (More information about the MTF study is available online at http://www.monitoringthefuture.org.)

The National Longitudinal Survey of Youth (NLSY) began surveying a nationally representative sample of 9,000 youth between the ages of 12 and 16 in 1997. The main purpose of the NLSY is to study school–labor market issues. The survey also asks youth to self-report having engaged in a variety of deviant and delinquent behaviors. The NLSY is conducted every 2 years. This survey is emerging as a valid source of self-reported delinquency trend data.

The Youth Risk Behavior Surveillance System (YRBSS) was designed to determine the prevalence and age of initiation of health risk behaviors; to assess whether health risk behaviors increase, decrease, or remain the same over time; and to provide comparable national, state, and local data. Developed by the Centers for Disease Control in collaboration with federal, state, and private sector partners, this voluntary system includes a national survey and surveys conducted by state and local education and health agencies. The YRBSS monitors six categories of priority health risk behaviors among youth and young adults, including behaviors that contribute to unintentional injuries and violence; tobacco use; alcohol and other drug use; sexual behaviors that contribute to unintended pregnancy and sexually transmitted diseases, including human immunodeficiency virus infections; unhealthy dietary behaviors; and physical inactivity. In addition, the YRBSS monitors general health status and the prevalence of overweight and asthma. Every 2 years, YRBSS provides data representative of 9th–12th graders in public and private schools nationwide. The most recent report

(Centers for Disease Control and Prevention, 2006) summarizes results from the national survey, 40 state surveys, and 21 local surveys conducted among students in grades 9–12 during October 2004–January 2006.

Self-report surveys that measure delinquency have limitations (McCord et al., 2001, pp. 30–31). First, the surveys of student samples (the MTF and YRBSS) miss three important groups of students: those who are absent from school when the surveys are taken, those who have dropped out of school, and homeless juveniles who are not attending school. Second, the behaviors covered in self-report surveys often are not directly comparable with arrest and court crime categories. Third, the validity of self-report data may not be consistent among people of different races and genders. Finally, self-report surveys of offending are susceptible to response errors in which respondents strategically overstate or underreport their offending (Lynch, 2002). Underreporting is apparent for homicide and rape offenses.

The Centers for Disease Control and Prevention's Youth Risk Behavior Survey (YRBS) is currently the most comprehensive survey of youth for indicators of at-risk behaviors in the United States (see Box 3.3). But its delinquency measures are limited to only two violence indicators and alcohol or other drug use. The following are important trends in youth risk behaviors from YRBSs covering the period 1991–2005. For each indicator, the Centers for Disease Control and Prevention (2006) reports trends in two segments of this 15-year survey period (Box 3.4).

IN FOCUS 3.4

Youth Risk Behavior Survey Results Covering the Period 1991–2005

- The percentage of students who reported lifetime alcohol use did not change significantly in 1991–1999 and then decreased in 1999–2005.
- The percentage of students who reported current alcohol use did not change significantly in 1991–1999 and then decreased in 1999–2005.
- The percentage of students who reported lifetime marijuana use increased in 1991–1999 and then decreased in 1999–2005.
- The percentage of students who reported current marijuana use increased in 1991–1999 and then decreased in 1999–2005.
- The percentage of students who reported lifetime cocaine use increased in 1991–1999 and then decreased in 1999–2005.
- The percentage of students who reported current cocaine use increased in 1991–2001 and then did not change significantly in 2001–2005.

The percentage of students who carried a weapon *decreased* in 1991–1999 and then *did not change* significantly in 1999–2005. In contrast, the percentage of students who were in a physical fight *decreased* in 1991–2003 and then *increased* in 2003–2005. *Increased* use of illicit drugs and alcohol was consistently reported in the 1990s, followed by *decreased* use in the first half of the current decade (see Box 3.4 for detailed results for alcohol, marijuana, and cocaine). These findings are mixed but generally point to decreased self-reported delinquency in the first half of the current decade (except for physical fighting). (Box 3.5 describes how nationwide data on the juvenile justice system are collected and reported.)

IN FOCUS 3.5
National Data on the Juvenile Justice System

The federal Office of Juvenile Justice and Delinquency Prevention (OJJDP) has statutory responsibility for collecting and reporting nationwide data on youths in the juvenile justice system. OJJDP maintains two reporting systems for this purpose: the National Juvenile Court Data Archive and the Census of Juveniles in Residential Placement (CJRP). To understand these data, one needs a fundamental understanding of the structure and processes of the juvenile justice system; Snyder and Sickmund (2006, pp. 104–107) provide a clear explanation, complete with a case flowchart illustrating the juvenile justice system's processing stages (p. 107). I have reprinted it in Chapter 12, Figure 12.1, because their representation of the juvenile justice system case flow emphasizes connections between the juvenile and adult criminal justice systems.

Juvenile Court Data

Juvenile court data are gathered for the National Juvenile Court Data Archive through a voluntary reporting system. The extent to which the data in this archive are representative of juvenile courts nationwide is unknown; in 2003–2004, data were collected from courts that had jurisdiction over 77% of the juvenile population in the United States in 2004 (Stahl et al., 2007). This archive makes available a wide variety of data on juvenile court referrals, methods of handling, and dispositions, including placements in detention centers and commitments to residential facilities.

Juvenile Corrections Data

The federal government no longer collects nationwide data on admissions of juveniles to detention and corrections facilities (for a brief history of federal juvenile correctional data collection, see Krisberg & Howell, 1998).

Therefore, the numbers and characteristics of juvenile admissions to detention and correctional facilities are unknown. The National Council on Crime and Delinquency collected such data in the early 1990s. See DeComo (1998) for an interesting analysis of racial and ethnic characteristics of youths admitted to detention and corrections facilities. This is the last report published on the Juveniles Taken into Custody reporting system.

In 1997, OJJDP launched an alternative reporting system, the 1-day Census of Juveniles in Residential Placement (CJRP). The CJRP collects individual data such as race, sex, and most serious offense on all juveniles held in residential facilities (short-term detention and long-term state correctional facilities) on a given day each year. In addition, facilities are asked to provide information about the legal status of each juvenile held. A Juvenile Residential Facility Census collects information on how facilities operate and the services they provide in alternate years with the CJRP, and a Survey of Youth in Residential Facilities collects information from confined juveniles and young adults (under age 21) held in juvenile facilities.

The biases that may exist in the CJRP data are unknown. Any census of incarcerated offenders taken on a single day has an inherent flaw: It overstates the proportion of more serious offenders because their confinement period is longer and therefore they are more likely to be there on the day the census is taken (Lynch & Sabol, 1997, p. 6; McCord et al., 2001).

Key Publications

In 1995, OJJDP began to publish a regular series of national reports on juvenile offenders and victims that include comprehensive information on existing data on the juvenile justice system from a wide variety of sources. Three such reports have been published to date (Snyder & Sickmund, 1995, 1999, 2006). The 2006 report, along with a statistical briefing book that contains valuable information on various aspects of juvenile justice system handling of children and adolescents, is available on OJJDP's Web site at http://ojjdp .ncjrs.gov/ojstatbb/index.html. In addition, the CJRP Databook (Sickmund, Sladkey, & Kang, 2004) contains a large set of predefined tables detailing the characteristics (age, sex, race or ethnicity, offense, type of facility, and placement status) of juvenile offenders in residential placement facilities. Tables are available for 1997, 1999, 2001, and 2003 at OJJDP's Web site at http://ojjdp.ncjrs.gov/ojstatbb/cjrp/.

In sum, juvenile arrests for violent crimes increased much more sharply than either violent victimizations or self-reported serious violent offenses in the period from the mid-1980s through the mid-1990s. These comparisons suggest that arrest data tend to exaggerate changes in violent juvenile offenses during this period. The tyranny of small numbers principle discussed in the next section appears to be an important factor in this regard.

The Tyranny of Small Numbers Principle

The phrase *tyranny of small numbers* refers to the fact that when a small increase occurs in a small number, a large percentage increase is shown. For example, if a person has one automobile and buys another one, this represents a 100% increase in the number of automobiles the person owns. Because only one-third of 1% of juveniles are arrested for violent offenses (Snyder, 2000), the base rate for juvenile violence is very low. Therefore, any change in either direction, when reported as a ratio or percentage, takes the form of a large number. Snyder and his colleagues (1996) illustrate the tyranny of small numbers principle as it applies to rates of juvenile violence:

> Of the 100 violent crimes committed in 1985 in a small town, assume that juveniles were responsible for 10, and adults for 90. If the number of juvenile crimes increased 70% by 1994, juveniles would be committing 17 (or 7 more) violent crimes. A 50% increase in adult violent crimes would mean that adults were committing 135 (or 45 more) violent crimes. If each crime resulted in an arrest, the percentage increase in juvenile arrests would be more than the adult increase (70% versus 50%). However, 87% of the increase in violent crime (45 of the 52 additional violent crimes) would have been committed by adults. Juvenile arrests represent a relatively small fraction of the total; consequently, larger percentage increases in juvenile arrests does not necessarily translate into a large contribution to overall crime growth. (p. 20)

Snyder and his colleagues show how the tyranny of small numbers principle applies in a comparison of juvenile and adult contributions to murders during the 1985–1994 period. They demonstrate that if juveniles had committed no more murders in 1994 than in 1985, murders in the United States would have increased 15% instead of 23%. Therefore, juveniles were responsible for about one-third of the increase in murders during the period 1985–1994. The tyranny of small numbers led the media and others to exaggerate the contribution of juveniles both to the total volume of violent crime in the United States and to the increase over the previous decade.

The tyranny of small numbers principle also applies to misinterpretation of the juvenile contribution to total increases in reported violent crimes. Using FBI-reported crime and clearance statistics, Snyder et al. (1996, p. 20) estimated that juveniles committed 137,000 more violent offenses in 1994 than in 1985, and adults committed an additional 398,000. Therefore, juveniles were responsible for about one-fourth (26%) of the growth in violent crime between 1985 and 1994, and adults were responsible for nearly three-fourths (74%) of the increase in violent crime clearances during this period.

Other Ways of Producing
Misleading Juvenile Delinquency Statistics

A common way in which some observers distort crime trend data is by focusing on a very short time period and ignoring long-term trends. As the preceding discussion shows, some observers dramatized the increase in juvenile homicide offenders between 1984 and 1994 as a tripling of the number. The effect of focusing only on the short period of the mid-1980s through the mid-1990s is an exaggeration of the magnitude of the increase. When viewed in a longer-term perspective, the increase in the juvenile homicide rate is not nearly as dramatic.

Zimring (1998a, pp. 31–47) made such a comparison for 13- to 17-year-olds from 1980 through 1995. He found that two of the four Violent Crime Index offenses were essentially trendless over that 16-year-period. Robberies and rapes fluctuated without any discernible long-range trend. Arrests for robbery dropped by 21%, and rape arrests remained at a low level. Aggravated assault increased 56% above the 1980 level, and a 34% gain was recorded for homicide. Thus the major change in violent juvenile arrests over this period was for aggravated assaults.

However, most of the increase in aggravated assault arrests from 1980 through 1995 occurred at the nonserious end of the seriousness scale (Zimring, 1998a, p. 41). As Zimring notes, the counting and classification of assaults are essentially matters of police discretion: "For the period since 1980, there is significant circumstantial evidence from many sources that changing police thresholds for when assault should be recorded and when the report should be for aggravated assault are the reason for most of the growth in arrest rates" (p. 39). Police standards for recording juvenile assaults shifted toward "upgrading" simple assaults to aggravated assaults in the 16-year period (p. 41). Zimring's conclusion is supported by Moone's (1994) analysis of juvenile victimization rates. Most of the increase in juvenile assault victimization rates in 1987–1992 was accounted for by an increase in minor assaults.

Another misleading way of depicting juvenile violence trends is to use the very lowest points in juvenile violence as the base year. As Zimring (1998a) observes, "Picking a low period in a cyclically fluctuating time series will generate the greatest difference between baseline rates and the current rates of violence, but it also risks confusing the up-and-down movements in a cyclical pattern with trends that represent changes in the average volume of violence to be expected over time" (p. 34). Several analysts have done this, picking 1984 or 1985 as their base year because it was a low point of juvenile violence rates (Blumstein, 1995a, 1995b; Fox, 1996b).

As a general observation, reliance on UCR arrest data to measure juvenile violence trends is very problematic. Because juveniles tend to commit crimes in groups, several adolescents may be arrested for a crime that only one of them committed. In one test of this supposition, the UCR data exaggerated the actual number of juveniles involved in a reported crime by about 40% (McCord & Conway, 2005). In another test, Snyder examined patterns in 21,000 robberies in seven states (Snyder & Sickmund, 2006, p. 124). The FBI's National Incident-Based Reporting System data from these states gave the victim's perception of the age of the offender and indicated whether the offender was arrested. Robberies by juveniles were 23% more likely to result in arrest than were robberies by adults. Therefore, the juvenile proportion of cleared robberies was substantially greater than the proportion of robberies actually committed by juveniles. Based on these two studies, it appears that UCR clearance percentages overestimate the juvenile responsibility for crime by about 23–40% because juvenile offenders are more likely to be arrested. It also is important to recognize that arrest data indicate society's *response* to juvenile delinquency, not the actual level of delinquency, so one needs to examine data from more direct measures of delinquency to assess whether an "epidemic" occurred. These data come from victimization surveys and delinquency self-report surveys.

A New Crime Wave?

Broadcast media are wont to characterize crime increases as "crime waves" (Fishman, 1978). The latest attempt to declare a new crime wave in the United States arguably began in a 2004 publication in which it was reported that "youth-gang related homicides have risen by more than 50 percent according to Professor James Alan Fox, a leading criminologist at Northeastern University. Gang homicides have climbed from 692 in 1999 to over 1,100" (Fight Crime: Invest in Kids, 2004, p. 3). Even though Fox's new numbers could not be substantiated with either UCR or National Youth Gang Survey data (Curry, Egley, & Howell, 2004), the notion that a huge increase in gang crime was occurring across the country appeared to stick. Soon, reports began to single out gang-involved juveniles as the driving force behind a new wave of crime in the United States (see Butts & Snyder, 2006; and Esbensen & Tusinski, 2007 for reviews of this media coverage).

   The number of arrests for violent crimes grew 2% between 2004 and 2005, and juvenile homicide arrests jumped 20% during this same period (Federal Bureau of Investigation, 2006). A Police Executive Research Forum (PERF) report, aptly titled *Chief Concerns: A Gathering Storm—Violent Crime in America*, reported (2006, p. 1) that

> For a growing number of cities across the United States, violent crime is accelerating at an alarming pace. The Federal Bureau of Investigation's (FBI) annual Uniform Crime Report (UCR) for 2005 reflects a significant increase in violent crime throughout the country compared to 2004 figures. Nationwide, the United States experienced increases in three of the four violent crime categories: homicide (3.4%), robberies

(3.9%) and aggravated assaults (1.8%). This rise in violent crime was experienced in all areas of the country. The FBI statistics reflect the largest single year percent increase in violent crime in 14 years. Importantly, statistics provided to the Police Executive Research Forum from numerous cities reflect that the rise in violent crime is continuing into 2006.

Police tied the jump in crime to juveniles (as young as 10 years of age), guns, and gangs (Johnson, 2006a, 2006b). The news prompted Attorney General Alberto Gonzales to order further information gathering from police chiefs in 18 cities. His summary of the reports he received emphasized three points (Gonzales, 2007):

- "The biggest concern for law enforcement is loosely organized local gangs or street crews" (p. 3).
- "Crimes committed with guns—particularly those committed by juveniles—are a concern to local law enforcement" (p. 4).
- "The third message we heard time and time again from police chiefs was a concern about the level of violence among their cities' youth. Many law enforcement officials reported that offenders appear to be younger and younger and their crimes are becoming more and more violent in nature" (p. 4).

The PERF released a second report in 2007 titled *Violent Crime in America: 24 Months of Alarming Trends*. It conveyed a more urgent message, that "violent crime increased last year, and many cities experienced double-digit or even triple-digit percentage increases in homicides and other violence" and that "the new crime statistics for 2006 show a worsening of a trend first identified by PERF in mid 2005, when PERF began to hear rumblings from its members that 'violent crime is making a comeback.' A number of cities, particularly in the middle part of the United States, were beginning to experience large increases in three major categories of violent crime: robberies, aggravated assaults, and homicides" (p. 1).

PERF convened a violent crime summit of more than 170 attendees including police chiefs and mayors from 50 cities, at which "participants agreed that young, disaffected youth—who are more likely to be attracted to gangs—are driving violent crime increases in many communities and that African-American and Hispanic youth are disproportionately both the victims and offenders" (p. 10).

Only time will tell whether these trends are supported empirically, but Butts and Snyder (2006) acknowledge that the crime drop may now be ending. For the first time in a decade, several of the most serious violent crimes tracked by national crime statistics increased between 2004 and 2005 (Butts & Snyder, 2006, p. 3). Murder arrests of adults grew 6%, and robbery arrests involving adults saw almost no change (an increase of only 1%). As noted earlier, among juveniles, or youth under age 18, the increase in some violent crime arrests was proportionally greater. Juvenile arrests for murder grew 20% between 2004 and 2005. Robbery arrests involving juveniles rose 11% in the same time period. However, juvenile arrests for aggravated assault did not increase, which seems odd, given the reported increase in murder and robbery, because trends in these offenses tend to coincide. In any event, Butts and Snyder conclude,

> Law enforcement organizations have expressed deep concern about a recent rise in violent crime statistics. Some of these concerns are well-founded, but others are exaggerated. The recent changes in violent crime are small compared with the scale of shifting crime over the past 30 years. It is premature to predict a coming wave of serious violent crime after 1 year of increase. It is incorrect to assume that future increases in violent crime are inevitable, and it is inappropriate to lay the blame for any increase that does occur on juveniles. (p. 8)

Several observations can be made about the alarming reports of a new crime wave. First, it is important to keep in mind that the "tyranny of small numbers" principle applies to national juvenile statistics—especially to violent crimes. Second, the observed increases appear to exist only in selected cities and for selected crimes, rather than a substantial overall increase. And the latest information on arrest trends is that violent crimes dropped slightly in the first half of 2007 (and murders in large cites decreased 6%) compared with the same period in 2006 (Johnson, 2008). Third, under the best circumstances, available data are sometimes inadequate to challenge published claims about crime trends (Egley & O'Donnell, 2007). Fourth, it is important to make a distinction between "youth crime" (below age 25) and "juvenile crime" (below age 18). Of all violent crime arrests in 2005, 16% involved juveniles under age 18, but 29% involved young adults between ages 18 and 24 (Butts & Snyder, 2007). Therefore, policies and programs that aim to reduce youth violence should target young adults as well as juveniles. Fifth, we must guard against creating crime "reporting waves" that look much like "crime waves." Interestingly, we criminologists cannot claim credit for this insight.

A sociologist (Fishman, 1978) was the first to discover and document a "crime reporting wave"—a presumed wave of juvenile muggings of older adults that turned out to be nothing more than what Fishman dubbed a crime reporting wave. He noted how additional media outlets ran the story after seeing the initial attention that it garnered and how the original story was embellished as it was repeated in another locality. But even the original story could not be substantiated with official crime data. There are also modern-day examples, including the superpredator myth and associated coming waves of violence (Chapter 1) and the crack cocaine epidemic (Hartman & Golub, 1999; Reeves & Campbell, 1994). This, then, brings me to the last point on this matter. As a practical matter, criminologists cannot keep pace with reporting waves. Alarming reports scoot across the airwaves and through print media with great speed, far faster than comprehensive and long-term data can be collected, analyzed, written up, peer reviewed, and reported. This is a main reason why Butts and Snyder say "it's too soon to tell."

What Do All These Data Suggest?

The decade from the mid-1980s through the mid-1990s saw sharp increases in violent crime rates among all age groups. When one examines the data from a short-term perspective, the increase in juvenile violence is exaggerated, in part because of the tyranny of small numbers principle. Long-term arrest data for the period from 1980 through 1996 show that only two of the four major violent juvenile crimes increased during this period: aggravated assault and murder. Aggravated assault arrests increased the most; however, most of this increase was at the nonserious end of the assault scale.

If we use more reliable measures of delinquency, we see a very different picture of violent juvenile crime trends. Available self-report data do not show a discernible trend between the late 1980s and the early 1990s, except for perhaps an increase in more serious violent offenses that could have been gang related. Victimization data show that violent juvenile victimizations resulting in serious injury actually declined from the late 1980s to early 1990s. (Of course, homicide cannot be measured in victim surveys.)

Thus the main feature of juvenile violence trends between the late 1980s and the early 1990s is the increase in gun use in homicides. Recall that nongun homicides did not evidence a similar increase. Much of the increase in adolescent and young adult homicides appears to be attributable to an increase in gang-related homicides. The contribution of gang-related violence and homicides to the total volume of juvenile and young adult violence is perhaps the most overlooked factor in analysis of crime trends. The size and number of youth gangs, overall gang violence, and gang-related homicides all grew enormously from the mid-1980s to the mid-1990s (see Chapter 6).

The recent reports of inconsistent increases in violence generally in the United States, and among juveniles in particular, appear to be premature and to have some of the characteristic features of reporting waves. But time and careful research will tell us whether this is so.

Nothing I have said in this chapter should be taken as an attempt to minimize the severity of juvenile violence. Rather, my aim is to put such violence into proper perspective, historically and in relation to adult crime. Juveniles are part and parcel of the very high rates of violence in the United States. Ours is an extremely violent country, and juvenile violence rates are particularly high—higher than in other industrialized countries (U.S. Department of Health and Human Services, 2001, p. 28). The rate of death from firearms in the United States is 3 times greater than in Canada, 6 times greater than in Australia, and nearly 38 times greater than in the United Kingdom (Krug, Dahlberg, Mercy, Zwi, & Lozano, 2002).

Discussion Topics

1. What are the three different data sources that observers use to gauge changes in the levels of serious and violent delinquency? What are the strengths and weaknesses of each of these sources?

2. What is the tyranny of small numbers principle? Why is it important to understand this principle when one is attempting to assess juvenile delinquency trends?

3. Aside from the inappropriate use of data sources, what are some other ways of producing misleading juvenile crime trend statistics?

4. What are the distinguishing features of juvenile violence? Why are these important?

5. Apply Fishman's principle of a "crime reporting wave" to the superpredator myth or the crack cocaine epidemic.

PART II

The Research Base on Juvenile Offenders and Gangs

This section provides current research on delinquency development in individuals and effective programs for forestalling or preventing delinquency and gang involvement. The chapters in Part II present an overview of juvenile delinquency development from three perspectives. Chapter 4 presents a developmental theory of delinquency and gang involvement, illustrating how the antisocial developmental process can produce both outcomes. Chapter 5 examines juvenile offender careers. The chapter shows the various types of juvenile offender careers that evolve from the delinquent developmental process. Chapter 6 examines youth gangs. This chapter provides an overview of youth gangs beginning with an examination of youth gang trends. The latest research is presented on various aspects of youth gangs. Chapter 7 provides solutions to youth gangs, emphasizing that a comprehensive approach is likely to be most successful. Research-based programs are also presented.

CHAPTER 4

A Theory of Juvenile Delinquency and Gang Involvement

The chapter begins with an explanation of the risk-protection framework that undergirds modern developmental theories of delinquency. This is followed by a review of the major risk factors for serious and violent delinquency. The chapter concludes with an illustration of how risk factors operate in a theoretical framework that provides an explanation of the social development process that leads to delinquency and gang involvement.

The Risk-Protection Framework

Risk- and protection-focused approaches to the prevention of particular problems were pioneered by public health professionals and have been successful in reducing problems as diverse as cardiovascular disease and traffic-related injuries (Institute of Medicine, 1994). Risk-focused strategies for the prevention of cardiovascular disease seek to convince people to reduce identified risk factors in their lives, such as smoking and diets high in fat, while enhancing protective factors, including regular exercise and balanced diet.

Risk factors predict increased risk for developing a problem or disorder and also serve as correlates or predictors of the pathways that some children and adolescents take, leading to juvenile delinquency and gang involvement. Just as actuarial tables that automobile insurance companies use do not predict any given person's driving experience, the presence or absence of specific risk factors does not guarantee the development or lack of development of the problem behaviors. Explaining why specific behaviors occur is very difficult because numerous factors are involved—even simultaneously—and social interactions shape behaviors and problems over time (Thornberry, 2005). Most problem behaviors have multiple determinants. That is, there can be many explanations for child and adolescent problems, none of which, by itself, is a complete explanation.

Researchers organize the risk factors for serious and violent delinquency according to five developmental domains (usually called risk factor domains): individual, family, school, peer group, and community. This framework is inspired by developmental psychologist Bronfenbrenner's (1979) conceptualization of the different spheres of influence that affect a child's behavior, such as relations in the family, the peer group, and schools. More recent research has expanded the scope of these developmental domains to include individual and community factors as well. In addition, research shows that risk and protective factors function as predictors of violence, crime, and substance abuse at different points in life, as affected by risk factors in the respective spheres of influence.

Unfortunately, the idea of risk reduction is sometimes misinterpreted as though it involves blaming youths for being at risk of delinquency involvement. Some youth development advocates urge a shift from risk- and protection-focused delinquency prevention to an emphasis on only the protection side of the equation, what they prefer to call "positive" youth development. They promote the exclusive use of what is sometimes called strength-based training, resilience strengthening, or asset building (Brendtro & Ness, 1995; Leffert, Saito, Blyth, & Kroenke, 1996). This is a narrow view of youth development.

On the contrary, risk- and protection-focused prevention does not involve blaming youths for their risk factors. Four of the five major risk factors for delinquency are clearly beyond the control of affected youths. Children do not choose the families into which they are born, the communities where they live, the schools they attend, or many of the individual problems they develop, such as mental illness. Therefore, risk reduction involves changing the conditions to which youth are exposed that negatively affect their life chances. It has been estimated that at least 25% of adolescents in America are at serious risk of not achieving productive adulthood (National Research Council & Institute of Medicine, 2002). A large proportion of them are victims of the failure of schools to educate them, victims of psychological abuse at school, and dropouts (Hyman & Perone, 1998; Hyman & Snook, 1999). As seen in Chapter 2, out-of-school youth are significantly more likely to become involved in physical fights, carry a weapon, and participate in a wide range of other delinquent behaviors.

Contrary to the view of asset-building advocates, the reality is that problem behaviors normally develop in people who have a preponderance of risk factors over protective factors (Browning & Huizinga, 1999; Stouthamer-Loeber, Loeber, Wei, Farrington, & Wikstrom, 2002; Thornberry, Huizinga, & Loeber, 1995). This principle applies for all types of delinquents—even child delinquents (Loeber & Farrington, 2001a, 2001c; Stouthamer-Loeber, Loeber, et al., 2002). However, in extremely high-risk conditions, people need more than a simple majority of protective factors to overcome multiple risk factors (Browning & Huizinga, 1999; Smith, Lizotte, Thornberry, & Krohn, 1995). Moreover, exposure to risk domains in the relative absence of protective domains "dramatically increases the risk of later persistent serious offending" (Stouthamer-Loeber, Loeber, et al., 2002, p. 120). Therefore, communities must reduce the presence of multiple risk factors to achieve significant reductions in delinquency and other health and social problems. The most effective approach is to reduce risk factors while increasing protective factors.

Risk factors function in a cumulative fashion; that is, the greater number of risk factors, the greater the likelihood of a negative outcome. There also is evidence that various problem behaviors are caused by common risk factors. This is a well-supported principle of prevention science (Institute of Medicine, 1990, 1994). For example, adolescent delinquency and violence cluster with other adolescent problems, such as drug abuse, teen pregnancy, and school misbehavior and dropout (Jessor, Donovan, & Costa, 1991). Table 4.1 illustrates this principle, showing that many problem behaviors and health problems are associated with each other and share common risk factors in the individual, peer group, school, family, and community domains. This table displays risk factors for eight major negative outcomes. This table also shows that multiple risk factors contribute to each problem behavior. These are common areas in which delinquency prevention specialists and youth developers can work together to reduce risk factors for delinquency and other problem behaviors. If risk reduction efforts address risk and protective factors at or slightly before the developmental points at which they begin to predict later delinquency or violence, they are more likely to be effective.

Mental health disorders have not been well researched as risk factors for delinquency. For many years, psychoanalysts have attempted to characterize, to no avail, juvenile offenders who have a "criminal mind" (Box 4.1). Despite the fact that it has been thoroughly debunked, DiIulio's infamous pejorative characterization of juvenile "superpredators" lives on today in clinical efforts to find a subgroup of youngsters similarly labeled as "psychopaths" (Steinberg, 2002), and clinicians use an unvalidated instrument, the Psychopathy Checklist–Youth Version (PCL-YV), in a futile quest to identify adolescent psychopaths. The PCL-YV is a research instrument and therefore inappropriate for clinical uses according to Lawrence Steinberg (2002), director of the MacArthur Foundation Research Network on Adolescent Development and Juvenile Justice. Moreover, as Professor

Table 4.1   Risk Factors for Eight Major Outcomes

	Outcomes							
Risk Factors	*Behavior Problems*	*School Failure*	*Poor Physical Health*	*Physical Injury*	*Physical Abuse*	*Pregnancy*	*Drug Use*	*AIDS*
Community								
Impoverished neighborhood	X	X	X	X	X	X	X	
Ineffective social policies	X	X	X		X	X	X	
School								
Poor-quality schools	X	X	X			X	X	X
Peer								
Negative peer pressure and modeling	X	X	X			X	X	X
Peer rejection	X				X			
Family								
Low socioeconomic status	X	X	X	X	X	X	X	X
Parental psychopathology	X	X	X	X	X	X	X	X
Marital discord	X	X			X	X	X	
Punitive child rearing	X	X	X	X	X		X	
Individual								
Early onset of target problem	X	X	X	X	X	X	X	X[a]
Problems in other areas	X	X	X	X	X	X	X	X
Other								
Stress[b]	X	X	X	X	X	X	X	X

a. Early sexual activity is a risk factor.

b. Stress can occur at all levels and affect children directly or indirectly through parents, peers, and teachers.

Steinberg points out, the PCL-YV is based on characteristics of psychopathic adults, and when these traits appear in juveniles, they could well be traits linked to a normal, immature adolescent mind, not a severe mental disturbance.

IN FOCUS 4.1

Mental Health Problems in Juvenile Justice System Clients

It is now well established that most youth in juvenile correctional facilities and programs, approximately 65–70%, suffer from mental health and substance use disorders, with 25% experiencing disorders so severe that their ability to function is significantly impaired (McReynolds et al., 2008; Skowyra & Cocozza, 2006; Teplin et al., 2006; Wasserman, McReynolds, et al., 2002; Wasserman et al., 2004). In contrast, 20% of youths in general population studies and 45% of formal probation referrals to juvenile court suffer from mental health and substance use disorders (McReynolds et al., 2008). In a multistate study of youths in 29 different community-based programs, detention centers, and residential facilities in Louisiana, Texas, and Washington (Skowyra & Cocozza, 2006), 70% met criteria for at least one mental health disorder. Some observers have questioned this large figure, wondering whether the inclusion of conduct problems in the measures inflates the affected numbers. Indeed, disruptive disorders were most common, followed by substance use disorders, anxiety disorders, and mood disorders. However, when conduct disorders were removed from the analysis, two-thirds (66%) of the youths still met criteria for a mental health disorder, and more than 60% met diagnostic criteria for three or more diagnoses. Co-occurring substance use disorders were most common among youths with a disruptive disorder, followed by youths with a mood disorder. The study found that girls were at significantly higher risk (80%) than boys (67%) for a mental health disorder. In another study of a random sample from a large population of juvenile detainees, two-thirds of males and three quarters of females had a psychiatric diagnosis (Teplin et al., 2006). Even when conduct problems were not considered, 60% of the youths continued to evidence a psychiatric disorder.

Guidelines have been developed for comprehensive assessment of mental health problems among children and adolescents in every sector of the child care and youth service systems (Columbia University Department of Child and Adolescent Psychiatry, 2003; Skowyra & Cocozza, 2006). A validated Diagnostic Interview Schedule for Children (DISC) and a well-tested, self-administered Voice DISC version of it are readily available for widespread use (Wasserman et al., 2004).

The Justice for Juveniles (JFJ) initiative, a joint effort by the National Mental Health Association and the National GAINS Center, provides information and practical assistance to communities to promote systemic change and improve service delivery for people with both substance abuse and mental disorders in contact with the justice system. The goal of the JFJ initiative

(Continued)

(Continued)

is to highlight, at both local and national levels, the issues and service needs of youth with co-occurring mental health and substance abuse disorders in contact with the juvenile justice system. The JFJ represents an important first step to identify these youth, their needs, the services available in communities around the country, and ways to improve how systems respond to treatment needs of youth.

A JFJ report, *Justice for Juveniles: How Communities Respond to Mental Health and Substance Abuse Needs of Youth in the Juvenile Justice System,* contains information that was collected in communities through a series of interviews with key stakeholders at both the state and local level, including directors of mental health, substance abuse, and juvenile justice agencies; family members; police; key service providers; judges; and advocacy groups. These interviews were conducted by self-selected Mental Health Association and Federation of Families affiliates who volunteered to collect data in their communities. The community assessment asked respondents about the policies and programs in place to address the treatment needs of youth in the juvenile justice system in their respective communities and their perspective on how well services are provided to youth. The final sample of communities included 15 counties and 9 states. The report is a general cross-site summary of all 111 interviews completed by the 24 sites participating in the initiative. Although this report cannot give a complete picture of the how communities respond to the mental health and substance abuse needs of youth involved in the juvenile justice system, it does provide a critical first step in an area where little or no information exists. This report is available at http://www1.nmha .org/children/justjuv/execsum.cfm. It is an excellent guide to child and adolescent mental health problems, solutions, and resources.

Protective Factors for Delinquency

Research on protective factors has been slower to develop than research on risk factors, in part because of conceptual issues. Factors typically are designated as either "risk" or "protective"; however, some factors may have risk effects but no protective effects and vice versa, and other factors may have both (Stouthamer-Loeber et al., 1993; Stouthamer-Loeber, Loeber, et al., 2002). It would help matters if protective factors were defined more explicitly. Farrington (2007, pp. 33–34) has identified three separate meanings of protective factors. The first definition suggests that a protective factor is merely the opposite end of the scale (or other side of the coin) to a risk factor. To illustrate, if low intelligence is a risk factor, high intelligence may be a protective factor. This definition of protective factors assumes a linear relationship between the factor and the specified outcome variable such as violence.

The second definition specifies protective factors that are free-standing, that is, without corresponding, symmetrically opposite risk factors (as in the first definition). This definition of protective factors does not assume a linear relationship between the factor and the specified outcome variable (e.g., violence).

The third definition of a protective factor identifies variables that interact with risk factors to minimize or buffer their effects. In other words, these risk factors may or may not be associated with violence themselves. Interaction effects can be studied in two ways (Farrington, 2007, pp. 33–34), "either by focusing on the effect of a risk variable in the presence of a protective factor or by focusing on the effect of a protective variable in the presence of a risk factor. For example, the effect of family income on violence could be studied in the presence of good parental supervision, or the effect of parental supervision on violence could be studied in the presence of low family income."

Other advanced work on the various relationships between risk and protective factors and variables they affect is under way in the Pittsburgh Youth Study, in a new book (Loeber, Farrington, Stouthamer-Loeber, & White, 2008). For example, Loeber's team of researchers has conceptualized and measured promotive factors that reduce delinquency onset and also promote desistance. They demonstrate in their new analyses how promotive factors have main effects in the same way that risk factors have been studied for decades. Promotive factors are defined as factors that either (a) predict a low probability of later offending in the general population and, possibly, have a direct effect on prosocial behavior, which they call *preventive promotive factors*; or (b) predict desistance from offending in populations of known delinquents, which they call *remedial promotive factors*. In addition, Loeber's team distinguishes two types of risk factors: aggravating risk factors (which predict later offending) and hindering risk factors (which influence desistance from offending). These conceptualizations add enormous precision to research in these immensely important areas.

Table 4.2 (Durlak, 1998) shows protective factors (biological factors are excluded) for eight major child and adolescent outcomes. The 1,200 prevention studies that Durlak reviewed suggest that all of the listed protective factors are potent in buffering youths against the eight major negative outcomes. Each of these protective factors is worthy of further study. Note also that many of the same factors provide protection against all of the negative outcomes. Durlak's review suggests that self-efficacy, a good parent–child relationship, and social support from helping parents, peers, and teachers may be the most important protective factors against delinquency and other problem behaviors.

I present Durlak's tables of risk and protective factors here to give readers a sense of how future work on risk factors might be organized and applied in communities. In the meantime, some progressive research is being done on protective factors that may be of interest to readers.

Table 4.2   Protective Factors for Eight Major Outcomes

Level of Analysis	Behavior Problems	School Failure	Poor Physical Health	Physical Injury	Physical Abuse	Pregnancy	Drug Use	AIDS
Community								
Social norms	X	X	X	X	X	X	X	X
Effective social policies	X	X	X	X	X	X	X	X
School								
High-quality schools	X	X				X	X	X
Peer								
Positive peer modeling	X	X		X		X	X	X
Family								
Good parent– child relations	X	X	X	X	X	X	X	X
Individual								
Personal and social skills	X	X	X	X	X	X	X	X
Self-efficacy	X	X				X	X	X
Other								
Social support[a]	X	X	X	X	X	X	X	X

a. Social support can occur at all levels and help children directly or indirectly by helping parents, peers, and teachers.

The researchers in the Pittsburgh Youth Study (Stouthamer-Loeber et al., 1993; Stouthamer-Loeber, Loeber, et al., 2002; Stouthamer-Loeber, Loeber, Stallings, & Lacourse, 2008) are conducting ingenious studies of risk and promotive (i.e., protective) factors to explore the relative influences of risk and protective factor domains (rather than single factors) on delinquency. This line of research is facilitated by the Centers for Disease Control, National Center for Injury Prevention and Control. The Centers for Disease Control has brought an interested group of researchers together for the purpose of carrying out coordinated analyses on existing data sets. This approach should yield a definitive set of protective factors for which there is strong empirical support.

Research to date has not considered certain protective factors. Religiosity is a good example. Research on the effects of religiosity as a protective factor against delinquency has been very sparse (Johnson, Li, Larson, & McCullough, 2000). The few well-designed studies that have been conducted on this topic have shown that religiosity is inversely related to delinquency (Chard-Wierschem, 1998; Jang & Johnson, 2001; Johnson et al., 2000) and that it may be more important for girls than boys (Resnick, Ireland, & Borowsky, 2004). But how religiosity operates to increase resilience is not clear. Its effects may be indirect (Chard-Wierschem, 1998). Alternatively, religiosity may operate directly, serving to instill moral values, trustworthiness, and ability to feel guilt for misdeeds. Both effects are likely. One major problem with this area of research is that studies typically measure religiosity only in terms of church attendance, which is not necessarily a good indicator of true religiosity. The fact that a person attends church regularly does not ensure that he or she accepts or applies key conceptual features of religion—values, beliefs, and other spiritual aspects—in his or her life. The preferred indicators of general religiosity are personal prayer practices and valuing religious observance (Resnick et al., 2004). Future research on protective factors and program development should consider religiosity to be an important element in delinquency reduction.

Two Key Features of Risk Factors

The first key characteristic of risk factors is that they vary over the developmental course of childhood and adolescence, depending on the age at which certain risk factors come into play. This is illustrated next.

Lipsey and Derzon (1998) were the first to organize risk factors and outcomes, as indicated in 66 reports of 34 longitudinal studies into two developmental time frames. Their review is also the first comprehensive meta-analysis of predictors of serious or violent offenses among children and adolescents. First, Lipsey and Derzon identified the main childhood (ages 6–11) predictors of serious or violent offenses at ages 15–25. Second, they identified the main adolescent (ages 12–14) predictors of serious or violent offenses at ages 15–25. The best predictors differ for the two age groups because certain risk factors have different degrees of influence at various developmental stages. In general, family influences are predominant early in life, followed by school factors, then peer group influences.

Lipsey and Derzon's findings may be summarized as follows:

- At ages 6–11, the best predictors of subsequent serious or violent offenses are involvement in delinquency (general offenses) at this early age and drug use. The second strongest group of predictors are being a male, living in a poor family (low socioeconomic status), and having antisocial parents. A history of aggression and ethnicity are in the third strongest group of predictors.
- For the 12–14 age group, lacking social ties and having antisocial peers are the strongest predictors of subsequent serious or violent offenses.

Involvement in delinquency (general offenses) is the one predictor in the second ranking group. Several predictors are in the third strongest group: a history of aggression, school attitude and performance, psychological condition (mental health), parent–adolescent relations, being a male, and a history of violence.

- Broken homes and abusive parents are among the weakest predictors of subsequent serious or violent offenses for both age groups.
- The significance of antisocial peers and substance abuse is reversed in the two age groups. Whereas having antisocial peers is the weakest predictor for the age 6–11 group, it is one of two very strong predictors for the 12–14 age group. Conversely, in the 6–11 age group, early onset of substance use is one of two very strong predictors; it is among the weakest predictors for the age 12–14 group.

This meta-analysis is important for what it reveals about the relative strengths of predictors for the two different age groups, children (ages 6–11) and adolescents (ages 12–14). The implications are important for prevention programming priorities. Early intervention efforts, with children, should target early delinquent behaviors, including drug use and displays of aggression, family poverty, and antisocial parents. In contrast, prevention efforts with adolescents should seek to reduce young people's associations with antisocial peers and involvement in delinquency, aggression, and physical violence while strengthening their social ties, improving their relationships with parents, and improving their mental health.

This is not to say that predictors in the fourth and fifth categories should be ignored. These, too, are significant predictors. A comprehensive prevention approach that addresses predictors in more than one risk factor domain (e.g., peer group and family) is likely to have the largest impact.

A second key feature of risk factors is that their influence is somehow thwarted by a unique characteristic of individuals, a trait called *resilience*. In a Washington, D.C., study, Chaiken (2000) found that almost one in five of a randomly selected sample of boys in census tracts with the highest rates of juvenile violence was resilient and avoided involvement in violent behavior. Psychologists Cairns and Cairns (1994) use the term *lifelines* to describe the various types of supports that promote adolescents' success in life, despite the odds against it. They identify the following as the main lifelines in the context of protection against adolescent problem behaviors: schools and mentors, social networks and friendships, families and neighborhoods, ethnicity and social class, individual characteristics, and new opportunities for living.

Why are some young people resilient? What protective factors immunize them against risk and increase their resilience? More to the point, how do most juveniles avoid delinquency and violence in the face of seemingly overwhelming odds? The findings from two studies provide partial answers to these questions.

In the first of two studies on this issue, conducted in Rochester, New York, the researchers found that in the short run, even during the peak age of delinquency involvement, protective factors did a very good job of insulating high-risk youth: 82% of the youth who had nine or more protective factors were resilient at ages 13–14 (Thornberry et al., 1995, pp. 230–232). The more protective factors youths had, the more resilient they were. But the positive effects did not enable the youngsters to remain resilient for long. By ages 15–17, high-risk youth with numerous protective factors were no more likely to be resilient and to avoid delinquency than youth with fewer protective factors.

The second study, part of the Denver Youth Survey, identified key protective factors against serious delinquency, and the findings also illustrate the relationship between risk factors and protective factors (Browning & Huizinga, 1999). When the number of risk factors exceeded the number of protective factors, the chance of a successful adolescence was very small. Indeed, the chance of a successful adolescence was not high until the number of protective factors far exceeded the number of risk factors. The researchers defined a successful adolescence as one with minimal involvement in serious delinquency, minimal problems resulting from drug use, age-appropriate grade in school or graduation from high school, and good self-esteem and self-efficacy.

A Developmental Theory of Delinquency and Gang Involvement

My main goal here is to demonstrate how common risk factors lead first to delinquent behavior, then to gang involvement. This is a clear case in which two related problem behaviors share the same risk factors. The theoretical model that follows (Figure 4.1; Howell & Egley, 2005b) draws on developmental theory (Loeber & Farrington, 1998, 2001a) in tying together risk factors in four developmental stages—preschool, school entry, childhood, and adolescence—in the pathway to delinquency and gang involvement. This theory also builds on Thornberry and Krohn's (2001) developmental model of delinquency, their theory of gang involvement (Thornberry, Krohn, Lizotte, Smith, & Tobin, 2003), and also Thornberry's (2005) brilliant exposition of his interactional theory. His far more complex theory seeks to explain the inevitable variations in delinquent career patterns. This topic will be examined in the next chapter.

This theory incorporates risk factors mainly from prospective longitudinal quantitative studies because the level of proof is higher in these kinds of studies. This is because longitudinal research designs permit measurement of the risk factors at an earlier time than the outcome variable—gang membership in this case. Thus, longitudinal research designs are stronger than cross-sectional studies for determining causal relationships. Because cross-sectional studies measure both risk factors and outcomes at the same time, the causal ordering cannot be determined with certainty; what appears to be a predictor

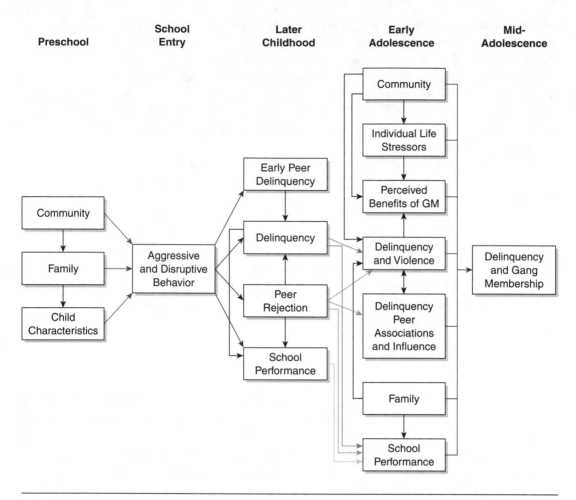

Figure 4.1   A Developmental Theory of Serious Delinquency and Gang Involvement

could well be an outcome of the dependent variable. Similarly, sorting out causal factors in ethnographic studies is a particularly difficult task because, for example, the focus of gang observational studies is on gang life, not on distinguishing adolescents who join from those who do not.

Table 4.3 contains risk factors for juvenile delinquency and gang involvement—almost all of which emanate from longitudinal quantitative studies—which I synthesized from a literature review. Note that these are organized by age level and that risk factors for gang involvement (almost all of which also predict general delinquency) are noted with an asterisk. A key point here is that delinquency and gang involvement share a common set of risk factors. Indeed, delinquency almost invariably precedes gang joining. Therefore, the theoretical model proposed here integrates developmental processes for delinquency involvement with gang membership. The risk factors shown in Table 4.3 also appear in an online database that was developed to help communities assess the prevalence of risk factors for these two problem behaviors and select research-based programs that address the specific risk factors. This online operating system is called the Strategic Planning Tool (http://www.iir.com/nygc/tool/). Because that tool was developed for practitioners' use in strategic community planning in conjunction with the implementation of a Gang Reduction Program, the theoretical framework presented here does not appear in the online tool. Nevertheless, the theory is implied in the manner in which local program planners and practitioners can operate the Strategic Planning Tool to serve their program development purposes.

As noted earlier, this theory suggests that there are four distinct developmental stages in the pathway to delinquency and gang involvement—preschool, school entry, childhood, and adolescence—and these are displayed in Figure 4.1. These and the key risk factors are described next.

The Preschool Stage

In this first developmental stage, child characteristics and community and family deficits produce aggressive and disruptive behavior disorders by the time of school entry (Burke, Loeber, & Birmaher, 2002; Coie & Miller-Johnson, 2001; Kalb & Loeber, 2003; Loeber & Farrington, 2001a) and, in turn, delinquency and school performance problems in later childhood (Loeber & Farrington, 2001a). The theoretical link between structural community (macro-level) factors and delinquency at the individual level is mediated primarily by family variables (Thornberry & Krohn, 2001).

At birth—or beginning in the prenatal period for some infants—the family of procreation is the central influence on infants and children. During the preschool years, and especially in the elementary school period and onward, the array of risk factors expands, as some children are exposed to negative peer influences outside the home (see Loeber & Farrington, 2001a). Some children are also exposed to additional risk factors situated in schools or in the community at large during this period.

When linked with certain family and child characteristics, concentrated disadvantage impedes socialization of children (Loeber, Farrington, & Petechuk, 2003; Tremblay, 2003). Important family variables in the preschool stage include low parental education (social capital) and a host of family problems (Loeber & Farrington, 2001a), including a broken home, parental criminality, poor family or child management, abuse and neglect, serious marital discord, and young motherhood (Pogarsky, Lizotte, & Thornberry, 2003). Pivotal child characteristics during the preschool period include a difficult temperament and impulsivity, typically described as aggressive, inattentive, and sensation-seeking behaviors (Keenan, 2001; Loeber & Farrington, 2001a).

A lack of "social capital" (Coleman, 1988, 1990) is a key byproduct of "concentrated disadvantage" (Sampson & Groves, 1989) in impoverished, distressed, and crime-ridden communities. When combined with family and child deficits, concentrated disadvantage increases the odds of disruptive behavior disorders in children by the time of school entry and delinquency

Table 4.3 Risk Factors for Delinquency, Violence, and Gang Involvement

Risk Factors Measured at Approximately Ages 0–3

Child

- Pregnancy and delivery complications
- Difficult temperament
- Hyperactivity, impulsivity, and attention problems

Family

- Having a teenage mother
- Maternal drug, alcohol, and tobacco use during pregnancy
- Maternal depression
- Parental substance abuse
- Parental criminality
- Poor parent–child communication
- Poverty or low socioeconomic status
- Serious marital discord

Risk Factors Measured at Approximately Ages 3–6

Child

- Aggressive or disruptive behavior
- Persistent lying
- Risk taking and sensation seeking
- Lack of guilt and empathy
- Low intelligence quotient

Family

- Harsh or erratic discipline practices
- Child maltreatment (abuse or neglect)

Risk Factors Measured at Approximately Ages 6–12

Child

- General delinquency involvement*
- Antisocial or delinquent beliefs*
- Aggression*
- Hyperactivity*
- Early and persistent antisocial behavior
- Psychological condition
- Medical or physical condition
- Few social ties (not involved in social activities, popularity)
- Authority conflict, rebellious, stubborn, disruptive, antisocial, conduct disorders*
- Early initiation of violent behavior*
- Victimization and exposure to violence
- Poor refusal skills*
- Substance use (especially marijuana and alcohol)*

Family

- Abusive parents
- Low family socioeconomic status

(Continued)

Table 4.3 (Continued)

- Antisocial parents
- Sibling antisocial behavior*
- Poor parent–child relations
- Poor parental supervision, control, monitoring, and child management*
- Family violence (child maltreatment, partner violence, conflict)
- Family poverty*
- Broken home*
- Parent proviolent attitudes*

School

- Low achievement in elementary school*
- Truancy and suspension
- Identified as learning disabled*
- Poorly organized and functioning schools
- Low school attachment*
- Low academic aspirations*

Peer

- Peer rejection
- Association with delinquent peers*
- Association with aggressive peers*

Community

- Residence in a disadvantaged or disorganized neighborhood*
- Availability of firearms*
- Availability or perceived access to drugs*
- Feeling unsafe in the neighborhood*
- Low neighborhood attachment*
- Neighborhood youth in trouble*

Risk Factors Measured at Approximately Ages 12–16

Adolescent

- Few social ties (involved in social activities, popularity)
- General delinquency involvement*
- Drug dealing
- Physical violence or aggression*
- Violent victimization*
- Mental health problems
- Conduct disorders (disruptive, antisocial)*[a]
- Illegal gun ownership or carrying*
- Early dating*
- Precocious sexual activity and early fatherhood*
- Antisocial or delinquent beliefs*
- Alcohol or drug use*
- Depression*
- Life stressors*[b]

(Continued)

Table 4.3 (Continued)

Family

- Poor parent–child relations or communication
- Antisocial parents
- Broken home or parent–child separation*
- Low family socioeconomic status or poverty*
- Family history of problem behavior or crime
- Delinquent siblings*
- Having a young mother
- Low attachment to child*
- Poor parental supervision, control, monitoring, and child management*
- Low parent education*
- Child maltreatment (abuse or neglect)*
- Family transitions (change in parent figures)*

School

- School attitude and performance
- Academic failure
- Low bonding and commitment to school*
- Truancy and dropping out of school
- Frequent school transitions
- Negative labeling by teachers (as either bad or disturbed)*
- Low academic aspirations*
- Low attachment to teachers*
- Low parent college expectations for child*
- Low math achievement test score (males)*

Peer

- Antisocial peers
- Association with delinquent peers*
- Association with aggressive peers*
- Peer drug use
- Gang membership

Community

- Community laws and norms that tolerate crime
- Poverty*
- Community disorganization*
- Availability and use of drugs in neighborhood*
- Exposure to violence and racial prejudice
- High-crime neighborhood*
- Availability of firearms*

---

* Risk factors for gang membership.

a. Conduct disorder symptoms included bullying, fighting, lying, cruelty toward animals, attacking people, running away from home, fire setting, theft, truancy, and vandalism (Lahey, Gordon, Loeber, Stouthamer-Loeber, and Farrington, 1999).

b. These consist of failing a course at school, being suspended or expelled from school, breaking up with a boyfriend or girlfriend, having a big fight or problem with a friend, or the death of someone close (Thornberry, Lizotte, Krohn, Smith, & Porter, 2003).

later during childhood. Families with a harsh child punishment profile are overrepresented in such disadvantaged neighborhoods, and serious delinquency tends to occur more quickly in youngsters residing in these communities (Loeber, Farrington, Stouthamer-Loeber, et al., 2003).

Taken together, concentrated disadvantage at the community level, family problems, and certain child characteristics lead to early childhood problems (aggression and disruptive behavior), and each of these four variables, in turn, increases the likelihood of delinquency in childhood and gang membership in adolescence.

The School Entry Stage

Early childhood aggression and disruptive behaviors (Coie & Miller-Johnson, 2001), including stubbornness, defiance and disobedience, and truancy after school entry are products of dysfunctional families (Kalb & Loeber, 2003), particularly in disadvantaged communities. Aggressive and disruptive behaviors are likely to be followed by rejection by prosocial peers, thus opening the door to antisocial or deviant peer influences, which predict delinquent activity in later childhood and early adolescence (Coie & Miller-Johnson, 2001). The link between physical aggression in childhood and violence in adolescence is particularly strong (Brame, Nagin, & Tremblay, 2001; Broidy et al., 2003).

Coie and Miller-Johnson (2001) propose a developmental model that emphasizes early peer rejection as an often-overlooked factor in the onset of child delinquency. Their model applies in particular to aggressive and disruptive children. Disruptive behavior disorders include conduct disorders, such as aggression and oppositional defiant disorder (Burke et al., 2002). Difficulties these children face in getting along with and being accepted by conventional peers may lead to increasing aggressiveness and more disruptive behavior. It appears that Coie and Miller-Johnson have identified a pivotal selection process that helps explain why aggressive and disruptive children are more likely to turn to delinquency and gang involvement: because their opportunities for prosocial peer relationships are limited.

It is important to note that most disruptive children do not become child delinquents, nor do most child delinquents engage in delinquency in adolescence. One-fourth to one-third of the disruptive children are at risk of becoming child delinquents, and about a third of all child delinquents later become serious, violent, and chronic offenders (Loeber & Farrington, 2001a). However, "the earlier the onset, the greater the continuity" (Thornberry & Krohn, 2001, p. 297).

Compared with later-onset delinquents, child delinquents tend to come from dysfunctional families with one or more of the following characteristics: family disruption (especially a succession of different caregivers), parental antisocial behavior, parental substance abuse, mother's depression, and child abuse and neglect (Wasserman & Seracini, 2001).

The Later Childhood Stage

In the third developmental stage, later childhood, other risk factors (causal variables) that explain gang membership begin to come into play. Children who are involved in delinquency, violence, and drug use at an early age are at higher risk for gang membership than other youngsters (Craig, Vitaro, & Tremblay, 2002; Hill, Howell, Hawkins, & Battin-Pearson, 1999; Lahey et al., 1999). More than one-third of the child delinquents in Montreal and Rochester samples became involved in crimes of a more serious and violent nature during adolescence, *including* gang fights (Krohn, Thornberry, Rivera, & Le Blanc, 2001). "In brief, very early onset offending is brought about by the *combination and interaction* of structural, individual, and parental influences" (Thornberry & Krohn, 2001, p. 295).

Peer rejection in the early school years may lead to greater susceptibility to the influence of deviant peers, including more aggressive youths (Coie & Miller-Johnson, 2001, p. 192). Aggressive and antisocial youths begin to affiliate with one another in childhood (Cairns & Cairns, 1991; Coie & Miller-Johnson, 2001), and this pattern of aggressive friendships may continue through adolescence (Cairns & Cairns, 1994). A Montreal study suggests that displays of aggression in delinquent acts at age 10 or perhaps younger may be a key factor leading to gang involvement (Craig et al., 2002). Peers rated gang members as significantly more aggressive than non–gang members at ages 10–14.

The negative consequence of delinquent peer associates is one of the most enduring findings in empirical delinquency studies (Warr, 2002). Associations with delinquent peers increase delinquency and the likelihood and frequency of physical aggression and violence (Lacourse et al., 2006), which in turn increases the likelihood of gang membership in early adolescence (Craig et al., 2002; Eitle, Gunkel, & Gundy, 2004; Hill et al., 1999). Weakened prosocial bonds as a result of delinquency may be an important interaction effect of this process (Thornberry & Krohn, 2001).

Poor school performance (poor grades and test scores) in later childhood is likely to result from prosocial peer rejection, child delinquency, and family problems (Thornberry & Krohn, 2001). Other school-related variables that lead to gang involvement include low achievement in elementary school (Craig et al., 2002; Hill et al., 1999), low school attachment, and having been identified as learning disabled (Hill et al., 1999).

Factors that weaken the student–school bond (commitment to school) in the later childhood stage contribute to delinquency and gang membership. The poor school performance of children is one side of the coin; poor-quality schools (poorly organized and functioning) is the other side (Hyman & Perone, 1998; Hyman & Snook, 1999; Lyons & Drew, 2006).

A contemporary indicator of poor-quality schools is zero tolerance policies that produce high suspension, expulsion, and dropout rates (see Chapter 2). Longitudinal studies have not directly examined the effects of these specific student statuses as a risk factor for gang membership. However, several of them have examined school failure, periods not in school, negative labeling by teachers, and bad behavior and attitudes toward school, all of which predict gang involvement and generally long-term membership in gangs (Craig et al., 2002; Esbensen, Huizinga, & Weiher, 1993; Hill et al., 1999; Thornberry, Krohn, et al., 2003). One of these studies (Thornberry, Krohn, et al., 2003) examined the effects of gang involvement on dropout rates, finding that gang membership (especially long term) greatly increased the odds of dropping out of school. In addition to alienating students from schools and teachers, thus weakening the student–school bond, zero tolerance policies release many youths from adult supervision during the day and after school, potentially exposing them to deviant influences on the streets (Vigil, 2002) and a higher likelihood of delinquency involvement themselves.

The Early Adolescence Stage

The remainder of our expanded theoretical model incorporates only risk factors that predict gang involvement. Children who are on a trajectory of worsening antisocial behavior are more likely to join gangs during adolescence (Esbensen & Huizinga, 1993; Hill et al., 1999; Lahey et al., 1999), and they tend to have more problems than non-gang members (Howell & Egley, 2005b). Gang entry might be thought of as the next developmental step in escalating delinquent behavior (Esbensen & Huizinga, 1993; see also Lahey et al., 1999). Future gang members not only evidence a large number of risk factors (Hill et al., 1999), they are likely to show risk factors in multiple developmental domains (Thornberry, Krohn, et al., 2003), including community or neighborhood, family problems, school problems, delinquent peer influence, and individual characteristics. Each of these risk domains is considered next.

Community or Neighborhood Risk Factors

As children grow older, they are more and more influenced by their environment, often negatively (Tremblay, 2003). Community or neighborhood risk factors that have been shown to predict gang membership in early adolescence include availability and perceived access to drugs, neighborhood youth in trouble, feeling unsafe in the neighborhood, and low neighborhood attachment (Hill et al., 1999; Hill, Lui, & Hawkins, 2001). Other important neighborhood risk factors include high community arrest rates, high drug use, and neighborhood disorganization (Table 4.3). Availability of firearms may also be an important community variable (Lizotte, Krohn, Howell, Tobin, & Howard, 2000). Exposure to firearm violence approximately doubles the probability that an adolescent will perpetrate serious violence over the subsequent 2 years (Bingenheimer, Brennan, & Earls, 2005).

Communities that suffer from concentrated disadvantage may lack the necessary "collective efficacy" (informal control and social cohesion) among residents to ameliorate the negative effects of concentrated disadvantage

(MacDonald & Gover, 2005; Morenoff, Sampson, & Raudenbush, 2001; Sampson & Laub, 1997). This condition is probably exacerbated by the prevalence of crime in the community, availability of drugs, and so on, all that weaken neighborhood attachment.

Family Risk Factors

Family-level factors can be divided into two groups: structural variables and social process variables. Nonintact family (not living with both biological parents) is a key structural variable, and family management problems typically characterize family process variables. However, structural variables are often mediated by family process variables, and thus typically are only indirectly associated with gang membership. For example, for Thornberry and colleagues (Thornberry & Krohn, 2001; Thornberry, Krohn, et al., 2003), structural adversity affects such factors as parenting deficits and the development of strong family bonds.

Family influences begin to fade in adolescence (Lahey et al., 1999; Lipsey & Derzon, 1998; Thornberry, Lizotte, et al., 2003), and studies do not distinguish clearly the family influences on gang membership that remain in adolescence from those that were potent at an earlier point. In the Rochester study, a nonintact family and low parent education predicted gang membership in early to mid-adolescence. Poor parental attachment to child, low parental supervision, and child maltreatment emerged as significant family process variables in the bivariate analysis of risk factors, but only for males (Thornberry, Krohn, et al., 2003, p. 66). Another family structural variable, family transitions (change in parent figures), predicted stable gang membership in a separate bivariate analysis (Thornberry, Krohn, et al., 2003, p. 71). Only one additional family structure variable (family poverty) has been examined in other longitudinal studies (Hill et al., 1999). Family process variables associated with gang membership in other quantitative longitudinal studies (Table 4.3) include sibling antisocial behavior, family financial stress, and parents' proviolent attitudes. Several ethnographic studies suggest that family conflict and child victimization in the home may have greater importance as risk factors for gang membership for girls than for boys (Fleisher, 1998; J. A. Miller, 2001; Moore, 1978; Moore & Hagedorn, 2001).

Important family risk factors for gang involvement are not limited to at-risk youths' family of origin; these also extend to the family that youths create. Among males, teenage fatherhood may predict gang membership (Loeber, Farrington, Stouthamer-Loeber, et al., 2003). Parental criminality may also prove to be an important variable; this factor has not been researched in longitudinal gang member risk factor studies.

School Risk Factors

Poor school performance on math tests predicts gang membership for males (Thornberry, Krohn, et al., 2003). Other school risk factors identified in the Rochester bivariate analysis include low academic aspirations, low attachment to teachers, low parent college expectations for their child, and low degree of commitment to school. Negative labeling by teachers (as either bad or disturbed) is another important predictor (Esbensen et al., 1993). Feeling unsafe at school may also predict gang involvement (Gottfredson & Gottfredson, 2001). Students who feel vulnerable at school may seek protection in the gang.

Peer Risk Factors

Along with peer delinquency, Thornberry, Krohn, et al. (2003) included delinquent beliefs as a component of antisocial influences in their gang membership theory, and the latter factor proved to be significantly related to gang membership whereas, surprisingly, delinquent peers did not. Other studies show that association with delinquent or antisocial peers and aggressive peers during childhood and early adolescence is a predictor of gang membership (Table 4.3).

Associates of gang members are also part and parcel of a community's gang problem because of their active involvement in delinquency (Curry, Decker, & Egley, 2002). Theories of gang membership must account for close associates of gang members because several variables distinguish associates of gang members from nongang youths (Eitle et al., 2004): preteen exposure to stress, early deviance, early peer deviance, and family attachment. Interestingly, increased preteen stress exposure was associated with increased gang involvement in this study even when the remaining three variables were controlled.

Individual Risk Factors

Studies have identified more individual risk factors for gang membership than in any other domain (Table 4.3). Early involvement in delinquency and violent behavior in the Seattle study and delinquency involvement in early adolescence in the Rochester study predicted gang membership. Both of these studies also show that the risk of gang involvement is elevated for youngsters who use alcohol or drugs and are involved in other forms of delinquency, and who hold antisocial or delinquent beliefs (Hill et al., 1999; Thornberry, Krohn, et al., 2003). Experiencing life stressors is another important individual risk factor at the early adolescence stage (Eitle et al., 2004; Thornberry, Krohn, et al., 2003).

Violent victimization is another potentially important individual variable (Lauritsen, 2003; Peterson et al., 2004), also seen in ethnographic studies (Decker & Van Winkle, 1996; Fleisher, 1998; J. A. Miller, 2001; Moore, 1991). This is a powerful predictor of individual violence (Loeber et al., 2008; Shaffer & Ruback, 2002), and personal victimization, involvement in violence, and aggression are predictors of gang membership (Craig et al. 2002; Hill et al., 1999; Lahey et al., 1999; Taylor, 2008).

Early dating predicted male gang membership in the Rochester gang theory (Thornberry, Krohn, et al., 2003), and this was also significant for females in the bivariate analysis. Precocious sexual activity was a significant risk factor for gang membership among males but not for females in the bivariate analysis in the Rochester study (Thornberry, Krohn, et al., 2003, p. 66). Depression showed a similar pattern. Interestingly, low self-esteem did not prove to be a statistically significant predictor in the Rochester study (p. 66). Also, Denver Youth Survey data show that youth who were involved in drug use, gang involvement, and delinquency tended to have *higher* self-esteem (Tiet & Huizinga, 2002).

Perceived Benefits of Joining a Gang

Although they are not a risk factor as such, personal reasons for joining a gang are an important source of motivation. Among the various reasons youth give for joining a gang, the following are most common: social reasons—youth join to be around friends and family members (especially siblings or cousins) who already are part of the gang; and protection—youth join for the safety they believe the gang can afford (Decker & Curry, 2000; Decker & Van Winkle, 1996; Peterson et al., 2004; Thornberry, Krohn, et al., 2003). Also reported by youth, albeit far less frequently, are more instrumental reasons for joining a gang such as drug selling or making money (Decker & Van Winkle, 1996).

This theory in its entirety has not been tested, although there is much research support for each of the individual components, some of which I have cited. Of course, there are many other competing theories of delinquency but few theories of gang involvement. Our purpose here was simply to illustrate how risk factors can increase the likelihood of given outcomes, juvenile delinquency and gang involvement in this case. Further theory development and research along these lines hold a great deal of utility for practical application because, as I'll show later, the risk-protection framework is available electronically to communities.

Discussion Topics

1. What are the key factors in defining the tipping point at which some youth turn from conformity to deviant behavior?

2. Explain why low self-esteem might not lead to gang involvement.

3. Which groups of risk factors for gang involvement do you think would influence you most in deciding whether to join a gang?

4. What are the shortcomings of the delinquency and gang theory presented here?

5. What is a major shortcoming of any theory of delinquency and crime?

CHAPTER 5

Juvenile Offender Careers

I n the previous chapter we demonstrated how risk factors can operate in key stages of development to produce deviant outcomes, namely, juvenile delinquency and gang involvement. In this chapter we examine various types of juvenile offender careers that evolve from the delinquent developmental process. All offenders do not have similar offense histories. They differ on several dimensions with age, such as the length of the delinquent career, the frequency of offending, the seriousness of the offenses that are committed, and desistance patterns.

A key issue in criminology concerns the most valid ways of characterizing offender careers. For many years, research suggested that offenders demonstrate such diversity in offenses over the life course that they could not be categorized into mutually exclusive taxonomic groups. Research tended to support more versatility than specialization in offender careers. But more recent studies have disproved this notion. Thanks to analyses of large, multiwave, longitudinal databases, more recent research is mapping offense histories.

My central purpose in this chapter is to show the practical utility of distinguishing everyday juvenile delinquents from serious, violent, and chronic juvenile offenders. In order for the juvenile justice system to target offenders successfully, its officials must be able to distinguish between juvenile offenders who are likely to desist from delinquency and those who are likely to persist in their delinquent careers and perhaps become more serious offenders. In this chapter, I describe the advances in research on serious, violent, and chronic juvenile offender careers that policy makers can use to improve juvenile justice system policies and practices.

I begin the chapter with an explanation of developmental theories of delinquency and then highlight important advances in these theories.

I discuss in particular Loeber's three-pathway model, which describes three pathways adolescents might follow in their orderly progression through adolescent problem behaviors and delinquency. I also present empirical descriptions of serious, violent, and chronic juvenile offender careers.

Throughout this chapter, I make numerous references to longitudinal studies of delinquents, principally the three ongoing longitudinal studies that make up Office of Juvenile Justice and Delinquency Prevention (OJJDP) Program of Research on the Causes and Correlates of Delinquency. These three studies, described in Box 5.1, have made substantial contributions to our knowledge about the causes and correlates of delinquency and gang involvement (see Chapter 6).

IN FOCUS 5.1

Longitudinal Studies in the Program of Research on the Causes and Correlates of Delinquency

This OJJDP program of research consists of three studies:

- The Pittsburgh Youth Study, directed by Drs. Rolf and Magda Loeber
- The Denver Youth Survey, directed by Dr. David Huizinga
- The Rochester Youth Development Study, directed by Dr. Terence P. Thornberry

Participants in the Pittsburgh Youth Study were boys randomly selected from the first, fourth, and seventh grades of public schools. For each grade cohort, the top 30% (about 250) of boys with the highest rates of predelinquent or delinquent behavior were selected, along with an equal number of boys randomly selected from the remaining 70% for comparison purposes. This resulted in a total sample of 1,517, with approximately 500 boys from each grade. Key publications from this study include Loeber, Farrington, Stouthamer-Loeber, and Van Kammen (1998), Loeber, Farrington, Stouthamer-Loeber, et al. (2003), Loeber, Farrington, Stouthamer-Loeber, and White (2008), and the entire Issue 2, Volume 12 (2002) of the journal *Criminal Behaviour and Mental Health*.

Subjects in the Denver Youth Survey (1,527 children and adolescents, both boys and girls) were randomly drawn from households in high-risk Denver neighborhoods. Subjects were ages 7, 9, 11, 13, and 15 when the study began. Key publications resulting from this study include Esbensen, Huizinga, and Weiher (1993), Huizinga and Jakob-Chien (1998), Esbensen, Huizinga, and Menard (1999), Huizinga, Loeber, Thornberry, and Cothern (2000), Espiritu, Huizinga, Crawford, and Loeber (2001), Huizinga and Schumann (2001), and Huizinga, Weiher, Espiritu, and Esbensen (2003).

Participants in the Rochester Youth Development Study (1,000 boys and girls) were randomly drawn from the seventh- and eighth-grade cohorts of Rochester public schools. To maximize the number of serious, chronic offenders in the study, the sample includes more youths from high-crime areas and fewer from low-crime areas. Key publications from this study include Thornberry, Krohn, Lizotte, and Chard-Wierschem (1993), Thornberry, Lizotte, Krohn, Farnworth, and Jang (1994), Krohn, Lizotte, Thornberry, Smith, and McDowall (1996), Lizotte et al. (2000), Thornberry and Porter (2001), Krohn et al. (2001), Bushway, Thornberry, and Krohn (2003), Pogarsky et al. (2003), Thornberry and Krohn (2003, 2005), Thornberry, Krohn, et al. (2003), and Thornberry (2005).

Although all of these three projects have unique features, they share several key elements:

- All three are longitudinal investigations that involve repeated contacts with the same juveniles over a substantial portion of their childhood years, throughout adolescence, and into adulthood. Thus all three are prospective studies (i.e., causal variables were measured in advance of outcomes).
- The three sites have collaborated to use a common measurement package, collecting data on a wide range of variables that make possible cross-site comparisons of similarities and differences.
- In all three studies, researchers have conducted face-to-face interviews with adolescents in private settings. By using self-report data rather than juvenile justice records, the researchers are able to come very close to measuring actual delinquent behaviors and ascertaining the distinctive features of delinquent careers.
- In all three studies, researchers obtain multiple perspectives on each child's development and behavior through interviews with the study subject, the child's primary caregiver, and the child's teachers and by reviewing official school, police, and court records.
- In all three studies, participants are interviewed at regular and frequent intervals (6 or 12 months).
- Sample retention has been high in all three studies. The average retention rate across all interview periods is 90%.

Data collection began in all three sites in 1987 and continues; thus all study subjects are now young adults. Eight key publications feature cross-site comparisons of similarities and differences in the findings across sites: Huizinga, Loeber, and Thornberry (1994), Kelley, Huizinga, Thornberry, and Loeber (1997), Loeber, Wei, Stouthamer-Loeber, Huizinga, and Thornberry (1999), Thornberry, Smith, Rivera, Huizinga, and Stouthamer-Loeber (1999), Huizinga et al. (2000), Smith, Krohn, Lizotte, McCluskey,

(Continued)

(Continued)

Stouthamer-Loeber, and Weiher (2000), Loeber, Kalb, and Huizinga (2001), and Thornberry, Huizinga, and Loeber (2004).

Researchers have conducted many other longitudinal studies on delinquency and related problem behaviors. For a list and descriptions of nearly 60 leading longitudinal studies on delinquency, substance use, sexual behavior, and mental health problems with childhood samples, see Kalb, Farrington, and Loeber (2001).

Developmental Criminology

The study of how offender careers develop in relation to age is called *developmental criminology*. Many criminologists have been slow to pick up on the promise that this area of study holds for our understanding of delinquent and criminal careers. By the late 1980s, a few criminologists had formulated developmental theories of juvenile delinquency (e.g., Becker, 1963; Elliott, Huizinga, & Menard, 1989; Hawkins & Weis, 1985; Lemert, 1951; Thornberry, 1987). Then some developmental psychologists who crossed over to criminology gave a boost to the adoption of this perspective in the late 1980s and early 1990s. Notably, Loeber (1988) called for the use of a developmental framework in the study of crime and delinquency; he and Le Blanc later coined the term *developmental criminology* to refer to this framework (Le Blanc & Loeber, 1998; Loeber & Le Blanc, 1990). In the first of their two developmental articles, Loeber and Le Blanc (1990) document the beginnings of this theoretical orientation toward crime and delinquency. In their later article, they summarize important contributions to developmental criminology, specifically describing individual changes in offending over time in terms of activation (onset), aggravation (escalation and stability maintenance), and desistance from crime. The developmental perspective focuses studies in two areas: the age links to such within-individual changes in offending and the risk or causal factors that explain changes in offending patterns over time.

Unfortunately, the search for causes of delinquency and crime has been dominated by cross-sectional studies (a research design in which, typically, one group is studied and a single measurement is taken at one point in time) and analyses of between-individual differences found through comparisons of deviants and nondeviants. As Le Blanc and Loeber (1993) have noted, such research "has led to a near standstill in the identification of those correlates or risk factors of offending that are also most likely to be causes [and] hindered the development of new, empirically based theories and the development of another generation of much-needed innovative intervention and prevention strategies for reducing delinquency" (p. 233). A major limitation of cross-sectional measurements is that "specialization in offenses and escalation in offending often cannot be inferred from them, because the concepts refer to repeated successive offenses or to increased seriousness over time" (Le Blanc & Loeber, 1998, p. 142). Thus developmental criminology uses longitudinal studies with repeated measurements to examine within-individual changes in offending over time.

Developmental criminology's theoretical orientation is achieving growing acceptance because of its usefulness for viewing the life course of offending. It involves the study of causal, or risk, factors that may explain onset, escalation, de-escalation, and desistance in individuals' delinquent and criminal careers. As Loeber and Stouthamer-Loeber (1996) observe, "In particular, a better understanding of individual differences in criminal careers can help to explain why some youths become involved in delinquency only marginally and others more deeply, and which groups of individuals start to desist in crime at which part of the life cycle" (p. 12).

Developmental criminology is spawning new theories of delinquency and crime at a rapid pace (see reviews in Cullen, Wright, & Blevins, 2006; Farrington, 2005; Thornberry & Krohn, 2003). Several of these theories have made important contributions to our understanding of juvenile delinquency. These include a developmental-ecological model (Loeber, Slot, & Stouthamer-Loeber, 2007; Loeber et al., 2008), child delinquency developmental theory (Coie & Dodge, 1998; Coie & Miller-Johnson, 2001), the social development model (Catalano & Hawkins, 1996), an interactional theory (Thornberry, 2005), a developmental explanation of gang involvement (Thornberry, Krohn, et al., 2003), an age-graded developmental theory (Sampson & Laub, 1993), an integrative theory (Farrington, 2005), and a revised strain theory (Agnew, 2005). Other scholars have also contributed to work on a developmental perspective on crime and delinquency; for example, see the contributions in four recent volumes edited by Farrington (2005), Flannery, Vazsonyi, and Waldman (2007), Loeber et al. (2008), and Thornberry and Krohn (2003).

Developmental Theories

Current developmental theories of delinquency and crime have grown out of a unique sociological framework for examining human experiences over time that is often called the *life-course perspective*.

The Life-Course Perspective

As formulated by Elder (1985a, 1985b), the life-course perspective views human development across the life span, focusing in particular on people's progress within culturally defined roles and social transitions that are age graded. For example, it is normal for a young person to complete his or her education, begin a career, then get married and begin a family. The terms *trajectories* and *pathways* are used to describe these long-term patterns of social development in social institutions, including families, schools, and occupations.

Thus a trajectory or pathway is an avenue of development over time, such as an occupational career or delinquency involvement. *Transitions* are short-term changes in social roles within long-term trajectories, such as dropping out of school, divorce, and desistance from delinquency.

Elder conceived of the life course as being structured by a web of interlocking trajectories that generally are consistent. They are interlocking in that changes in one life domain, or pathway, may well affect other domains. On occasion, these pathways are interrupted by life events (short-term transitions) such as being arrested, getting married, or graduating from college. "Off-age" transitions (i.e., those that are not age appropriate, such as becoming a teenage parent) can produce disorder in the life course (Thornberry, Krohn, et al., 2003). Individual adaptations to these changes are important because they may lead to different trajectories. For example, some transitions may propel people into pathways leading them to a life of crime, whereas others may propel people from delinquency into a life of general compliance with legal rules (Sampson & Laub, 1993).

In the life-course perspective, childhood, adolescent, and adult experiences are viewed as a continuous process of change, depending on the consequences of earlier patterns of behavior and the influence of risk factors in several important domains (mainly the family, school, peer groups, and communities). In addition, individual characteristics (e.g., intelligence and personality traits such as resilience) affect how people respond to influences in these experiential domains. Studies of juvenile offenders have shown that offense onset, escalation, and desistance do not occur merely as functions of offenders' chronological age. For some, predelinquent behaviors begin in early childhood, and these children often continue offending throughout most of their lives. For others, onset of delinquent behaviors occurs in late childhood or early adolescence. Desistance takes place in childhood and adolescence for some people but much later for others (Stouthamer-Loeber, Loeber, Stallings, & Lacourse, 2008).

Life-Course–Persistent and Adolescence-Limited Offenders

Moffitt (1993) and others identified two main groups of offenders in the childhood and adolescent period: life-course–persistent offenders and adolescence-limited offenders (see also Patterson, Capaldi, & Bank, 1991). Life-course–persistent offenders begin offending in childhood, and adolescence- limited offenders begin their offending later.

According to Moffitt (1993, pp. 675–679), life-course–persistent offenders make up only a small proportion (about 5%) of the entire population of juvenile offenders. She describes the offense history of a typical such offender: He engages in biting and hitting at age 4, shoplifting and truancy at age 10, selling drugs and stealing cars at age 16, robbery and rape at age 22, and fraud and child abuse at age 30. Past age 40, the co-occurring problems of life-course–persistent offenders include drug and alcohol addiction; unsatisfactory employment; unpaid debts; normlessness; drunk driving; violent assault; multiple and unstable relationships; spouse battery; abandoned, neglected, or abused children; and psychiatric illnesses. Thus such offenders exhibit changing manifestations of antisocial behavior across the life course as age and circumstances alter their opportunities for antisocial involvement. Four characteristics distinguish life-course–persistent offenders: early onset of offending, active offending during adolescence, escalation of offense seriousness, and persistence in crime in adulthood.

In contrast, adolescence-limited offenders represent a far larger proportion of the adolescent peak in the age-crime curve (Farrington, 1986). These offenders do not have childhood histories of antisocial behavior; rather, they engage in antisocial behavior only during adolescence. As teenagers, they may show inconsistency in their behavior across situations. For example, they may shoplift while with a group of friends but obey school and family rules. As Moffitt (1993) describes them, they "are likely to engage in antisocial behavior in situations where such responses seem profitable to them, but they are also able to abandon antisocial behavior when prosocial styles are more rewarding" (p. 686).

Other researchers have identified life-course–persistent and adolescence-limited groups of offenders and other adolescent groups as well (see Moffitt, 2007). Actually, it has become clear that several subgroups of offenders are identifiable, and new research in Rochester, New York, shows that there may be as many as eight trajectory groups (Thornberry, 2005), although most research has revealed four to six distinguishable groups (Loeber et al., 2008).

Moffitt's typology is an interesting one nevertheless, and it has stimulated a number of investigations into the actual existence of various subgroups with distinct offending patterns. However, her central argument, that the main cause of life-course–persistent offending is the interaction of neuropsychological deficits with adverse environmental conditions in early childhood, has not become widely accepted. Most children with neuropsychological deficits overcome them and do not become life-course–persistent offenders (Loeber & Farrington, 2001b; Wasserman & Seracini, 2001). There is substantial empirical evidence of multiple-factor influences on behavior, in a developmental fashion, over the life course (Lipsey & Derzon, 1998; Loeber & Farrington, 2001a; Thornberry & Krohn, 2003). Moreover, strong empirical evidence suggests that multiple pathways to juvenile delinquency produce unique offender career patterns that can be characterized in different terms, such as involvement in property and violent offending, or in more general severity terms, such as serious, violent, and chronic careers.

We next review Thornberry's interactional theory for an introduction to some key features of offender careers, which should provide some insights into how offenders' delinquent careers evolve into general patterns. Serious, violent, and chronic careers are reviewed next, followed by consideration of specific steps that lead to these types of offender careers.

Thornberry's Interactional Theory

Thornberry (2005, pp. 157–159) argues that the most central aspects of offender careers that developmental theories should explain involve patterns of *onset, course,* and *desistance. Onset* refers to "the fundamental question of etiology: Why do only some members of a population engage in delinquent and criminal behavior?" (p. 158). However, he insists that a worthwhile developmental theory must also account for age of onset. This, of course, is more difficult.

The *course* of a delinquent career refers to persistence: how long the career lasts and the association with frequency and seriousness of offenses (p. 158). A valid developmental theory must explain the processes that maintain offending for some offenders and lead some of them to escalate in terms of frequency and seriousness, and it must also provide a causal explanation of the association between age of onset and the persistence of offending. In other words, why are offenders who start early somewhat more likely to persist longer?

Last, he argues, a developmental theory should include an explanation of the social and psychological processes that lead to *desistance.* Two key issues must be addressed here (p. 159). First, does desistance occur suddenly, or does it unfold as a more gradual developmental process? Second, are the causes of desistance simply the reverse of those associated with onset, a different set of influences entirely, or some combination of these influences?

Thornberry's (2005) interactional theory explains child, adolescent, and young adult involvement in general antisocial behavior and delinquency (see also Thornberry & Krohn, 2001, 2005). The reader is invited to study his research-based interactional theory (Thornberry, 2005, pp. 166–189). I will highlight only a few explanations of delinquent behavior in his theory here. It incorporates four broad developmental stages: the preschool years, childhood, adolescence, and late adolescence and emerging adulthood. However, Thornberry does not view these stages as having sharp boundaries. Rather, "they are regions of the more gradual, continuous process of human development" (p. 166). A basic premise of interactional theory is that antisocial behavior is not a product of fixed antecedents; rather, it becomes enmeshed in mutually reinforcing causal loops over time (p. 173). To illustrate this principle, delinquency makes family life worse, which may stimulate more delinquency, which may make family life worse, and so on.

Thornberry's (2005) interactional theory offers the following expectations about onset (pp. 159–161).

- First, offending is common; that is, a substantial majority of the population will be involved in antisocial behavior.
- Second, few offenders will have extensive criminal careers.
- Third, onset is continuously distributed, from childhood at least through early adulthood. "Offending can start earlier or later, but onset is not divided into neat patterns of *early starters* and *late starters*" (p. 160).

- Put in other words, "rather than viewing antisocial behavior as starting early *or* later as implied by typological theories [such as Moffitt's], the data suggest that it starts *earlier* or *later*" (Thornberry & Krohn, 2001, p. 302).

The course of offender careers can vary enormously; those who initiate offending can exhibit a wide range of different careers during their period of active involvement (Thornberry, 2005). "Some careers will be of short duration, almost of an episodic nature, while others will be quite persistent. Some persistent careers will involve high-frequency offending, others low-level sporadic offending. Yet other careers will be intermittent" (p. 160). Put differently, Thornberry contends that offending patterns do not emerge in a uniform pattern, unfolding in a similar shape over an invariant life course, as implied by more rigid theories such as Gottfredson and Hirschi's (1990) control theory.

With respect to desistance, "Interactional theory views desistance as composed of two developmental processes. The first reflects the downward movement from the peak level of involvement to the start of noninvolvement. The second process reflects the maintenance of behavior at a zero or near-zero level of offending" (Thornberry, 2005, p. 161). Thus he contends that "the more typical pattern is a gradual movement away from offending as the person's environmental and interactional patterns change. Thus, interactional theory does not anticipate sharp turning points that quickly deflect offending trajectories from high levels to zero (p. 161). Explanations for these differing patterns vary. "Desistance is more likely a product of changing life circumstances" (p. 161; cf. Stouthamer-Loeber et al., 2008).

Supporting evidence of many of these theoretical propositions can readily be seen in the trajectory maps for males in the Rochester Youth Development Study, shown in Figure 5.1. This technique for mapping offender careers—the trajectory approach—was developed by Nagin and Land (1993) to summarize developmental patterns of behavior, including criminal behavior. Technically, the map describes the relationship between levels of offending and age over time. Nagin's method is ideal for problems that do not have a normal growth curve, such as depression and delinquency, which are not constant personal attributes.

Perhaps the most revealing observation from Figure 5.1 is the discovery of eight groups with diverging patterns of offending in the Rochester Youth Development Study data. Thus patterns of offending do not divide neatly into two dominant groups, as suggested by Moffitt and colleagues, because we see eight unique trajectory groups instead of just two groups of early and late starters. The continuous nature of onset is also reflected in the pattern of onset for the trajectory groups. The members of the low-level offender group who do offend have the latest age of onset, with a mean of 15.1 years; only 17% began before age 13. In contrast, the mean age of onset for the persistent high-level offenders is 9.4 years, and 84% of them began before age 13. Onset for the other groups is arrayed between these extremes.

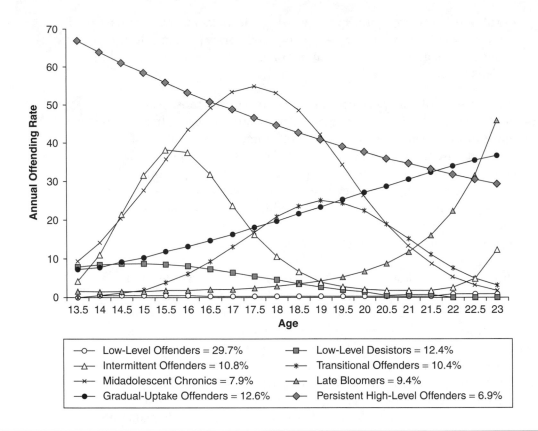

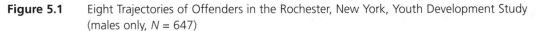

Figure 5.1 Eight Trajectories of Offenders in the Rochester, New York, Youth Development Study (males only, *N* = 647)

Second, the modest correlation between age of onset and persistence is seen in any number of the offender groups shown in Figure 5.1. For example, both the late bloomers and the persistent high-level offenders exhibit similar patterns of persistent, high-rate offending from the late teens onward, but these two groups have vastly different onset patterns.

Third, offending patterns do not progress in the same maturational pattern, resembling the age–crime curve (Farrington, 1986), as suggested by Gottfredson and Hirschi. A casual observation of Figure 5.2, which is a different snapshot of the identical Rochester juvenile offenders, suggests that the standard age–crime curve applies to the data. However, that assumption would be misleading. Age of onset is but one dimension of offender careers. Developmental patterns or group trajectories discussed earlier (shown in Figure 5.1) illuminate the remaining story of offender careers that can be displayed from Thornberry's analysis using Nagin's method.

Fourth, as predicted by Thornberry's (2005) interactional theory, offending is rather common in the Rochester sample. More than 9 out of 10 (94%) of the total sample of Rochester youth self-report some involvement in

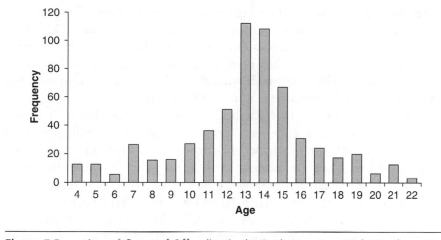

Figure 5.2   Age of Onset of Offending in the Rochester, New York, Youth
Development Study (males only)

delinquent behavior by their early 20s, and 70% report more than sporadic
involvement. At the other extreme, persistent, chronic offending is rare;
only 6.9% fall into the highest-rate group.

Last, the process of desistance occurs at various ages, not only at the transition from adolescence to adulthood as implied by the population age–crime
curve. In the present case, desistance appears to begin at age 15 for the low-
level desistors, 16 for the intermittent offenders, 17.5 for the midadolescent
chronics, and 19 for the transitional offenders (assuming the latter two patterns remain near zero).

Juvenile Offender Careers

Another way of describing juvenile delinquency involvement is to view
the entire offense history of groups of offenders. A useful way of describing
these histories is in simple and straightforward terms, consistent with the
language of juvenile justice officials and staff. Three offense categories are
predominant in the statutory codes that juvenile court and correctional
agencies implement: property, violent, and chronic offenses. These agencies
also use formal risk and need assessment instruments to guide offender
placements and develop comprehensive treatment plans that aim to fore-
stall further progression in delinquent careers and promote desistance. This
way of describing the main offender subgroups provides a benchmark that
helps juvenile justice officials plan services, monitor offender placements,
and modify program structures. Identifying these groups of offenders
should be of interest to prevention agencies and organizations as well,
because they are ideal targets for these organizations' efforts to prevent the
spread of delinquency and violence in adolescence.

Snyder (1998) conducted an ingenious analysis that revealed predominant offender careers among 16 groups of juvenile court referrals in Maricopa County, Arizona (which includes Phoenix and smaller cities). More specifically, Snyder's sample consisted of all people born in Maricopa County in each of 16 years who continued living there through their 17th birthday (Box 5.2). The rich Maricopa County database enabled Snyder to examine juvenile offender careers by compiling all court referrals that each person had during his or her juvenile years (ages 10–17). After compiling the court careers of the total group, Snyder then sorted the careers into four types. Ordinary delinquent careers consisted of the juveniles who never had more than three court referrals (i.e., nonchronic), never had a court referral for a "serious" offense (see note, Box 5.2), and had no referrals for any of the specific violent offenses. See Box 5.2 for definitions of the three remaining groups. Thus Snyder created four groups of offender careers—"ordinary delinquents," "chronic offenders" (four or more court referrals), "serious offenders," "violent offenders"—and the combined "serious, violent, and chronic offenders."

IN FOCUS 5.2
Snyder's Maricopa County, Arizona, Study

Sample: All people born from 1962 through 1977 (birth cohorts) who were referred to the juvenile court in Maricopa County, Arizona, for a delinquency offense before their 18th birthday. Thus the analysis focused on members of 16 annual birth cohorts who turned age 18 in the years 1980–1995, which generated a sample of 151,209 court careers.

Key findings: Almost two-thirds (64%) of juvenile court careers were nonchronic (fewer than four referrals) and did not include any serious or violent offenses; 18% of all careers had serious (but nonviolent) offenses, 8% had violent offenses, and 3% of the careers had serious, violent, and chronic offenses.

Note: Violent offenses included murder and nonnegligent manslaughter, kidnapping, violent sexual assault, robbery, and aggravated assault. Serious nonviolent offenses included burglary, serious larceny, motor vehicle theft, arson, weapon offenses, and drug trafficking. Nonserious delinquent offenses included simple assault, possession of a controlled substance, disorderly conduct, vandalism, nonviolent sex offenses, minor larceny, liquor law offenses, and all other delinquent offenses (Snyder, 1998, p. 429). Chronic offenders were classified as those with four or more court referrals.

Figure 5.3 shows the relative size of each of the four groups (a Venn diagram of the relationships between them). The entire circle in Figure 5.3 represents all people in 16 birth cohorts who were referred to juvenile courts from ages 10 through 17—more than 150,000 adolescents. There is a standing policy in Maricopa County that all arrested youth must be referred to juvenile court for screening. Therefore, the court records in that county provide complete histories of all youthful offenders' official contacts with the juvenile justice system (Snyder & Sickmund, 1999, p. 80).

The group with "ordinary delinquent" careers is actually the largest group, and these are represented in the outer section of the circle. This group of offenders represented about two-thirds (64%) of all juvenile court careers in Snyder's 16 samples. (Note that it is inappropriate to total these percentages because an individual offender can be represented in more than one career.)

In sum, Figure 5.3 illustrates that about 3% of the careers were serious, violent, *and* chronic. Much overlap is seen between the subgroups. Nearly a third (29%) of the chronic offenders were also violent offenders, about a third (35%) of the serious offenders were also chronic offenders, and about half (53%) of the violent offenders were also chronic offenders. Several other analyses of juvenile justice databases have identified similar subgroups of juvenile offenders (Howell, 2003b).

A key finding in Snyder's study is that very few juvenile offenders have serious, violent, *and* chronic offender careers. A logical question that follows is this: What are the stepping stones to that pinnacle of delinquency involvement?

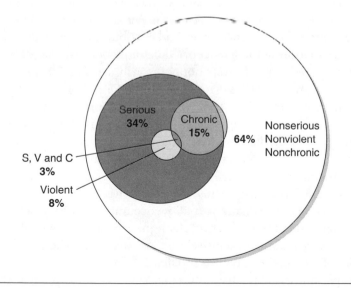

Figure 5.3   Overlap of Serious, Violent, and Chronic Offender Careers

NOTE: From Maricopa County study, *N* = 151,209.

Pathways to Serious, Violent, and Chronic Delinquency

How can the progression from predelinquent behaviors in childhood to serious, violent, and chronic delinquency best be characterized? The trajectory models are valuable, but they have an important limitation in that they do not describe the escalation processes from minor to more serious offenses in a proportion of delinquent youth (Loeber et al., 2008). Explanatory models that chart pathways in which delinquency involvement escalates have potentially enormous value. Let us first think about the importance of this progression from the standpoint of the juvenile justice system. The limited offense history information available in official records is of little help to these officials in distinguishing serious, violent, and chronic offenders from others. Self-report studies of delinquency involvement indicate that these records provide an incomplete picture of serious offenders' delinquent histories (Elliott, 1995; Huizinga, Esbensen, & Weiher, 1996; Stouthamer-Loeber, Loeber, Van Kammen, & Zhang, 1995). Most of the delinquent acts that youngsters commit are never brought to the attention of police or juvenile courts.

In contrast, most serious and violent offenders eventually are arrested, but not necessarily for their most serious offenses. Huizinga, Loeber, and Thornberry (1995) report on studies in Rochester, Denver, and Pittsburgh that found that by age 14, most chronic violent adolescents (81% in Rochester, 97% in Denver, and 74% in Pittsburgh) had begun committing violent offenses, but only small proportions of the youths in these groups had been arrested (slightly more than one-third of them in Rochester and Denver, and about half in Pittsburgh). However, most chronic violent offenders are arrested at some point (two-thirds were arrested in Rochester and about three-fourths in Denver and Pittsburgh; Huizinga et al., 1995, p. 26). Examination of the self-reported delinquency histories of the Denver subjects indicated that they were not necessarily arrested for their most serious offenses, however (Huizinga et al., 1996). Only 6% of the serious violent offenders in the Denver study were arrested for the most serious violent offenses they reported having committed. About one-fourth were arrested before they committed any serious violent offenses, about one-fourth were arrested during the same year in which they committed these types of offenses, and about one-fourth were arrested after they had initiated their serious violent offending. Thus, by themselves, arrest records do not provide sufficient information to allow accurate classification of juvenile offenders and depiction of their delinquency careers. As Elliott (1995) observes, "To rely almost exclusively on arrest studies when describing the dynamics of criminal behavior is indefensible" (p. 21).

I will present evidence from developmental studies to show that child delinquents do not emerge from families as full-blown life-course–persistent offenders. As Thornberry (2005, p. 160) puts it, "Onset is not destiny. Regardless of when one starts, careers can take on different lengths and shapes, depending on later aspects of life-course development." In fact, the developmental process that produces a juvenile delinquent is affected by numerous factors in childhood and adolescence.

Loeber's Three-Pathway Model

When a young offender is first referred to juvenile court, juvenile justice system officials get a very limited view, or snapshot, of that person's entire offending career in the form of official records. This limited view makes it very difficult for officials to distinguish between potential chronic–serious or chronic–violent offenders and adolescence-limited offenders. Risk assessment instruments are key tools for helping juvenile justice officials make such distinctions (see Chapter 10). If we can arrive at a better understanding of the pathways to serious, violent, and chronic offending, we can improve these instruments so that they can much more accurately distinguish between types of offenders.

Loeber prefers to use the term *developmental pathway* to describe a segment of a delinquent or criminal career trajectory that progresses from less serious problem behaviors to more serious offenses (Loeber et al., 2008, p. 7). This may also be thought of as "the stages of behavior that unfold over time in a predictable order" (Loeber, Keenan, & Zhang, 1997, p. 322). Loeber's pathway model also distinguishes chronic offenders ("persisters," in Loeber's terminology) from nonchronic offenders ("experimenters"; Loeber et al., 1997). This model also distinguishes between nonserious, serious, and violent offenders.

The model of pathways to problem behavior and delinquency shown in Figure 5.4 has three important dimensions. First, the model shows an orderly progression over time from less serious to more serious status offenses and delinquent behaviors. Second, the progressively narrowing width of the triangles in the figure illustrates the decreasing proportion of youth (from "many" to "few") involved in particular problem behavior and delinquent offenses. Finally, the model shows the general age of onset (from "early" to "late").

Loeber and his colleagues (Loeber & Hay, 1997; Loeber, Wei, et al., 1999) discovered an empirically based set of three main but overlapping pathways in the development of delinquency from childhood to adolescence among boys (Figure 5.4). These are the authority conflict pathway, the covert pathway, and the overt pathway. The authority conflict pathway consists of predelinquent offenses, the covert pathway consists of concealing and serious property offenses, and the overt pathway consists of violent offenses. Gang involvement (gang fighting) is an intermediate step in Loeber's overt pathway. The pathways are hierarchical in that those who have advanced to the most serious behavior in each of the pathways usually have displayed persistent problem behaviors characteristic of the earlier stages in each pathway.

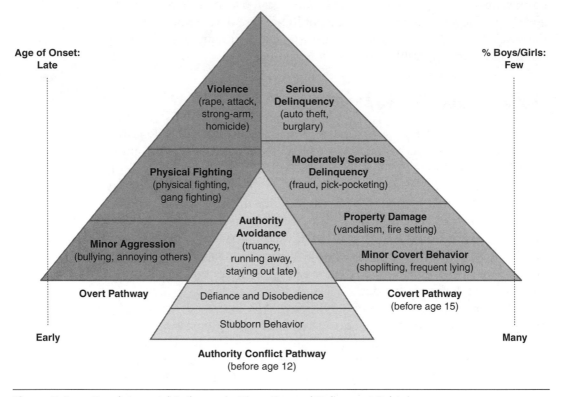

Figure 5.4   Developmental Pathways in Disruptive and Delinquent Behavior

Indeed, Loeber and his colleagues discovered that youngsters follow in a remarkably orderly progression from less to more serious problem behaviors and delinquency from childhood to adolescence (Loeber et al., 1993, 1997). Problem behavior typically begins in the authority conflict pathway with stubborn behavior, followed by defiance or disobedience, then truancy, running away, or staying out late. Persistent offenders then typically move into either the overt pathway or the covert pathway. The first stage of the covert pathway is minor covert behavior (shoplifting, frequent lying); this is followed by property damage (vandalism, fire setting) and then moderately serious (fraud, pickpocketing) and serious delinquency (auto theft, burglary). The first stage of the overt pathway is minor aggression (bullying, annoying others); this is followed by physical fighting (often including gang fighting) and then more serious violence (rape, physical attacks, strong-arm robbery).

In a major discovery, researchers (Loeber et al., 2008) have debunked a long-held notion that juvenile offenders are not selective, that their offense pattern is commonly "cafeteria-style," as proposed by Malcolm Klein and others. Interestingly, serious violent offenders were more likely than theft offenders to specialize in offense patterns. Half of the serious violent offenders in both cohorts were specialized offenders, compared with a third of the serious theft offenders.

The pathway model has been validated in Denver and Rochester samples (Loeber, Wei, et al., 1999) and also in a Chicago study and the National Youth Survey (Tolan & Gorman-Smith, 1998). In addition, Tolan, Gorman-Smith, and Loeber (2000) have replicated the triple-pathway model in a sample of African American and Hispanic adolescents in Chicago and in a nationally representative U.S. sample of adolescents. The pathway model is also applicable for antisocial girls (Gorman-Smith & Loeber, 2005; Loeber, Slot, & Stouthamer-Loeber, 2007), although the evidence is not yet as strong as for boys.

Knowledge of developmental pathways is important to the juvenile justice system because such knowledge is an important step toward identifying youth who are at risk for escalation to more serious behavior (Loeber, Wei, et al. 1999, p. 246). Figure 5.5 displays the cumulative onset of moderate and serious levels of reported violence for the oldest cohort in the Pittsburgh Youth Study. Before age 12, this information in the oldest cohort was obtained from retrospective questions (in the screening phase). Possibly because of this, the retrospectively reported cumulative onset of violence in the oldest cohort was very low up to age 11. Nevertheless, the percentage of children who engaged in both moderate and serious violence escalated rapidly from ages 5 to 19. By age 20, more than 40% of the cohort was involved in serious violence. In other words, nearly half of the Pittsburgh youngsters advanced in the violence pathway. The peak period of onset occurred between ages 10 and 20. The reader should note that this figure shows a different perspective on serious offender career development than the view that was shown in Figure 5.2, the age of onset in the Rochester data.

Loeber's explicit pathway model is particularly well suited for practice in the juvenile justice system. As noted earlier, the covert and overt pathways correspond to the serious and violent offense categories, respectively. Taking into account offense progression in the three pathways over time, Loeber's theoretical model also accounts for chronic offending. The next step in the practical application of Loeber's model is to link predictors (risk factors and promotive factors) with offenders who advance in the covert (serious-chronic) and overt (violent-chronic) pathways, and this work is under way (Loeber et al., 2007).

Following this work, I anticipate that Loeber and his colleagues will link other problem behaviors with progression in the pathways, which they suggest in their new book (Loeber et al., 2008). For example, they acknowledge that it has long been known that delinquents use drugs more than non-delinquents and that a significant proportion of delinquents deal drugs, become gang members, and carry guns. Yet, they note, little is known about the developmental sequences of these problem behaviors and violence and serious property offenses.

Early Onset Versus Later

The profile of offender careers differs enormously when age of onset is taken into consideration. In the previous section, we saw how Loeber and

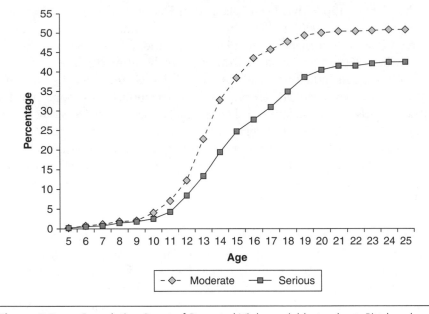

Figure 5.5   Cumulative Onset of Reported Violence (oldest cohort, Pittsburgh Youth Study)

colleagues mapped the progression of offender careers from a very early age into mid- to late adolescence. Offenders who advanced onward and moved into the serious and violent pathways became serious, violent, *and* chronic offenders. A national Study Group on Very Young Offenders (Loeber & Farrington, 2001a) produced some very interesting findings about the characteristics of child delinquents, also called "very young offenders."

We first examine a Venn diagram (Figure 5.6) of the relationships between serious, violent, and chronic offender careers among children who began offending at a very early age or later in adolescence in the Maricopa County, Arizona, data set described earlier (Box 5.2). The very young offenders have a much larger percentage of serious, violent, and chronic offender careers. Research findings uniformly agree that the risk of later violence, serious offenses, and chronic offending is two to three times higher for early-onset offenders than for later-onset offenders (Loeber & Farrington, 2001b). Compared with offenders who start their career at a later age, child delinquents are also more likely to carry weapons, including guns, to become gang members, or engage in substance use.

What proportion of child delinquents persist in their delinquency? In an analysis of the youngest members of the Denver and Pittsburgh samples, Espiritu et al. (2001) found that although most engaged in some form of aggression or minor violence (mainly throwing objects, hitting other students, and—to a much lesser extent—involvement in gang fights), only about 25% of the child delinquents persisted in minor violence, property offenses, or drug use for 5 years or more. The Denver sample included

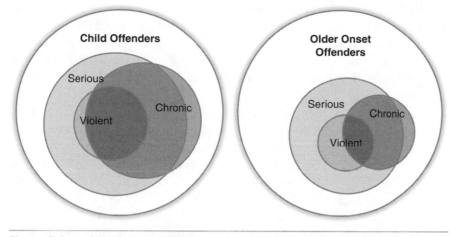

Figure 5.6   Comparison of the Characteristics of Very Young and Later-Onset Offender Careers

females, and the Pittsburgh sample did not. Other studies have shown that about a third of all child delinquents later become serious, violent, and chronic offenders (Loeber & Farrington, 2001b).

A key question about child delinquents is whether they are more likely to become typical juvenile delinquents or violent delinquents than are youngsters who begin their delinquent careers at older ages. All 21 of the longitudinal studies that have included child delinquents have reported a significant relationship between early onset and later crime and delinquency (for an excellent review of these studies, see Krohn et al., 2001, pp. 74–81). The findings for females have been similar to those for males.

Krohn et al. (2001) explored whether offenders who begin their delinquent behavior very early (onset at age 10 or under) have more serious and violent offender careers in their adolescent and young adult years than do later-onset delinquents. Specifically, the researchers hypothesized that child delinquents' criminal careers are of greater duration, extending further into the life course, that child delinquents go on to commit more offenses and have higher individual offending rates over the life course, and that their offenses tend to be more serious and more violent than those of late-onset offenders. All three of these hypotheses were confirmed for the very youngest offenders in Krohn et al.'s analyses of data from the longitudinal studies in Rochester and Montreal, although data from the Montreal study were less consistent. The analyses included females in only the Montreal study.

In the Rochester sample, the very youngest onset group (onset at 4 to 10 years of age) had the highest prevalence rate for both serious and violent offenses during the early adult years, roughly ages 19 to 22 (Krohn et al., 2001, p. 83). More than a third (39%) of this group reported involvement in serious and violent offenses in young adulthood, compared with 20% of the youngsters with onset at ages 11–12 and 23% of those with onset at ages 13–14.

The following observations can be made, based on this research and other studies of very young offenders (Loeber & Farrington, 2001b):

- Child delinquents in the juvenile justice system are a small group of youth who present a disproportionate threat to public safety in the long run.
- Because child delinquents often are multiproblem youth, they consume a disproportionate amount of resources of the juvenile justice system, child welfare system, schools, and mental health services.
- A focus on child delinquents, in contrast to a focus on older chronic offenders, provides an opportunity to intervene early and reduce overall levels of crime in the community.

The study group compiled the following list of warning signs for later problems among disruptive children during the preschool years (Loeber & Farrington, 2001b, p. xxiv):

- Disruptive behavior that is either more frequent or more severe than that of other children of the same age and is displayed in multiple settings (especially in the home *and* at preschool or elementary school)
- Disruptive behavior such as temper tantrums and aggression that persists beyond the first 2 to 3 years of life
- A history of aggressive, inattentive, or sensation-seeking behavior in the preschool years

Co-occurrence of Serious and Violent Offending and Other Problem Behaviors

I now turn to adolescent offenders to examine the extent to which they manifest other problem behaviors in addition to delinquency. Those who do are most likely to have begun their delinquent careers in childhood. Many studies have shown that several adolescent problem behaviors share a number of risk factors in the family, school, peer group, community, and individual domains (see Chapter 4). Until recently, however, the extent of the overlap in problem behaviors among serious and violent offenders was not well researched. The key issue here is the extent to which multiple-problem youth are serious and violent offenders and vice versa. Huizinga and Jakob-Chien (1998) reviewed evidence from the Denver Youth Survey on the co-occurrence of serious (serious nonviolent or serious violent) offending and other problem behaviors. They found a clear relationship between combinations of problems and serious violent delinquency. In the total Denver adolescent sample, 68% of those who had drug problems, mental health problems, and school problems and had been victimized were serious violent offenders.

This study prompted Huizinga et al. (2000), researchers in the OJJDP Program of Research on the Causes and Correlates of Delinquency, to conduct a joint analysis of problem co-occurrence in all three of the research program's longitudinal studies. I summarize the findings from this analysis in this section, along with other research results as appropriate. In this study, the research team—consisting of Denver, Rochester, and Pittsburgh researchers—examined multiple problem behaviors among "persistent serious delinquents," which they defined as self-reported offenders in serious assault or serious property offenses in at least 2 of the first 3 years of the respective projects.

This study shows that the relationship between persistent serious delinquency and combinations of other persistent problem behaviors was fairly consistent across the three study sites. For most male serious offenders, involvement in persistent serious delinquency and other problems go together. Yet serious delinquency does not always co-occur with other problems; that is, a youth who experiences other persistent problems is not necessarily a persistent serious delinquent.

More than half of the male serious delinquents in the Denver and Pittsburgh samples and more than half of the female serious delinquents in the Denver sample displayed other problems; in Rochester, the proportion was roughly 40% for both genders. Among those with multiple problems, as the number of problems increased, so did the chance of being a persistent serious delinquent. More than half (55–73%) of those with two or more problems were also persistent serious delinquents. For females, the relationship between combinations of persistent problems was different and varied in the two sites that sampled females, so Huizinga et al. caution that generalizations are unwarranted. In sum, a combination of persistent drug, school, and mental health problems greatly increase the likelihood of persistent serious delinquency.

Of the high-risk males in the three sites, 25% were persistent serious delinquents, 15% were drug users, 7% had school problems, and 10% had mental health problems. Of the high-risk females in the two sites, about 5% were persistent serious delinquents, 11–12% were drug users, 10–21% had school problems, and 6–11% had mental health problems. Females were not studied in the Pittsburgh site. All three sites studied only high-risk children and adolescents.

The most common pattern of occurrence of persistent serious delinquency, drug use, school problems, and mental health problems was an intermittent one across the three study sites. For all sites, the most common temporal pattern of each problem behavior was that it occurred for only 1 year, followed by 2 years, then 3 years.

Persistent Serious Delinquency and Drug Use

In this analysis across the Denver, Rochester, and Pittsburgh sites, Huizinga et al. (2000) found a statistically significant relationship between persistent delinquency and persistent drug use for both males and females (across all three sites for males and in two sites for females). Indeed, persistent drug use is the problem that co-occurs most frequently with persistent serious delinquency. Smith et al. (2000) have also found that the combination of delinquency involvement and marijuana use can have serious negative consequences throughout the life course. However, Huizinga et al. found that a majority of persistent serious offenders were not persistent drug users (34–44% for males in the three sites and 46–48% for females in two sites). Thus slightly more than a third of persistent serious male delinquents, and nearly half of all persistent serious female delinquents, were drug users.

Conversely, for males, the majority of persistent drug users were persistent serious delinquents (54–70% in the three sites). This was not the case for females; only 20–23% of the persistent drug-using females were persistent serious delinquents in the two sites. Thus, among females, delinquency is a stronger indicator of drug use than drug use is an indicator of delinquency. For both genders, the majority of persistent serious offenders were not drug users.

Persistent Serious Delinquency and Mental Health Problems

Huizinga et al. (2000) found that the relationship between mental health problems and persistent serious delinquency was statistically significant for males at all three sites. For males, the presence of mental health problems is a better indicator of serious delinquency than serious delinquency is an indicator of mental health problems. Only 13–21% of male persistent serious delinquents in the three sites displayed mental health problems. On the other hand, of those with mental health problems, almost one-third in Rochester (31%) and almost one-half at each of the other two sites (46%) were persistent serious delinquents.

The relationship was statistically significant for females in Rochester but not in Denver. In Rochester, one-third of females (34%) who were persistent serious delinquents also had mental health problems. Conversely, only 17% of those with mental health problems were persistent serious delinquents. This relationship is the reverse of that seen in males. Thus neither male nor female persistent serious delinquents can be characterized as having mental health problems. Conversely, it would be erroneous to characterize most adolescents with mental health problems as persistent serious delinquents.

Interestingly, in an analysis of the Denver data, Huizinga and Jakob-Chien (1998) found that low self-esteem did not appear to be related to serious violent delinquency. Rather, consistent with research suggesting a link between self-esteem and violence (Baumeister, Smart, & Boden, 1996; Brezina, Agnew, Cullen, & Wright, 2004), Huizinga and Jakob-Chien suggest that high self-esteem and threats to this self-esteem may lead to violence. This finding could well apply to gang members (Peterson, Taylor, & Esbensen, 2004).

Persistent Serious Delinquency and School Problems

Huizinga et al. (2000) found that the three sites differed substantially in the evidence they yielded about the prevalence of school problems. The sites also differed in terms of the extent of co-occurrence of persistent school problems (poor academic performance, truancy, and dropping out) and persistent serious delinquency. For example, the proportion of persistent serious male delinquents who had persistent school problems ranged from 9% in Pittsburgh to 41% in Denver. Similarly, the proportion of persistent serious female delinquents who had persistent school problems ranged from 11% in Denver to 55% in Rochester. Site differences of similar magnitude were observed in the proportions of those with school problems who are delinquents. Thus broad generalizations about the relationship between persistent serious delinquency and other persistent school problems are unwarranted. In sum, persistent serious delinquents should not be characterized as having school problems, nor should those with school problems be characterized as persistent serious delinquents. School failure problems vary by locality; these three cities may not have particularly high overall rates of school failure.

Effects of Multiple Problems

Huizinga and colleagues (2000) conclude that the degree of co-occurrence between persistent serious delinquency and other persistent problems is not overwhelming, but the size of the overlap suggests that a large number of persistent serious delinquents face additional problems that need to be addressed. It is crucial that juvenile justice system officials carefully identify the unique configurations of problems that individual youths have experienced. To do this, they need to use well-designed assessment instruments to determine the particular treatment needs of each delinquent and to help them craft an individualized treatment plan that fits those needs (see Chapter 10).

Effects of Personal Victimization on Subsequent Violence

In the three-site study described earlier, Huizinga et al. (2000) did not examine the overlap of persistent serious delinquency and victimization; however, Huizinga and Jakob-Chien (1998) did in their Denver study. That analysis showed that violent victimization is a key risk factor for serious violent delinquency. As the seriousness of offending increases, so does the probability of being violently victimized: 49% of male serious, violent juvenile offenders were violently victimized, compared with 12% of nondelinquents. For males, being a victim of violence was related to seriousness of delinquent offending and especially to violent offending. For girls, being a victim of violence was related more to general delinquency than to violent offending in this study.

Loeber et al. (2001) examined risk factors for violent victimization in the Pittsburgh Youth Study and the Denver Youth Survey and found that being a victim of violence that resulted in serious injuries was related to seriousness of delinquent offending and especially to violent offending among males and females. Across both studies and for each gender, the combination of committing assaults and carrying a weapon was particularly associated with elevated levels of victimization. Involvement in gang fights was one of the strongest risky behaviors for subsequent violent victimization (p. 4). At both sites, members of minority groups, especially African American males, were more likely to have been victims.

Another longitudinal self-report study, conducted by Woodward and Fergusson (2000), shows the effects of violent victimization on personal levels of violent offending. Interestingly, these researchers found that the individual and family risk factors that placed young people at risk of physical assault were the same across both gender groups. "These results suggested that the behavior and lifestyle characteristics associated with male and female assault may be the same" (p. 246). These results are compatible with findings on the physical assault experiences of young people in the Dunedin longitudinal study (Martin et al., 1998) and other seminal research (Lauritsen, 2003; Lauritsen & Quinet, 1995; Lauritsen & White, 2001; Menard, 2002).

Victimized adolescents are not usually innocent bystanders, although prior victimization is a strong predictor of subsequent victimization for males (Esbensen et al., 1999; Peterson et al., 2004). Violent offending in adolescence is one of the strongest predictors of both violent offending and violent victimization in adulthood (Menard, 2002), as are violent victimization and marijuana use. Involvement in these offenses in adolescence also has deleterious long-term consequences. Menard (2002) examined their effects on a successful transition to adulthood, measured by employment or financial stability, conventional aspirations or beliefs, involvement in a conventional support network, and abstinence from serious criminal behavior and substance use. The strongest predictors of nonsuccess in adulthood were frequency of marijuana use and violent offending and most recent grade point average, followed closely by violent victimization in adolescence. Consistent with past research, Menard found that violent victimization in adolescence has pervasive effects on problem outcomes in adulthood (p. 14). It increases the odds that, in adulthood, a person will be a perpetrator or a victim of both violence in general and domestic violence. It nearly doubles the odds of problem drug use in adulthood, and it also increases the odds of adult property offending. Thus the establishment of problem behavior patterns in adolescence greatly increases the likelihood of the persistence of these patterns into adulthood.

It appears that the more violent altercations and risky behaviors that street youths participate in, the greater their risk of violent victimization. For example, Hoyt, Ryan, and Cauce (1999) found that adolescent victimization was predicted by street exposure—time on the streets, substance abuse, and gang involvement—in addition to prior victimization. In another analysis—of Pittsburgh Youth Study data—Loeber, DeLamatre, Tita, Stouthamer-Loeber, and Farrington (1999) found that almost all of the juveniles who were killed or wounded by guns had been highly delinquent themselves. The victims of serious violence tended to have histories of engaging in serious delinquency, gang fights, and drug selling. They also tended to carry guns. Victims tended to do poorly academically, receive less parental supervision, and have poorer communication with their parents and long histories of behavior problems.

Violent victimization has also been linked with gang involvement (Decker, 2007; Decker, Katz, & Webb, 2008; Peterson et al., 2004). In the most recent study among these, the researchers (Decker et al., 2007) found that the more organized the gang, even at low levels of organization, the more likely it is that members will be involved in violent offenses, drug sales, and violent victimizations.

Do Girls Have a Unique Pathway to Serious, Violent, and Chronic Offending?

Although girls appear to follow the same delinquency pathways as boys (Gorman-Smith & Loeber, 2005), is it possible that the influence of risk factors and related problem behaviors differs in some important respects? Most studies show that girls have a lower prevalence and incidence of conduct disorders than boys (Loeber, Burke, Lahey, Winters, & Zera, 2000, p. 7), although there are exceptions (e.g., Tiet, Wasserman, Loeber, McReynolds, & Miller, 2001). However, conduct disorders appear to have more serious consequences for girls than for boys, in the form of other problem behaviors (Loeber et al., 2000, p. 7). Adolescent girls with conduct disorders are more at risk than boys for anxiety, depression, and, in turn, substance use and possibly suicidal behavior (Loeber et al., 2000, pp. 11–12). Even though girls show a lower prevalence of alcohol abuse, if they also experience depression, their level of aggression may well approach the level seen in boys. In a new large-scale Pittsburgh study of girls, Hipwell et al. (2002, p. 112) found that more than 8% of the girls in the entire sample qualified for psychiatric diagnoses between ages 5 and 8.

Research has established that more males than females are involved in serious and violent delinquency and adult crime. For example, national self-report data show that serious and violent delinquency prevalence rates throughout the adolescent years are two to three times higher for males than for females: 7–8% for males annually, compared with 2–3% for females (Elliott, Huizinga, & Morse, 1986, p. 485). Over a longer period, from adolescence to young adulthood (up to age 27), 42% of males and 16% of females are involved in serious violent offenses (Elliott, 1994a, p. 8). Elliott (p. 5) summarizes the essential gender prevalence differences: The peak age in prevalence is earlier for females, the desistance rate is steeper for females, and the gender difference becomes greater over time.

Given the higher prevalence rates among males, it is obvious that male gender is a far stronger predictor of general delinquency, and also serious or violent delinquency, than female gender. In their Philadelphia study that examined continuity in offending among serious, violent, and chronic juvenile offender subgroups, Kempf-Leonard, Tracy, and Howell (2001) found that the male-to-female ratio was 3:1 among serious offenders (serious property and violent offenders), 4:1 among violent offenders, and 3:1 among chronic offenders. They found even larger gender differences when they examined repeated serious and violent offending. For serious and chronic delinquents the male-to-female ratio was 6:1; for violent and chronic delinquents it was 7:1.

Some people might be tempted to conclude that life-course–persistent female offenders should not be taken as seriously as their male counterparts, given that females are less prevalent than males in the adolescent delinquent population. But when we look at the relative proportions of adult crimes for which the two genders account, we can see that female juvenile offenders should not be ignored. Kempf-Leonard and colleagues (2001) found that serious and chronic juvenile offenders constituted just 3.5% of the female delinquents in their sample, yet 44% of this group had officially recorded police contacts in adulthood and accounted for 16% of all police encounters with women (see p. 462, Table 1). Thus this small group of serious and chronic female delinquents was responsible for a share of adult crime 4.4 times as great as the group's size would suggest. In contrast, serious and chronic male delinquents made up 21% of the male offenders in the sample, but they were responsible for only 30% of the adult male criminality, just 1.4 times as much as the group's size would suggest.

Even more startling is the fact that violent and chronic female delinquents constituted just 2% of all the female delinquents in Kempf-Leonard et al.'s (2001) sample, but 44% had adult careers in crime, accounting for 11% of the total number of police encounters. Here, the violent and chronic female share is 5.5 times as great as parity would suggest. Again, the males do not show the same share of adult crimes. Violent and chronic male delinquents represented 14% of the male delinquents but committed only 21% of the adult male crimes. This share is only 1.5 times as great as parity would suggest. This study clearly shows that males have a greater propensity to commit serious and violent crimes in their delinquency careers, but it is for females that this involvement carries the greatest risk of adult crime. This study suggests that serious, violent, and chronic female offender careers deserve far more attention in research concerning criminal careers than they have received in the past.

In sum, boys are more likely than girls to be serious, violent, and chronic juvenile offenders. However, this does not mean that the serious, violent, and chronic offender careers of girls should be taken lightly. Although the proportion of adolescent girls who become serious, violent, and chronic juvenile offenders is very small, girls in these groups go on to commit more than their share of adult crimes. Thornberry et al. (2003) have published similar findings about female gang members. Although female gang members represented only 16% of all girls in the Rochester sample in early adolescence, they accounted for 64% of the serious violent acts committed by all the girls. Thus developmental criminology must address gender-specific patterns in offender careers over the life course (Kempf-Leonard & Tracy, 2000). Before we can propose a possibly unique pathway to serious, violent, and chronic juvenile offender careers for girls, we first need to answer the question of whether the risk factors for delinquency are different for boys and girls.

Risk Factors

Some researchers contend that the risk factors that influence the onset and persistence of violent behavior are different for boys and girls and that boys and girls undergo different developmental processes (Kelley et al., 1997, p. 9). However, unique risk factors for female and male delinquency have not yet been identified, and few studies have compared the two genders. In an earlier review of gender differences in a wide variety of antisocial behaviors, Rutter, Giller, and Hagell (1998) found that "risk factors associated with offending in girls are generally similar to those found to apply in boys" (p. 255). Other scholars agree (e.g., Kempf-Leonard & Tracy, 2000). Indeed, a key longitudinal comparison of males and females concerning risk factors for delinquency and other antisocial behaviors, in the Dunedin Multidisciplinary Health and Development Study, strongly supports this conclusion. Moffitt, Caspi, Rutter, and Silva (2001) measured risk factors and problem behaviors over the first two decades of life and found that the same risk factors predict antisocial behaviors (conduct problems) in both males and females. The gender differences found in self-reported delinquency were accounted for by males' greater exposure to risk factors; that is, males experienced more of the risk factors that predicted serious and persistent antisocial behavior. However, this study did not measure child physical or sexual abuse. Research has shown that girls are more likely than boys to suffer physical and sexual abuse throughout childhood and adolescence (Finkelhor & Dziuba-Leatherman, 1994, p. 180) and may have more difficulty adapting socially as a result.

It also is disappointing that the Dunedin study did not separate serious and violent acts from other conduct disorders. Psychologists commonly measure "conduct disorders" as defined by the American Psychiatric Association (2000); that definition includes several serious forms of delinquency (destroying property, carrying weapons, breaking and entering, forced sex, and physical fights) and other less serious problem behaviors (running away, telling lies, truancy, stealing, bullying, setting fires, cruelty to people or animals, and staying out late). Thus the Dunedin study did not examine specifically the relationship between risk factors and serious violent delinquency among girls. Only three longitudinal prospective studies have done so: the Rochester Youth Development Study, the Denver Youth Survey, and the Christchurch Health and Development Study. In an examination of the results of the first two of these studies, Huizinga et al. (2000) compared male and female adolescents on key predictors of serious property and serious assault offenses and found that gender differences were small in both study sites when they compared drug use, problems in school, and mental health problems (see also Loeber et al., 2001).

In another longitudinal study, the Christchurch Health and Development Study in New Zealand, Woodward and Fergusson (2000) found that males and females shared similar childhood risk factors (early conduct problems, childhood family environment, and adolescent lifestyle) for violence in adolescence. They note, "For both males and females, the profile of those at greatest risk was that of a young, conduct-disordered adolescent reared by physically punitive and substance-abusing parents, who upon reaching adolescence, engaged in antisocial and other risk-taking behavior" (p. 254).

Although general delinquency and other antisocial behaviors in girls and boys appear to be influenced by a common set of risk factors, the levels of certain risk factors—particularly history of physical and sexual abuse and certain mental health problems—may be higher among girls than among boys, as I discuss in the next section. It is possible that these particular risk factors have more important developmental consequences for girls than for boys. However, this possibility has not been tested; thus it remains to be seen whether girls and boys evidence different developmental processes in their progression toward serious, violent, and chronic juvenile offender careers.

A Unique Pathway

I would like to propose six stepping-stones for a subgroup of girls' pathway to serious, violent, and chronic juvenile offender careers: child physical and sexual abuse, mental health problems, drug abuse, running (or being thrown) away, youth gang membership, and detention or incarceration. Except for child abuse, boys and girls suffer these experiences about equally; however, the combination of all these experiences may have greater negative effects on girls than on boys, propelling a subgroup of girls toward serious, violent, and chronic juvenile offender careers. My central proposition is that the gendered nature (Chesney-Lind, 1997, p. 176) of these risk factors and environments may well have a greater impact on girls than on boys for the most severe delinquency outcomes—that is, serious, violent, and chronic juvenile offender careers. However, this is an empirical question.

Child abuse is the first stepping-stone. Girls are more likely than boys to suffer physical abuse up to about age 4, and they are about twice as likely as boys to suffer sexual abuse throughout childhood and adolescence (Finkelhor & Dziuba-Leatherman, 1994, p. 180). There are similar differences when abuse and neglect are considered together. For example, Ireland, Smith, and Thornberry (2002) found in the Rochester study that by age 18, 16% of the males and 27% of the females had substantiated cases of maltreatment.

The effects of such childhood victimization on developmental pathways may be unique for girls (Acoca, 1998a, 1998b, p. 562; Chesney-Lind, 1997; Chesney-Lind & Sheldon, 1998). As we reported in Chapter 4, research has found that a history of childhood maltreatment (abuse and neglect) significantly increases the likelihood of later self-reported juvenile involvement in moderately serious, serious, and violent delinquency for both girls and boys (Smith & Thornberry, 1995). However, Widom and Maxfield (2001) report that when they compared abused and neglected girls with girls who had not been victimized in that way, they found that the abused and neglected girls were significantly more likely to have been arrested for violence as juveniles and as adults; they did not find this pattern for males.

The second stepping-stone for girls on the pathway to delinquency is mental health problems. Adolescent females tend to have higher rates of psychiatric disorders than adolescent males (Romano, Tremblay, Vitaro, Zoccolillo, & Pagani, 2001), but this may not be true for serious and violent female offenders (Huizinga et al., 2000). Among children age 12 and older in the juvenile justice system, a multistate study (Skowyra & Cocozza, 2006) found that girls were at significantly higher risk (80%) than boys (67%) for a mental health disorder (see also Cauffman, 2004; McReynolds et al., 2008). In another study of a random sample of a large population of juvenile detainees, two-thirds of males and three-quarters of females had a psychiatric diagnosis (Teplin, Abram, McClelland, Dulcan, & Washburn, 2006). Even when conduct problems were not considered, 60% of the youth continued to evidence a psychiatric disorder.

Some research suggests a sharp rise in the onset of depression in girls in the adolescent period (Kovacs, 1996; Renouf & Harter, 1990). During childhood the depression rate is about the same in boys and girls, but after the onset of puberty, the rate among girls is about twice the rate among boys (Brent & Birmaher, 2002). This condition may contribute to the higher rate of relational aggression among girls than among boys (see Chesney-Lind & Brown, 1999; Crick & Grotpeter, 1995; Lerman & Pottick, 1995).

Boys and girls may also differ with respect to the impact of depression on violent behavior. In preliminary research for the Project on Human Development in Chicago Neighborhoods, Obeidallah and Earls (1999) found that, compared with nondepressed girls, mildly to moderately depressed girls had higher rates of aggressive behavior and crimes against people. Thus depression may be a central pathway through which girls' serious antisocial behavior develops, so it may be a precursor to delinquency and violence. Early pubertal maturation might be a precursor for the onset of both depression and antisocial behavior among girls (Brooks-Gunn, Graber, & Paikoff, 1994; Stattin & Magnusson, 1991), so this may be an important screening point.

Drug abuse is the third stepping-stone. There is evidence that the trend for earlier initiation of alcohol use is more pronounced among girls than among boys and that girls may be more vulnerable to persistent use, alcohol abuse, and dependence at an early age (Hipwell et al., 2005). In adolescence, prior delinquency involvement is a stronger indicator of drug use among girls than vice versa, but nearly half of the persistent serious female delinquents are drug users (Huizinga et al., 2000). But little research has been conducted on children younger than age 12. Among children age 12 and older in the juvenile justice system, girls are more likely than boys to have substance use disorders (Zahn, 2007).

Running (or being thrown) away is the fourth stepping-stone. The proportion of girls (11%) who run away from home is about the same as that for boys (10%) (Hammer, Finkelhor, & Sedlak, 2002; Snyder & Sickmund, 1999, p. 58; Tyler & Bersani, 2008). The relationship between running away, or being thrown away, and subsequent delinquency is well established (for an excellent review of this literature, see Kaufman & Widom, 1999, pp. 349–351). Kaufman and Widom (1999) found that childhood victimization (sexual or physical abuse and neglect) increases the runaway risk and that both childhood victimization and running away increase the likelihood of juvenile justice system involvement. Theirs and other studies have found that running away is correlated with subsequent high-risk outcomes (Tyler & Bersani, 2008). Life on the streets is risky for homeless children (Hagan & McCarthy, 1997), leading to substance abuse, association with deviants, risky sexual behaviors, and violent victimization (Hoyt et al., 1999). In a study of homeless and runaway adolescents in four Midwestern states, Whitbeck, Hoyt, and Yoder (1999) found that such street experiences also amplified the effects of early family abuse on victimization and depressive symptoms for young women. Moreover, in a subsequent analysis of only the girls in the initial study sample, Tyler, Hoyt, and Whitbeck (2000) found that girls who leave home to escape sexual abuse are often sexually victimized on the streets. Tyler and colleagues explain the pathway as follows: Exposure to dysfunctional and disorganized families early in life places youths on a trajectory of early independence; this early independence on the streets, along with the homeless or runaway lifestyle, exposes them to dangerous people and places; and this environment and the absence of conventional ties put them at increased risk of sexual victimization (p. 238).

Youth gang activity is the fifth stepping-stone. Child abuse, early dating, and precocious sexual activity increase the risk of gang involvement for both girls and boys (Thornberry, Krohn, et al., 2003). Several studies suggest that family conflict and child victimization in the home may have greater importance as risk factors for gang membership for girls than for boys (Fleisher, 1998; Maxson, Whitlock, & Klein, 1998; J. A. Miller, 2001; Moore, 1978; Moore & Hagedorn, 2001). In a study of gang girls, J. A. Miller (2001) found that girls with serious family problems—especially violence between adults in the home, parental drug or alcohol abuse, jailed family members, and physical or sexual abuse—often choose gangs as a means of avoiding chaotic family life and meeting their own social and developmental needs. For many of the young women in Miller's study, "home was not a particularly safe place" (p. 47), and these unsafe conditions helped drive them into the streets and into gangs. Unfortunately, gang involvement increases girls' risk of victimization, particularly assault and possibly sexual victimization (Fleisher, 1998; J. A. Miller, 2001). Ironically, they feel protected by older males in gender-mixed gangs, yet they are often victimized by them (J. A. Miller, 2001).

Girls who are actively involved in gangs become the most serious, violent, and chronic juvenile offenders of all girls (Thornberry, Krohn, et al., 2003). As reported in Chapter 4, gang membership has similar detrimental long-term impacts on adolescent developmental processes for both boys and girls. Thornberry, Krohn, et al. (2003) have observed that, over and above increasing the "criminal embeddedness" of gang members, gangs cut youngsters off from conventional pursuits. Thus gang involvement has disruptive life-course consequences for females and males alike. According to Thornberry, Krohn, et al. (2003), the gang effect is particularly strong for females in the areas of early pregnancy, teen motherhood, and unstable employment. Gang membership also increases the odds of continued involvement in criminal activity throughout adolescence and into adulthood for both young men and young women.

Juvenile justice system involvement is the sixth stepping-stone on girls' pathway to delinquency. Girls are far more likely than boys to enter the juvenile justice system via arrests for running away from home, and this group of runaway girls also has high rates of substance abuse problems and gang involvement (Kempf-Leonard & Johansson, 2007). Although only a little more than one-fourth (29%) of juveniles arrested in 2003 were girls, they represented more than half (59%) of the juvenile arrests for running away (Snyder & Sickmund, 2006, p. 125). Once girls are placed on probation—typically for status offenses, such as running away or liquor law violations—"any subsequent offense [becomes] a vector for their greater involvement in the juvenile justice system" through probation violations and new offenses (Acoca, 1999, p. 7). Girls are far more likely than boys to be held in detention centers for minor offenses, particularly for probation and parole violations (American Bar Association & National Bar Association, 2001). Girls are also more likely than boys to be detained for contempt of court, increasing the likelihood of their return to detention centers, providing more opportunities for further victimization.

Although intervention with treatment programs early in offender careers is beneficial (Farrington & Welsh, 2007; Loeber & Farrington, 2001a), incarceration in detention centers and reformatories rarely is (Holman & Ziedenberg, 2006). As a matter of fact, incarceration, ironically, often leads to further victimization. As Acoca (1998b) notes, "The abuses that a majority of girl offenders have experienced in their homes, in their schools, or on the streets often are mirrored and compounded by injuries they receive [in these facilities] within the juvenile justice system" (p. 562). When girls are placed in detention centers, they are often subjected to further victimization in the forms of emotional abuse; emotional distress from isolation; physical abuse, threats, and intimidation from staff; and unhealthy conditions of confinement (Acoca, 1998). Overcrowding in such facilities is a major factor contributing to unhealthy conditions. Juvenile detention centers across the country are experiencing serious overcrowding (Snyder & Sickmund, 2006, p. 223), especially in girls' detention units (American Bar Association & National Bar Association, 2001). It is not unusual for such facilities to use common rooms with floor mats as sleeping areas. The limited resources of these detention centers are strained as they attempt to meet the basic physical and mental health needs of the girls in their custody, and the conditions of confinement are sometimes deplorable (American Bar Association & National Bar Association, 2001, pp. 21–22).

Girls in correctional facilities show multiple serious disorders and problem behaviors. In an examination of the records of girls held in a secure Colorado facility, Rubin (2000) found that 100% of them suffered from posttraumatic stress disorder. Other disorders in this population included substance abuse (80%), psychiatric disorders (conduct disorder, major depression, bipolar disorder, and oppositional defiant disorder; 67%), and eating disorders (50%). As Rubin states, "These behavior problems manifest themselves in poor impulse control, poor concentration, poor communication skills, poor anger expression, physical aggression, property destruction, inhibited social skills, distorted thinking, uninhibited sexual activity, low tolerance for frustration, inhibited ability to delay gratification, and, of course, low self-esteem" (p. 2). In addition, 64% had been victims of sexual abuse, 47% practiced self-harm or self-mutilation, and 14% were already mothers. In a study of all boys and girls committed to Virginia's long-term state training schools in 1993–1998, McGarvey and Waite (2000) found that 24% of the females and 5% of the males had previously attempted suicide. Nearly half of the girls (49%) and more than a third (36%) of the boys had used psychotropic medications. It is difficult to imagine how girls with problems such as these could benefit from incarceration in a reformatory.

The relevance of several of the stepping-stones described in this chapter is illustrated by Acoca's (1998) findings from an interview study with nearly 200 girls in four California detention centers (see also Acoca & Dedel, 1998). For many of these girls, the pathway to delinquency began with childhood victimization. More than 9 out of 10 (92%) had experienced one or more forms of physical, sexual, or emotional abuse, often on multiple occasions, and 40% of them had been sexually assaulted (p. 565). More than half (53%) of them had experienced one or more forms of sexual abuse, beginning with molestation at about age 5. More than 45% had been beaten or burned by caregivers at least once, generally between the ages of 11 and 13. About 25% were victims of parental neglect.

A typical girl's story could be described as follows: At age 13 or 14 she first began risky behaviors, including running away from home, polydrug and alcohol use, school failure, and truancy, followed by expulsion from school. She became sexually active at age 13 and was a victim of sexual assault in the same year. She was first shot or stabbed at age 14, the same age at which she delivered her first child (29% of the total sample had been pregnant, 16% while in custody). About half of the girls in this sample became affiliated with gangs at ages 13–15, and more than two-thirds of the gang members became very involved in gang life.

Because Acoca's study was cross-sectional, there is no way to specify with certainty the temporal ordering of these stepping-stones. Indeed, it is not known whether the pathways I have proposed are predominant ones for life-course serious, violent, and chronic female juvenile offenders. More research is needed on this proposed developmental pathway. Welcome illumination of girls' pathways to delinquency is forthcoming from the first major U.S. longitudinal study exclusively of girls (the Pittsburgh Girls Study, $N = 2,451$). It is under way in the Pittsburgh Life History Studies (directed by Drs. Rolf and Magda Loeber). Headed by Allison Hipwell, it was launched in the fall of 2000 (Hipwell et al., 2002, 2005, 2007).

Discussion Topics

1. Which type of offender career mapping do you think is most useful? Why?

2. What factors have the most influence on the shape of offender careers?

3. If you were a juvenile justice official, would you rather know about Snyder's depiction of serious, violent, and chronic offenders or Loeber's pathways? Why?

4. What are the limitations of Loeber's pathways?

5. Which model best explains juvenile offender careers: Thornberry's interactional theory or Loeber's pathways?

CHAPTER 6

Youth Gangs

The terms *street gang* and *youth gang* are used interchangeably. These seemingly similar terms can embrace widely varying gangs (Box 6.1). At one end of the spectrum, researchers define youth gangs very restrictively. To illustrate, the following are widely accepted criteria among researchers for classifying groups as youth gangs (or street gangs):

- The group must have three or more members, generally ages 12–24.
- Members must share some sense of identity, especially symbols and a name.
- Members must view themselves as a gang and be recognized by others as a gang.
- They must have some permanence and a degree of organization.
- They must have verbal and nonverbal forms of communication.
- They are involved in an elevated level of criminal activity (Curry & Decker, 2003; Esbensen, Winfree, He, & Taylor, 2001; Klein, 1995).

IN FOCUS 6.1
Youth Gang Definitions and Characterizations

The term gang tends to designate collectivities that are marginal members of mainstream society, loosely organized, and without a clear, social purpose. (Ball & Curry, 1995, p. 227)

The Fremont Hustlers gang was a haphazardly assembled social unit composed of deviant adolescents who shared social and economic needs and the propensity for resolving those needs in a similar way. (Fleisher, 1998, p. 264)

(Continued)

(Continued)

Gangs are one delinquent subgroup along with other homogeneous adolescent subgroups: skaters, preps, hip-hop, ravers, postgrunge, goths and stoners. (Fleisher, 1998, p. 257)

[For control and prevention efforts, gangs are] a shifting, elusive target, permeable and elastic . . . not a cohesive force but, rather, a spongelike resilience. (Klein & Maxson, 1989, p. 211)

The gang is an interstitial group (between childhood and maturity) originally formed spontaneously, and then integrated through conflict. (Thrasher, 1927, p. 18)

[A gang is] any denotable adolescent group of youngsters who a) are generally perceived as a distinct aggregation by others in the neighborhood, b) recognize themselves as a denotable group (almost invariably with a group name), and c) have been involved in a sufficient number of delinquent incidents to call forth a consistently negative response from neighborhood residents and/or law enforcement agencies. (Klein, 1971, p. 13)

A youth gang is a self-formed association of peers united by mutual interests with identifiable leadership and internal organization who act collectively or as individuals to achieve specific purposes, including the conduct of illegal activity and control of a particular territory, facility, or enterprise. (Miller, 1992, p. 21)

[Gangs are] groups that are complexly organized although sometimes diffuse, sometimes cohesive with established leadership and membership rules, operating within a framework of norms and values in respect to mutual support, conflict relations with other gangs, and a tradition often of turf, colors, signs, and symbols. (Curry & Spergel, 1988, p. 382)

[A gang is] an age-graded peer group that exhibits some permanence, engages in criminal activity, and has some symbolic representation of membership. (Decker & Van Winkle, 1996, p. 31)

Gang characteristics consist of a gang name and recognizable symbols, a geographic territory, a regular meeting pattern, and an organized, continuous course of criminality. (Chicago Police Department, 1992, p. 1)

A Criminal Street Gang is any ongoing organization, association, or group of three or more persons, whether formal or informal, having as one of its primary activities the commission of criminal acts. (Street Terrorism Enforcement and Prevention Act, 1988, California Penal Code sec. 186.22[f])

[A gang is] a self-identified group of kids who act corporately, at least sometimes, and violently, at least sometimes. (Kennedy, Piehl, & Braga, 1996, p. 158)

What makes these criteria so restrictive is not only the sheer number of them but also that they can be used to winnow a broad range of adolescent groups down to those that are bona fide youth gangs (see Box 6.2; Esbensen, Winfree, et al., 2001). This ingenious process for sifting out nongangs that Esbensen and colleagues developed reduces the remaining gangs to those that have a name, are somewhat organized, and are involved in delinquent or criminal activity. Their research shows that these are central features of the most highly delinquent and organized gangs. The researchers found that as each more restrictive definitional criterion was added, the proportion of qualifying gang members was reduced. The fact that nearly half of the eighth graders who claimed gang membership ("ever involved") were no longer active members confirms that gang membership is short-lived for most very young members.

IN FOCUS 6.2
Indicators of Bona Fide Gangs

Youth gang researchers have devised a way to measure adolescents' involvement in youth gangs by determining their degree of bonding to the gangs (Esbensen, Winfree, et al., 2001). These researchers' study sample consisted of some 6,000 eighth graders (average age nearly 14) in known gang problem localities. The study measured gang bonding on a continuum of five levels of involvement in progressively more serious gangs:

1. Level 1: Ever involved in a gang (17%)

2. Level 2: Currently a gang member (9%)

3. Level 3: Currently a member of a *delinquent gang* (8%)

4. Level 4: Currently a member of a delinquent gang that is *organized* (5%)

5. Level 5: Currently a *core* member of a delinquent gang that is organized (2%)

Esbensen and colleagues also discovered that members of gangs that were somewhat "organized" (i.e., had initiation rites, established leaders, and symbols or colors) self-reported higher rates of delinquency and involvement in more serious delinquent acts than other youths. Another study tested the influence of gang organization on members' involvement in violent crime and drug sales (Decker, Katz, & Webb, 2008). The researchers found that people who were members of more organized gangs in three Arizona cities reported higher victimization counts, more gang sales of different kinds of drugs, and more violent offending by the gang than did members of less organized gangs.

At the other end of the spectrum, many state legislatures and law enforcement agencies define gangs very broadly to include a variety of adult criminal organizations including drug cartels and ongoing criminal enterprises. For example, as seen in Box 6.1, California's gang law defines a "criminal street gang" as any ongoing organization, association, or group of three or more people, whether formal or informal, having as one of its primary activities the commission of criminal acts (Street Terrorism Enforcement and Prevention Act, 1988, California Penal Code sec. 186.22[f]). Several states have modeled their gang definitions after this broad one even though it encompasses adult criminal enterprises ("organized crime") that typically are not considered to be street gangs. When law enforcement agencies estimate the number of gangs in their jurisdiction, they often include a variety of gangs that encompass the two extremes discussed here (Howell, Egley, & Gleason, 2000).

This chapter provides an overview of youth gang problems in the United States. It begins with an examination of youth gang trends. The next two sections shed light on the relative seriousness of gang problems in American cities, towns, and rural areas. More transitory gang problems in sparsely populated areas are examined first, followed by more persistent gang activity in the most densely populated centers. That information is important for the section to follow, which examines myths about youth gangs. These tend to apply mainly to gangs in smaller cities and towns and rural areas, where gang problems are less entrenched. The chapter concludes with a pitch for measured response to gangs based on a local assessment rather than overreaction with law enforcement suppression strategies.

Youth Gang Trends

The National Youth Gang Center (NYGC), established by the Office of Juvenile Justice and Delinquency Prevention, has chronicled the distribution and level of the U.S. gang problem since its first systematic National Youth Gang Survey (NYGS) in 1996 (Figure 6.1). In the mid-1990s, gang problems in the United States increased to an unprecedented level (Miller, 2001). A precipitous decline followed. From 1996 to 2001, the systematic NYGS revealed year-to-year declines or a leveling off of the number of jurisdictions reporting youth gang problems (Egley, Howell, & Major, 2006). Between 1996 and 2002, the estimated number of gang members declined 14%, and the estimated number of gangs decreased nearly 30%. Still, gang crime problems plague large numbers of U.S. cities, towns, and counties.

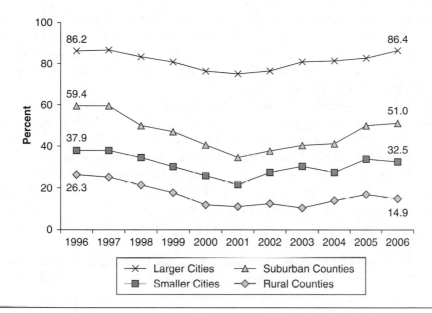

Figure 6.1   Prevalence of Gang Problems in the United States, 1996–2006

This downturn was followed by a substantial upturn in youth gang problems reported in the NYGC from 2002 to 2005, particularly in rural counties and suburban counties (Table 6.1, Curry & Howell, 2007; Egley, O'Donnell, & Curry, 2007). Overall, 20% more localities reported gang activity in 2005 than in 2002. Three other indicators of gang activity buttress this observed trend. First, the NYGS respondents are asked each year

Table 6.1   Law Enforcement Agencies Reporting Gang Problems, 2002 and 2005

Area Type	2002 Total	2005 Total	Percentage Change
Rural counties	53	89	68
Smaller cities	178	210	18
Suburban counties	143	189	32
Larger cities	320	346	8
Total	694	834	20

NOTE: Rural counties and smaller cities estimated from samples.

whether gang problems are "getting better," "getting worse," or "staying about the same." In 1999, 25% of jurisdictions classified their gang problem as "getting worse," and this statistic increased to about 50% in 2005 (Egley et al., 2007), indicating a doubling of the proportion of agencies that regard their gang problem as worsening.

Second, the estimated number of gangs reported by NYGS respondents increased at a similar pace (up 21% from 2002 to 2005), but the estimated number of gang members increased by much less (8%) during this period (Egley & Major, 2004; Egley et al., 2007). The slower increase in the growth of gang members is attributable to the fact that most of the increase in gang activity was reported in rural counties (68%), where the number of gang members is small. Cities with a population of 50,000 or more and suburban counties accounted for approximately 85% of the estimated number of gang members in 2002 (Egley et al., 2006).

Third, gang homicides increased across the United States in the early 2000s (Curry et al., 2004). To use the most reliable indicator, researchers examined the number of gang homicides reported in municipal areas with populations of 100,000 or more. In these areas, gang homicides increased 34% from 1999 to 2003. The 2003 figure (1,451 reported homicides) was about the same as the number in the peak year for the 1990s (1,447). Reported gang homicides declined from 1997 to 2000, after which the increase commenced.

An independent validation of the increase in reported gang activity cited here is seen in the trend in student reports of gang activity in schools. Pertinent data were collected in the School Crime Supplement to the National Crime Victimization Survey. In the mid-1990s, 28% of the national sample of students reported that gangs were present in their schools (Chandler, Chapman, Rand, & Taylor, 1998). This amount dropped to 17% in 1999 and then began to increase to 24% in 2005, almost to the level reported a decade earlier (Dinkes et al., 2006). Although these two surveys have important differences—mainly that the student survey gauges the youngest segment of gang participants (Curry, 2000)—they reveal a similar trend, a decrease in gang activity in the late 1990s and an increase in the opening years of this century.

It is too soon to say whether the recent increase in gang activity is a lasting trend. Gang problems in the United States as a whole appear to occur in spurts or cycles, and the length of the upswings and downturns cannot be predicted. Miller (1992) describes this pattern as like "a wave that strikes with great fury at one part of the shore, recedes, strikes again at another, ebbs away, strikes once more, and so on." Indeed, variations from one geographic area to another are common—even within the same city—depending on the existence of recurring gang conflicts that create peaks and valleys in gang crimes (Block & Block, 1993; Decker & Van Winkle, 1996).

Transitory Gang Problems

Figure 6.2   People See Gangs in Different Ways

Many small cities and towns and rural areas experienced gang problems for the first time in recent years (Egley et al., 2007; Howell & Egley, 2005a). The heightened public awareness of gangs and reports of a pervasive gang presence in different parts of the country has complicated community reactions. The visibility of adolescent groups in shopping malls and on street corners and their frequent troublesome behavior may suggest gang involvement. Another factor that may lead to the mistaken conclusion that a gang problem exists is the recent transfusion of gang culture into the larger youth culture. Certain clothing styles and colors commonly worn by gang members have become faddish in the popular youth culture. One need only watch MTV for a short period of time to see the popularity of what once were considered exclusively gang symbols. Identifying a group as a gang isn't always easy (Figure 6.2 and Box 6.3). Knowing their history helps (Howell, 1998d).

IN FOCUS 6.3

What Makes a Gang a Gang?

Peggy Sanday (1990) described in detail the events that led to a gang rape allegedly committed by several members of a fairly well-organized, cohesive group of older adolescents in Philadelphia. Even before this particular incident, the XYZs (the fictitious name Sanday gave the group) had already developed a reputation throughout the neighborhood for making trouble. They often congregated on benches situated in front of their clubhouse, which the XYZs claimed as their turf. On more than one occasion, women

(Continued)

(Continued)

had reported verbal harassment by members of the gang when they passed by. New members of the community were commonly warned about the group, and women were urged to take precautions if they attended parties that were regularly thrown by the gang.

This short description has many of the indicators of traditional descriptions of a gang, that is, "a group of inner-city adolescents, a concern with turf, harassment of local residents, an organizational structure, some degree of solidarity, and mutual participation in serious forms of illegal behavior. . . . However, we have left one very important piece of information out of our short summary of Sanday's study: these were all members of a prominent fraternity at a prestigious upper-middle-class university" (Bursik & Grasmick, 1993, p. 8).

Differential Impacts of Gangs on Communities

Cities, towns, and rural counties can be grouped into three categories with respect to their youth gang problems. The scope and severity of their gang problem corresponds closely to the size of their population. In the first category—rural areas and small towns with populations under 25,000—very few of the gangs are well organized, and few of them seem to survive. Only 4 in 100 rural counties and 10 in 100 small cities and towns report a persistent gang problem (Howell & Egley, 2005a). In these sparsely populated areas, the typical community with reported gang problems has on average three to six gangs and 50–100 members. If they do not report a gang problem year after year, their estimates are on the low side of both of these indicators.

Localities in the second group (cities and suburbs with populations between 25,000 and 100,000) are the most difficult to classify with certainty because many of them experience a gang problem at some point, but this may not be a permanent or serious condition (Howell, Moore, & Egley, 2002). In contrast, the likelihood of gang problems—and more persistent and serious gang problems—is much higher for the third category, cities and suburban areas with populations greater than 100,000 (Howell, 2006). In fact, all cities with populations greater than 250,000 consistently report gang problems year after year (Egley, Howell, & Major, 2006).

Table 6.2 shows how the reported number of gangs and gang members grows larger as city size increases, from 3–6 gangs and 50–100 members in rural counties and towns under 25,000 population to an average of 7–30 gangs with 200 or more members in larger cities (100,000–250,000 population). Nationwide, the bulk of all gang members are found in the very largest cities (250,000 population and greater), where more than 30 gangs are typically reported, and the majority of these cities typically have more than 1,000 gang members (Howell, 2006; Howell & Egley, 2005a).

Table 6.2 Estimated Number of Gangs and Gang Members and Population Size

Estimated Number of Gangs	Estimated Number of Gang Members
Populations under 25,000	
3–6	50–100
Populations between 25,000 and 100,000	
4–15	50–200
Populations between 100,000 and 250,000	
7–30	200+
Populations greater than 250,000	
30+	1,000+

The youth gang myths that are previewed in the next section apply mainly in the first and second categories, the less entrenched gang problem communities that are just beginning to experience a youth gang problem (or suspect that they are) and other localities that have an ongoing gang problem that is not particularly persistent or serious. Community leaders in these circumstances often are susceptible to misleading information about youth gangs and often feel uncertain about what an appropriate response might be. It is very common for uncertain community officials and others to overreact to youth gangs.

Youth Gangs: Myths and Realities

Felson (2006) argues that the gangs themselves create myths as part of what he calls their "Big Gang Theory." As Felson explains it, youths sometimes feel that they need protection on the streets in their communities. The gang provides this service. However, few gangs are nasty enough to be particularly effective in protecting youths. Therefore, they need to appear more dangerous than they actually are to provide maximum protection. Felson observes that gangs use a ploy found in nature to maximize the protection they seek to provide. In order to scare off threatening predators, some harmless animals and insects mimic a more dangerous member of their species. In turn, predators learn to avoid all species—both harmless and dangerous—that look alike. For example, Felson notes that the coral snake, an extremely dangerous viper, is mimicked by the scarlet king snake, which is often called the "false coral snake" because of its similar colors and patterns. Although the latter snake is not venomous at all, it scares off potential predators by virtue of its appearance.

Felson suggests that gangs use the same strategy, providing signals for local gang members to help make their gangs resemble truly dangerous big-city gangs. These standardized signals or symbols typically consist of hand signs, colors, graffiti, clothes, and language content. Indeed, gang membership is often more symbolic than real (Espelage, Wasserman, & Fleisher, 2007).

Armed with indicators of truly bad gangs, members of harmless gangs can display scary signals at will to create a more menacing image (Felson, 2006). Graffiti is often used, but it's not always gang related (Table 6.3; Weisel, 2004). Using a famous gang name helps gangs propagate a menacing image that may intimidate others. Once enough people believe their overblown dangerous image, it becomes accepted as reality.

The myth that local gangs are affiliated with big-city gangs also supports the exaggerated dangerousness of gangs in small cities and towns. This image persists because of the similarity of local gangs' names and symbols, which is explained by mimicry or imitation. An analogy helps reveal the reality of the situation. Local Little League baseball teams may appear to be affiliated with major league baseball teams because of similar names and uniforms, but there is no connection between local youth teams and professional baseball clubs. So it is with gangs; there rarely is any connection between local gangs and big-city gangs known by the same names. The reality is that local gangs often cut and paste bits of Hollywood images of gangs and big-city gang lore into their local versions of gangs (Starbuck, Howell, & Lindquist, 2001). And they often do a poor job of this copying, perhaps using the wrong colors, distorting the original gang's symbols, and so on. To illustrate the point, a gang of youth in Kansas City said they were affiliated with the Chicago Folks gang, but when asked about the nature of their affiliation, they couldn't explain it. They said that they just liked to draw the Folks' pitchfork symbol (Fleisher, 1998, p. 26).

One example illustrating this point is the broadcasting of the names of local groups that claim to be gangs—such as Crips or Bloods that have a legendary image as Los Angeles gangs—which helps validate scary images of the local gangs. Unfortunately, the broadcast media sometimes unwittingly help local gangs promote their Big Gang Theory. Misrepresentations of gangs in the print media have been well documented in a study covering articles published in the past quarter century (Esbensen & Tusinski, 2007). These researchers found that the leading newsweeklies consider gangs to be a monolithic phenomenon and do not describe the diversity among distinctively different types of gangs, such as prison gangs, drug gangs, and youth gangs. They also portray gangs as highly organized groups that have spread to new areas as part of a conspiracy to establish satellite sets across the country.

Although gang coverage by broadcast electronic media has not been systematically analyzed through the method by which Esbensen and Tusinski examined newsweeklies, it appears that the gang phenomenon is often exaggerated and grossly misrepresented. Similar distortions of other crime problems by the broadcast media are not uncommon. The exaggeration of the

Table 6.3   Types of Graffiti and Associated Motives

Type of Graffiti	Features	Motives
Gang[a]	• Gang name or symbol, including hand signs. • Gang member names or nicknames, or sometimes a roll-call list of members. • Numbers: Offenders commonly use numbers as code in gang graffiti. A number may represent the corresponding letter in the alphabet (e.g., 13 = M, for the Mexican Mafia) or represent a penal or police radio code. • Distinctive, stylized alphabets: These include bubble letters, block letters, backwards letters, and Old English script. • Key visible locations. • Enemy names and symbols or allies' names.	• Mark turf • Threaten violence • Boast of achievements • Honor the slain • Insult or taunt other gangs
Common tagger[b]	• High-volume, accessible locations. • High-visibility, hard-to-reach locations. • May be stylized but simple name or nickname tag or symbols: The single-line writing of a name is usually known as a tag, whereas slightly more complex tags, including those with two colors or bubble letters, are known as throw-ups. • Tenacious (keeps retagging).	• Notoriety or prestige • Defiance of authority
Artistic tagger	• Colorful and complex pictures known as masterpieces or pieces.	• Artistic • Prestige or recognition
Conventional graffiti	• Spontaneous. • Sporadic episodes or isolated incidents. • Malicious or vindictive. • Sporadic, isolated, or systematic incidents.	• Play • Rite of passage • Excitement • Impulse • Anger • Boredom • Resentment • Failure • Despair
Ideological	• Offensive content or symbols. • Racial, ethnic, or religious slurs. • Specific targets, such as synagogues. • Highly legible. • Slogans.	• Anger • Hate • Political • Hostility • Defiance

a. Copycat graffiti looks like gang graffiti and may be the work of gang wannabes or youths seeking excitement.

b. Tagbangers, a derivative of tagging crews and gangs, are characterized by competition with other crews. Therefore, crossed-out tags are features of their graffiti.

crack cocaine "epidemic" of the late 1980s and early 1990s is a case in point (see Brownstein, 1996, and Reeves & Campbell, 1994, for well-researched analyses of that coverage). There were cocaine "wars" (Eddy, Sabogal, & Walden, 1988), to be sure, but they mainly involved adult criminal organizations (see also Gugliotta & Leen, 1989). Almost invariably, newspaper accounts, popular magazine articles, and electronic media broadcasts on youth gangs contain at least one myth or fallacy (Box 6.4). These and several other gang myths are analyzed in detail elsewhere (Howell, 2007). Objective assessments of gang activity—or suspected gang presence—usually will debunk most of the gang myths.

IN FOCUS 6.4
Top 10 Gang Myths

1. Gangs are highly organized criminal enterprises.

2. Gangs migrate across the country to establish satellite sets.

3. Small local gangs are spawned by big-city gangs.

4. Gangs, drugs, and violence usually go together.

5. All gangs are alike.

6. Youth usually join a gang because of peer pressure.

7. Adolescents are often recruited by adults to join gangs.

8. Once kids join a gang, they're lost for good.

9. Once a gang forms, it's probably permanent.

10. Male gangs dominate gang girls.

When allowed to persist, gang myths tend to influence gang prevention and control policies (Archbold & Meyer, 2000; S. Moore, 2007; Toch, 2007), often leading to excessive use of gang suppression strategies and tactics. Two researchers carefully documented the process by which violent youth crimes were defined by the police as a gang-related problem in the community and the conditions that lead to a moral panic in a midsized Midwestern town of approximately 50,000 people (Archbold & Meyer, 2000). Similar gang-related moral panics have been documented elsewhere (Jackson & Rudman, 1993; McCorkle & Miethe, 2002; Zatz, 1987). One reason for panicking over suspected gang activity is that community leaders often are uncertain as to what youth gangs are all about. In addition to the absence of a commonly shared gang definition, the widely varying definitions of them (Box 6.1), and the numerous myths that are perpetuated in gang lore (Box 6.4), gangs are also confusing for other reasons that Felson identifies (Box 6.5). This situation is far more likely to exist in less populated areas where gang problems are intermittent because community conditions are not sufficient to sustain them (see Chapter 7).

IN FOCUS 6.5
Why Youth Gangs Are Confusing, According to Felson

- The *gang* word has many meanings: drug gangs, prison gangs, organized crime, juvenile gangs, etc.
- Different gangs use the same name.
- Gangs are unstable; they often change.
- Many gangs get too much credit for their dangerousness.
- It is often difficult to find the gang's structure.
- Gang leadership may change with activities.
- The "Big Gang Theory" can exaggerate the size and danger of juvenile gangs.

Bad community conditions may only produce delinquent groups, however. The tipping point (Klein, 1995, pp. 29–30) at which an adolescent group becomes a gang requires two "signposts," according to Klein. The first one is a commitment to a criminal orientation (or willingness to use violence; Decker & Van Winkle, 1996). The second signpost is when the gang to-be takes on a collective criminal orientation as a group, a gang, that is set apart from others. "Very often, part of this process is an acceptance of intergroup, now intergang, rivalries and hostilities. It's hard to find a one-gang city; gang cohesiveness thrives on gang-to-gang hostilities" (Klein, 1995, p. 30). Self-recognition is almost always fostered by a group name, signs, clothing, symbols, and territorial graffiti.

Persistent Gang Problems

As noted earlier, *persistent gang problems* are viewed as gang activity that is reported year after year and is more easily recognized. This likelihood is much greater in cities and suburban areas with populations greater than 100,000, in which gang problems date back many years (Howell & Egley, 2005a). There, more gangs and larger ones are commonly found (for an excellent overview of these gangs see Valdez, 2007). The following sections examine their impacts in several contexts: on communities, in schools, females in gangs, gang migration and immigration, and gang members returning from prison.

General Community Impacts of Youth Gangs

Although residents' major concern is with the more organized and violent gangs, the startup gangs also instill fear in residents when their troublesome behaviors involve intimidation, vandalism, graffiti, and occasional drug sales (Weisel, 2002, 2004). Nevertheless, community residents' fear of gangs and of becoming victims of gang crime is very great in the most gang-infested communities. A study in Orange County, California, that interviewed a random sample of residents illustrates this case (Lane & Meeker, 2000). Fear of crime and gangs was an immediate, daily experience for people who lived in lower-income neighborhoods where gangs were more prevalent and dangerous. But for people in other areas, fear was generally an abstract concern about the future that became immediate only when they entered certain pockets of the county. In the most gang-ridden areas, many residents reported having avoided gang areas because they are afraid of gangs and criminal victimization. Others talked about avoiding certain streets and taking a circuitous route to shopping areas at night to avoid gangs that operate in certain neighborhoods. Intimidation of other youths, adults, and business owners is not uncommon, and intimidation of witnesses or potential witnesses is particularly serious because it undermines the justice process (Bureau of Justice Assistance, 1997).

Gangs have a formidable presence in many of this country's major metropolitan areas (Coughlin & Venkatesh, 2003; Egley et al., 2004). A recent nationwide study of reported drive-by shootings found that almost half (46%) of them appeared to be gang-related (Violence Policy Center, 2007). Venkatesh (1996) describes one of the worst cases of gang dominance in Chicago's Robert Taylor Homes, a low-income public housing development. In the early 1990s, gangs in the housing development were transformed from turf gangs to drug gangs, and an escalation of gang violence resulted. Use of zip guns and hand-to-hand fighting of the past had given way to powerful handguns, drive-by shootings, and some use of assault weapons. The residents' safety was jeopardized, with a high risk of being caught in gang crossfire. Other drug gangs operating as organized criminal groups have had devastating impacts on communities. New York City's Puerto Rican Black Park Gang, so named because it shot out lights surrounding its base of operations in a park to avoid police detection (Bureau of Justice Assistance, 1997) is a classic example. It was a very violent drug gang—believed to be responsible for 15 murders—that trafficked in drugs and used the proceeds to buy legitimate businesses through which it laundered drug profits. In addition to drug trafficking and violent crimes, it was involved in trafficking or using illegally obtained firearms and using force to intimidate witnesses and victims. Urban gang problems are formidable, to be sure, yet modern-day urban gangs seem to be ever-changing (Coughlin & Venkatesh, 2003).

Impact of Gangs in Schools

Where they have a substantial community presence, youth gangs are linked with serious delinquency problems in elementary and secondary schools across the United States (Chandler et al., 1998). This study of data gathered in the School Crime Supplement to the 1995 National Crime Victim Survey documented several examples. First, there is a strong correlation between gang presence in schools and both guns in schools and availability of drugs in school. Second, higher percentages of students report knowing a student who brought a gun to school when students report gang presence (25%) than when gangs were not present (8%). In addition, gang presence at a student's school is related to seeing a student with a gun at school: 12% report having seen a student with a gun in school when gangs are present, compared with 3% when gangs are not present. Third, students who report that any drugs (marijuana, cocaine, crack, or uppers or downers) are readily available at school are much more likely to report gangs at their school (35%) than those who say that no drugs are available (14%). Fourth, the presence of gangs more than doubles the likelihood of violent victimization at school (nearly 8% vs. 3%). The presence of gangs at school also can be very disruptive to the school environment because they may not only create fear among students but also increase the level of violence in school (Laub & Lauritsen, 1998). Gang presence is also an important contributor to overall levels of student victimization at school (Howell & Lynch, 2000).

Unfortunately, school administrators' reports of gang activity in school do not correspond with other reports (Gottfredson & Gottfredson, 2001; Naber, May, Decker, Minor, & Wells, 2006). In a national study, in the 10% of schools with the highest student gang participation rates, only 18% of principals reported that gangs are a problem in the school (Gottfredson & Gottfredson, 2001, p. 3).

School administrations have taken greater security measures in response to the gang problem, but their effectiveness is subject to debate (Howell & Lynch, 2000). "The presence of security officers, metal detectors, and security cameras may deter some students from committing acts of violence, but this presence also serves to heighten fear among students and teachers, while increasing the power of some gangs and the perceived need some students have for joining gangs" (Thompkins, 2000, p. 54). It is also important to be aware that school-related gang crime extends beyond the boundaries of school buildings themselves to contexts in which youths congregate before and after school; in fact, gang crime begins to escalate very early on school days (Wiebe, Meeker, & Vila, 1999).

Females in Gangs

Female participation in youth gangs has increased in the past decade or more (Curry, 1998; Fleisher, 1998; Moore & Hagedorn, 2001). In some localities, girls represent one-fourth to one-third of the current gang members (Esbensen, Deschenes, & Winfree, 1999; Thornberry, Krohn, et al., 2003). In the 1997 National Longitudinal Survey of Youth, a nationally representative sample of 9,000 youth between the ages of 12 and 16, found that 8% had belonged to a gang. The male to female ratio in this group was approximately 2:1 (11% vs. 6%) (Snyder & Sickmund, 2006, p. 70). Even law enforcement officials, who historically have minimized female participation in gangs, have begun to recognize their increased presence in the NYGS (Figure 6.3). This is an important issue because a multicity study found that criminal activity is elevated in gangs that have gender-balanced membership (Peterson, Miller, & Esbensen, 2001).

Gang Migration and Immigration

The impact of gang migration on local gang problems is not as large as commonly perceived. First, there is very little evidence supporting the notion that youth gangs have the capacity to set up satellite operations in distant cities (Decker, Bynum, & Weisel, 1998; Howell & Decker, 1999). Recent studies debunk the popular belief that gangs are engaged in a systematic, organized effort to spread their influence internationally (McGuire, 2007; Ribando, 2005). Second, "gang migration" almost exclusively involves relocation of gang members with their families (Maxson, 1998).

However, migration of gang *members* can present substantial problems (Ribando, 2005). The 2004 NYGS asked law enforcement respondents about gang member migration, or the movement of actively involved gang youth

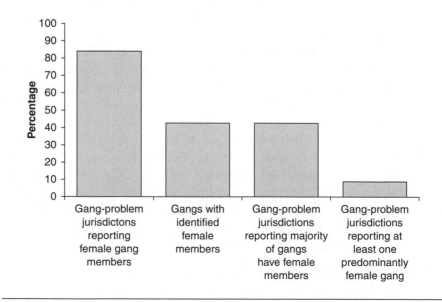

Figure 6.3   Female Participation in Youth Gangs According to Law Enforcement Views

from other jurisdictions. An analysis of survey results (Egley & Ritz, 2006) showed that a small number of agencies (10%) reported that more than half of the documented gang members in their jurisdiction had migrated from other areas, and a majority (60%) of respondents reported none or few (less than 25%) gang member migrants. Among agencies experiencing a higher percentage of gang member migration, 45% reported that social reasons (e.g., members moving with families, pursuit of legitimate employment opportunities) affected local migration patterns "very much." Also reported, but to a lesser degree, were drug market opportunities (23%), avoidance of law enforcement crackdowns (21%), and participation in other illegal ventures (18%). Social reasons were significantly more likely to be reported among agencies experiencing higher levels of gang member migration (Figure 6.4). The 2006 NYGS requested each respondent to indicate the factors that influenced gang-related violence in the respondent's jurisdiction. Although not ranked among the most important factors, gang member migration across U.S. jurisdictions was perceived to be a more important factor in local gang violence than gang member migration from outside the United States (Egley & O'Donnell, 2008).

Nevertheless, heavy immigration, particularly from Latin America and Asia, has introduced extremely violent gangs such as Mara Salvatrucha (MS) to the United States (Johnson, 2005; Triplett, 2004). Johnson (2005) suggests that two California-based groups have drawn on the ebb and flow of migrants to become substantial threats to public safety: the 18th Street and MS gangs. The MS identify themselves with tattoos such as the number 13, meaning *trece* in Spanish, shown as "MS-13." The MS gang is said to be involved in a variety of criminal enterprises, and they show no fear of law enforcement (Valdez, 2000).They seem willing to commit almost any crime, and MS gang members tend to have a higher level of criminal involvement than other gang members. Valdez reports that MS members have been involved in burglaries, auto thefts, narcotic sales, home invasion robberies, weapon smuggling, carjacking, extortion, murder, rape, witness intimidation, illegal firearm sales, car theft, aggravated assaults, and drug trafficking. They also have been known to place a "tax" on prostitutes and non–gang member drug dealers who are working on MS turf. Failure to pay up usually results in violence. Valdez also reports that MS gang members are involved in exporting stolen U.S. cars to South America. The cars are often traded for contraband when dealing with drug cartels. He estimated that 80% of the cars on El Salvador streets were stolen in the United States.

Gang Members Returning From Prison

The return of gang inmates to their communities of origin is another instance of gang member relocation that presents special problems. It is widely recognized that national prison data seriously underestimate the proportion of inmates who are gang involved (because of inmates' reluctance to

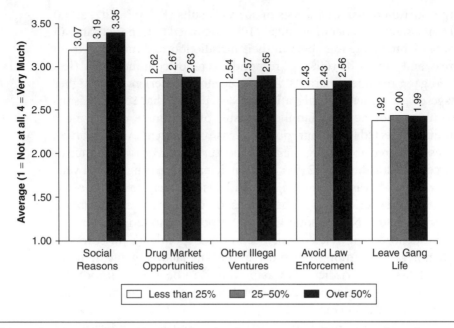

Figure 6.4   Reasons for Gang Member Migration (by percentage of gang member migrants, 2004 National Youth Gang Survey)

divulge their gang affiliations). However, in recent years the issue of gang members returning from secure confinement has received greater attention, in part because of the growing numbers of inmates who are released annually. A recent estimate is that nearly 700,000 prison inmates arrive in communities throughout the United States each year (Sabol, Minton, & Harrison, 2007).

Recent NYGS findings reveal that returning members are a noticeable problem for approximately two-thirds of the gang problem jurisdictions nationwide (Egley et al., 2006). Of the agencies reporting the return of gang members from confinement in 2001, nearly two-thirds (63%) reported that returning members "somewhat" or "very much" contributed to an increase in violent crime among local gangs; 69% reported the same for drug trafficking. Respondents said returning members had less of an impact on local gang activities such as property crimes and weapon procurement: 10% or less reported that returning members influenced each of these areas "very much." According to these respondents, the effect of returning members was typically observed in increases in violent crime and drug trafficking among local gangs.

An Illinois study supports these perceptions of law enforcement professionals. In this study of more than 2,500 adult inmates released from prison across the state in 2000, nearly one-quarter of them were identified as gang members (Olson & Dooley, 2006). More than half (55%) of the gang members were readmitted to Illinois prisons within the 2-year follow-up period, compared with 46% of the non-gang members. Gang members were more likely than nonmembers to be arrested, were rearrested more quickly after release from prison, were rearrested more frequently, and were more likely to be arrested for violent and drug offenses than were non-gang members.

Reducing Gang Problems

This final section examines priority aspects of gang problems that must be reduced, beginning with their economic impact, and the criminal and violent crimes for which they are responsible. The increase in a youth's involvement in criminality after joining a gang is then considered, followed by a review of how gangs increase the level of criminal violence in cities and thus account for more violence than nongang groups. Last, the impact of gangs on the participants themselves is considered.

Economic Impact of Gangs

An informed estimate of the economic cost of gang crimes cannot be made because gang crimes are not routinely and systematically recorded by most law enforcement agencies. Therefore, the proportion of all crimes attributable to gangs is unknown. In addition, the medical and financial consequences of gang violence per se are often overlooked. The total volume of crime is estimated to cost Americans $655 billion each year (Fight Crime: Invest in Kids, 2004), and gangs are responsible for a substantial proportion of this cost.

A study of admissions to a Los Angeles hospital trauma center found that the costs of treating 272 gang-related gunshot victims totaled nearly $5 million (emergency room, surgical procedures, intensive care, and surgical ward stay), which equated to $5,550 per patient per day (Song, Naude, Gilmore, & Mongard, 1996). More than a decade ago, the total medical cost of gang violence in Los Angeles County alone was estimated to exceed $1 billion annually (Hutson, Anglin, & Mallon, 1992). Nationwide, the complete costs of gun violence indicate a value of approximately $1 million per assault-related gunshot injury (Cook & Ludwig, 2006). A single adolescent criminal career of about 10 years can cost taxpayers between $1.7 and $2.3 million (Cohen, 1998), or $110 million per 500 boys (Walsh et al., 2008).

Criminal and Violent Gang Activity

National law enforcement data on gang-related crimes are not available because less than half (47%) of these agencies record gang crimes (Egley et al., 2006). In several of its annual surveys, the NYGC has elicited information from law enforcement agencies about their *estimates* of gang involvement in serious crimes, including aggravated assault, robbery, larceny or theft, burglary or breaking and entering, and motor vehicle theft.

Generally speaking, many gangs were involved in a variety of these crimes (Howell & Gleason, 1999). However, gangs in very large cities that emerged by the early 1980s were far more actively involved in violent crimes than late-onset gang jurisdictions, particularly aggravated assault and robbery (Howell, Egley, & Gleason, 2002). In contrast, gang members in the latest-onset jurisdictions were most likely to be involved in burglary or breaking and entering and larceny or theft.

NYGS respondents estimated the proportion of gang members who engaged in the following six serious or violent offenses in 2001: aggravated assault, robbery, burglary, motor vehicle theft, larceny or theft, and drug sales. Two clear patterns were seen (Egley et al., 2006). First, a large majority of agencies noted some gang member involvement in all six of the measured crimes. Second, the most common response was that none of these crimes was committed by a large proportion of gang members in the jurisdiction, indicating wide variability among gang members in terms of offending. Agencies that said a large proportion of gang members were involved in one or more of these offenses most often reported drug sales. A clear majority of law enforcement agencies in the NYGS report that although gang and drug problems overlap, it is typically only a subset of gang members in their jurisdiction who are actively involved in drug sales. These findings correspond with other research that finds a weak causal relationship between gang activity, the drug trade, and violence (Bjerregaard, 2008) and an extensive amount of variation in the types of crimes in which gangs are involved (Klein, 1995).

Of course, homicide is the crime of greatest concern to everyone. Reports of gang-related homicides are concentrated mostly in the largest cities in the United States, where there are long-standing and persistent gang problems and a greater number of documented gang members, most of whom are identified by law enforcement as young adults (Howell, 1999; Maxson, Curry, & Howell, 2002). In the 2002 and 2003 National Youth Gang Surveys, nearly 4 out of 10 very large cities (populations of 250,000 or more) reported 10 or more gang homicides (Egley, 2005). However, 2 out of 10 respondents could not determine whether they had any gang homicides.

Youth gangs are responsible for a disproportionate number of homicides. In two cities, Los Angeles and Chicago—arguably the most gang-populated cities in the United States—more than half of the combined nearly 1,000 homicides reported in the NYGS in 2004 were attributed to gangs (Egley & Ritz, 2006). Of the remaining 171 cities, approximately one-fourth of all the homicides were considered gang related. More than 80% of gang problem agencies in both smaller cities and rural counties recorded no gang homicides.

Jurisdictions experiencing higher levels of gang violence—evidenced by reports of multiple gang-related homicides over survey years—were significantly more likely than those experiencing no gang homicides to report that firearms were "used often" by gang members in assault crimes (47% vs. 4% of the jurisdictions, respectively) (Egley et al., 2006). Areas with longer-standing gang problems and a larger number of identified gang members—most often those with more adult-aged gang members—were also more likely to report greater firearm use by gang members in assault crimes.

Although the proportion of all crimes committed by gang members is unknown, analyses of reported violent crimes in several cities reveal that their members often represent a large proportion of the high-rate violent offenders (Braga, Kennedy, & Tita, 2002). Lethal violence related to gangs tends to be concentrated in the largest cities that are mired with larger and ongoing gang problems. Frequent firearm use in assault crimes is typically reported in these larger cities.

Gangs Increase a Youth's Involvement in Criminality

Surprisingly, a couple of criminologists have suggested that gangs do not increase a youth's involvement in criminality (Katz & Jackson-Jacobs, 2004). Their contention has been refuted by very rigorous scientific studies of prospective longitudinal panels of child and adolescent subjects in four large U.S. cities (Pittsburgh, Pennsylvania; Rochester, New York; Denver, Colorado; and Seattle, Washington) and also in two cities in other countries (Montreal, Canada; and Bergen, Norway). The research teams in Pittsburgh, Rochester, Denver, and Seattle recorded delinquent acts reported to them by study youths from as early as the first grade into adulthood. These long-term data permitted them to analyze delinquency rates before, during, and after gang involvement. The researchers found that although future gang members tend to be aggressive and involved in fights and other violent acts at a very young age (Craig et al., 2002; Lahey et al., 1999), they do commit many more serious and violent acts while they are gang members than before joining and after leaving the gang (Bendixen, Endresen, & Olweus, 2006; Esbensen & Huizinga, 1993; Gatti, Tremblay, Vitaro, & McDuff, 2005; Gordon et al., 2004; Thornberry, Krohn, et al., 2003). Figures 6.5 and 6.6 show this pattern in the Norway study (Bendixen et al., 2006), in which surveyed students were ages 13–14 at Time 1, ages 14–15 at Time 2, and 15–16 at Time 3. Moreover, the violence facilitation function of gangs persists even beyond the influence of risk factors for gang membership (Battin, Hill, Abbott, Catalano, & Hawkins, 1998; Thornberry, Krohn, et al., 2003) and neighborhood conditions (Hall, Thornberry, & Lizotte, 2006). This finding, that gang involvement increases youths' criminality, has been noted as "one of the most robust and consistent observations in criminological research" (Thornberry, 1998, p. 147). Since Thornberry made this astute observation, this important finding has been further replicated in the United States and also in Canada (Gatti et al., 2005) and Norway (Bendixen et al., 2006).

Gangs Increase the Level of Criminal Violence in Cities

The second notion promulgated by the same criminologists (Katz & Jackson-Jacobs, 2004) is that gangs do not increase the level of criminal

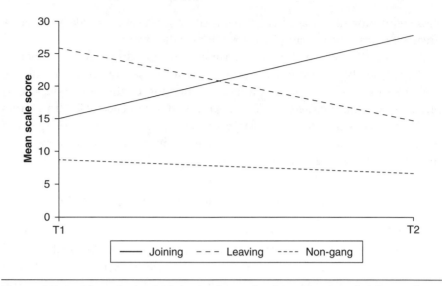

Figure 6.5   Mean Antisocial Behavior Scores for Gang Members (Joining and Leaving) and Non–Gang Members, Time 1 and Time 2

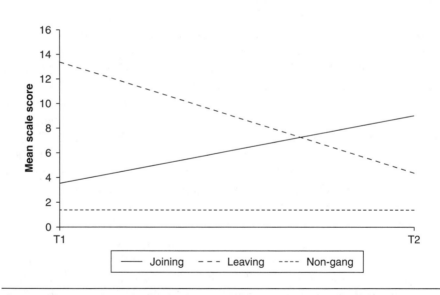

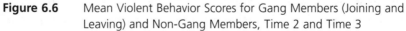

Figure 6.6   Mean Violent Behavior Scores for Gang Members (Joining and Leaving) and Non-Gang Members, Time 2 and Time 3

violence in cities. This unusual view was debunked when researchers in the aforementioned longitudinal studies compared violent crime rates of gang and nongang youths in these urban samples. If the rates of the gang youths were higher, then it would be difficult to deny that gangs increase the level of criminal violence in society. As it turns out, gang members' violence rates were up to seven times higher than the violent crime rates of adolescents who were not in gangs in longitudinal data sets in five cities: Denver, Montreal, Pittsburgh, Seattle, and Rochester, New York (Esbensen & Huizinga, 1993; Gatti et al., 2005; Gordon et al., 2004; Hill et al., 2001; Thornberry, Krohn, et al., 2003).

The following data on youths in three of these cities show that gang members were responsible for a large proportion of all self-reported violent offenses committed by the entire sample during the adolescent years. Rochester gang members (30% of the sample) self-reported committing 68% of all adolescent violent offenses; in Seattle, gang members (15% of the sample) self-reported committing 85% of adolescent robberies; and in Denver, gang members (14% of the sample) self-reported committing 79% of all serious violent adolescent offenses (Thornberry, 1998). In the Rochester adolescent sample, two-thirds (66%) of the chronic violent offenders were gang members (Thornberry et al., 1995). Given these significantly higher violent crime rates among gang members compared with nongang youths, it is difficult to imagine how the level of violent crime in these cities would not be higher from the presence of highly delinquent gangs.

Gangs Account for More of the Violence

Katz and Jackson-Jacobs (2004) also suggest that other delinquent groups could well account for more violence than the gang youths. Researchers examined this a decade ago. In four of the longitudinal studies, in Seattle, Rochester, Denver, and Montreal, the influence of gang membership on levels of violence was found to be greater than the influence of other highly delinquent peers (Battin et al., 1998; Gatti et al., 2005; Huizinga et al., 2003; Thornberry, Krohn, et al., 2003). During periods of active gang membership, the Rochester gang members were responsible for, on average, four times as many offenses as their share of the total study population would suggest (Thornberry, Krohn, et al., 2003). Two empirical studies have found that police-identified gang members are significantly more delinquent, including higher levels of involvement in serious and violent offenses, than a comparison group of nongang youth with prior arrests (Curry, 2000; Katz, Webb, & Schaefer, 2000). Given the consistency of the findings on this point in prospective longitudinal studies in multiple sites, this too must be accepted as a notably robust finding in criminological research.

Impact of Gangs on Participants

Most youths who join gangs have already been involved in delinquency and drug use. Once in the gang, they are quite likely to become more actively involved in delinquency, drug use, and violence, and they are more likely to be victimized themselves (Peterson et al., 2004; Taylor, 2008). Their problems do not end here. They are at greater risk of arrest, juvenile court referral, detention, confinement in a juvenile correctional facility, and, later, imprisonment. For the gang to have devastating consequences, it doesn't necessarily have to be a large formal gang. Even low levels of gang organization have important consequences for involvement in crime and victimization (Decker et al., 2008; Esbensen, Winfree, et al., 2001; Taylor 2008).

Gang involvement has a way of limiting youngsters' life chances, particularly if they remain active in the gang for several years (Thornberry, Krohn, et al., 2003). Over and above embedding its members in criminal activity, the gang acts as a powerful social network in constraining the behavior of members, limiting access to prosocial networks, and cutting members off from conventional pursuits (Thornberry, Krohn, et al., 2003). These effects of the gang tend to produce precocious, off-time, and unsuccessful transitions that bring disorder to the life course in a cascading series of difficulties, including school dropout, early pregnancy or early impregnation, teen motherhood, and unstable employment.

This section has considered the impacts of gangs on communities and the levels of violence and other crimes in cities where they are most prevalent and dangerous. We also have examined the various criminal and life-course impacts of gangs on their members. The many excellent gang studies lead "to one inescapable conclusion: if we are to be successful in our efforts to reduce delinquency and youth violence, we have to intervene successfully in the criminal careers of gang members" (Thornberry, Krohn, et al., 2003, p. 193). This means that programs and strategies must address the risk factors and treatment needs of gang members and also prevent and control gang activity in the contexts where their criminality is most prevalent. Promising and effective programs and strategies are reviewed in the next chapter.

Discussion Topics

1. How many of the gang definitions in Box 6.1 would qualify the XYZs as a gang?

2. Pick five gang articles from the archives of a local newspaper (or that of a larger city nearby) and see how many gang myths can be found in each article (consult the gang myths article, Howell, 2007).

3. From the articles you reviewed, pick the gang that appears to be the most dangerous. Determine how many of the criteria for classifying groups as youth gangs (presented in the opening paragraph of this chapter) that gang would meet.

4. Why are gangs so difficult for communities to control?

5. Why do gangs have more devastating impacts on the life-course of adolescents than other delinquent groups?

CHAPTER 7

Effective Programs for Preventing and Reducing Youth Gang Problems

C hapter 6 contrasted cities, towns, and rural areas with transitory gang problems with larger cities and suburban areas in which gang problems are far more persistent and entrenched. These two extremes in severity of gang problems suggest two important implications for successful responses. First, each community's gang programs and strategies must be based on an objective assessment of its specific gang problem. As we saw in Chapter 6, gangs are confusing to many observers (see Box 6.5). Moreover, community representatives often see gangs differently when thinking about combating them. Police tend to describe them as a hierarchichal organization with formal leaders and well-defined roles, much like a military organization (Figure 7.1). In contrast, gangs typically consist of clusters of subgroups, often called sets or cliques, with some associates on the periphery who may never join (Figure 7.2). Second, if a community's gang problem is at the lower level of severity, mainly prevention and intervention programs and strategies would be most appropriate. On the other hand, if its gang problem is at the upper level of severity, prevention, intervention, and suppression programs and strategies will be needed. Research suggests that a continuum of programs and strategies is most likely to be effective (Decker & Curry, 2002, 2003; Spergel, Wa, & Sosa, 2006; Tita, Riley, & Greenwood, 2003).

Another key principle helps guide the choice of programs for inclusion in each community's continuum. All programs need not specifically target gang members to be effective with them. Gang members and other delinquents

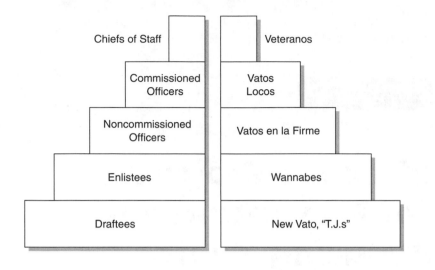

Figure 7.1 A Comparison of Hispanic Gangs and Military Structure

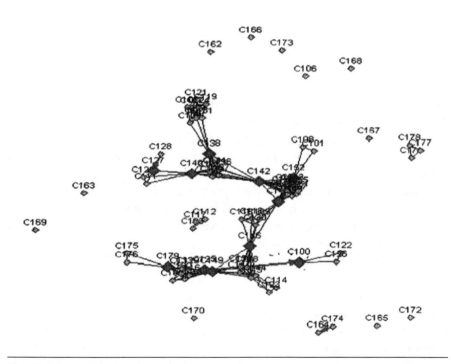

Figure 7.2 Crip Sets in Newark, New Jersey

share the same risk factors; the major distinction is that gang members tend to have more of them (Howell & Egley, 2005b). Youth who have no gang affiliation and gang members who are not criminally committed to a gang lifestyle or strongly bonded to a gang can benefit from the same prevention and intervention programming (Schram & Gaines, 2005). Even for gang-involved youth, programs that reduce delinquency and other risky behaviors such as alcohol and drug use should also help reduce victimization and gang involvement (Taylor, 2008; see also Chapter 4).

But intervening with gangs successfully at the upper level of severity is a formidable challenge, for three main reasons: gang members' criminal embeddedness, gangs' community roots, and the availability of firearms. Youth street gangs encourage and reinforce the criminal tendencies of their members in many ways, effectively embedding them in a criminal lifestyle (Lien, 2005; Thornberry, Krohn, et al., 2003). Thus it is not surprising that these gangs are the most criminally active groups to which a substantial proportion of adolescents and young adults in the United States belong. They also commit more homicides than any other identifiable youth groups.

Furthermore, youth street gangs are rooted in weakened social structures (Moore, 1998; Vigil, 2002), that is, in the cracks of our social institutions. Joan W. Moore (1998), a prominent gang researcher, asserts that for a youth group to become established as a youth gang, certain conditions must exist. First, conventional socializing agents, such as families and schools, and social services must be ineffective and alienating (which often is the case where gangs exist). Under these conditions, conventional adult supervision is largely missing, inconsistent, and irrelevant. Second, the adolescents must have a great deal of free time that is not consumed by other roles; they just hang out. Third, for the gang to become at least partly institutionalized—if not fully institutionalized across generations—members must have limited access to appealing conventional career lines (i.e., good adult jobs). Finally, the young people must have a place to congregate, usually a well-defined neighborhood, at a mall, in a park, or at school. These conditions must be changed to prevent and reduce gang problems.

The Firearm Factor

One key factor dramatically changed gangs beginning in the 1970s: increased availability of more lethal guns (Block & Block, 1993; Cook & Ludwig, 2006; Decker, 2007; Miller, 1992). Modern-day street gangs recruit youths who possess firearms, and these are generally readily available to members (Box 7.1). A permit is not required to buy a handgun and guns need not be registered in 38 of our states, and legislatures in 26 states bar cities from passing gun laws tougher than statewide statutes (Moore, 2005). The Brady Handgun Violence Prevention Act (Public Law 103-159) requires instant criminal history background checks on people who apply to buy any type of firearm from federally licensed dealers (U.S. General Accounting Office, 2002). If the background check is not completed within 3 days, the transfer (sale) is permitted by default. The act prohibits the transfer of a firearm to felons and certain other people, including fugitives, people convicted of a misdemeanor crime of domestic violence, and juveniles. Approximately 8.5 million background checks are made each year (U.S. General Accounting Office, 2005). However, in the secondary market of firearms not sold by federal firearm licensees, private citizens may sell their firearms without a license, and local firearm shows are a common source in the secondary market. Private citizens are not supposed to knowingly sell firearms to people in excluded categories, and several states require background checks for private sales; however, private sales are not federally regulated. Theft is another major source of unauthorized firearm access. Firearm theft is so pervasive that even the places deemed most secure—police departments—are sometimes susceptible (Leahy, 2007). Not surprisingly, greater gun availability is associated with higher homicide rates (Cook & Ludwig, 2006; Grossman et al., 2005). Gang violence, particularly gun homicide, is the most intractable component of the urban gang problem in the United States.

IN FOCUS 7.1
Availability of Firearms

- Approximately 4.5 million new (i.e., not previously owned) firearms are sold each year in the United States, including 2 million handguns.
- Estimates of annual secondhand firearm transactions range from 2 to 4.5 million.
- It is estimated that approximately one-half million firearms are stolen annually.
- The estimated total number of firearm transactions ranges from 7 to 9.5 million per year, of which between 47% and 64% are new firearms.
- An average of 81 firearm-related deaths occur per day in the United States, and rates of firearm-related homicide, suicide, and unintentional death in the United States exceed those of 25 other high-income nations (Hahn et al., 2005, p. 40).
- Firearm-related homicides cost approximately $100 billion per year.
- From 1973 through 1994, the number of guns in private ownership in the United States rose by 87 million (Malcom, 2002), to an estimated 200 million (Reich et al., 2002).
- The growing number of privately owned guns continued unabated in the next decade, and the latest estimate is 258 million privately owned firearms, of which 93 million are handguns (Wellford et al., 2005).

Gun availability fuels gang violence (Block & Block, 1993). Consider that, despite the sharp drop in lethal violence among young people in the United States over the past decade, the number of gang homicides reported by law enforcement respondents to the National Youth Gang Survey increased 34% from 1999 to 2003 in cities with populations of 100,000 or more (Curry et al., 2004). Gang-related gun violence can be understood in terms of self and identity that are heavily rooted in self-concepts of masculinity and reinforced by other gang members (Stretesky & Pogrebin, 2007). Prolonged intergang wars are not uncommon in some of the very largest U.S. cities, where most gang homicides occur (Egley et al., 2006; Howell, 1999).

Gang violence also has its roots in characteristics of communities, including concentrated economic and social disadvantage (Decker, 2007). But Decker contends that social processes play a very important role. Violence is considered normal behavior in gangs (Decker, 1996). "Much gang violence appears to have a contagious character, spreading from one neighborhood to another and outliving the initial source" of the beef that precipitated the specific violent episode (Decker, 2007, p. 398). Therefore, gang programming in large cities, where gang problems are more entrenched and gangs are quick to defend their turf or reputation with violence, requires outreach and workers who are skilled in intervening in potentially violent situations. Effective and promising gang programs are reviewed in this chapter. First, however, consideration must be given to mobilizing your community to address a presumed gang problem.

Community Mobilization

A key to successfully dealing with youth gangs is to first mobilize the community. The reality is that communities respond to problems that their key leaders or stakeholders perceive to be important. The range of problems is broad, including natural disasters, public health problems, external threats, drugs, delinquency, and gangs. A literature review that my colleague and I conducted (Howell & Curry, 2005) suggests several essential elements of successful community mobilization. These are organized in chronological order in Box 7.2, as suggested in the reviewed literature, but it is important to recognize that the sequence of steps may vary in different communities. For example, if a community already is well organized to deal with a variety of youth problems—often by an existing coalition of some sort—it would be advisable to take advantage of this existing infrastructure to address a gang problem. This situation would preclude the need to take several of the preliminary steps outlined in what follows. The sequence of steps suggested here assumes that the community has a low degree of organization to address such social problems.

IN FOCUS 7.2
Essential Elements of Successful Community Mobilization

1. The current or potential gang problem must be recognized as a major threat to community safety and security.

2. Identify key neighborhood leaders in the community.

(Continued)

(Continued)

3. Contact key neighborhood leaders, local agencies, and community groups to discuss their concerns and to inquire about their interest in a collective effort.

4. Cultivate a natural leader, a community organizer, within the community. He or she must express deep feelings and impress on others that a problem exists and that something must be done about it.

5. The community leader or organizer should urge the broadcast media to become involved in all aspects of the mobilization process as early as possible.

6. Convene a meeting of community representatives and discuss emerging concerns. Think of these as community network meetings to formulate a cohesive plan.

7. Hold numerous individual meetings with many stakeholders to seek their support and refine priority problems.

8. Convene a second community-wide meeting. Think of this as a neighborhood involvement activity to heighten awareness of how community entities can interact to bring about a gang-free environment.

9. The community or agency leaders, with the aid of the community organizer, should then begin to involve and solicit the support of a variety of local agencies or community groups, former gang influentials, and even selected gang youth to alert the community to the gang problem.

10. Create or designate a formal community organization to act on behalf of the community group.

11. Conduct an objective assessment of the potential gang problem.

12. Set specific goals and objectives together with a timeline for their accomplishment. Seek to achieve small wins at the outset.

The term *collective efficacy* is used to describe a useful way of thinking about community mobilization and social control (Sampson, 2002; Sampson, Raudenbush, & Earls, 1997). Collective efficacy does not mean crime control generated from the top down, as in policing. Instead it refers to informal social control from the bottom up through citizen and community organizational involvement. Therefore, as will be seen shortly, the Comprehensive Gang Model emphasizes community mobilization (organization) as a key strategy. There is empirical support for this. In a Chicago study, Sampson and colleagues (1997) discovered that relationships between poverty and residential instability and violent crime were diminished by the presence of higher levels of collective efficacy. This research suggests that community organization can help improve community conditions that give rise to and support gang activity (Howell & Curry, 2005).

A community should not even think about programs and strategies for responding to gangs before it has assessed its own gang problem. The National Youth Gang Center (NYGC) has developed an assessment protocol (National Youth Gang Center, 2002a) that any community can use to assess its gang problem, which guides development of a comprehensive, community-wide plan of gang prevention, intervention, and suppression (National Youth Gang Center, 2002b). *Prevention* programs are needed to target youths at risk of gang involvement, to reduce the number of youths who join gangs; *intervention* programs and strategies are needed to provide sanctions and services for younger youths who are actively involved in gangs to separate them from gangs; and law enforcement *suppression* strategies are needed to target the most violent gangs and older, most criminally active gang members. Because nearly all youth gangs are homegrown in the torn fabric of our communities, cutting off the head of the monster (so to speak) with suppression alone is not likely to have a lasting impact without programming that simultaneously reduces the number of youths who join gangs, removes younger members from gangs, and strengthens our core social institutions.

Selected programs and strategies must be tailored specifically to the local gang problem, and it is critically important for each community to take ownership of its gang assessment and the programs and strategies it adopts. It may be necessary to conduct a broader assessment of youth violence instead of a gang assessment, for two reasons. First, uncertainty may exist as to whether the community actually has a gang problem. Second, it is common for some stakeholders to deny the existence of a gang problem. In either event the assessment should be guided by a flexible gang definition. Stakeholders must agree on the specific definition that will be used to guide the assessment. A useful definition for discussion is shown in Box 7.3. I will return to the next steps in developing a continuum of gang prevention, intervention, and suppression programs after my review of evaluated gang-related programs.

IN FOCUS 7.3

A Good Gang Definition for Community Assessment Purposes

The following definition of a youth gang is recommended. It is a slightly simplified version of the youth gang definition provided in Chapter 6.

- The group has three or more members.
- Members have symbols and a name.

(Continued)

(Continued)

- Members view themselves as a gang, and they are recognized by others as a gang.
- The group has some permanence and a degree of organization.
- The group is involved in a high level of delinquent or criminal activity.

This definition is offered as a preliminary one, subject to review and discussion by community stakeholders. Reaching consensus on a practical gang definition that will be used uniformly is extremely important. In addition, definitions of a gang member (including identification criteria) and a gang incident must be developed and agreed upon.

A Measured Response to Gangs

All too often, a community's first response to gangs is law enforcement suppression. Street sweeps using huge police forces are not uncommon (Klein, 1995, 2004). In the modern version of gang sweeps, the use of task forces of law enforcement representatives in targeted arrests of gang members originated in Boston (Kennedy, 1999). But "communities will not support any indiscriminate, highly aggressive crackdowns that put nonviolent youth at risk of being swept into the criminal justice system" (Braga, 2004, p. 19). In the original Boston version, high-rate violent gang members (mainly adults) were rounded up via "notifications" that law enforcement knew they were gang members and personally assured them of very long sentences if they committed another crime, no matter how minor. With time, these "round-ups" or "call-ins" have become more widespread and come to target less bona fide gang-involved youth and career criminals. North Carolina is a case in point, where suspected juvenile gang members—most of whom have not been convicted of committing a crime—have been the subject of the "call-ins" in a couple of cities. Of course, constitutional (due process) issues come into play when a nebulous status such as *gang member* is used as evidence for enhanced criminal sentences (S. Moore, 2007; Wright, 2006). Constitutional due process issues apply especially to juveniles, given that more than half of young gang members will be out of the gang within a year (Gatti et al., 2005; Hill et al., 2001; Peterson et al., 2004; Thornberry, Krohn, et al., 2003). Specifically, Wright (2006) argues that placing a person in gang or criminal intelligence databases increases the likelihood of a criminal conviction and a longer sentence, and this may violate the due process requirements of the fifth and fourteenth amendments. He suggests that a properly managed database might attend to due process requirements but that a predocumentation or postdocumentation hearing is the best remedy.

As a first step, every community that suspects it has a gang problem should make an objective, community-wide assessment to determine whether a gang problem exists and the dimensions of the problem if gangs are present. Without the benefit of an empirical assessment, community stakeholders run a high risk of being seriously mistaken about the nature of their gang problem (McCorkle & Miethe, 2002). Every effort must be made in this assessment to discard preconceived notions because many of them are based on gang myths. Community resources often are committed to suppression approaches that could be used advantageously for more appropriate intervention and prevention efforts that better match the nature of the gang problem that actually exists.

A Review of Evaluated Gang Programs

The history of gang intervention is littered with programs that failed outright or were of questionable effectiveness, from the first evaluation in the 1930s (Thrasher, 1936) through the 1970s (Howell, 2000). The scope of this review, however is limited to studies conducted in the past decade (or were begun earlier and remain operational) that have shown promise or demonstrated effectiveness. (See Howell, 1998b or 2000, for a list of gang program evaluations during the period 1936–1999.)

Several of the programs referenced here did not have gang reduction as a program goal, but they reduced gang involvement or gang crime as a result of addressing general delinquency involvement or targeting chronic, serious, or violent delinquents, many of whom are gang members in many communities. These programs are included here because programs need not produce dramatic results to have practical utility in dealing with gang problems. In fact, few such programs do show large effects, for reasons discussed earlier in this chapter.

Each of the programs that follow has been scored and classified using scientific criteria that are used to rate programs for inclusion in a national database of programs that address child and adolescent problem behaviors. This database is connected to the *Helping America's Youth (HAY) Community Guide* (Box 7.4), which nine federal agencies worked together to develop in 2005.

IN FOCUS 7.4

Instructions for Using the *Helping America's Youth Community Guide*

Using this guide, almost any community can assess risk factors for delinquency and gang involvement and strengthen its continuum of services. Steps to follow:

1. Go to http://helpingamericasyouth.gov/.

2. Click on the link "The Community Guide to Helping America's Youth."

(Continued)

(Continued)

3. Click on the link "Assess Your Community and Connect Its Resources."

4. The section "Conduct a Community Assessment" will show you how to take a step-by-step approach to learning more about your community that will help you choose the right strategy for action.

5. Using the online mapping tool will provide useful census data about your community, help you see where the people you would most like to serve live in your community, and show you what federal resources are already available. For information about additional funding opportunities available through the 9 collaborating federal agencies in Helping America's Youth, visit http://www.grants.gov.

6. The Community Resource Inventory provides a database tool to help you with your community assessment and strategic planning. You can identify and include partners, community programs, and assets that are already available in your community.

7. Go back to "Assess Your Community and Connect Its Resources."

8. Click on the link "Conduct a Community Assessment."

9. Scroll down to "Now, let's get started" and follow these steps:
   • "Step 1: Establish the What, Where, and Who"
   • "Step 2: Learn More About the What, Where, and Who"

The online mapping tool will provide census data about your community, help you see where the people you would most like to serve live in your community, and show you what federal resources are already available. Unfortunately, the online mapping tool can't give you all the information you will need about your community. Some of that must come from your own research. Form a small working group to take on this job. Remember that others in your community may already have done some data collection. Look around and see what results of surveys, focus groups, community forums, or other data are already available to you. How has the information been summarized and made available to the public? What does the information tell you about local problems, issues, and resources? Looking at this material may also help you assess how ready your community is to take the next step.

   • "Step 3: Identify Resources in Your Community"
   • "Step 4: Analyze and Learn From the Data You've Collected"

The priority activity at this point is preparation for "Step 5: Develop a Plan of Action." Analyzing and learning from the data you've collected will position you to set priorities, particularly with regard to target groups and risk and protective factors.

- "Step 5: Develop a Plan of Action"

You are now ready to develop your strategic plan, a continuum of prevention and intervention programs. You are ready to use the Program Tool. You can use the data you've collected on indicators or the risk and protective factors that concern you the most to help you select an appropriate program. It is very important to go back to your Community Resource Inventory to answer questions about how a newly selected program will fit with what is currently in place in your county.

- "Step 6: Share What You've Learned"

This is a suggested outline for your community assessment report:

I. **Introduction:** State why you performed an assessment. Tell what you set out to do and how you went about doing it. Summarize the information that you have to share.

II. **Key findings:** Present the major findings from your assessment and the central problems that emerged.

III. **Additional factors:** Present the associated risks that were identified. Speak about the community perceptions that must be considered in addressing these problems.

IV. **Strengths and Resources:** Map out the resources that are available in the community to address these issues.

V. **Action Plan:** Lay out your plan of action. The plan should include, as specifically and comprehensively as possible, the strategies you will implement to address the needs you uncovered.

VI. **Measures of Success:** Propose the ways you will determine the success of the implementation of your plan.

VII. **Challenges:** Identify the challenges to be addressed in order for this effort to be a success.

VIII. **Conclusions:** Present your conclusions and invite your audience to get involved.

The program rating criteria were agreed on by the participating agencies, and programs in the database fall into one of the following classifications:

Level 1 programs have been scientifically demonstrated to prevent delinquency, reduce risk factors, or enhance protective factors for delinquency and other child and youthful problems using a research design of the highest quality (i.e., an experimental design and random assignment of subjects). In other program rating schemes, programs in this category are designated "exemplary" or "model programs."

Level 2 programs have been scientifically demonstrated to prevent delinquency, reduce risk factors, or enhance protective factors for delinquency and other child and youthful problems using an experimental or quasi-experimental research design, with a comparison group, and the evidence suggests program effectiveness, but the evidence is not as strong as for the Level 1 programs.

Level 3 programs display a strong theoretical base and have been demonstrated to prevent delinquency and other child and youthful problems or to reduce risk factors or enhance protective factors using limited research methods (with at least single-group pretreatment and posttreatment measurements). The programs in this category appear promising but must be confirmed using more rigorous scientific techniques. The main reason is that a control group is not required in the research design.

Using this classification scheme, Level 1 programs are considered effective, Level 2 programs are also considered effective although the evidence is less convincing, and Level 3 programs are considered promising. The effectiveness level of programs that follow is shown in parentheses as L-1, L-2, or L-3.

This program rating procedure has two important limitations, however. These traditional types of program rating criteria create an odd situation when police suppression initiatives are rated. The reviewer is required to think about punishment as if it were a treatment ingredient. This unusual circumstance is further complicated by the absence of information on punishment dosages for individuals in most suppression studies, which typically examine only successful prosecutions or criminal convictions.

Second, traditional program rating criteria such as these rate mainly the scientific strength of the evaluation of program services and do not take into account an important prerequisite of gang intervention, the role of program structures that may not include therapeutic services. The latter contexts or settings are extremely worthwhile for stabilizing gang offenders' behavior sufficiently to give treatment a chance to work. Graduated sanctions are a prime example. Sanctions themselves do not address the treatment needs of offenders. Therefore, sanctions should be viewed as providing only the setting for service delivery; it is the intervention within the setting that has the actual power to produce change in offenders (Bonta, 1996). Intensive probation supervision using police and probation officer teams is one example. Creating a "neutral zone" through the use of "no gang" contracts (Roush, Miesner, & Winslow, 2002) in secure juvenile corrections settings is another case. Detention or confinement may be appropriate. Gang activity must be restricted to ensure public safety and to give therapeutic interventions a reasonable opportunity to work. Whenever feasible, program services should be provided in program structures for maximum impact.

Traditional program rating criteria that score only individual programs also ignore the value of strengthening the overall continuum of program services and program structures. There is no quantified method for scoring the strength of a community's continuum of prevention, intervention, and suppression programs and strategies. This must be determined by experimental evaluation.

Engaging community stakeholders and institutions in risk- and protection-focused prevention that addresses undesirable community conditions is an excellent starting point (Wyrick, 2006; Wyrick & Howell, 2004). A continuum of sanctions and services is needed that parallels offender careers, beginning with prevention and early intervention in predelinquent and delinquent careers and then juvenile justice system intervention using graduated sanctions, linked with a continuum of rehabilitation interventions (Figure 7.3). This continuum can be organized to prevent further development of offender careers toward serious, violent, chronic offending and gang involvement. As seen in the theory presented in Chapter 4, delinquent behavior is a precursor to gang involvement. Moreover, delinquency typically is preceded by conduct problems and school failure. Therefore, a strong community continuum of delinquency prevention and early intervention programs can reduce gang membership (Howell, 2003b, pp. 87–102).

Active juvenile delinquents are also a key target group. Advanced management decision-making tools are available to assist juvenile justice system professionals in developing a continuum of graduated sanctions that can be linked with a continuum of treatment options, both components of which can be matched with precision to offenders' recidivism risk level and treatment needs (Chapter 10). However, effective program services must be used if the graduated sanctions system and linked interventions can be expected to produce worthwhile positive outcomes. Table 7.1 shows 19 promising or effective gang-related programs. Only one program, the Montreal Preventive Treatment Program (L-1), has been rated as very effective or as an "exemplary" or "model program," and seven can be considered effective (L-2). Nine programs have been rated only promising. The inclusion of two unrated programs is explained later.

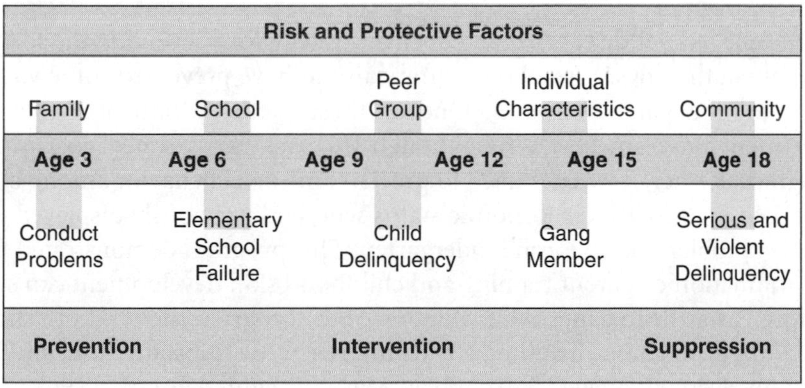

Risk and Protective Factors				
Family	School	Peer Group	Individual Characteristics	Community
Age 3	**Age 6**	**Age 9** **Age 12**	**Age 15**	**Age 18**
Conduct Problems	Elementary School Failure	Child Delinquency	Gang Member	Serious and Violent Delinquency
Prevention		**Intervention**		**Suppression**

Figure 7.3   A Continuum of Gang Prevention, Intervention, and Suppression Components

Table 7.1   Effective and Promising Gang-Related Programs

Type of Program	Program
Prevention Programs	• Montreal Preventive Treatment Program (L-1)* • Gang Resistance Education and Training (L-2)** • Gang Resistance Is Paramount (L-3)* • Boys and Girls Club Gang Prevention Through Targeted Outreach (L-3)* • Movimiento Ascendencia ("Upward Movement") (L-3)*
Intervention Programs	• Little Village Gang Violence Reduction Program** • Building Resources for the Intervention and Deterrence of Gang Engagement** • Aggression Replacement Training (L-2)* • Operation New Hope (formerly Lifeskills '95) (L-2)* • Multidisciplinary Team Home Run Program (L-3)* • Philadelphia Youth Violence Reduction Partnership (L-3)* • Boys and Girls Club Gang Intervention Through Targeted Outreach (L-3)** • Broader Urban Involvement and Leadership Development Detention Program (L-3)*
Suppression Programs	• Hardcore Gang Investigations Unit (L-2)* • Tri-Agency Resource Gang Enforcement Team (L-2)* • Chicago Alternative Policing Strategy (L-2)* • Operation Ceasefire (L-3)* • Dallas Anti-Gang Initiative (L-3)**
Comprehensive Programs	• Comprehensive Gang Model (L-2)*

NOTE: L-1 = model or exemplary program; L-2 = effective program; L-3 = promising program.

*For program information, see http://guide.helpingamericasyouth.gov.
**For program information, see http://www.iir.com/nygc/tool.

Gang Prevention

No one has yet discovered an effective strategy for preventing the formation of youth gangs. Several programs claim to have prevented some youths from joining gangs, however. One of these is the Montreal Preventive Treatment Program (L-1), even though this was not a stated goal of the program. Rather, it was designed to prevent antisocial behavior among boys, ages 7 to 9, of low socioeconomic status who had previously displayed disruptive problem behavior in kindergarten. This program demonstrated that a combination of parent training and childhood skill development can steer children away from gangs. An evaluation of the program showed both short- and long-term gains, including less delinquency, less substance use, and less gang involvement at age 15 (Tremblay, Masse, Pagani, & Vitaro, 1996).

A specifically designed gang prevention program, Gang Resistance Education and Training (GREAT) (L-2), showed a small but systematic beneficial program effect (Esbensen, Osgood, Taylor, Peterson, & Freng, 2001,

p. 102) on participants in terms of reduced victimization, more negative views about gangs, improved attitudes toward police, more prosocial peers, and less risk seeking but not on gang involvement, drug use, or delinquency. A second GREAT program evaluation is under way, conducted by Esbensen and colleagues at the University of Missouri at St. Louis. This second study gauges the effectiveness of a revised and expanded GREAT curriculum.

Other promising gang prevention programs include the Boys and Girls Club Gang Prevention Through Targeted Outreach (L-3) (Arbreton & McClanahan, 2002), Gang Resistance Is Paramount (L-3) (Solis, Schwartz, & Hinton, 2003), and a program for girls, Movimiento Ascendencia ("Upward Movement") (L-3) (Williams, Curry, & Cohen, 2002). Gang Resistance Is Paramount (GRIP) is unique for its practical approach. In addition to a school-based antigang curriculum, GRIP provides recreational activities, gang awareness education for parents, and counseling of parents and youths regarding the youths' gang activities.

Gang Intervention

Among prevention, intervention, and suppression experiments, intervention initiatives have produced the most consistently positive results, particularly those that incorporated an interagency intervention team. Each of these has a common denominator: providing serious offenders under court supervision an intensively delivered combination of sanctions and services.

Two successful gang programs have not been rated for inclusion in the *Helping America's Youth Community Guide* because the Office of Juvenile Justice and Delinquency Prevention (OJJDP) chose to rate only the Comprehensive Gang Model as a whole and not the individual sites that have implemented it. The first of these, the Little Village Gang Violence Reduction Program, targeted mainly older members (ages 17 to 24) of two of the area's most violent Hispanic gangs, the Latin Kings and the Two Six (Spergel, 2007). Specifically, the Little Village program targeted more than 200 of the "shooters," also called influential persons, or leaders of the two gangs. The intervention team (mainly outreach youth workers, police, and probation officers) convened biweekly and used a case management approach in working with active gang members, supported by the outreach youth workers. Suppression contacts, made mainly by Chicago police, reduced the youths' interest in and attachment to the gang. Services such as job placement reduced gang youths' time spent with other gang members. Self-reports of criminal involvement showed that the program reduced serious violent and property crimes, and sharp declines were also seen in the frequencies of various types of offenses (Spergel, 2007). The program was more effective with older, high-rate violent gang offenders than with younger, less violent offenders. Active gang involvement was also reduced among project youths, but mostly for older members, and this change was associated with less criminal activity. Had this program been rated on HAY criteria, it probably would have scored at Level 2.

The Building Resources for the Intervention and Deterrence of Gang Engagement (BRIDGE) program in Riverside, California, is another successful gang program that used an intervention team. It targeted gang-involved youth between the ages of 12 and 22 in two communities. Formation of an intervention team was a key to the success of the program (Spergel et al., 2006). It consisted of several core members, including the project coordinator, police, probation and parole officers, the outreach worker, the social service provider, and others. In daily meetings, the intervention team shared information that provided opportunities for intervention with project youth. Case management involved development of a treatment plan by the intervention team. Had this program been rated on HAY criteria, it probably would have scored at Level 3.

Aggression Replacement Training (ART) (L-2) is another effective intervention program. It is a 10-week, 30-hour cognitive–behavioral program administered to groups of 8 to 12 juvenile offenders three times per week. During these 10 weeks, participating youths typically attend three 1-hour sessions per week, one session each of skill streaming, anger control training, and training in moral reasoning. ART has produced impressive results working with gangs in Brooklyn, New York, communities (Goldstein, Glick, & Gibbs, 1998). An evaluation of ART implementation in Washington State (with general delinquents) found that when it was competently delivered, ART reduced 18-month felony recidivism rates by 24% (Barnoski, 2004b).

One correctional aftercare program has produced positive short-term effects for gang members: the Operation New Hope program (formerly called Lifeskills '95) (L-2), which was implemented in California's San Bernardino and Riverside Counties (Josi & Sechrest, 1999). This program was designed for high-risk, chronic juvenile offenders released from the California Youth Authority. In addition to reintegrating these youths into communities, the New Hope program aimed to reduce their need for gang participation and affiliation as a support mechanism (Degnan, 1994; Degnan & Degnan, 1993). An evaluation of the program's results found that participating youths were far less likely to have frequent associations with former gang associates than were members of the control group. In addition, youths assigned to the control group were about twice as likely as program participants to have been arrested, to be unemployed, and to have abused drugs or alcohol frequently since their release.

The Multidisciplinary Team (MDT) Home Run program (L-3) in San Bernardino County, California, is an excellent example of a nongang program that successfully served gang members with an intervention team, although it is rated promising. Four professionals make up each MDT: a probation officer, a licensed therapist, a social worker, and a public health nurse. High-risk youthful offenders (including gang members) and their families are referred by probation officers. Each team provides intensive and comprehensive wrap-around services to high-risk youth and offenders and their families for 6 months. An evaluation (Schram & Gaines, 2005) compared outcomes for randomly selected gang and nongang offenders from among all youths served in the MDT program. Both groups showed significant improvements on school measures (increased grade point average, lower number of school absences, and reduced number of suspensions), family functioning, alcohol and substance abuse, and reported arrests after the program.

Gang Suppression

Suppression strategies, loosely based on deterrence principles, have dominated gang interventions for a quarter century and continue to do so (Klein, 1995, 2004). Legislators and policy makers in the United States have a tendency to "declare war" on social problems, and their "solutions" often are characterized by aggression. In the last half century, the U.S. government has launched "wars" on poverty, crime, drugs, gangs, and juveniles (Howell, 2003b). This curious proclivity, combined with the growth of youth street gangs from the mid-1980s to the mid-1990s, gangs' concomitant growing use of firearms noted earlier, and popular myths about gangs and juvenile "superpredators," prompted President Clinton to declare a "war on gangs" in his 1997 State of the Union address. Of course, his action spurred gang suppression initiatives.

But gang suppression actually began earlier. The first program to evidence substantial success in suppressing gangs, Operation Hardcore (L-2) (which targeted habitual gang offenders for vertical prosecution), proved effective in producing more convictions, fewer dismissals, more convictions to the most serious charge, and a higher rate of prison confinement of gang members (Dahmann, 1983). Other outcomes were not measured. The second large-scale suppression initiative, the Los Angeles Police Department's infamous street gang sweeps, were never evaluated but could not be considered successful by any measure—particularly not the "Operation Hammer" street sweeps (Klein, 1995, pp. 161–163; see Chapter 11). A wide variety of gang suppression measures showing little success followed, including forming cul-de-sacs with concrete barriers to alter the flow of gang-driven vehicles, antiloitering statutes, civil injunctions, traffic checkpoints, curfew and truancy enforcement, and crackdowns on gun violations (Weisel, 2002).

More targeted gang suppression has shown some success. A three pronged suppression strategy of selective incarceration of the most violent and repeat older gang offenders in the most violent gangs; enforcement of probation controls (graduated sanctions and intensive supervision) on younger, less violent gang offenders; and arrests of gang leaders in hotspots of gang activity proved somewhat effective in the Tri-Agency Resource Gang Enforcement Team (TARGET) (L-2) program in Orange County, California (Kent, Donaldson, Wyrick, & Smith, 2000). Another targeted program, the Dallas, Texas, Anti-Gang Initiative (L-3), also showed some success in using aggressive curfew and truancy enforcement while targeting geographic areas that were home to seven of the city's most violent gangs (Fritsch, Caeti, & Taylor, 2003).

Community policing, a "softer" form of police suppression (Klein, 1995), implemented in the Chicago Alternative Policing Strategy (CAPS) (L-2), has shown success in reducing adult crimes. In the first phase of CAPS, gang problems were reduced in two of the three experimental police districts (Skogan & Hartnett, 1997), but once CAPS was implemented city-wide, successes with gang problems were largely limited to perceptions of African American residents (Skogan & Steiner, 2004).

Boston's Operation Ceasefire is a promising deterrence strategy (L-3) that applied the cross-agency "problem analysis" approach originally dubbed "problem-oriented policing" (Goldstein, 1979). Claims of a "Boston Miracle" (Braga, Kennedy, Waring, & Piehl, 2001; Kennedy, 2007) have been questioned in others' evaluations (Fagan, 2002; Ludwig, 2005; Rosenfeld, Fornango, & Baumer, 2005), and the results of replications in larger cities have been less successful (Ludwig, 2005; Tita, Riley, & Greenwood, 2003). Project Safe Neighborhoods (PSN) in Chicago appeared to have been effective (Papachristos, Meares, & Fagan, 2005), but the evaluation overlooked Chicago's Operation Ceasefire (http://www.ceasefirechicago.org/), which was operating in the same areas where PSN was implemented, and at the same time, with "violence interrupters" who very skillfully intervene in anticipated gang shootings (Skogan, Hartnett, Bump, & Dubois, 2008). The latter initiative probably produced the observed positive outcomes. The use of singular suppression tactics in combating gangs and gun crime still has a mixed report card (Decker, 2003, p. 290; see also Bynum & Varano, 2003; Fagan, 2002; Ludwig, 2005) and calls often are made for better implementation of problem-oriented or problem-solving policing (Manning, 2005; Box 7.5).

IN FOCUS 7.5

Questions Researchers Should Ask About Problem-Solving Policing

- Do officers receive systematic training in the process of problem solving?
- Do their supervisors, at the sergeant level and above, receive training to guide, supervise, and evaluate the process?
- Do sergeants wish to do so routinely?
- Are there role models and examples in departments?
- Is the necessary oral culture present that supports the value of the approach and how to carry it out (see Manning, 2003)?
- How much time is spent on the job in activities labeled as problem solving?
- What rewards exist for problem solving, and are they visibly displayed?
- Has the peer culture changed to support problem solving with carrying the load, being a good street cop, and leaving the shift with a "clean patch" or turf?
- Does the organization provide time for activities other than responding to 911 calls?

- Do unions, devoted to control of the conditions of work, impede transfers and rewards based on skill?
- What, if any, is the role of investigators and special units?
- Does top command publicly espouse and reward problem solving?
- Are lower participants dubious, see it as "the flavor of the month," and fully expect another policy to be announced shortly?
- Are there negative consequences for officers who refuse, finesse, obfuscate, or avoid problem solving and continue to patrol, respond to calls, and value short-term soothing responses?

A Comprehensive Gang Model

Spergel's Comprehensive Gang Prevention, Intervention, and Suppression Model (L-2) (referred to herein as the Comprehensive Gang Model) is based on a nationwide assessment of youth gang problems and programs, funded by the OJJDP. Conducted in the late 1980s (Spergel, 1995; Spergel & Curry, 1990, 1993), this study identified the main strategies that are commonly used in community responses to gang problems. Spergel incorporated the following five strategies into a framework for addressing gang problems at the community level (Spergel, 1995, pp. 171–296) (Figure 7.4).

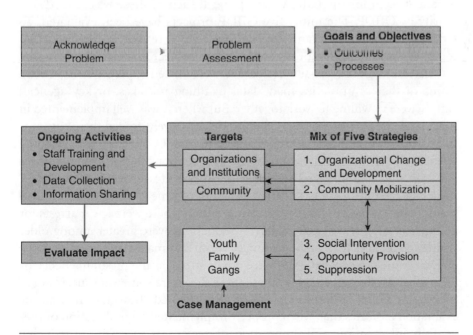

Figure 7.4   Comprehensive Gang Model

Community mobilization: Involvement of local citizens, including former gang youth, community groups, and agencies, and the coordination of programs and staff functions within and across agencies.

Opportunity provision: The development of a variety of specific education, training, and employment programs targeting gang-involved youth.

Social intervention: Involvement of youth-serving agencies, schools, grassroots groups, faith-based organizations, police, and other juvenile and criminal justice organizations in reaching out to gang-involved youth and their families, linking them with the conventional world and needed services.

Suppression: Formal and informal social control procedures, including close supervision and monitoring of gang-involved youth by agencies of the juvenile and criminal justice system and also by community-based agencies, schools, and grassroots groups.

Organizational change and development: Development and implementation of policies and procedures that result in the most effective use of available and potential resources, within and across agencies, to better address the gang problem.

This brief review of Spergel's model considers the evaluation of his model in Chicago's Little Village (Spergel, 2007) and outcomes from that project as well as in five other implementation sites. Spergel's Comprehensive Gang Model has guided experiments in 20 sites in the past decade. Except for the Little Village project, each of these was funded primarily by OJJDP. The initial five OJJDP projects have been evaluated. To facilitate drawing program implications, these results are summarized together with outcomes for the Little Village project in Chicago.

The results of the six-site evaluation were mixed (Spergel et al., 2006). Three of the communities made fatal planning mistakes, or key agencies simply were unwilling to work together. But when it was well implemented in three sites, the Comprehensive Gang Model effectively guided these communities (in Chicago; Mesa, Arizona; and Riverside, California) in developing services and strategies that contributed to reductions in both gang violence (in three sites) and drug-related offenses (in two sites) (Spergel et al., 2006). At the successful sites, a key factor was length of time in the program. When youths were in the program for 2 or more years, there were fewer arrests for all types of offenses. In general, arrest reductions were greater among older youth and females than among younger youth and males. General deterrence effects (at the project area level) were not as strong as the program effects for individual youths; nevertheless, these three sites were somewhat successful in integrating police suppression with service-oriented strategies. In sum, the evaluation indicates that, when properly implemented, a combination of prevention, intervention, and suppression strategies was successful in reducing the gang problem (L-2; Spergel et al., 2006).

Spergel and his colleagues assessed program elements, strategies, and operating principles in terms of their importance to successful implementation of the Comprehensive Gang Model, based on interviews with program staff and youths, service tracking records, and field observations. None of the sites fully implemented these three critical program implementation requirements. The three sites that showed the largest reductions in violence and drug-related crimes implemented more of them.

Lessons Learned

The evaluations of Spergel's model have identified eight factors that are deemed extremely important to successful implementation (the ideal organizational structure is shown in Figure 7.5). These factors have been modified to incorporate the views of NYGC staff, who have worked directly with at least 14 other sites that have implemented the Comprehensive Gang Model or are in the process of doing so. The purpose of soliciting the NYGC staff's views was to draw on their experiences in a much larger number of sites, thus increasing the specificity and generalizability of the factors associated with effective implementation.

- A project director or coordinator who has professional respect, is well regarded by all agency leaders and others working on the project, and has a broad base of skills for performing diverse tasks, including coordinating with agency heads and elected officials, supervising outreach workers, and data collection and analysis (or at least a basic understanding of how it is done, why it is needed, and the requirements of a data-driven problem-solving approach).
- Management capacity of the lead agency and its commitment to a data-driven problem-solving approach. This means using the data on an ongoing basis to set priorities for the project and to maintain effective targeting of services. If the lead agency is too far removed—both geographically and bureaucratically—from the community implementing the model, the project often suffers. The lead agency should be respected by all involved community agencies but should never be perceived by others as running the project.

Figure 7.5   Comprehensive Gang Model Organization

- An effective, representative steering committee that is committed to a data-driven problem-solving approach. All members must be knowledgeable about the Comprehensive Gang Model and support their agency's participation and time allocation to the project, whether on the steering committee, on the intervention team, or through other agency programs or services provided to project clients.
- City and county government leaders who are committed to the Comprehensive Gang Model and are able to provide for the sustainability of the project, with or without federal funds, or the ability of the project coordinator and steering committee to access additional funds. Without this support, projects die.
- The development of an interdisciplinary intervention team (which includes police and probation agents as key players) and the coordination of outreach worker efforts.
- An objective assessment of the community's gang problem that provides the basis for a data-driven problem-solving approach.
- Targeting of gang members and at-risk youths.
- A combination and balance of prevention, intervention, and suppression strategies, and implementation of all five of the Comprehensive Gang Model strategies.

Three of these lessons merit special attention. A combination and balance of prevention, intervention, and suppression strategies is particularly important for success in any community (see Wyrick, 2006; Wyrick & Howell, 2004). *Prevention programs* are needed to target youths at risk of gang involvement, to reduce the number of youths who join gangs; *intervention programs and strategies* are needed to provide sanctions and services for younger youths who are actively involved in gangs to separate them from gangs; and law enforcement *suppression strategies* are needed to target the most violent gangs and older, criminally active gang members. This continuum sets the Comprehensive Gang Model apart from single-dimensional gang suppression models.

The development of intervention teams is also critical. In most sites, interdisciplinary intervention teams have proved to be the main organizational change vehicle. These teams appear to integrate the services of diverse community agencies in a manner that they could not accomplish on their own while targeting a specific subset of gang members, those who are not so entrenched in gang life that they cannot be redirected. This approach has proved effective in other sites that have targeted potential serious, violent, and chronic juvenile offenders. Three examples are described herein: the Little Village program, the MDT Home Run Program and the BRIDGE program. This is another feature that clearly distinguishes the Comprehensive Gang Model from popular gang suppression initiatives.

Another extremely important lesson learned from the numerous Spergel model sites is the necessity of objective and comprehensive community assessments of gang problems—that involve all sectors of the community—to provide a factual database for strategic planning. Few of them found the gang problem to have the expected characteristic features, and several interesting findings in reports of Little Village project workers counter conventional wisdom (Spergel, 2007). Although many of the gang members were involved in drug dealing and sometimes had peripheral or direct connection with organized crime in the area (e.g., making a drug run), most of the youth gang members were not disciplined, organized crime apprentices. In fact, drug selling and drug use were about as likely to involve nongang peers as gang members. As seen in studies elsewhere, serious gang violence in Little Village had little to do with drug trafficking; instead, it was concentrated on the borders of gang turfs and around the high schools. Assessments to determine actual gang activities are vital for sound strategic planning.

This review of youth gang programs refutes the myth that nothing works with gangs or gang members. A recent review of gang programs (Klein & Maxson, 2006) has been widely interpreted as drawing this conclusion. (Their actual summary statement, based on their review, is that "past efforts at gang control have been demonstrably ineffective or—at best—untested for their effectiveness" [p. 12].) But they claim that the essence of their message is that none of the gang programs they reviewed has been conclusively *proven* effective. Although Klein and Maxson may have used criteria similar to those used to rate programs in the Helping America's Youth initiative, they did not numerically score programs based on evaluation reports, which could explain the outcome of their review.

Another limitation of Klein and Maxson's review is that they did not include several programs that have reduced gang member crimes but were not specifically intended as gang programs. Prevention science shows that multiple problem behaviors can be prevented or reduced in the course of addressing common underlying causes (Chapter 4). Because delinquency and gang involvement share many of the same risk factors (Howell & Egley, 2005b), a delinquency prevention program can also reduce involvement in delinquent behavior among gang members.

Klein and Maxson also seem unwilling to give programs credit for degrees of effectiveness. For example, they are highly critical of the GREAT program because the initial version of it did not prevent gang joining. It would be a miracle of social science if one hour of an antigang curriculum delivered only 9 weeks to students in a school classroom prevented gang joining. The GREAT program deserves recognition for having reduced victimization, instilled more negative views about gangs among youth, improved attitudes toward police, and increased the numbers of prosocial peers. These multiple outcomes—even though the effect sizes were not large—are noteworthy for such a minimally intrusive and inexpensive program.

Another major issue concerns Klein and Maxson's critique of the Comprehensive Gang Model in that they equate implementation failures with program failure. This indicates a major misunderstanding on their part of the essence of the Comprehensive Gang Model. It is *not* a prescriptive program intervention model that either works or doesn't to reduce gang crime. Rather, it is a strategic planning framework—a process for reducing gang problems. Failure to implement a strategic planning process is a shortcoming of community stakeholders, a product of denial that a gang problem exists or refusal to work together (Decker & Curry, 2002), neither of which is a fault of the model itself.

The NYGC has developed a Strategic Planning Tool, an operating system that communities can use to assess their gang problem and use with the Comprehensive Gang Model to develop a prevention, intervention, and suppression continuum (http://www.iir.com/nygc/tool). This tool includes research-based risk factors and indicators and information on promising and effective juvenile delinquency and gang programs and strategies that address specific risk factors among various age groups. It incorporates a problem-solving approach to gang-related crime, for example, in engaging participating sites in an analysis of crime trends involving gang members, identification of hotspots, and the targeting of high-rate gang offenders and violent gangs.

To complement use of the Strategic Planning Tool, an assessment protocol is available that any community can use to assess its gang problem and promote the development of a data-driven continuum of gang prevention, intervention, and suppression programs and strategies (National Youth Gang Center, 2002a). Resource materials that assist communities in developing an action plan to implement the Comprehensive Gang Model are also available (National Youth Gang Center, 2002b). (Both of these resources are available online at http://www.iir.com/nygc/acgp/default.htm). This operating system does not reference the Comprehensive Gang Model as if it were a prescriptive program model; rather, it contains user-friendly tools that empower communities to assess their gang problem, inventory existing program resources, identify gaps, and select preferred solutions from a menu of research-based programs and strategy options. Gang programs should be integrated with communities' continuum of delinquency programs. A plethora of such programs is available online (http://guide.helpingamericasyouth.gov).

Discussion Topics

1. What makes working with gang members so difficult?

2. What implications does the gang theory in Chapter 6 have for working with gang members?

3. Given the multiple problem behaviors of gang members, what are reasonable outcomes for programs that attempt to intervene with them?

4. What makes gangs so intractable? What is most likely to work with them?

5. Construct a continuum of delinquency and gang programs using the Helping America's Youth Community Guide (Box 7.4).

PART III

Programmatic and Policy Responses to Juvenile Delinquency

This section provides current research on what works and what doesn't in preventing and reducing juvenile delinquency. The chapters in Part III address this comprehensive topic from four perspectives. Chapter 8 presents principles and characteristics of best practice programs. It lays the foundation for the more specific examination of effective programs that follows. Chapter 9 describes effective prevention and rehabilitation programs. The chapter draws on systematic reviews and meta-analyses to identify the specific services that are likely to be most effective. Chapter 10 illustrates a comprehensive strategy framework that can help organize evidence-based programs in a continuum for greater impact. Two chapters address ineffective programs and strategies. Chapter 11 broadly covers what doesn't work in preventing and reducing juvenile delinquency, and Chapter 12 is devoted to one practice that is especially ineffective: transfer of juveniles to the criminal justice system.

CHAPTER 8

Principles and Characteristics of Best Practice Programs

The business of identifying and disseminating effective programs and matching them with offenders who will benefit most from them is yet in its infancy. How could this be? Isn't this a fundamental mission of criminology? Of course it is, but little attention has been given to this enterprise. The main reason for lack of progress in this expected role of criminology is that policy makers, legislators, and practitioners have been preoccupied with punishment for nearly 40 years, and incarceration has been the main crime control strategy since the mid-1980s (Blumstein, 1983; Blumstein et al., 1986). In a brilliant essay, Cullen (2007) offers five reasons why rehabilitation should be adopted as corrections' guiding paradigm. These are summarized briefly here.

1. **Reason 1:** Rejecting rehabilitation was a mistake (Cullen, 2007, pp. 718–719).

Beginning in the late 1960s, criminologists joined with left-wing political forces to reject the rehabilitative ideal in favor of a "justice model" that would limit corrections officials' discretion with offenders and institute due process rights and determinate sentencing. This movement was buttressed by a negative review of program evaluations in juvenile and criminal justice systems (Lipton, Martinson, & Wilks, 1975; Martinson, 1974). The most-quoted conclusion from this review is Martinson's (1974) statement that "with few isolated exceptions, the rehabilitative efforts that have been reported so far have no appreciable effect on recidivism" (p. 25). Even in the mid-1980s, leading criminologists clung to the view of null effects of treatment (Blumstein, 1983).

2. **Reason 2:** Punishment does not work (Cullen, 2007, pp. 719–720).

"Locking up over two million offenders is bound to prevent some crime" (p. 719), but there is growing evidence that "get-tough" strategies, including punishment and imprisonment, are related to higher levels of recidivism. The favorite programs engineered by "just deserts" model advocates such as control-oriented intensive supervision, scared straight, and boot camp programs "have no overall impacts on recidivism" (p. 719) (see Chapter 11).

3. **Reason 3:** Rehabilitation does work (Cullen, 2007, pp. 720–721).

The myth that nothing works persisted until it was gradually overturned by 12 "disciples of rehabilitation" (as Cullen, 2005, dubs them) of highly skilled scholars who used tools of science to examine the evidence more carefully and systematically over the past 30 years (Table 8.1). Cullen (2005) cites much of the research that he and others produced that shows that rehabilitation works, and there are other key reviews that debunk the "nothing works" myth (see especially Andrews & Bonta, 2006; Cullen, 2007; Cullen & Gendreau, 2000; Gendreau, Smith, & French, 2006; Lipsey, 1999a, 1999b; Lipsey & Cullen, 2007; Lipsey & Wilson, 1998; MacKenzie, 2006; McGuire, 2002; Palmer, 1992; Petrosino, 2005). Yet some observers still question the effectiveness of rehabilitation (Farabee, 2005).

4. **Reason 4:** The public likes rehabilitation . . . even if it is a liberal idea (Cullen, 2007, p. 721).

Public opinion pollsters have underestimated the insights of Americans. Most citizens favor "a balanced approach, one that exacts a measure of justice, protects the public against serious offenders, and makes every effort to change offenders while they are within the grasp of the state" (Cullen, 2007, p. 721). Numerous public opinion polls show that, for juveniles, the public believes that treatment is particularly important and especially favors early

Table 8.1   Twelve Disciples Who Saved Rehabilitation

Disciples	Main Contribution
Ted Palmer	Challenged Martinson's "nothing works" doctrine
Frank Cullen	Reaffirmed rehabilitation
Paul Gendreau	Detailed reviews of correctional literature
Don Andrews and James Bonta	Principles of effective correctional intervention
Mark Lipsey and David Wilson	Persuasive evidence from meta-analyses
Joan Petersilia and Doris MacKenzie	Showed what does not work
Scott Henggeler	Revisited child saving
Ed Latessa and Patricia Van Voorhis	Spread good news of effective correctional intervention

intervention programs (Cullen, 2006; Cullen, Bose, Jonson, & Unnever, 2007). Not only that, the public is willing to pay for juvenile rehabilitation and early intervention programs (Nagin, Piquero, Scott, & Steinberg, 2006).

5. **Reason 5:** Rehabilitation is the moral thing to do (Cullen, 2007, pp. 721–722).

Conservative advocates of punishment argue that rehabilitation sends the wrong message to offenders: that they are not responsible for their actions. "This reasoning has surface appeal, but it also borders on the ridiculous—for three reasons" (p. 721): (a) Offenders who choose crime are very much bound by the circumstances into which they are born, which they certainly do not choose; (b) rehabilitation does not excuse victimization but demands that offenders work to change the parts of themselves that lead to criminal involvement; and (c) rehabilitation does not demean human dignity but instead encourages personal growth. "What the punishment paradigm has wrought . . . over the past decades is disquieting. . . . It is time to take a new pathway—one that draws on Americans' long-standing cultural belief in offender reformation and on the emergent 'what works' literature" (p. 722).

How Research Is Translated Into Practice

Before addressing the issue of how research is translated into practice, readers are advised to think about various ways of defining key terms for this discussion. Box 8.1 provides recommended definitions (now codified in the cited Tennessee law) that distinguish levels or degrees of what we refer to herein as best practice programs. In the Tennessee legislation, four best practice levels are noted from the highest level (evidence-based) to the lowest (theory-based). Admittedly, these are fine-grained distinctions, but they are important ones, and these definitions should be used to guide best practice research, guideline development, and programming.

IN FOCUS 8.1

Tennessee Code Annotated, Title 37, Chapter 5, Part 1, Section 1

The Tennessee Code . . . is amended by inserting the following as a new, appropriately designated section thereto:

(a) As used in this section, unless the context otherwise requires:

   (1) "Evidence-based" means a program or practice that meets the following requirements:

(Continued)

(Continued)

(A) The program or practice is governed by a program manual or protocol that specifies the nature, quality, and amount of service that constitutes the program; and

(B) Scientific research using methods that meet high scientific standards for evaluating the effects of such programs must have demonstrated with two (2) or more separate client samples that the program improves client outcomes central to the purpose of the program;

(2) "Pilot program" means a temporary research-based or theory-based program or project that is eligible for funding from any source to determine whether or not evidence supports its continuation beyond the fixed evaluation period. A pilot program must provide for and include:

(A) Development of a program manual or protocol that specifies the nature, quality, and amount of service that constitutes the program; and

(B) Scientific research using methods that meet high scientific standards for evaluating the effects of such programs must demonstrate on at least an annual basis whether or not the program improves client outcomes central to the purpose of the program;

(3) "Research-based" means a program or practice that has some research demonstrating effectiveness, but that does not yet meet the standard of evidence-based; and

(4) "Theory-based" means a program or practice that has general support among treatment providers and experts, based on experience or professional literature, may have anecdotal or case study support, and has potential for becoming a research-based program or practice.

The business of increasing the use of scientific knowledge to solve problems is not new. It has a long history, and many names are used to describe this process, including *technology transfer, information or research utilization, dissemination,* and *organizational change* (Backer, 1993). Backer documents three distinct American applications of these sorts: agricultural innovations (1920–1960), use of defense and space-related research (1960–1980), and improvements in health, education, and human resources. Recently, support for best practice crime prevention and rehabilitation has begun to grow, following the leads set in medicine and education (Welsh & Farrington, 2006).

The mental health field also has been challenged to deliver effective, evidence-based programs, dating back to Jane Knitzer's (1982) call for a system of care. Yet much of the individual programming in all fairness must be characterized as "treatment as usual," defined as the best clinical judgment without the use of evidence or manuals, and the research suggests that everyday practice has had no effect on specific disorders (Knitzer & Cooper, 2006). These observers also note that evidence-based care implemented in community-based settings (as opposed to R&D sites) has produced less promising effects than under R&D conditions. "Early data show that evidence-based treatments are being applied in the field with varying degrees of consistency and fidelity. Familiarity with empirically supported practices varies, but even where practitioners received on-the-job training, systematic implementation was not assured" (Knitzer & Cooper, 2006, pp. 673–674). Littell's (2006) review of independent replications of Multisystemic Therapy found considerable loss in fidelity when such therapy was implemented in distant sites (but see Henggeler, Schoenwald, Borduin, & Swenson, 2006, for a rejoinder).

There are three major approaches for translating research evidence about effective programs into practice for everyday use by practitioners and policy makers (Lipsey, 2005). The first one is to evaluate the effects of your program as it is implemented. The second one is to draw on lists of model programs, with evidence of effectiveness. A third approach is systematic synthesis or meta-analysis. Regardless of the approach followed, studies on which "what works" conclusions are based must meet very high standards of methodological quality on four criteria: statistical conclusion validity, internal validity, construct validity, and external validity (see Welsh & Farrington, 2006, pp. 2 5).

Evaluate the Effects of Your Program as It Is Implemented

It is particularly important to field an independent evaluation of programs under two conditions. The first is when the program constitutes a new experimental undertaking, that is, a pilot program. The second situation is when a new statewide initiative is launched that represents a large investment of federal, state, or county funds. The only scientifically credible method for assessing the effectiveness of an active or planned program is with a research design that compares recidivism rates for offenders exposed to the intervention with those for a substantially similar control group not exposed to it (Lipsey & Cullen, 2007). The strongest designs have three key features (p. 4). First, they assign large numbers of offenders randomly to intervention and control conditions. Second, they maintain high fidelity to the treatment protocol. Third, they manage to have little attrition of subjects from the assigned conditions or the data collection on the recidivism measures. The second and third approaches to translating research into practice that follow draw on high-quality studies that have these features. Each of these criteria can be incorporated into program review instruments for multiple program reviews.

A Model Program Approach

This approach, which entails selecting a recommended program from a list of research-supported programs and adapting it to local circumstances, is exemplified by the Blueprints Project (Mihalic, Irwin, Elliott, Fagan, & Hansen, 2001) described in Chapter 9 (see Table 9.1 for a list of such programs). In this approach, what typically are called model or exemplary programs are identified in single program reviews. This approach has a distinct advantage in that the recommended programs are specific and individualized (Lipsey, 2005). Thus practitioners and policy makers who want to adopt one of these programs typically are able to obtain a very prescriptive model to follow and, in most cases, contact information for reaching a program developer or sponsor for operational details, if not a specific treatment protocol.

However, if the prescriptive protocols that are available for the very best programs are not followed with high fidelity, this condition tends to greatly diminish the expectation that outcomes comparable to those found in the supporting research will follow (Lipsey, 2005). Such a situation means that the transportability of the model is problematic (Henggeler et al., 2006). Therefore, it is important when implementing a model program to monitor not just implementation but also outcomes to ensure that sponsors are getting what they want out of it. The best approach would be to import model programs as if they were a pilot to be evaluated in an everyday practice context before expanding, like the Washington State experiment with Functional Family Therapy (Barnoski, 2004a). An alternative strategy for translating research into practice is examined in Chapter 9.

Systematic Reviews and Meta-Analysis

The third major approach to the translation of research evidence about effective programs into practice for everyday use by practitioners and policy makers is systematic reviews, including meta-analyses of large groups of studies. Although there are several methods for assessing program research evidence—and they vary in terms of strengths and weaknesses—the key difference is between single program reviews that focus on identifying specific programs that work (i.e., exemplary or model programs) and reviews that aim to synthesize principles of program effectiveness or features of effective programs across the large body of well-evaluated programs.

Systematic reviews with meta-analytic review methods are the most rigorous for determining what works (Lipsey, 2005). The best systematic reviews "use rigorous methods for locating, appraising, and synthesizing evidence from prior evaluation studies, and they are reported with the same level of detail that characterizes high quality reports of original research" (Welsh & Farrington, 2006, p. 8). The key features of systematic reviews are as follows (pp. 8–9):

- Explicit objectives.
- Explicit eligibility criteria.
- Each study is screened according to the eligibility criteria.
- Assembly of the most complete data possible.
- Use of quantitative techniques, including meta-analysis, whenever possible.
- Structured and detailed reporting.

The Campbell Collaboration is at the forefront of systematic reviews in criminology and criminal justice (Welsh & Farrington, 2006, pp. 11–14). The prestigious Cochrane Collaboration has long conducted systematic reviews in the public health arena. The Campbell Collaboration recently created the Crime and Justice Group to prepare rigorous and systematic reviews in the criminology and criminal justice domains. Several of these will be referenced in Chapter 9.

Meta-analysis is typically used in systematic reviews. This review method involves the preparation of statistical summaries of large groups of studies (Box 8.2). The idea of combining many smaller studies into one big study was pioneered by Glass (1976) and dubbed meta-analysis. However, Mark Lipsey and a group of Canadian criminologists get credit for popularizing use of meta-analytic techniques in criminology.

IN FOCUS 8.2
Meta-Analysis

Originally developed in the field of medicine and further developed by educators (Glass, McGaw, & Smith, 1981), meta-analysis is a quantitative technique for coding, analyzing, and summarizing research evidence. In conducting a meta-analysis, a researcher uses statistical procedures to synthesize and compare clusters of studies on a given topic. Meta-analysis enables a researcher to examine a wider range of program evaluations in a more systematic manner than is possible in a conventional program-by-program review. This procedure is now widely accepted "as a sophisticated way to extract, analyze, and summarize the empirical findings of a collection of related research studies" (Lipsey, 1999b, p. 616). The methods used to conduct meta-analyses are very similar to those used in good survey research (Lipsey, 1999b, pp. 617–618). In a meta-analysis, the database is developed by trained coders who are guided in their review of existing research by questionnaires concerning data elements and program characteristics. Depending on the subject matter of the inquiry, a population of research studies is defined for the analysis, and a sample of relevant studies is

(Continued)

(Continued)

drawn—or the entire universe of studies in a given field may be retrieved for review and synthesis. Once the data are extracted, they are analyzed and synthesized through the use of statistical methods.

In the case of program evaluations, meta-analysts standardize program intervention effects (known as the effect sizes) to permit comparisons across studies. The effect size is the standardized statistic representing the magnitude of the difference between the mean value on the outcome variable (recidivism) for the individuals receiving intervention (the treatment group) and the mean value for a comparable group (the control group) (Lipsey, 1999b, pp. 616–617). Thus the result of a program meta-analysis "is a rather complete statement of currently available research evidence about the effects of rehabilitative interventions on the recidivism of juvenile offenders" (Lipsey, 1999a, p. 162). Two common criticisms of meta-analysis are that this review technique "cannot overcome problems of poor research design" (McCord et al., 2001, p. 191) and that summarizing studies with different methodological features creates an "apples and oranges" problem (Sharpe, 1997). These are not insurmountable problems. Meta-analysts can handle research design nuances quite adequately with multivariate analyses that permit method adjustments in effect sizes to control for between-study differences, although better multivariate analysis techniques are needed (Lipsey & Wilson, 1998, 2000). There are many other program evaluation particulars that may have far more important influences on outcomes than broad design quality ratings (Durlak & Lipsey, 1991; Lipsey, 2000a). These include attrition, type of delinquency outcome measure, sample size, statistical power (Lipsey & Wilson, 1998, 2001), and the involvement of researchers in the design, delivery, and supervision of treatment in demonstration programs (Lipsey, 1999b; Petrosino & Soydan, 2005). Nevertheless, these influences on outcomes can be identified and assessed in meta-analyses (Lipsey & Wilson, 2000), something that cannot be done in conventional narrative reviews.

Meta-analysis has many other advantages as well. As Lipsey (1999b) notes, "Most striking, perhaps, is the power of meta-analysis to identify intervention effects not clearly visible to traditional reviewers" (p. 619; see also Lipsey & Wilson, 1993; Schmidt, 1992). Lipsey's (1999b) discovery of the delinquency reduction potential of "practical" juvenile justice program interventions is an excellent example. Another advantage of meta-analysis is that this technique enables users to assess program effectiveness easily on a number of other dimensions, such as the types of offenders with which program interventions work best, gender effects of different interventions, and supplementary program interventions that work well with particular interventions. These are program features that cannot be assessed comprehensively in program-by-program reviews. Thus the narrative review method lacks the scope and depth of meta-analysis procedures (Redondo, Sanchez-Meca, & Garrido, 1999). In addition, meta-analysis study results are far easier to translate into everyday practice than are narrative review results, as will be seen later in this chapter.

The main grist of a meta-analysis is a statistic called the effect size (Lipsey & Wilson, 2001). This statistic represents the difference between the treatment and control group on a specified outcome such as recidivism (Figure 8.1). Effect sizes typically are weighted according to the sample size on which they are based and other study characteristics. A main purpose of a meta-analysis of program evaluations is to determine which characteristics of programs are most strongly related to the positive effects. Lipsey and his colleagues statistically control differences in the rigor of study methods to level the playing field and then examine the contribution of the juveniles' characteristics, program implementation, and type of intervention to large program effects (Lipsey, 2002; Lipsey & Wilson, 2001).

Lipsey (2000b) shows the average effect sizes on recidivism for juvenile offenders in juvenile justice system outcome studies in his meta-analytic database, which numbered 556 studies at that time (Figure 8.2). The majority (57%) reduced recidivism. Thus it can be said that *most* juvenile justice system programs reduce recidivism. This is an important point that counters the myth of ineffective juvenile justice system programs discussed in Chapter 9. On the other hand, almost half (43%) of the programs made little or no difference: About one quarter (26%) of them showed increases in recidivism, and 17% showed no differences. Statistically significant differences are shown in the shaded portions of the bars in Figure 8.2. The more reliable differences will appear prominently in meta-analyses that identify the features of the most effective programs.

Programs that are designed specifically to demonstrate the effectiveness of particular interventions—called research and development programs—typically produce the largest positive program effects. Indeed, the mean effect size for the practical programs (.07) is only about half that for the average R&D program (.13) (Lipsey, 2002). This is largely because the interventions in such programs are tested under favorable conditions.

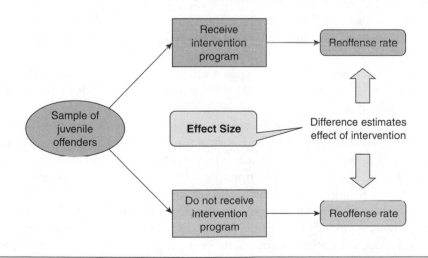

Figure 8.1   Control-Comparison Group Research Design for Estimating the Effects of Intervention

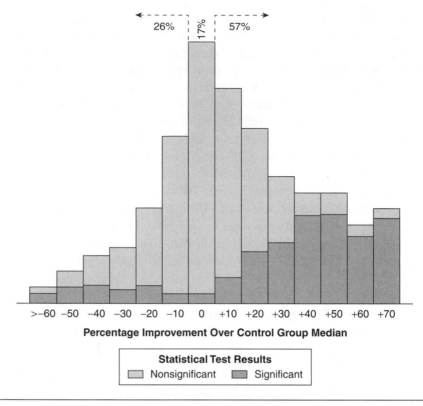

Figure 8.2 Recidivism Results of 556 Delinquency Outcome Studies

A distinguishing feature of research and development programs is active research team involvement in planning and implementing the program. In addition, research and development programs typically are highly structured around specific and systematically administered treatment protocols. Service providers in such programs usually are well trained in service delivery, and treatments are closely monitored.

However, one of the strengths of meta-analysis is that it allows the analyst to include the full range of well-designed program evaluations. Meticulous meta-analysis procedures that assign more weight to studies with stronger research designs enable analysts to include more studies in their reviews and thus make more confident statements about what works in everyday practice.

Lipsey (1999b) next conducted a meta-analysis to determine whether effective "practical" juvenile justice programs (routine programs designed and managed by system professionals) are worthwhile. From his database of juvenile justice program evaluations, he selected for this analysis programs that had a rehabilitative orientation, did not involve researchers directly, were sponsored by public or private agencies, and had clients who came to the programs through public or private agencies rather than being recruited by researchers. In other words, these were programs that had a rehabilitation orientation but were not R&D programs.

Lipsey (1999b) analyzed these 196 evaluations of practical juvenile justice system programs in his database that met the aforementioned criteria and found that nearly half (44%) of them reduced recidivism between 10% and 25% (Table 8.2). He also found that some practical programs (about 17% of the nearly 200 programs) produced very worthwhile reductions in recidivism rates, about 21–25%. However, 57% either showed negligible positive effects or that many of the offenders in them got worse.

Lipsey (1999b) found that four main characteristics of practical programs were associated with the largest recidivism reductions: the provision of certain services, a distinct role for the juvenile justice system, a sufficient amount of service, and administration of services to the most appropriate juvenile subpopulation.

In addition, comparable positive program effects were found for samples in which all the juveniles had prior offenses, or high proportions were adjudicated or institutionalized delinquents and high proportions were reported to have histories of aggressive or violent behavior.

The Cumulative Impacts of Practical Programs With Effective Characteristics

To examine the cumulative impact of these more effective program characteristics, Lipsey (1999b) analyzed their impacts in tandem by separating the 196 practical programs in the database into categories according to whether they scored high on none, one, or more of the four program characteristics described earlier (see Table 8.2). Programs that had none of the four characteristics (7% of the programs) *increased* recidivism somewhat.

Table 8.2   Proportion of Practical Programs With Different Numbers of Favorable Characteristics and Associated Improvement in Recidivism Rates Relative to Control

Number of Favorable Characteristics	Distribution of Programs (%)	Percentage Change in Recidivism
0	7	+12
1	50	−2
2	27	−10
3	15	−21
4	2	−25

NOTE: Favorable program characteristics are as follows: uses one of the more effective types of service, juvenile justice–administered program conducted in non–juvenile justice facility, good program implementation with high amount of service, juveniles' ages 15+, and mixed prior offenses.

Those that had only one of the four characteristics (50% of the programs) reduced recidivism insignificantly (only 2%). However, those that had two of the four characteristics (27% of the programs) reduced recidivism 10%, those with three of the four characteristics (15% of the programs) reduced recidivism 21%, and those with all four of the highly effective program characteristics (2% of the programs) reduced recidivism 25%. Thus the presence of three or four of the desired program characteristics produced a very substantial impact on recidivism. Programs with additional features of effective programs reduce recidivism more. This analysis prompted Lipsey to pursue a way of engaging practitioners and service providers in improving practical programs.

Principles of Effective Programs Based on Lipsey's Meta-Analyses

The following are findings from Lipsey's more recent meta-analyses of more than 500 evaluations of prevention and rehabilitation programs for juvenile offenders in which a control group was used (Lipsey, 2006, 2007; Lipsey & Wilson, 1998; Wilson, Lipsey, & Soydan, 2003).

Principle 1: Most programs have small but not negligible effects.

The "nothing works" claim that programs for juvenile offenders are ineffective is false. The mean reduction in recidivism for all well-evaluated juvenile justice programs is just 8%. But approximately one-fourth of the studies show recidivism reductions of 30% or more.

Principle 2: Programs are about equally effective with boys and girls, minority and nonminority youths, and aggressive and nonaggressive youth.

However, effects are somewhat larger for higher-risk cases (including committed juveniles receiving treatment while incarcerated).

Principle 3: There are some important differences with interventions for committed offenders.

- The setting influences the effects of intervention: Other things being equal, research suggests that effects on recidivism are more than twice as large when juveniles are treated in group homes, boarding schools, cottages, and other such smaller-scale living units than in larger institutional facilities.
- The professional role of the treatment provider is related to the effects on recidivism: Other things equal, effects are larger when the "therapists" are

mental health or other such personnel than when they are juvenile justice personnel supervising the youth.

Principle 4: Some programs can make recidivism worse.

Intuitions and "common sense" about what should work are not good guides to effective programs. Scared straight, shock incarceration, and boot camps are programs with a very strong intuitive appeal (largely because of a presumed deterrent effect), but they are not effective.

*Principle 5: Some programs have large
effects that represent significant reductions
in recidivism, but large effects are not happenstance;
they are systematically related to program characteristics.*

Treatment choices really matter in juvenile justice. Matching properly configured services with offenders who will benefit most is challenging.

*Principle 6: The type of program matters;
different programs cluster in terms of effectiveness.*

Clusters of programs for serious and violent juvenile offenders can be grouped according to degrees of effectiveness based on a meta-analysis; see Table 9.3 in Chapter 9 (Lipsey & Wilson, 1998).

*Principle 7: Implementation is
as important as program type.*

The evidence supporting this statement is shown in Table 8.3. For this analysis, Lipsey (2006) chose 509 of the juvenile justice programs in his database (some of the 556 did not provide sufficient detailed information for this purpose). In this illustration, when implemented with high fidelity, programs in group 4 (least effective) reduce delinquency (by 24%), about the same as the very best programs (group 1) when implemented with low fidelity. Lipsey emphasizes that it is a mistake to think of program effectiveness entirely in terms of the type of program used. How well it is implemented is equally important. Programs with less inherent effectiveness that are well implemented can show effects as large as those of better programs weakly implemented. The largest effects, of course, are for the best program types, well implemented.

*Principle 8: Everyday practice programs
show smaller effects than R&D programs.*

Although real-world programs show average positive effects, as noted earlier, they are only about half the size of the effects seen for R&D

programs. Much of what the R&D programs are doing could be emulated in practice, however. They also serve as a benchmark to gauge what might be possible for good programs that are well implemented.

Principle 9: Most everyday juvenile justice programs reduce recidivism, but not by much.

About half of the evaluated practical juvenile justice programs do not produce meaningful reductions in recidivism. Thus, there's potential for much more effective practical programs—research shows it is possible—but there is little indication that actual juvenile justice programs are attaining anything near that potential. To improve this situation, juvenile justice practitioners must use best practice services and in configurations that, on average, produce larger reductions in recidivism. Lipsey has developed an ingenious method for rating them across the board against best practice research guidelines and engaging them in making indicated improvements, as presented in Chapter 9.

Principle 10: There is enough research to characterize best practice for most interventions but not all of them.

In Chapter 9, a prototype instrument, the Standardized Program Evaluation Protocol (SPEP), will be described. It itemizes the characteristics of effective programs and consists of a rating scheme that assigns points to specific program characteristics according to their relationship to recidivism outcomes in the available research. Different ratings and point allocations are defined for different programs, classified according to the primary service they provide. In experiments that are under way in two states, we were able to classify almost all of the service programs using Lipsey's SPEP instruments.

Table 8.3 The Relationship Between Programs' Effectiveness Rank and Average Recidivism Reduction

Program Type, by Rank	Program Implementation: Amount of Service, Quality of Delivery (%)		
	Low	Medium	High
Group 1 (best)	24	34	46
Group 2	16	30	40
Group 3	6	20	32
Group 4 (poorest)	0	12	24

Features of R&D programs can be emulated in juvenile justice and youth service agencies. However, Lipsey (1999b) cautions that "such beneficial effects do not come automatically. A concerted effort must be made to configure the programs in the most favorable manner and to provide the types of services that have been shown to be effective, and avoid those shown to be ineffective" (p. 641).

There are many other lessons to be learned from meta-analysis (see Box 8.3 for several of them). We now turn to another major source of principles of effective programs.

IN FOCUS 8.3
Lessons From Lipsey's Meta-Analyses

Degree of effectiveness: Many social programs are more effective than expected.

Individual outcome evaluations can be misleading: Failure to attain statistical significance in an underpowered outcome evaluation means only that the research failed to reject the null hypothesis of no effects, not that it has confirmed the absence of effects.

Sources of program effectiveness: The critical features of program effectiveness are not necessarily unique to any particular program but show general patterns across programs.

There is safety in numbers: The consistency of effects across a large number of studies gives practitioners some assurance that program effects may be robust enough to appear despite inexact replication of a specific program model.

Method matters: About as much effect size variation is associated with the methodological differences between studies as with program characteristics. The mean effect size for nonrandomized control or comparison group designs is actually slightly smaller than for randomized designs. The inclusion of lower-quality studies would, on average, have the effect of slightly lowering the overall mean effect size, not inflating it. One-group pretest–posttest designs are capable of upwardly biasing the mean effect size.

Published versus unpublished studies: Published studies are more likely to report stronger effects than unpublished studies.

Eight Principles of Effective Correctional Intervention

Canadian scholars have joined with American criminologists at the University of Cincinnati to identify principles of effective (and ineffective) correctional interventions based on traditional program reviews and selected meta-analyses. The main focus of the Canadian and American researchers has been on using correctional outcome studies to develop a best practice model that integrates clinical and management practices in corrections. These best practices are stated as principles of effective correctional intervention (Andrews, 2006; Andrews & Bonta, 1998; Cullen & Gendreau, 2000).

The following version of principles of effective correctional intervention was compiled by the Crime and Justice Institute (2004) with support from the National Institute of Corrections. These principles are organized into the approximate order that they should be addressed in a corrections system, and they are based on a large body of research that has accumulated over the past 40 years or more (Crime and Justice Institute, 2004, pp. 18–21). Readers should be aware that these principles are based on reviews of the adult and juvenile correctional literature, so differences in their application to these two distinct offender groups are unknown. It should also be noted that there are other versions of the principles of effective correctional intervention (Box 8.4). The Crime and Justice Institute version that follows contains eight major principles, and the text supporting each of them was extracted from that report.

IN FOCUS 8.4
Principles of Effective Correctional Intervention

Andrews (2006, pp. 596–600) presents these as follows:

1. Use structured and validated risk or need assessment instruments.

2. Never assign low-risk cases to intensive service.

3. Reserve intensive services for moderate and higher-risk cases.

4. Always target a preponderance of relevant criminogenic needs.

5. Always use cognitive-behavioral and social learning interpersonal influence strategies.

6. Managers and supervisors must attend to the relationship and structural skills of service delivery staff.

7. Clinical supervision entails regular ongoing high-level modeling and reinforcement of relationship and structuring skills.

8. Make monitoring, feedback, and corrective action routine, as a matter of policy.

Principle 1: Assess actuarial risk and
needs (Crime and Justice Institute, 2004, p. 3).

Develop and maintain a complete system of ongoing offender risk screening or triage and need assessments. Assessing offenders in a reliable and valid manner is a prerequisite for the effective management (i.e., supervision and treatment) of offenders. Timely, relevant measures of offender risk and need at the individual and aggregate levels are essential for the implementation of numerous principles of best practice in corrections (e.g., risk, need, and responsivity). Offender assessments are most reliable and valid when staff are formally trained to administer tools. Screening and assessment tools that focus on dynamic and static risk factors, profile criminogenic needs, and have been validated on similar populations are preferred. They should also be supported by sufficiently detailed and accurately written procedures.

Principle 2: Enhance intrinsic motivation
(Crime and Justice Institute, 2004, p. 4).

Staff should relate to offenders in interpersonally sensitive and constructive ways to enhance intrinsic motivation in offenders. Behavioral change is an *inside job;* for lasting change to occur, a level of intrinsic motivation is needed. Motivation to change is dynamic, and the probability that change may occur is strongly influenced by interpersonal interactions, such as those with probation officers, treatment providers, and institution staff. Feelings of ambivalence that usually accompany change can be explored through motivational interviewing, a style and method of communication used to help people overcome their ambivalence about behavior changes. "Research strongly suggests that motivational interviewing techniques, rather than persuasion tactics, effectively enhance motivation for initiating and maintaining behavior changes" (p. 4). (But see Chapter 11.)

Principle 3: Target interventions (Crime and Justice
Institute, 2004, pp. 4–5). This principle has five components.

(a) **Risk principle (Crime and Justice Institute, 2004, p. 4).** Prioritize primary supervision and treatment resources for offenders who are at higher risk to reoffend. Research indicates that supervision and treatment resources that are focused on lower-risk offenders tend to produce little or no net positive effect on recidivism rates. Shifting these resources to higher-risk offenders promotes harm reduction and public safety because these offenders have greater need for prosocial skills and thinking and are more likely to be frequent offenders. Reducing the recidivism rates of these higher-risk offenders reaps a much larger bang for the buck. Successfully addressing this population requires smaller caseloads, the application of well-developed case plans, and placement of offenders into sufficiently intense cognitive–behavioral interventions that target their specific criminogenic needs.

(b) **Criminogenic need principle (Crime and Justice Institute, 2004, p. 4).** Address offenders' greatest criminogenic needs. Offenders have a variety of needs, some of which are directly linked to criminal behavior. These criminogenic needs are dynamic risk factors that, when addressed or changed, affect the offender's risk of recidivism. Examples of criminogenic needs are criminal personality; antisocial attitudes, values, and beliefs; low self-control; criminal peers; substance abuse; and dysfunctional family. Based on an assessment of the offender, these criminogenic needs can be prioritized so that services are focused on the greatest criminogenic needs.

(c) **Responsivity principle (Crime and Justice Institute, 2004, p. 5).** Responsivity requires consideration of individual characteristics when matching offenders to services. These characteristics include culture, gender, motivational stages, developmental stages, and learning styles. These factors influence an offender's responsiveness to different types of treatment. The principle of responsivity also requires that offenders be provided with treatment that is proven effective with the offender population. Certain treatment strategies, such as cognitive–behavioral methods, have consistently produced reductions in recidivism with offenders under rigorous research conditions. Providing appropriate responsivity to offenders involves selecting services in accordance with these factors, including matching treatment type to offender and matching style and methods of communication to offender's stage of change readiness.

(d) **Dosage (Crime and Justice Institute, 2004, p. 5).** Providing appropriate doses of services, prosocial structure, and supervision is a strategic application of resources. Higher-risk offenders need significantly more initial structure and services than lower-risk offenders. During the initial 3 to 9 months after release, 40–70% of their free time should be occupied with delineated routine and appropriate services (e.g., outpatient treatment, employment assistance, education). Certain offender subpopulations (e.g., severely mentally ill, chronic dual diagnosed) commonly need strategic, extensive, and extended services. However, too often individuals within these subpopulations are neither explicitly identified nor provided a coordinated package of supervision and services. The evidence indicates that incomplete or uncoordinated approaches can have negative effects, often wasting resources.

(e) **Treatment principle (Crime and Justice Institute, 2004, p. 5).** Treatment, particularly cognitive–behavioral types, should be applied as an integral part of the sentence and sanction process. Integrate treatment into sentence and sanction requirements through assertive case management (taking a proactive and strategic approach to supervision and case planning). Delivering targeted and timely treatment interventions will provide the greatest long-term benefit to the community, the victim, and the offender. This does not necessarily apply to lower-risk offenders, who should be diverted from the criminal justice and corrections systems whenever possible.

Principle 4: Skill train with directed practice (using cognitive–behavioral treatment methods) communities (Crime and Justice Institute, 2004, p. 6).

Provide best practice programming that emphasizes cognitive–behavioral strategies and is delivered by well-trained staff. To successfully deliver this treatment to offenders, staff must understand antisocial thinking, social learning, and appropriate communication techniques. Skills not only are taught to the offender but also are practiced or role-played, and the resulting prosocial attitudes and behaviors are positively reinforced by staff. Correctional agencies should prioritize, plan, and predominantly implement programs that have been scientifically proven to reduce recidivism.

Principle 5: Increase positive reinforcement communities (Crime and Justice Institute, 2004, p. 6).

When learning new skills and making behavioral changes, people appear to respond better and maintain learned behaviors for longer periods of time when approached with *carrots* (positive reinforcements or rewards) rather than *sticks* (punishments or negative reinforcements). Behaviorists recommend applying a higher ratio of positive reinforcements to negative reinforcements in order to achieve more sustained behavioral change. These rewards do not have to be applied consistently to be effective (as negative reinforcement does) but can be applied randomly. Increasing positive reinforcement should not be done at the expense of or undermine swift, certain, and meaningful responses for negative and unacceptable behavior.

Principle 6: Engage ongoing support in natural communities (Crime and Justice Institute, 2004, p. 6).

Realign and actively engage prosocial supports for offenders in their communities. Research indicates that many successful interventions with extreme populations (e.g., inner-city substance abusers, homeless, dual diagnosed) actively recruit and use family members, spouses, and supportive others in the offender's immediate environment to positively reinforce desired new behaviors. This Community Reinforcement Approach has been found effective for a variety of behaviors (e.g., unemployment, alcoholism, substance abuse, and marital conflicts).

Principle 7: Measure relevant processes and practices (Crime and Justice Institute, 2004, p. 7).

Accurate and detailed documentation of case information, along with a formal and valid mechanism for measuring outcomes, is the foundation of best practices. Agencies must routinely assess offender change in cognitive and skill development and evaluate offender recidivism if services are to remain effective. In addition to routine measurement and documentation of offender change, staff performance should also be regularly assessed. Staffs that are periodically evaluated for performance achieve greater fidelity to program design, service delivery principles, and outcomes. Staff whose performance is not consistently monitored, measured, and subsequently reinforced work less cohesively and more often at cross-purposes and provide less support to the agency mission.

Principle 8: Provide measurement feedback (Crime and Justice Institute, 2004, p. 7).

Once a method for measuring relevant processes and practices is in place (Principle 7), the information must be used to monitor process and change. Providing feedback to offenders about their progress builds accountability and is associated with greater motivation for change, lower treatment attrition, and improved outcomes (e.g., reduced drink or drug days, treatment engagement, goal achievement). The same is true within an organization. Monitoring delivery of services and fidelity to procedures helps build accountability and maintain integrity to the agency's mission. Regular performance audits and case reviews with an eye toward improved outcomes keep staff focused on the ultimate goal of reduced recidivism through the use of best practices.

The Crime and Justice Institute advises that the framework of principles and the organizational development model they make up should be operationalized at three critical levels: the individual case, the agency, and the system. At each of these levels, thorough, comprehensive, and strategic planning is necessary for success. Identifying, prioritizing, and formulating well-timed plans are tasks requiring system collaboration and a focus on organizational development (Crime and Justice Institute, 2004, p. 8).

Implementation Issues With Best Practice Programming

Attention to implementation issues is at the forefront of best practice programming. New initiatives have been undertaken to facilitate fidelity in best practice program implementation. Four noteworthy examples are described here.

First, implementation issues are best illustrated in the Safe and Drug-Free Schools State Grants program of the U.S. Department of Education. It requires grant recipients at the state and local level to implement activities that are based on scientific research under its Principles of Effectiveness policy (Hallfors & Godette, 2002). However, early research shows that schools continue to select heavily marketed curricula that either have not proven to be effective or have not been evaluated at all, such as DARE, Here's Looking at You, and McGruff Drug Prevention (Hallfors & Godette, 2002). The latter three programs were most frequently funded by school districts, and only 59% of the school district coordinators reported that their district used any of the six research-based programs that the U.S. Department of Education had disseminated to them under its Principles of Effectiveness initiative (p. 465). Results from a sample of 104 school districts in 12 states indicated that many districts were selecting research-based curricula but that the quality of implementation was low: Only 19% of the responding district coordinators indicated that their schools were implementing a research-based curriculum with fidelity (p. 461). A study of the implementation of one of the six research-based programs (Reconnecting Youth, a school-based drug prevention program) in 10 schools in two school districts in the United States did not produce successful outcomes (Hallfors et al., 2006). A companion study (Thaker et al., 2007) revealed several obstacles that appeared to contribute to poor implementation. Certain program characteristics made it difficult to implement Reconnecting Youth, and these meant that schools had to significantly change their usual practices to implement the program. Organizational barriers included a lack of financial resources and a lack of school leadership in support of the program. Finally, staff turnover and district-wide scheduling and curriculum changes all resulted in high levels of organizational turbulence at most schools, further hindering program implementation.

Second, the Blueprints Project achieved a high level of fidelity (Elliott & Mihalic, 2004; Mihalic & Irwin, 2003) in a study of implementation integrity in 147 sites (violence prevention programs were implemented at 42 sites and Life Skills Training, a drug prevention program, was implemented at 105 sites). To check on sustainability, telephone interviews with each of the 42 site coordinators of the violence prevention programs (6 months after funding for the initiative ended) indicated that 35 sites were still implementing the programs (Elliott & Mihalic, 2004). The researchers attributed this high level of sustainability "to careful site selection, provision of training and technical assistance, and monitoring of the quality and level of implementation with immediate feedback to the local site implementers" (p. 50).

However, replication of the 10 Blueprint programs was hampered by lack of capacity of the program developers to facilitate the process. Only 4 of the 10 programs had the organizational capacity to deliver their programs to 10 or more sites a year. Other factors also enhanced or impeded successful implementation of the programs. The researchers concluded that most replication failures can be traced to limited site capacity, inadequate site preparation, or lack of readiness. Many of the sites were not ready to undertake implementation of a Blueprint Program (see Table 9.1). The researchers concluded, "Our own experience shows that sites are seldom prepared to implement and sustain programs. We believe that any statewide or national prevention initiative must include ample time and money for local capacity building prior to implementing programs and that some independent monitoring of the quality of training, technical assistance, and fidelity is essential if the potential prevention effects are to be realized" (Elliott & Mihalic, 2004, p. 51).

Fidelity (or integrity) of implementation is a major impediment to successful transfer of all types of evidence-based programs into practice (Gambrill, 2006). Ely and his colleagues (2002) identified 56 different obstacles to evidence-based practice in medicine alone. Future research must address not only impediments to achieving initial implementation fidelity but also obstacles to maintaining fidelity. This latter issue has not been researched at all. Henggeler and colleagues (2006) suggest that R&D program models should be researched for transportability, which addresses conditions that affect the implementation and outcomes of a particular treatment model when it is implemented in practice conditions. They buttress their argument with outcomes for Multisystemic Therapy in Norway and Canada (p. 452). In Norway, three of the four sites in the transportability trial demonstrated positive effects; in contrast, only one of the four sites in the Canadian transportability trial did so (see also Littell, 2006). The slippage reported when Blueprint projects were implemented in Washington State (Barnoski, 2004b) is another reminder that even the best programs encounter problems in transferring research to practice settings.

Backer (1993) identified four conditions that are necessary for program transfers to be effective:

- Appropriate innovations must be brought to the attention of organizations and be made accessible for dissemination.
- Evidence must show that the use of the innovation is feasible and effective.
- Resources must be adequate.
- Interventions must be provided that encourage organizations to change.

No doubt, there are many other obstacles to transportability. Funding sources may dry up. It is difficult to retain highly trained staff in competitive job markets. Another attractive program sometimes comes along. State or local program managers or administrators may change, bringing in officials who themselves somehow know what works without consulting research, or prefer to use the "watermelon thumping" method (Box 9.1, Chapter 9). Simpson (2002, pp. 174–176) provides a straightforward program change model, a heuristic framework, or steps involved in transferring research to practice. He identifies four action steps (exposure, adoption, implementation, and practice):

1. *Exposure* is the first stage, usually involving training through lecture, self-study, workshops, or expert consultants.

2. The second stage, *adoption,* represents an intention by management to try an innovation.

3. *Implementation,* the third stage of change, calls for the addition of resources and an atmosphere conducive to acting on a decision to adopt an innovation.

4. In the final stage, *practice,* is the action of incorporating an innovation into regular use and sustaining it.

Organizations are being formed to address fidelity problems. The Coalition for Evidence-Based Policy (2003) recommends the establishment of a federal "what works" clearinghouse "that provides authoritative, user-friendly information to practitioners on evidence-backed interventions" (p. 17). One such clearinghouse has been established at the direction of the White House, called the Helping America's Youth Community Guide (see Chapter 7 and Box 7.4).

Third, an Association for the Advancement of Evidence Based Practice (http://www.aaebp.org/) has been formed. The AAEBP's mission is to promote the development, adoption, and effective implementation of best practice programs for at-risk youth and families and increase the number of youth and families served by such programs. Although this organization looks similar to the Blueprints Project, which promotes mainly a few R&D program models, the AAEBP has assured interested parties that it will have a broader objective of helping providers and program developers to design, develop, test, and implement more effective best practice programs and practices. Similarly, the National Implementation Research Network (http://nirn.fmhi.usf.edu/) has as its stated purpose to advance the science of implementation across domains (e.g., mental health, substance abuse, education, juvenile justice) by

- Conducting implementation research and evaluation
- Developing and updating syntheses of relevant implementation research and practice descriptions

Fourth, some states have created centers to promote the implementation of best practices for youth with mental health disorders in communities throughout their states. These centers provide information, assistance, and training to communities interested in implementing best practices and often serve as liaisons to program developers to ensure that implementation efforts are structured and adhere to the recommended protocols associated with each particular intervention. These centers typically are supported by a combination of public and private funds. States that have created such centers include Connecticut, Ohio, Pennsylvania, and Colorado (National Center for Mental Health and Juvenile Justice, http://www.ncmhjj.com/Blueprint/default.shtml).

The SPEP that Mark Lipsey has developed will be unveiled in Chapter 9. Statewide evaluations of juvenile justice programs have been conducted with this tool in two states that have participated in its development. This tool holds a great deal of promise for achieving best practices on a statewide basis.

The most promising approach seems to be to embed best practices in a comprehensive framework that comprises the entire juvenile justice continuum. We offer a framework in Chapter 10 that is driven by local program gaps, need assessments data on offenders, and a strategic system-wide planning process. Such a framework provides a platform for evaluating programs across the board and making system-wide program improvements.

Discussion Topics

1. What are the strengths and weaknesses of the various approaches to translating the best programs into everyday practice?

2. Why are program providers and state program administrators reluctant to make and implement research-based decisions?

3. If you were a correctional administrator of a system that is in disarray, what steps would you take to institute best practices?

4. Where does the juvenile justice system stand in terms of achieving a balance between punishment and rehabilitation of offenders?

5. Why do some of the best programs increase recidivism when poorly implemented?

CHAPTER 9

Effective Prevention and Rehabilitation Programs

I begin this chapter with a discussion of four key myths about juvenile justice programs. The discussion of these myths also highlights research on juvenile justice programs. I then provide examples of effective programs for juvenile offenders, followed by a review of important research on the costs and benefits of juvenile justice programs. The chapter concludes with a brief illustration of how communities can use the growing knowledge base concerning the most effective ways to improve juvenile justice system programs.

Myths Versus Research Evidence

Four key myths dominate public opinion about juvenile justice programs. The first one—that nothing works—has been predominant for more than three decades, as we saw in Chapter 8. I address this myth in this section, as well as the other three key myths: that the juvenile courts are not effective, that the juvenile justice system is not effective with serious and violent juvenile offenders, and that community-based programs that serve as alternatives to incarceration for serious and violent juveniles are ineffective. These myths are central to ending the debate over the future role of the juvenile court.

Myth: Nothing Works With Juvenile Offenders

As seen in Chapter 8, the "nothing works" myth has dominated the field since the mid-1970s, when a review of program evaluations in juvenile and criminal justice systems was released (Lipton et al., 1975; Martinson, 1974).

This view was buttressed by scary predictions of a coming wave of super-predators and a bloodbath and by the ensuing despair that the juvenile justice system could not stem the tide. But studies of the relative effectiveness of juvenile justice programs have consistently been positive since the early 1980s, for two main reasons. First, the program evaluation base has expanded significantly, providing a deeper and more detailed body of empirical evidence about the effects of rehabilitative programs for juvenile offenders (Lipsey, 1999b, p. 613). Second, the quantitative technique of meta-analysis emerged; this technique allows researchers to analyze and synthesize data so that they can summarize program evaluation results. It also enables them to examine a wider range of program evaluations in a more systematic manner than was possible in the past (Lipsey & Wilson, 2000; see Box 8.2 for a discussion of meta-analysis).

More than a dozen meta-analyses have been conducted on evaluations of the effects of rehabilitative programs on recidivism, especially for juvenile offenders (for a complete reference list, see Lipsey & Cullen, 2007). As Lipsey (1999b) noted earlier, these are important because "it is no exaggeration to say that meta-analysis of research on the effectiveness of rehabilitative programming has reversed the conclusion of the prior generation of [program-by-program] reviews on this topic" (p. 614). This is particularly true with respect to juvenile offender programs. Nevertheless, the myth of ineffective juvenile justice programs continues to be perpetuated in the juvenile justice literature (see Feld, 2003; Hsia & Beyer, 2000; Schwartz et al., 1998).

Lipsey's (1992; see also Lipsey, 1995, 2007) meta-analyses have been instrumental in debunking the "nothing works" myth with respect to juvenile rehabilitation programs. His initial meta-analysis included nearly 400 experimentally designed studies of general delinquency treatment published since 1950. Contrary to the myth, Lipsey found that juveniles in treatment groups had recidivism rates about 10% lower than those of untreated juveniles. The best intervention programs produced up to a 37% reduction in recidivism rates and similar improvements in other outcomes. These treatment programs typically focused on changing overt behavior through structured training or behavior modification interventions designed to improve interpersonal relations, self-control, school achievement, and specific job skills. Treatment programs found to be most effective were "more structured and focused treatments (e.g., behavioral, skill-oriented) and multi-modal treatments seem to be more effective than the less structured and unfocused treatments (e.g., counseling)" (Lipsey, 1992, p. 123). After completing his review, Lipsey (1995) observed,

> It is no longer constructive for researchers, practitioners, and policy-makers to argue about whether delinquency treatment and related rehabilitative approaches "work," as if that were a question that could be answered with a simple "yes" or "no." As a generality, treatment clearly works. We must get on with the business of developing and identifying the treatment models that will be most effective and providing them to the juveniles they will benefit. (p. 78)

Myth: The Juvenile Justice System Is Not Effective

Lipsey's work has also helped to debunk the myth that juvenile courts are not effective. In a meta-analysis of more than 500 juvenile justice programs, Lipsey (2007) found that most of them reduce recidivism. Recidivism rates (new offenses) in more than 200 court supervision programs ranged from 21% to 34%, depending on how closely the evaluated programs corresponded with features of the most effective programs in the meta-analytic database. Another review of court data from selected localities found that, on average, only 15% of juvenile probationers were re-adjudicated for offenses committed while they were under court supervision (Snyder & Sickmund, 2006, p. 235). Recidivism among youths released from secure juvenile correctional facilities is higher, of course, ranging from 25% (reconfined rate) to 55% (rearrested rate) (p. 234). These recidivism rates compare very favorably with rates for the adult criminal justice system (see Chapter 11).

Myth: The Juvenile Justice System Is Ineffective With Serious, Violent, and Chronic Offenders

The myth that the juvenile justice system cannot handle serious, violent, and chronic juvenile offenders has emanated mainly from the general public's acceptance of the "superpredator" image of juvenile offenders. As described in Chapter 1, a number of observers have disseminated the myth of this hypothetical "new breed" of juvenile offenders who are beyond redemption (and thus presumably cannot be rehabilitated). In addition, this new generation of juvenile offenders presumably includes a larger proportion of serious and violent offenders than earlier generations; these offenders are said to commit more crimes and to begin committing violent and serious offenses at younger ages than their predecessors. But, as I have also noted in Chapter 1, the research evidence does not support these presumptions (Snyder, 1998; Snyder & Sickmund, 2000; Zimring, 1998a).

Several studies have shown that the juvenile justice system is effective with violent and chronic offenders. In an Arizona study, Snyder (1988) found that only 17% of the offenders initially referred to the Maricopa County court for violent offenses returned for a second violent offense. Thus these courts prevented the overwhelming majority of violent offenders from becoming repeat violent offenders.

Lipsey and Wilson's (1998) meta-analysis of 200 programs for serious and violent juvenile offenders is the most comprehensive study on this topic (see also Lipsey, Wilson, & Cothern, 2000). This analysis showed that the average juvenile justice system program serving serious and violent juveniles reduced recidivism about 12% in comparison with control groups, a slightly larger effect than programs for delinquents in general, which an earlier meta-analysis found to be about 10% (Lipsey, 1992, 1995). The best programs for serious and violent delinquents were capable of reducing recidivism rates by as much as 49%, a 12% larger reduction than the best programs for delinquents in general (up to 37%; Lipsey, 1995). These very best programs tended to be highly structured; focus on developing skills (interpersonal skills, academic and employment skills); use behavioral and cognitive–behavioral methods (with follow-up reinforcements), including social learning techniques such as modeling, role playing, and graduated practice; and use multiple components to address offenders' problems in multiple domains (e.g., individual, family, school, peer group, and community). As Lipsey and Wilson observe, "If anything, then, it would appear that the typical intervention in these studies is more effective with serious offenders than with less serious offenders" (p. 332)—just the opposite of the myth.

Myth: Community-Based Programs for Juveniles Are Ineffective

The history of the juvenile justice system is distinctive for its vacillation between policies supporting incarceration and the use of community-based alternatives to confinement (Finestone, 1976). Increased use of incarceration typically follows moral panics (Bernard, 1992). As I have shown in Chapter 3, more use of confinement has been a predominant response to the current moral panic over juvenile delinquency.

The promise of alternatives to incarceration for juvenile offenders has changed dramatically over the past 25 years. A major issue remained unresolved, however: Are community-based alternatives more effective than juvenile reformatories, particularly with serious and violent offenders? For more than two decades after the "nothing works" report (Lipton et al., 1975), the conclusion that prevailed was that community-based programs are only about as effective as juvenile correctional programs (Krisberg, Currie, Onek, & Wiebush, 1995). Now community alternatives can be used more widely, based on Lipsey and Wilson's (1998) meta-analysis showing that they can be effective even with serious violent offenders. In addition, Aos, Phipps, Barnoski, and Lieb (2001) have conducted a comprehensive cost–benefit study, and their results indicate that community-based programs are far more cost beneficial than institution-based treatment.

Translating Knowledge of What Works Into Practice

Implementation of effective human service is not simply a matter of selecting an evidence-based program off the shelf.

—Andrews (2006, p. 595)

At present, we have little evidence about the effects of taking best practice programs to scale in public health and related areas of mental health, education, welfare, and criminal justice. . . . The simple truth is that we do not yet know much about how best to translate research findings into advice for practitioners that they can and will actually use effectively.

—Lipsey (2005, p. 3)

These two quotations remind us that applying research knowledge of what works into practice is not a straightforward process and that large-scale transfers have not yet been successful.

This section reviews two of the three major approaches for moving research into practice: the model program approach and systematic reviews. The third option, evaluating your program as you implement it, is unnecessary in many cases because of the rich body of knowledge that is available from the model program approach and systematic reviews. I will also show in this chapter that there is such a rich body of knowledge on effective programs that program managers should never import untested programs. Edward Latessa has dubbed this method "watermelon thumping" (Box 9.1). Now several repositories of model programs and systematic reviews exist (Box 9.2). It is clear that systematic reviews are gaining popularity, and they are featured in this chapter.

IN FOCUS 9.1

Watermelon Thumping for Success

Widely respected criminologist Edward Latessa is well known for his humorous characterizations of criminal justice practices, which he uses so effectively in public presentations. A favorite is the following one, in which he likens state administrators' selection of program models to watermelon thumping. When he was a child, Ed's dad allowed him to tag along on trips to the farmer's market to purchase a watermelon. Ed watched his father as he thumped several watermelons. Time and again, Ed asked his father why he thumped them. Invariably, his father simply said, "I'm selecting the best one." Because of his father's success, his method impressed Ed so much that he later began thumping watermelons when he went to the market to purchase a watermelon, with his kids in tow. Sure enough, Ed's children asked him the same question that he asked of his dad: "What are you doing, Dad?" Of course, Ed relied on his father's response: "I'm selecting the best one." But, Ed confesses, "I have no earthly idea what I'm listening for." It is most unfortunate for kids, Ed says, that the main method state officials commonly use to select programs is much like watermelon thumping.

IN FOCUS 9.2

Repositories of Model Programs and Systematic Reviews

Model Programs

- Helping America's Youth Community Guide: http://guide.helpingamer icasyouth.gov/
- Model Programs Guide (Office of Juvenile Justice and Delinquency Prevention): http://www.dsgonline.com/mpg2.5/mpg_index.htm
- Blueprints for Violence Prevention: http://www.colorado.edu/cspv/index.html
- National Registry of Effective Programs and Practices (Substance Abuse and Mental Health Services Administration, U.S. Department of Health and Human Services): http://modelprograms.samhsa.gov
- Exemplary and Promising Safe, Disciplined and Drug-Free Schools Programs (U.S. Department of Education): http://www.ed.gov/admins/lead/safety/exem plary01/index.html
- What Works Clearinghouse, U.S. Department of Education (on educational interventions, some of which address youth violence and substance abuse prevention): http://ies.ed.gov/ncee/wwc/

Systematic Reviews

- *The University of Maryland* (Sherman, Farrington, MacKenzie, & Welsh, 2006)
- *Community Guide to Community Preventive Services,* Centers for Disease Control and Prevention (on community, population, and healthcare system strategies to address a variety of public health and health promotion topics for violence prevention, including reduction of firearm violence, therapeutic foster care, and universal school-based programs): http://www.thecommunityguide.org/violence/default.htm
- Principles of Effective Correctional Intervention (University of Cincinnati Corrections Institute): http://www.uc.edu/corrections/training.html
- The Campbell Crime and Justice Coordinating Group: http://www.aic .gov.au/campbellcj/reviews/titles.html
- Center for Evaluation Research and Methodology, Vanderbilt Institute for Public Policy Studies: http://www.vanderbilt.edu/cerm/ (contact: Dr. Mark Lipsey)

One Model Program Approach

The Center for the Study and Prevention of Violence (CSPV) conducted a program-by-program review of a wide range of prevention and rehabilitation programs for children and adolescents (Mihalic et al., 2001).

Although the acclaimed effective programs were called violence prevention programs, the list was not limited to prevention or violence. Drug treatment programs and general delinquency reduction programs were also included. The researchers used rigorous scientific criteria to identify effective programs in a literature review. A program had to meet the following criteria to be declared effective: a strong research design with evidence of a deterrent effect on violence, delinquency, or substance abuse; sustained effects at least 1 year beyond treatment; and replication with demonstrated effects at more than one site for at least 1 year after treatment. These very restrictive indicators of successful programs netted fewer than a dozen programs, many of which are research and demonstration programs. Unfortunately, these criteria excluded from consideration most evaluated juvenile justice system programs, which typically do not have the necessary resources for replication in other sites. Nevertheless, because of the restrictive review criteria, the blueprint programs are considered the most effective or "exemplary" youth programs known to date. As a drawback, though, most research and development programs are evaluated by the developers (Petrosino & Soydan, 2005), which raises some skepticism about the outcomes. But numerous other possible explanations for the greater success of research and demonstration programs were noted in Chapter 8.

The CSPV study identified 11 programs that meet the above criteria (Table 9.1), and 19 other programs were found to be promising. The 11 designated effective programs (one is no longer recognized as a Blueprint program, but another one has been added) have been written up in the form of "blueprints" for jurisdictions interested in replicating them (see Mihalic et al., 2001). The federal Office of Juvenile Justice and Delinquency Prevention supported extensive training and technical assistance to jurisdictions wanting to implement any of the 10 programs.

I must attach several caveats to the CSPV's list of effective programs. First, the eligibility criteria are so stringent that few (if any) everyday, practical programs could ever qualify, because of lack of program resources. Second, it is likely that success with these programs would be noteworthy, but it is very difficult to replicate research and development programs, for reasons that I will discuss shortly. Third, one program that the CSPV declared effective, the 1991 Olweus Bullying Prevention Program, actually has had mixed results (Baldry & Farrington, 2007; Rigby, 2004). One meta-analysis of all types of evaluated bullying prevention programs concluded that "the effectiveness of antibullying programs is not proven" (Baldry & Farrington, 2007, p. 201), and another one concluded that the positive effects are too small to have practical benefits (Ferguson, Miguel, Kilburn, & Sanchez, 2007).

The client outcomes of full-scale blueprint replications have not yet been reported, with the exception of statewide implementation of 2 of the 11 programs in Washington State. Information on that initiative follows.

The Washington State legislature mandated that only effective programs shall be funded and implemented in the state. It commissioned the Washington State Institute for Public Policy (WSIPP) to undertake

Table 9.1   Blueprint Programs

Effective Programs

- Midwestern Prevention Project
- Big Brothers Big Sisters of America
- Functional Family Therapy
- Quantum Opportunities Program*
- Life Skills Training
- Multisystemic Therapy
- Nurse-Family Partnership
- Multidimensional Treatment Foster Care
- Olweus Bullying Prevention Program
- Promoting Alternative Thinking Strategies
- The Incredible Years: Parent, Teacher, and Child Training Series
- Project Towards No Drug Abuse

*No longer a Blueprint program.

NOTE: Information on all of the programs listed in this table can be accessed online at http://www.colorado.edu/cspv/blueprints.

an exhaustive cost–benefit analysis of juvenile rehabilitation programs to identify those that would be cost beneficial (Aos et al., 2001). Based on the WSIPP's (2002) recommendations, localities chose to implement one or more among three well-known and research-based programs, the first two of which are Blueprint programs: Functional Family Therapy (FFT), Multisystemic Therapy (MST), and Aggression Replacement Training (ART). The basic findings from the WSIPP evaluation follow (Barnoski, 2004b, p. 1).

- When FFT was delivered competently, the program reduced felony recidivism by 38%. The cost–benefit analyses found that FFT generates $2.77 in savings (avoided crime costs) for each taxpayer dollar spent on the program, regardless of therapist competence. For competent FFT therapists, the savings would be greater: $10.69 in benefits for each taxpayer dollar spent.
- When competently delivered, ART had positive outcomes, with estimated reductions in 18-month felony recidivism of 24% and a benefit to cost ratio of $11.66.
- Because of problems implementing the WSIPP evaluation design, no findings were associated with MST.

However, both the FFT and ART programs actually increased recidivism in sites across Washington State when they were poorly implemented. Figure 9.1 shows the outcomes for FFT. Three outcome measures are shown, and the results are similar for each measure. When FFT therapist groups delivered FFT competently (with a high degree of fidelity, shown in the third bar of each set) recidivism in the treatment group was lower than in the control group (the first bar of each set). But when low fidelity was evident (not competent), recidivism was higher than in the control group; in other words, the FFT services appeared to cause an increase in delinquency under this condition. Similar outcomes were seen for ART, which performed as well as FFT when implemented with high fidelity, and delinquency increases were seen with low fidelity. Outcomes of the many other Blueprint project replications across the United States have not yet been reported.

Correctional Program Assessment Inventory

A second source of information on what works is the Correctional Program Assessment Inventory (CPAI, now called the Correctional Program Checklist). The CPAI (Gendreau & Andrews, 1996, 2001; Gendreau, Goggin, & Smith, 2001; Matthews, Hubbard, & Latessa, 2001) is based on the Canadian and American principles of effective correctional intervention described in Chapter 8. It provides specifications for successful adult and juvenile correctional programs. For example, following the research-based principles, such a program "should focus on higher risk offenders; deliver cognitive–behavioral or behavioral interventions that focus on relevant criminogenic needs; attend to the qualifications, skills, and values of staff; and evaluate what they do" (Lowenkamp, Latessa, & Smith, 2006, p. 577; see also Jones & Wyant, 2007). The CPAI was developed to gauge adherence to these principles of effective correctional intervention— that is, program fidelity. Its utility is enhanced even more when it is used in

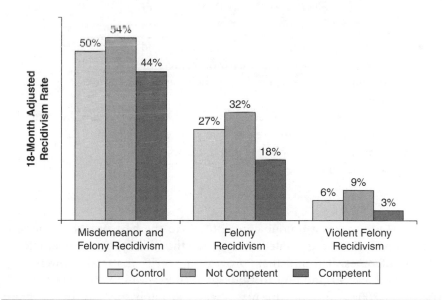

Figure 9.1   Functional Family Therapy Recidivism Rates

conjunction with the Youth Level of Service/Case Management Inventory (YLS/CMI). Developers of the YLS/CMI report that it creates typologies of youthful offenders based on their risk and needs that reliably predict reoffending (Flores, Travis, & Latessa, 2003).

A recent study (Lowenkamp et al., 2006) investigated the relationship between the CPAI and program outcome using program integrity indicators and offender data from 38 halfway houses in Ohio (Box 9.3). Adult parolees from prison (the Ohio Department of Rehabilitation and Correction) comprised the offender sample. Three recidivism measures were used (return to prison, a new offense, and technical violations) and offenders were tracked over a two-year follow-up period. The central purpose of this study was to determine whether or not the proposed characteristics of effective correctional programs actually correlated highly with offender outcomes. The CPAI was used to structure data collection and analysis variables related to program integrity. An abbreviated version of the CPAI was used that covered the following areas: program implementation, client pre-service assessment, program characteristics, evaluation (how well a program evaluates itself on quality assurance and outcomes), and an "other" category containing miscellaneous items. Indeed, the researchers found a "fairly strong" correlation between the total CPAI score and all three outcome measures, indicating that "program implementation, offender assessment, and evaluation are all important in determining the effectiveness of a correctional program" (p. 588).

IN FOCUS 9.3

How the CPAI Process Works

- Pre- and post-evaluations of existing services and practices are made to see how they align with the "what works" literature.
- A risk and criminogenic need assessment instrument is used to classify offenders.
- Training is provided in effective strategies in the "what works" literature.
- Ongoing technical assistance assists in service improvement.
- Performance data are collected and tracked.
- Process and outcome evaluations are done.

This study makes a unique contribution to the best practice programming. It is the first large-scale fidelity study that links program characteristics to outcomes. It found that "program integrity matters" (Lowenkamp et al., 2006, p. 590), adding to findings in the Washington State research (Barnoski, 2004b). Second, this new research strongly suggests that program features can be manipulated to achieve better outcomes (lower recidivism).

This prospect holds considerable promise in suggesting that better outcomes can be produced by improving existing programs. Unfortunately, juveniles were not included in the study, but the findings should apply to them as well. As is the case with juvenile programs, there is much room for improvement in adult treatment and rehabilitation programs. Gendreau et al.'s (2001) summary of the overall findings of the three largest CPAI surveys revealed that 70% of all programs failed according to the CPAI. Low intensity (frequency) of treatment was a key factor accounting for specific program deficits.

Lipsey's Practical Program Evaluation Tool

Mark Lipsey has amassed by far the most comprehensive database of delinquency prevention and juvenile justice system program evaluations. His is the only complete database of juvenile justice program evaluations, and he is an international leader of meta-analysis, having perfected the uses of this remarkable method of synthesizing program research on a large body of studies. His database consists of all known published and unpublished studies of juvenile justice program evaluations since 1950 on which reports are available in English. Out of more than 10,000 studies that Lipsey and his staff reviewed, nearly 650 of them used control groups. Lipsey winnowed the studies that qualified for inclusion in his meta-analytic database down to 509 studies (Table 9.2).

As shown in Chapter 8, Lipsey demonstrated the enormous variability in program outcomes for juvenile justice studies (see Figure 8.2). He also showed that although many everyday programs are quite effective, there's plenty of room for improvement in most of them (see Table 8.2). These findings inspired him to develop a tool that incorporates the features of the most effective juvenile justice programs and use it to score programs against best practice guidelines and engage service providers in improving existing programs.

A significant advantage of the synthesis approach over the model program approach is that it generally draws on a much larger number of

Table 9.2   Lipsey's Current Database on the Effects of Intervention With Juvenile Offenders

Offenders	Number of Studies
Preadjudication (at risk)	178
Court supervision (probation)	216
Committed	90
Aftercare	25
Total	509

studies to reveal the common denominators in effective programs. "If the synthesis finds reasonable consistency in the effects across this diversity, practitioners and policymakers have some assurance that program effects may be robust enough to appear despite inexact replication of a given program model" (Lipsey, 2005, p. 2).

If the synthesis finds differential effects with program variation, Lipsey (2005) envisioned that it may be possible to determine which characteristics are associated with the strongest effects and to translate those relationships into program guidelines for practitioners and policy makers. "The meta-analysis techniques now available for such applications provide sophisticated tools for investigating both the consistency of effects and the characteristics associated with their differences" (p. 2) (see also Lipsey & Wilson, 2000).

In his meta-analysis of 509 juvenile justice programs, Lipsey (2007) identified five main features of effective juvenile delinquency prevention and treatment programs:

- *Primary service:* The primary service (most predominant therapeutic element) is effective, independent of its use with another intervention.
- *Supplementary services:* Adding another service component to a primary service often increases its effectiveness.
- *Treatment amount:* The amount of service provided is sufficient, as indicated by service frequency, program duration, and program quality.
- *Treatment quality:* Service quality and quality of implementation influence effectiveness.
- *Youth risk level:* Programs are generally more effective with high-risk offenders than for low-risk offenders.

These are key features of effective programs across the entire juvenile justice continuum: prevention, court intervention, and correctional programs. Lipsey discovered that the configurations of programs have a considerable impact on their effectiveness. It is commonly assumed that the juvenile justice system treatment enterprise is organized in a series of large-scale programs. In reality, this is not the case. For example, in the aforementioned meta-analysis the average evaluated program incorporated 5.6 treatment elements. Rather, communities typically tie multiple interventions together in myriad combinations. In Lipsey's meta-analytic approach, what constitutes a program typically is defined more broadly in terms of effective primary services (i.e., the active treatment ingredients) that are used in many programs (Lipsey, 2007).

The Standardized Program Evaluation Protocol

The Standardized Program Evaluation Protocol (or SPEP) is an evidence-based rating scheme for assessing the effectiveness of programs for reducing the recidivism of juvenile offenders (Lipsey, 2007; Lipsey, Howell, & Tidd, 2003). It assigns points to specific program characteristics according to their relationship to recidivism outcomes in the available research (Howell & Lipsey, 2004a, 2004b). Different ratings and point allocations are defined for different types of program services, classified and scored according to the primary and supplemental services they provide, the amount of service provided (measured in terms of frequency, duration, and proportion of clients who receive them), treatment quality, and the risk level of the clients who receive specific services.

Some funded programs cannot be rated with a SPEP instrument. These are purely structures, without therapeutic content. That is, they provide a setting or context that fulfills specific intervention needs or requirements other than service delivery (e.g., a detention facility, shelter care, foster care, graduated sanctions). These structures do not have a specific therapeutic content (interactions with clients specifically intended to bring about behavioral change), so they are not rated by an SPEP. However, program structures such as these are very important to have in a community and should be acknowledged in descriptions and assessments of the juvenile justice continuum.

Table 9.3 shows a grouping of juvenile delinquency treatment programs for serious and violent offenders according to their relative effectiveness (based on effect sizes shown in parentheses) in a meta-analysis (Lipsey & Wilson, 1998). Note the differences in service effectiveness rankings for the two categories of offenders: noninstitutionalized and institutionalized. This is an indication of what works best for whom in these two treatment settings. Lipsey's discovery of a wide variation in effect sizes shown here was important because it suggested to him that he could assign proportional values to service types based on the research showing their relative effectiveness.

Lipsey conducted subsequent meta-analyses to identify effective programs for general delinquents. The results of these meta-analyses have also permitted him to drill down into these effective programs and isolate the specific features of effective programs. A major discovery of his is that specific services—primary services and supplementary services—account for a large amount of the delinquency reduction potential of programs. He also has identified common features of the most effective programs in the research, which can be used to rate existing programs in terms of their expected effectiveness.

Table 9.4 shows the three major program effectiveness criteria and the point values associated with each of them. About 40% of the variation in recidivism effects is associated with type of program, so each SPEP allocates a maximum of 35 points for the primary service with the option of another 5 points for an eligible supplementary service that boosts the effectiveness of that particular primary service. Another 40% of the total value of a program is associated with the second criterion, fidelity of program implementation, which is measured in terms of amount of service (frequency and duration, 25%) and quality of service (15%). The third criterion, risk level of all juveniles who are served in the program, is allocated up to 20 points. All SPEPs used across the entire juvenile justice system continuum contain

Table 9.3   Effectiveness of Interventions for Serious and Violent Juvenile
Offenders

Type of Treatment Used With Noninstitutionalized Offenders	Type of Treatment Used With Institutionalized Offenders
Positive Effects, Consistent Evidence	
Individual counseling (.46)	Interpersonal skills (.39)
Interpersonal skills (.44)	Teaching family homes (.34)
Behavioral programs (.42)	
Positive Effects, Less Consistent Evidence	
Multiple services (.29)	Behavioral programs (.33)
Restitution with probation or parole (.15)	Community residential (.28)
	Multiple services (.20)
Mixed But Generally Positive Effects, Inconsistent Evidence	
Employment related (.22)	Individual counseling (.15)
Academic programs (.20)	Guided group counseling (.09)
Advocacy or casework (.19)	Group counseling (.05)
Family counseling (.19)	
Group counseling (.10)	
Weak or No Effects, Inconsistent Evidence	
Reduced caseload, probation or parole (−.04)	Employment related (.15)
	Drug abstinence (.08)
	Wilderness challenge (.07)
Weak or No Effects, Consistent Evidence	
Wilderness challenge (.12)	Milieu therapy (.08)
Early release, probation, or parole (.03)	
Deterrence programs (−.06)	
Vocational programs (−.18)	

NOTE: The midpoints of estimated effect sizes are shown in parentheses.

these three common denominators of effective programs, that is, the features of the most effective evaluated programs in Lipsey's database.

Based on his meta-analyses of programs for general delinquents, Lipsey groups programs according to their relative effectiveness for prevention clients, juvenile offenders on probation, and institutionalized offenders. As shown in Table 9.5, Lipsey divides the primary service types (found in the delinquency program evaluation literature) for juveniles on probation into three groups, on the basis of their average effect sizes: above-average effects, average effects, and below-average effects. The top group is allocated a

Table 9.4   The Relative Contribution of Different Program Factors to Recidivism Reduction

- 40% Type of program (major service type and supplemental services)
- 40% Program implementation
  - o   25% Amount of service
  - o   15% Treatment quality
- 20% Risk level of juveniles

maximum of 100 points. The average effects group can score a maximum of 90 points (because their primary services earn only 25 points) and the below-average effects programs can reach a maximum of 80 points (because their primary services earn only 15 points). These maximum scores also depend on how many points each program earns in the other three sections of the SPEP instrument, the general form of which is shown in Figure 9.2. It is important to note that once the primary and supplemental services are determined, SPEP program ratings can be performed by computer using client tracking and demographic data that typically are maintained in a management information system.

Table 9.5   Primary Services With Above-Average, Average, or Below-Average Effects for Juvenile Probationers

Amount of Effect	Service
Above-Average Effects	<ul><li>Cognitive-behavioral therapy</li><li>Group counseling</li><li>Vocational training</li><li>Mentoring</li><li>Some drug abuse treatment</li><li>Some sex offender treatment</li></ul>
Average Effects	<ul><li>Family counseling or therapy</li><li>Individual counseling</li><li>Integrated multimodal (e.g., multisystemic therapy)</li><li>Remedial education or tutoring</li><li>Life skills</li><li>Some drug abuse treatment</li><li>Some sex offender treatment</li></ul>
Below-Average Effects	<ul><li>Recreation</li><li>Restitution</li><li>Challenge programs</li><li>Intensive supervision</li><li>Some drug abuse treatment</li><li>Some sex offender treatment</li></ul>

Figure 9.2 shows the point values of an SPEP rating instrument that scores services for juvenile offenders who have been placed on probation (i.e., for adjudicated offenders) in any state. The generic version of the SPEP instrument shown here incorporates the five main features of effective juvenile delinquency prevention and treatment programs as program rating elements. Lipsey adjusted the incremental contributions that each of the

Standardized Program Evaluation Protocol (SPEP) for Services to Probation Youth	Possible Points	Received Points
Primary Service:		
High average effect service (35 points) Moderate average effect service (25 points) Low average effect service (15 points)	35	
Supplemental Service:		
Qualifying supplemental service used (5 points)	5	
Treatment Amount:		

Duration:
 % of youth that received target number of weeks of service or more:
     0% (0 points)   60% (6 points)
     20% (2 points)   80% (8 points)
     40% (4 points)   100% (10 points)
	10	

Contact Hours:
 % of youth that received target hours of service or more:
     0% (0 points)   60% (6 points)
     20% (3 points)   80% (12 points)
     40% (6 points)   100% (15 points)
	15	

Treatment Quality:		
Rated quality of services delivered: Low (5 points) Medium (10 points) High (15 points)	15	
Youth Risk Level:		

% of youth with the target risk score or higher:
     25% (5 points)   75% (15 points)
     50% (10 points)   99% (20 points)
	20	

Provider's Total SPEP Score:	100	[INSERT SCORE]

Figure 9.2   General Form of the SPEP Rating Instrument

aforementioned five features of the most effective evaluated programs makes to recidivism outcomes to reflect their value in terms of a numerical score. Lipsey tailors this generic SPEP instrument to each primary service found in the probation program literature to specify point values in each section of the instrument. Next, I'll examine each section of the SPEP instrument.

The first section of this generic SPEP scores the primary service. Table 9.5 shows the grouping of evidence-based services for probationers into "above average," "average," and "below average" effect categories. The above-average primary services are allocated 35 points, average primary services are awarded 25 points, and below-average programs are allocated 15 points.

The second section of the generic SPEP awards five points to a program for various services shown in the research to boost the effectiveness of primary services. The program being rated can receive credit for only one supplemental service because of a common limitation of studies, which rarely examine the impact of more than one supplemental service. Each of the primary services shown in Table 9.5 is an eligible supplemental service.

The third section of the SPEP scores services for probationers in terms of treatment amount. Studies show that the amount of service produces larger delinquency reductions in two ways: duration of service (the actual period of time that clients received services) and frequency of service (number of face-to-face contact hours in a given period of time). The optimal duration period and frequency of services for added increments of recidivism reduction vary from one primary service to another, and these would be specified on each SPEP instrument. Note that Dr. Lipsey can adjust point values on this particular factor so as to represent them in terms of the percentage of youths in the program who receive the optimal duration and frequency of service (e.g., 30 contact hours over 15 weeks).

This fourth section of the SPEP scores programs in terms of treatment quality. This section of the SPEP instrument is still under development, but key indicators include staff background and training and monitoring staff delivery of the service. The risk level of program clients is scored in the fifth section of the generic SPEP instrument. More points are awarded in proportion to the higher risk level of clients.

SPEP Implementation

Research is under way on SPEP implementation in two states, North Carolina and Arizona. Two key research questions are addressed in these implementation experiments. The first question is whether the SPEP ratings of the represented service programs are related to the recidivism outcomes for the juveniles they served. Programs with higher SPEP ratings are expected to show better outcomes. Evidence of this relationship would support the validity of the SPEP and the utility of initiatives to implement it as a tool for program evaluation and improvement. SPEP experiments in the two states show that that the SPEP scores are working as expected and do show promising empirical validity as guides to effective programming for juvenile offenders in North Carolina (Lipsey, Howell, & Tidd, 2007a, 2007b) and Arizona (Lipsey, 2008; also see the Arizona Juvenile Justice Services Division's SPEP Web page at http://www.supreme.state.az.us/jjsd/SPEP/default.htm). The second research question is whether program improvements recommended in the SPEP guidelines produce corresponding reductions in delinquency. This research is the next step for the SPEP experiments.

An analysis by Lipsey (2007; Table 9.6) illustrates the incremental gains in expected recidivism for juvenile court programs with successively more favorable intervention characteristics. It shows that the average recidivism rate for control groups is 40%, compared with 34% for juveniles in the average court supervision program in Lipsey's database. When one of the most effective (above average) services is used, the average recidivism rate drops to 32%. Lower recidivism rates are associated with each addition of a favorable program characteristic, from 28% for programs using a best supplemental service to only 21% for those with all five favorable program characteristics. Again, the more favorable characteristics a program has, the more it reduces recidivism in the studies in Lipsey's database. Incremental improvements can add up to a significant recidivism reduction. This is an innovative approach to program improvement that has a great deal of practical application. Program improvements can be made whenever feasible. This approach fits nicely with states' best practice legislation that requires gradual compliance with best practice guidelines such as those in Tennessee (25% the first year, 50% the second year, 75% in the third year, and 100% in the fourth year, under the new statute, SB 1790, 2007).

In summary, from a practical standpoint, efforts to improve juvenile treatment and rehabilitation programs necessarily must focus on improvements in program configurations and implementation fidelity. When better combinations of service elements (primary and supplemental services) are delivered to appropriate clients (especially higher-risk youth) with high

Table 9.6   Expected Recidivism With Features of Effective Court Delinquency
Programs

Control group (juveniles not in a program)	40%
Average supervision program in database	34%
Effective, above average service (AAS)	32%
AAS + best supplemental service (BSS)	28%
AAS + BSS + optimal service amount (OSA)	24%
AAS + BSS + OSA + appropriate clients	21%

fidelity (service frequency, program duration, and program quality), greater program effectiveness should be shown in recidivism data. A system-wide evaluation approach is recommended (see Chapter 10).

A unique strength of the SPEP is that it supports continuum building with its focus on the broad array of programs in juvenile justice systems, including prevention, court services for probationers, and correctional programs for committed offenders. Dr. Lipsey already has done preliminary meta-analyses on programs for committed offenders and prevention programs. With the understanding that he will update these earlier meta-analyses, I present these preliminary results here for two reasons. First, I want to give readers a preview of the types of program services that are effective at the front and back ends of juvenile justice systems and permit a comparison with court services that have been firmly established (while recognizing that those too will need to be updated in the distant future, after many more studies are available). Second, I want readers to consider the importance of expanding one's program scope to encompass the entire system and the potential value of making program improvements across the system sectors simultaneously.

Prevention Program Services

Table 9.7 presents the effective primary services for delinquency prevention clients—that is, nonadjudicated youths—in Lipsey's (2005) meta-analyses. In contrast to the aforementioned list of the most highly effective primary service types for court-supervised juvenile offenders, these overlap very little with priority services for at-risk clients or with the top services for committed offenders. The best services for prevention clients are interpersonal skills training, parent training, and tutoring or remedial education.

Table 9.7   Primary Services With Above-Average, Average, or Below-Average Effects for Prevention Clients (youth who have not been adjudicated delinquent)

Amount of Effect	Service
Better Than Average	• Interpersonal skills • Parent training or counseling • Tutoring; remedial education
Average	• Drug, alcohol therapy or counseling • Employment or job training
Smaller Effects (but still effective)	• Mentoring • Family counseling • Individual counseling

Committed Juvenile Offender Program Services

Table 9.8 shows the primary service types that Lipsey (2005) has found to be effective for institutionalized juvenile offenders. Note that the top-rated primary services; that is, those program types that are most effective (i.e., that, on average, produce the largest effect sizes) tend to be the most highly structured programs, such as behavior management and cognitive–behavioral therapy. As a general observation, the best practice services for juvenile justice system clients increase in the degree of structured services all along the continuum.

Program Areas

The meta-analytic technique and other systematic review methods permit analysts to probe program evaluations on particular topics for other important implications about service delivery. The following topics are intended to give the reader a feel for the richness of knowledge of best practices and system-wide program implications that can be generated in systematic reviews, particularly when meta-analyses are used (see also Welsh & Farrington, 2006, for an excellent collection, consisting of preliminary Campbell Collaboration reviews; a brief introduction to this volume is found in Welsh & Farrington, 2007).

School-Based Programs

Science-based deliquency prevention programs are needed in many American schools. Because of the urgent need to ameliorate the conditions described in Chapter 2, so schools can more effectively prevent delinquency problems, this section presents systematic syntheses of research on

Table 9.8   Primary Services With Above-Average, Average, or Below-Average Effects for Committed Juvenile Offenders

Amount of Effect	Service
Above-Average Effects	• Behavior management • Cognitive-behavioral therapy • Employment or job training • Interpersonal skills training
Average Effects	• Family counseling • Group counseling • Individual counseling
Below-Average Effects (but still effective)	• Career or vocational counseling • Tutoring or remedial education

school-related programs. Violence in schools is manageable. Significant violent events in the schools have declined significantly for more than a decade, and the victimization rate of students ages 12–18 at school declined between 1992 and 2005 (National Center for Education Statistics, 2007).

Previous studies that have found dramatic peaks in violent juvenile delinquency during after-school hours may have overestimated the after-school peak because of reliance on officially recorded crime in police reports (Gottfredson & Soule, 2005). The fact is that, considering all forms of crime, more crime victimization occurs at school or on the way to and from school than elsewhere on school days (Gottfredson & Gottfredson, 2007).

Recent reviews and meta-analyses of school-based prevention (Gottfredson, 2001; Gottfredson & Wilson, 2003; Gottfredson, Wilson, & Najaka, 2002a; Hahn et al., 2007; Wilson, Gottfredson, & Najaka, 2001) have identified effective strategies and specific programs that have been shown to reduce crime and antisocial behavior. Strategies supported by multiple studies include programs or practices that (1) enhance school management in general (e.g., by engaging the school in systematic planning and implementation of school improvement activities) and specifically improve the clarity of school rules and the consistency of their enforcement, (2) clarify and communicate norms about behaviors, (3) teach youths a range of social competency skills (e.g., developing self-control, stress management, responsible decision making, social problem solving, and communication skills), and (4) use cognitive behavioral or behavior techniques to teach these same social competency skills, especially to youths at high risk for problem behavior. Some evidence also suggests that mentoring programs and efforts to reorganize schools into smaller units might reduce crime and antisocial behavior. Making use of these well-tested approaches to reducing youth crime during the times when such crime is most prevalent is likely to reduce juvenile delinquency overall.

A national study found that schools that were more *communally organized* had lower levels of teacher victimization and student delinquency (Payne, Gottfredson, & Gottfredson, 2003). These schools had more students who were bonded to the school, and these higher bonding levels, in turn, led to less delinquency. A communally organized school emphasizes informal social relations, common norms and experiences, and collaboration and participation; in contrast, more bureaucratic schools emphasize formal participation, technical knowledge, and regulation and standardization. Schools that have a high sense of community are those in which members know, care about, and support one another and have common goals and a sense of shared purpose and to which they actively contribute and feel personally committed (p. 751).

Program services can also be implemented in schools to prevent aggression that would fit nicely in communally organized schools. Lipsey and his colleagues performed a meta-analysis of 221 evaluated school-based programs that prevent or reduce aggressive behavior (Wilson, Lipsey, & Derzon, 2003; see also Wilson & Lipsey, 2007, for an update). This systematic synthesis provides new information on the types of programs that have proved effective and also common features of them and key factors in their implementation.

The most effective programs as revealed in this comprehensive study, in descending order of effectiveness, are

- Behavioral, classroom management
- Therapy, counseling
- Schools within schools (separate schools or classrooms)
- Academic services
- Social competence, cognitive–behavioral
- Social competence, no cognitive–behavioral component

Some of these programs were implemented in preschool, but most of them were placed in elementary schools, followed by middle schools and high schools. Interestingly, programs that targeted very young children (5 years and under in preschool and kindergarten) and adolescents (14 years and up in high schools) tended to show greater reductions in aggression—more than programs for elementary and middle school children. Programs that targeted high-risk students tended to show greater reductions in aggression. In addition, programs were most effective in settings where the base rates of aggressive behavior were high. Otherwise, the effects of school-based programs did not vary greatly with the age, gender, or ethnic mix of the research samples. Specific school-based program models can be found in the online repositories of effective programs and services (see Box 9.2).

A key issue is this: Are these program types effective when implemented in the course of routine practice? Most of the 221 studies evaluated research and development programs, in which there was significant researcher involvement in training and supervision of service delivery personnel. These produced very large reductions in aggressive behavior rates. In contrast, the research to date suggests that school-based routine practice programs have minimal effects on aggressive behavior in children and adolescents. Why is this? Routine practice programs implemented in schools typically are poorly implemented (Gottfredson & Gottfredson, 2002). Thus schools, perhaps more than other juvenile justice settings—for whatever reasons—need to pay very close attention to program fidelity when implementing new programs.

Many school districts across the country are implementing the highly acclaimed Positive Behavior Intervention and Support (PBIS), also called Positive Behavioral Support (PBS) or School-Wide Positive Behavior Support (SW-PBS). This is a very promising framework with the potential of improving school climate and linking students with serious behavioral problems to needed services, although results to date do not qualify PBS as an evidence-based practice (Kutash, Duchnowski, & Lynn, 2006, p. 32). Most experts in the field agree that PBS is in its infancy, and the most promising results to date have been found when PBS was implemented in conjunction with functional behavioral assessments for serious behavioral problems (p. 32).

The PBS is endorsed by the U.S. Office of Special Education Programs (see OSEP Center on Positive Behavioral Interventions and Supports, 2004), and empirical support for PBS is growing (Freeman et al., 2006). The basic thesis of the PBS model is that effective prevention efforts necessarily include primary, secondary, and tertiary intervention levels (OSEP Center on Positive Behavioral Interventions and Supports, 2004, p. 17; Freeman et al., 2006, p. 4; Table 9.9):

- Primary prevention involves all students and adults in the school and is implemented across all school and school-related settings. This component is school-wide and is expected to reach 80% of the students.
- Secondary prevention is intended to support students who have learning, behavior, or life histories that put them at risk of engaging in more serious problem behavior. This component is expected to target only 15% of the students, who display at-risk behavior.

Table 9.9   School-Wide Positive Behavior Support Components and Core Elements

Prevention Tier	Core Elements
Primary	Behavioral expectations defined
	Behavioral expectations taught
	Reward system for appropriate behavior
	Continuum of consequences for problem behavior
	Continuous collection and use of data for decision making
Secondary	Universal screening
	Progress monitoring for at-risk students
	System for increasing structure and predictability
	System for increasing contingent adult feedback
	System for linking academic and behavioral performance
	System for increasing home and school communication
	Collection and use of data for decision making
Tertiary	Functional behavioral assessment
	Team-based comprehensive assessment
	Linking of academic and behavior supports
	Individualized intervention based on assessment information focusing on (a) prevention of problem contexts, (b) instruction on functionally equivalent skills and instruction on desired performance skills, (c) strategies for placing problem behavior on extinction, (d) strategies for enhancing contingence reward of desired behavior, and (e) use of negative or safety consequences if needed
	Collection and use of data for decision making

- Tertiary prevention strategies focus on the smaller number of students who engage in serious or chronic problem behavior (only 5%) and whose needs are more individualized and require comprehensive plans to address their unique needs.

The OSEP Center on Positive Behavioral Interventions and Supports (2004) acknowledges that schools that are implementing PBIS are just beginning to design systems for students with "the most challenging behaviors" and that when students need additional services "beyond school-wide programs aimed at primary prevention of problem behavior, their needs are identified in the same ways as their general education peers (e.g. teacher referral)" (pp. 3, 5). If assessment centers were established in schools to screen the most troubled youth (with mental health problems, drug abuse, alcohol abuse, or gang involvement), those most in need could be identified and referred to essential services. This would strengthen the overall PBIS. In addition, PBIS can help schools address excessive suspension, expulsion, and high dropout rates and contributing zero tolerance policies (Chapter 2).

After-School Programs

Another key need in school programming is for effective after-school programs. This is a special case in which few research-based programs are available. A meta-analysis of after-school programs (Gottfredson, Gerstenblith, Soule, Womer, & Lu, 2004) found that middle school programs reduced delinquency but elementary school programs did not. In line with the aforementioned meta-analysis (Wilson et al., 2003), most effective programs were structured ones that focused on social competency (e.g., developing self-control) or interpersonal skill development.

The after-school period is a critical opportunity for delinquency prevention because the lack of adult supervision of youngsters is conducive to delinquency (Osgood & Anderson, 2004). In fact, the situations that are most conducive to delinquency are unstructured socializing with peers away from authority figures. Worse yet, such unstructured socializing increases delinquency opportunities for all adolescents in that group (Osgood & Anderson, 2004).

Aside from their potential for delinquency prevention, after-school programs enhance the well-being of children and contribute to their safety during the critical period of school days in which many children and adolescents might otherwise be unsupervised by adults. An exhaustive RAND Corp. review of research on after-school programs (Beckett, Hawken, & Jacknowitz, 2001) identified evidence-based good practice standards for successful programs (e.g., educational attainment, emotional development, and health). The RAND researchers identified 17 good practice standards of successful after-school programs in the research literature (Box 9.4).

IN FOCUS 9.4

Seventeen Good Practice Standards of Successful After-School Programs

Staff Management Practices

- Training staff
- Hiring and retaining educated staff
- Providing attractive compensation

Program Management Practices

- Providing of a sufficient variety of activities
- Ensuring that programming is flexible
- Establishing and maintaining a favorable emotional climate
- Maintaining a low child-to-staff ratio
- Keeping total enrollment low
- Having a mix of younger and older children
- Providing age-appropriate activities and materials
- Providing adequate space
- Maintaining continuity and complementarities with regular day school
- Establishing clear goals and program evaluation
- Paying adequate attention to safety and health of students

Community Contacts

- Involving families
- Using volunteers
- Using community-based organizations and facilities

The Wallace–Reader's Digest Fund replicated four well-known after-school programs in its Extended Service Schools Initiative (the Beacon, Bridges to Success, Community Schools, and the West Philadelphia Improvement Corporation). They all operate programs in school buildings, involve partnerships between community-based organizations (or universities) and schools, and offer a range of activities to the children and youth who participate, including academic and enrichment activities, sports, and recreation. Participating youth reported less often that they had initiated alcohol use and reported more often than nonparticipating youth that they handled their anger in socially appropriate ways. The report on this experiment details the four models that were implemented and evaluated in 20 communities (Grossman et al., 2002).

A more recent experiment evaluated statewide after-school programs in Maryland (Gottfredson, Cross, & Soule, 2007), producing important findings on their structure and management. Smaller programs, those that include well-structured programming (i.e., a published curriculum), and programs that employ more highly educated staff produced reductions in one or more problem behaviors. The most commonly used curriculum was Botvin's Life Skills Training (see Table 9.1).

Early Intervention With Disruptive Children and Child Delinquents

As noted in Chapter 4, one-fourth to one-third of disruptive children may become child delinquents, and about a third of all child delinquents may later become serious, violent, and chronic offenders. Yet, as Loeber and Farrington (2000) observe, "We know less about [the numbers and characteristics of such] children in the United States than about farm animals" (p. 756). There are no annual surveys of the numbers of persistent disruptive children in elementary schools or in child welfare and protection agencies. Police referral data are scant, and juvenile courts have not been expected to handle them for more than a quarter of a century. Policy makers are more likely to fund programs for adolescents and costly residential corrections for older juveniles than to fund programs for child delinquents (Loeber & Farrington, 2000).

There are three fundamental strategies for early intervention with delinquents (Farrington & Welsh, 2007; Welsh & Farrington, 2007). The first is to intervene at the individual level with at-risk children, particularly disruptive children. This has proven to be an effective early intervention strategy, according to Farrington and Welsh and to other reviews in their 2007 book. Preschool intellectual enrichment and child skill training programs are noteworthy for their highly favorable results. These programs typically target children with low intelligence and attainment. and they show improvements in school readiness, cognitive skills, and social and emotional development. Other effective individual programs target risk factors of impulsivity, low empathy, and self-centeredness.

The Child Development Institute's (formerly Earlscourt Child and Family Centre) Under 12 Outreach Project (ORP) was developed as an early intervention for child delinquents. In Canada, children under 12 who commit offenses fall under the authority of provincial child welfare agencies rather than the juvenile justice system. ORP serves boys ages 6–11 who have had police contact or were referred from other sources and also are clinically assessed as engaging in above-average levels of aggressive, destructive, or other antisocial behavior. ORP uses a multisystem approach, combining interventions that target the child, the family, and the community. The program uses a variety of established interventions: skill training; training in cognitive problem solving, self-control strategies, and cognitive self-instruction; family management skill training; and parent training. Both the

ORP and its parallel gender-sensitive program for girls, Earlscourt Girls Connection, are fully manualized and are in various stages of replication. ORP has received the highest rating (Level 1) on program effectiveness in a nationwide U.S. review of research-based programs (*Helping America's Youth Community Guide;* see Chapter 7 and Box 7.4; also Augimeri et al., 2006).

Family prevention is the second recommended strategy (Farrington & Welsh, 2007; Welsh & Farrington, 2007). In this strategy, programs intervene with high-risk families that are most likely to produce child delinquents. A combination of home visiting and parent training is the most effective approach with these families. The single most popular program, and a very effective one, is the Nurse Family Partnership, which provides first-time, low-income mothers with home visitation services. This program has shown reductions in child abuse and neglect, reduced delinquency among the children, and produced other favorable outcomes (Blueprints Program, Table 9.1; see also Bilukha et al., 2005).

School- and community-level prevention is the third recommended strategy (Farrington & Welsh, 2007; Welsh & Farrington, 2007). School and after-school strategies were reviewed earlier. In addition, mentoring is an excellent community-level prevention program. These programs provide adult mentors who work one on one with troubled children and adolescents in a supportive, nonjudgmental manner while acting as role models. Although results of evaluated programs are mixed, the overall weight of evidence supports mentoring (Farrington & Welsh, 2007), but these programs are more effective as a secondary prevention or intervention strategy (working with delinquent youth) than in a primary prevention format (see Table 9.5).

Programs for Girls

Contrary to some exaggerated reports, the juvenile justice system is not being flooded with girls, although there is an increase in referred females (Snyder & Sickmund, 2006). But, based on major longitudinal studies of youth violence, the gender gap is not closing (Steffensmeier, Schwartz, Zhong, & Ackerman, 2005). As seen in Chapter 8, meta-analyses of the entire field of juvenile justice show that program services are about equally effective with boys and girls. This finding suggests two implications. First, a separate track of programs specifically for girls is not needed. The evidence-based core services (primary services) in juvenile justice programs (cognitive-behavioral therapy, individual counseling, and the like) appear to work as well for girls as boys. Second, this is not to say that certain gender-specific services are not needed. Of course, they are. Examples include services for pregnant teenagers, counseling in handling relationships with sexually aggressive boys, and programs for sex offenders. Effective programs that include girls or serve them along with boys can be found in the *Helping America's Youth Community Guide* (Box 7.4). An excellent example of one that effectively serves both boys and girls in parallel tracks is the Earlscourt

Girls Connection in the Under 12 Outreach Project. However, it appears that specialized training of juvenile justice system staff on gender-specific issues is necessary to adequately address the needs of girls in the system (Bloom, Owen, Deschenes, & Rosenbaum, 2002).

Discussion Topics

1. Is it surprising to you that we do not know much about how best to translate research findings into advice for practitioners?

2. What are the main reasons that we do not know much about this?

3. What are the most important recent developments on this front?

4. Why is meta-analysis a unique analytical technique for determining what works?

5. Why do you think service providers and juvenile justice officials sometimes resist using best practices?

CHAPTER 10

The Comprehensive Strategy Framework

An Illustration

The Comprehensive Strategy for Serious, Violent, and Chronic Juvenile Offenders (Wilson & Howell, 1993) was developed at the federal Office of Juvenile Justice and Delinquency Prevention (OJJDP) in the early 1990s. It was the product of an OJJDP review of research on juvenile offenders, best practices, and effective programs. This review culminated in the Comprehensive Strategy (CS).

The seventh U.S. "moral panic" over juvenile delinquency (Chapter 2) instigated the OJJDP review and development of the CS. Reported juvenile violence—particularly homicides (and also suicides)—had increased sharply beginning in the late 1980s, and a "moral panic" over juvenile delinquency was in full bloom. The "get tough on juveniles" movement was growing along with a penchant among policy makers for quick fixes, piecemeal solutions that often were stimulated by the so-called epidemic of juvenile violence.

The OJJDP review (Wilson & Howell, 1993) found basis for optimism that juvenile delinquency could be prevented and controlled, using a balanced approach of prevention, rehabilitation, and control measures (Box 10.1). The CS attempted to strike a balance between calls for more punishment of juvenile offenders on one hand and prevention and treatment on the other. It was disseminated along with supporting research, promising and effective programs, and tools for improving juvenile justice system management of juvenile offenders in a practitioner guide (Howell, 1995) that was designed to assist states and communities in implementing the CS.

IN FOCUS 10.1

Benefits of Using the Comprehensive Strategy

- Increased prevention of delinquency (and thus fewer young people enter the juvenile justice system)
- Enhanced responsiveness from the juvenile justice system
- Greater accountability on the part of youth
- Decreased costs of juvenile corrections
- A more responsible juvenile justice system
- More effective juvenile justice programs
- Less delinquency
- Fewer delinquents becoming serious, violent, and chronic (SVC) offenders
- Fewer delinquents becoming adult offenders

Thus the CS is a juvenile justice "diffusion" framework. *Diffusion* has been defined as the process by which members of a particular social system—the juvenile justice, delinquency prevention, and social service systems in this case—learn about, make decisions about, and act on ideas and practices they perceive as new (Hallfors & Godette, 2002). The CS is based on the premise that local ownership of programs and strategies is imperative for optimal system effectiveness. Therefore, each community, city, or state must develop its own comprehensive plan, in a strategic planning process (Box 10.2). Selected cases described as follows illustrate how the CS framework can be adapted to state and local needs (interested readers can find other examples in Howell, 2003b).

IN FOCUS 10.2

The Planning Process

Training and technical assistance providers use the CS curriculum to guide communities through the system reform process. The CS planning process consists of the following four phases:

- *Mobilization:* Community leaders are enlisted and organized to participate in the CS planning process. A formal community planning team is created to receive training and technical assistance and to develop a 5-year strategic plan. Representatives of all sectors of the community are engaged in the planning process, including youth development agencies, citizen volunteers, private organizations, schools, law enforcement agencies, prosecutors, courts, corrections agencies, social service agencies, civic organizations, religious groups, parents, and teens.

- *Assessment:* Quantitative data are gathered and analyzed for use in the development of a baseline profile of the community's risk and need factors and a comprehensive juvenile justice profile. The data can guide decision making about long-term program planning, coordination, and optimum resource allocation.

- *Planning:* A 5-year strategic plan is created for building a continuum of services to address the community's priority risk and need factors, based on best practices. The plan clearly articulates the community's vision, mission, goals, and objectives.

- *Implementation and evaluation:* Systems and programs are developed according to the 5-year strategic plan; these include a seamless continuum of prevention, intervention, and graduated sanctions and programs. Evaluation mechanisms and procedures are established.

The Comprehensive Strategy

The CS is a succinct statement, consisting of its guiding principles, rationale, description, and illustration of the prevention and intervention components and promising and effective programs (Wilson & Howell, 1993). Because the CS has been reprinted in two sources (Howell, 1995, 1997), it is not repeated here. An implementation guide (Howell, 1995) further translates research into practice and guides communities and states in a process of implementing prevention and treatment science using the CS framework. Furthermore, this book serves the same purpose.

CS Principles

The CS calls for a proactive and balanced approach that integrates prevention and control It is based on the following five core principles (Wilson & Howell, 1993):

- We must strengthen the family in its primary responsibility to instill moral values and provide guidance and support to children. Where there is no functional family unit, we must establish a family surrogate and help that entity to guide and nurture the child.
- We must support core social institutions such as schools, religious institutions, and community organizations in their roles of developing capable, mature, and responsible youth. A goal of each of these societal

institutions should be to ensure that children have the opportunity and support to mature into productive, law-abiding citizens. In a nurturing community environment, core social institutions are actively involved in the lives of youth.

- We must promote delinquency prevention as the most cost-effective approach to reducing juvenile delinquency. Families, schools, religious institutions, and community organizations, including citizen volunteers and the private sector, must be enlisted in the nation's delinquency prevention efforts. These core socializing institutions must be strengthened and assisted in their efforts to ensure that children have the opportunity to become capable and responsible citizens. When children engage in acting-out behavior, such as status offenses, the family and community, in concert with child welfare agencies, must respond with appropriate treatment and support services. Communities must take the lead in designing and building comprehensive prevention approaches that address known risk factors and target other youth at risk of delinquency.

- We must intervene immediately and effectively when delinquent behavior occurs to prevent delinquent offenders from becoming chronic offenders or committing progressively more serious and violent crimes. Initial intervention efforts, under an umbrella of system authorities (police, intake, and probation), should be centered in the family and other core societal institutions. Juvenile justice system authorities should ensure that an appropriate response occurs and act quickly and firmly if the need for formal system adjudication and sanctions is demonstrated.

- We must identify and control the small group of SVC juvenile offenders who have committed felony offenses or have failed to respond to intervention and nonsecure community-based treatment and rehabilitation services offered by the juvenile justice system. Measures to address delinquent offenders who are a threat to community safety may include placement in secure community-based facilities, training schools, and other secure juvenile facilities. Even the most violent or intractable juveniles should not be moved into the criminal justice system before they graduate from the jurisdiction of the juvenile justice system.

Each of these core CS principles is supported in research summarized in the earlier chapters of this book (in particular, Chapters 4 and 5; see also Loeber et al., 2008, pp. 329–333, for updated research findings on delinquent careers pertinent to each of these core principles). Implementation of them will help officials develop balanced juvenile justice systems (see Box 10.3 for conditions that the CS counters). The CS framework will also prove useful in this enterprise.

IN FOCUS 10.3
Common Juvenile Justice System Conditions

- Unbalanced emphasis on prevention versus graduated sanctions
- Overreliance on detention, incarceration, and residential programs
- Poor targeting of SVC juvenile offenders
- Poor matching of offenders with appropriate levels of supervision, sanctions, and programs
- Use of ineffective programs
- Poor program planning
- Lack of continuity between juvenile court and corrections system operations
- Underdeveloped parole supervision or aftercare and transitional services
- Ineffective allocation of court and correctional resources
- Lack of a clear focus on the use of and objectives for confinement resources (often demonstrated in poor classification systems and excessive numbers of lengthy placements)
- Inadequate data collection on offenders in the system, management information systems, and information sharing
- Lack of good policy guidance in the development of institutional classification, length of commitment, and release criteria
- Lack of good policy guidance for state executive, legislative, and judicial stakeholders in the development of legislation, standards, and other policy directives that create data-driven, outcome-based, and result-oriented juvenile justice policy reforms

The CS Framework

The CS is a two-tiered system for responding proactively to juvenile delinquency (Figure 10.1). In the first tier, delinquency prevention, youth development, and early intervention programs are relied on to prevent delinquency and reduce the likelihood of delinquent career development among children who display conduct disorders and other problem behaviors. If these efforts fail, then the juvenile justice system, the second tier, must make proactive responses to juvenile delinquency by addressing the risk factors for recidivism and associated treatment needs of delinquents, particularly those with a high likelihood of becoming SVC offenders. A continuum of sanctions and services is needed for them that reduces this likelihood while protecting the public. The CS guides jurisdictions in developing a continuum of responses that parallel offender careers, beginning with prevention and early intervention in predelinquent and delinquent careers and then juvenile justice system intervention using graduated sanctions, linked with a continuum of treatment programs. These two components can be organized to prevent further development of offender careers toward SVC status.

The CS framework consists of six levels of program interventions and sanctions, moving from least to most restrictive:

- Prevention of delinquency by reducing risk and enhancing protection
- Early intervention with predelinquent and child delinquents and their families
- Immediate intervention for first-time delinquent offenders (misdemeanors and nonviolent felonies) and nonserious repeat offenders
- Intermediate sanctions for first-time serious or violent offenders, including intensive supervision for SVC offenders
- Secure corrections for the most serious, violent, and chronic offenders
- Aftercare or reentry

The theoretical foundation of the CS is detailed in Howell (2003b). The public health model and developmental criminology are overarching theoretical models. The prevention component incorporates an adaptation of the public health model for reducing risk factors and increasing promotive and protective factors for delinquency and other problem behaviors.

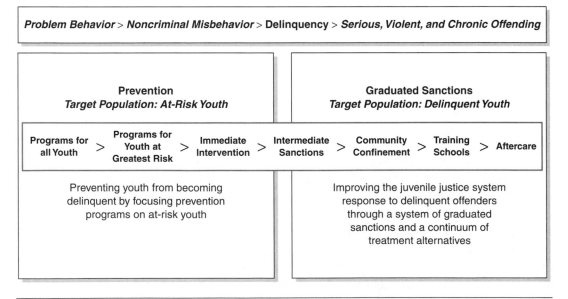

Figure 10.1   Comprehensive Strategy for Serious, Violent, and Chronic Juvenile Offenders

Developmental or life-course criminology is reflected in both CS components. Both learning theories and control theory are reflected in the key principles of the CS.

CS Linchpins

The CS is activated by three activities that are considered linchpins for effective implementation. First, communities must conduct a comprehensive assessment of risk and protective factors for delinquency in their specific jurisdictions, instead of arbitrarily selecting prevention programs that may miss the mark. Second, juvenile justice system agencies must assess their delinquent populations for risk and treatment needs and strengths in order to classify and position offenders within a structured system of graduated sanctions to best protect the public, and to properly place offenders in program interventions that are appropriate for their treatment needs and strengths. Successful accomplishment of these two tasks not only *engages* communities in research-based practices, thus raising the comfort level, but also helps them see the potential value of using evidence-based program interventions. Third, community engagement and long-term strategic planning entail four sequential steps: *mobilization, assessment, planning,* and *implementation* (Figure 10.2).

These activities are initiated (with outside technical assistance and training, if necessary) by a community planning team that develops a 5-year

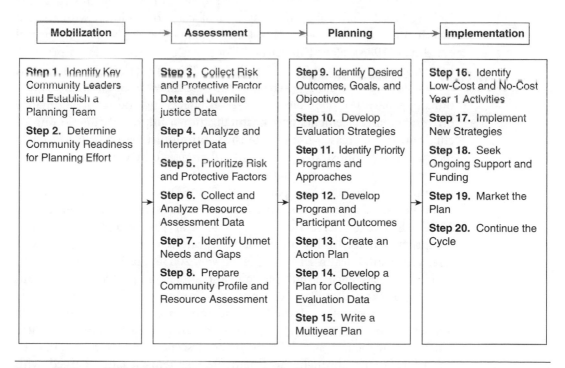

Figure 10.2   Comprehensive Strategy Community Planning Process

strategic plan. This multiyear plan should place top priority on the development of risk and need assessment instruments and a disposition matrix for all juvenile court delinquency case dispositions. These tools would dramatically reduce unnecessary and costly confinement of juvenile offenders. The reader will see later in this chapter how the North Carolina Department of Juvenile Justice and Delinquency Prevention used these tools to sharply reduce confinement without endangering public safety.

There is a compelling need to effectively integrate mental health, child welfare, education, substance abuse, and juvenile justice system services (Howell, Kelly, Palmer, & Mangum, 2004). This is imperative because the extremely costly and largely ineffective residential facilities of the child welfare (Kortenkamp & Ehrle, 2002), mental health (Lerman, 2002), and juvenile justice systems (see Chapter 2) are all overloaded. Both public and private agencies are overreliant on residential care. Moreover, these agencies "are too crisis-oriented, too rigid in their classification of problems, too specialized, too isolated from other services, too inflexible to craft comprehensive solutions, too insufficiently funded, and they are mismanaged" (Roush, 1996b, p. 29). Thus a major objective is confinement reduction through use of less costly and more effective family- and child-centered treatment interventions.

This is not as simple as it sounds, however. Most children and youths destined for the deep end of these systems have evidenced problems and juvenile or social service system mishandling for several years (Burns et al., 2001; Stouthamer-Loeber & Loeber, 2002). But the prospect of integrated, multiagency services remains more of an ideal than an actual practice. Jane Knitzer (1982) first called for a system of care for children with mental health problems, and her concept was further developed by Stroul and Friedman (1986). Now, Knitzer and Cooper (2006) have assessed progress in developing systems of care (SOCs) at the 20-year mark. Their assessment is that although system-level effects with SOCs have been good, individual outcomes have not. Notable system-level effects include reduced reliance on residential placements and hospitalizations, improved functioning of children, and increased use of intensive community-based services. Yet "a recent study demonstrated consistent adherence to SOC principles in initiative sites but no improvements in children's outcomes and no advantage in improved outcomes compared with non-SOC sites using services that embodied similar principles" (p. 671; see Stephens, Holden, & Hernandez, 2004). Thus *integrated* services continue to be an elusive goal with but a few exceptions, notably in initiatives that integrated juvenile justice, child welfare, and mental health services (see Howell, 2003b, pp. 233–239).

The co-occurrence of multiple child and adolescent problems is the main basis for integrated multisystem initiatives. Youths' problems tend to come bundled together, often stacked on one another over time (Loeber, 1990; Loeber & Farrington, 2001c). The need for an integrated response is also buttressed by the fact that children and adolescents are often routed in haphazard pathways through the fragmented systems legally charged with responsibility for addressing their problems (Armstrong, 1998). Integration of the necessary services is further complicated by U.S. schools that often funnel youth into the juvenile justice system and its detention centers instead of linking them with needed services (Weisel & Howell, 2007). Ineffective programs are commonly used in all youth service systems, and the failure rate is highest for youths in residential facilities, principally because of the ineffectiveness of bed-driven treatment (Chapter 11).

Ideally, the community planning team also would develop an interagency teamwork protocol (for information exchange and cross-agency client referrals) and build an infrastructure to implement the 5-year strategic plan to address these common problems. An effective infrastructure ideally would consist of four levels, beginning with multiple-agency child–family treatment teams (led by a case manager) at the local level. An interagency council could garner or pool community resources for comprehensive care and ensure that local public, private, and community decision makers work together as a team. A state collaborative could bring state agency decision makers together as a team to promote or develop policies that support local interagency councils and treatment teams. The infrastructure should ensure that the door through which clients enter the service delivery system does not limit service access.

The Prevention Component

The prevention component of the CS consists of the two initial program levels of the continuum: prevention and early intervention. In this framework, *prevention* refers to primary prevention. Early intervention programs in this component target predelinquent and delinquent children and their families, outside the juvenile justice system.

Use of the science-based risk and protection framework of the public health model helps structure the delinquency prevention enterprise in communities. The public health model is a user-friendly model for practitioners because of widespread familiarity with applications in the health arena. These practitioners are well aware that juvenile delinquency and other child and adolescent problem behaviors share common risk and protective factors (Durlak, 1998; Loeber & Farrington, 1998). Thus multiple research-based prevention programs and activities can be successfully promoted by providing community members with training and technical assistance in risk–protection assessment and strategic prevention planning. Adoption of the risk–protection framework in the broad juvenile justice arena has progressed on two fronts with two different sorts of implementation tools. Generally speaking, the risk–protection model has been used more widely in preventing delinquency and drug use than in treating or reducing recidivism of youth afflicted with these problem behaviors.

Congress established Incentive Grants for Local Delinquency Prevention Programs in Subchapter V of its 1992 reauthorization of the Juvenile Justice and Delinquency Prevention Act of 1974. The Title V Community Prevention Grants Program, as it is now known, provides communities with funding and a guiding framework for developing and implementing comprehensive juvenile delinquency prevention plans. Title V supports the development and implementation of risk- and protection-focused prevention strategies that meet the unique circumstances and risk conditions of local communities nationwide. The Community Prevention Grants Program provides funding to participating states and territories, which then make subgrants to qualified units of local government (Caliber Associates, 2006). However, these typically are only about $65,000. Therefore, to help communities plan and implement risk- and protection-focused prevention programs, the limited grant funds have been supplemented with some training and technical assistance. However, this has been very limited (pp. 235–238).

In the early 1990s, the OJJDP promoted implementation of a delinquency prevention model, Communities That Care (CTC), in its state block grant prevention program. The CTC operating system required local planners to assess the presence of risk factors and urged them to consider adoption of research-based protection enhancement programs. Experiences with CTC implementation demonstrate that local planners can be successfully guided in collecting and analyzing risk and protective factor data from their communities and using these data to make decisions about the selection of research-based policies and programs to address their unique profiles of risk and protection (Hawkins, 1999). However, the programs funded in this planning process did not demonstrate delinquency reductions in experimental studies.

After the commercial marketing of CTC in the late 1990s, OJJDP developed other tools to promote research-based, data-driven strategic prevention planning in conjunction with the OJJDP state block grant prevention program. In 2000, OJJDP provided states with a new curriculum that places a stronger emphasis on selecting and evaluating research-based prevention strategies (Caliber Associates, 2006). To assist communities in these activities, three tools were developed: the Model Programs Guide, the Model Programs Guide Database (Box 9.2), and the Community Data Collection Manual. Yet few successful risk- and protection-focused programs have been reported (Caliber Associates, 2006). Even the "more experienced communities also were challenged in the translation from theory to practice" (p. 231). Community mobilization and service integration remain problematic. It is "one thing to understand the concept of collaboration, but it is something altogether different to try to implement it with real people in actual community settings" (p. 231).

In 2005, a more comprehensive Web-based application was created in a joint effort by nine federal agencies that also promoted the risk–protection model in community planning, focused broadly on multiple child and adolescent problem behaviors. This tool, called the Helping America's Youth (HAY) *Community Guide* (Chapter 7, Box 7.4), was constructed from a prototype Strategic Planning Tool (http://www.iir.com/nygc/tool/) that was developed under OJJDP support at the National Youth Gang Center to help communities systematically assess and address gang problems with risk-focused planning and a continuum of sanctions and research-based programs. Indicators and data sources of risk factors for delinquency and gang involvement are provided in the Strategic Planning Tool. The HAY *Community Guide* expanded the National Youth Gang Center Strategic Planning Tool to cover the broad array of child and adolescent problem behaviors. The guide links research-based programs to both risk and potentially protective factors in all five risk factor domains (Chapter 4).

How much of this technology and information base communities have the capacity to incorporate into everyday practice remains to be seen. Regional orientations for community groups that were convened around the United States in 2007–2008 suggest that the HAY tool is more user friendly than any previous system for engaging local communities in risk- and protection-focused planning. Although communities have shown the capacity to perform research-based risk assessments, their capacity to implement protection enhancements has not been as successful, in part because this enterprise has been based largely on theoretical protective factors, unlike the risk assessment process, which has been guided by a list of empirically supported risk factors. However, communities can successfully inventory their resources (programs) and launch a broad collaborative initiative that integrates many services on their own if they access the *Community Guide* on the HAY Web site (Box 7.4).

Every community should have in its continuum of prevention programs specific services for children who are exposed to violence—and victims themselves—at a very young age in their homes, neighborhoods, and at school and going to and from school (Flannery, Singer, van Dulmen, Kretschmar, & Belliston, 2007; see also Eitle & Turner, 2002). Flannery and colleagues identify several program priorities (p. 315):

- Mental health professionals should be placed in schools to immediately identify children who need services and deliver or coordinate them.
- Interventions must include families and peer groups.
- Prevention services must address risk and protection at multiple levels and across multiple systems.
- Prevention services must also give priority to development of positive coping skills, competencies, and problem-solving skills that will help children and adolescents deal effectively with high levels of exposure to violence and victimization.

This latter point is underscored by recent pioneering research in which Lauritsen (2003) linked self-reports of victimizations reported by youth ages 12–17 and their family information with data on the communities in which the youth lived. Lauritsen found that children are at greater risk of victimization when they have lower levels of parental supervision, live in a community with high proportions of young people, and have not yet learned the neighborhood's rules and problem areas because they are new to the community. A clear implication from this research is that prevention services must focus on places and circumstances with elevated risk outside the school context—in families and communities, as well as within schools—and the earlier the better, just as Flannery and colleagues suggest.

The Intervention Component

A hallmark of the juvenile justice system is individualized treatment of offenders. By using formal decision-making tools, a community can facilitate better matching of offenders' risk profiles with the appropriate sanction levels to protect the public and better matching of offender treatment needs with interventions. This work is accomplished in the intervention component of the CS. It consists of the last four levels of the overall CS framework: immediate intervention, intermediate sanctions, secure corrections, and aftercare. Three main formal decision-making tools (Wiebush, 2002) are used in this system and illustrated in this chapter: risk and need assessments and a placement matrix. Other key formal decision-making tools are shown in Box 10.4.

IN FOCUS 10.4

Four Components of the Formal Decision-Making Model

1. Structured case assessments:
   - Detention screening instrument (to determine eligibility of placements)
   - Research-based risk assessment
   - Objective assessment of child and family strengths and needs
   - Placement matrix for recommending court dispositions
   - Standardized case plans
   - Routine assessment of case plan progress

2. Differentiated service standards based on risk, severity, and the youth's need for treatment intervention

3. A workload accounting system to support agency staff allocation, service planning, and budgeting

4. A management information system to provide case data for service delivery quality assurance, planning, and evaluation

---

Because official records contain an incomplete picture of offenders' delinquent histories (Farrington, Jolliffe, Loeber, & Homish, 2007), risk assessment instruments are used to estimate the level of sanctions that is needed to protect the public (Box 10.5). Although tools are not available to reliably screen at-risk youths and predict specific individuals' onset of delinquency, this limitation should not be confused with the predictive utility of risk assessment for recidivism (Andrews, Bonta, & Wormith, 2006; Wiebush, 2002). The reality is that formal decision-making tools such as risk assessment and need assessment instruments are not widely used in juvenile justice practice (Sarri et al., 2001; Young, Moline, Farrell, & Bierie, 2006) despite the fact that excellent instruments are readily available (DeComo & Wiebush, 2005; Gottfredson & Moriarty, 2006; Wiebush, 2002). One reason is that the field is preoccupied with various methodological issues surrounding risk assessment (Gottfredson & Moriarty, 2006).

IN FOCUS 10.5
Risk Assessment Instrument Development

From the time of their creation, juvenile courts and correctional agencies have used some means of assessing offenders' risk levels. There are four basic approaches to risk assessment: staff judgments, clinical or psychological assessments, consensus-based assessments, and assessments using actuarial (research-based) instruments (Gottfredson & Moriarty, 2006; Wiebush, 2002). Two of these are not reliable at all: Informal staff judgments result in overclassification (i.e., too many false positives), and clinical predictions have been shown to be significantly less accurate than assessments based on the use of empirically derived tools (Gottfredson & Moriarty, 2006). In a comparison of clinical judgments with actuarial approaches, actuarial methods performed better than clinical procedures in 46% of the studies and equally well in 10%, whereas clinical judgments outperformed actuarial prediction in only 6% of the studies (Grove et al., 1990; for a summary of this study, see Grove & Meehl, 1996). Consensus-based risk assessments (i.e., assessments using structured tools that incorporate items agreed on by a group of agency staff) are also less accurate than assessments made using actuarial instruments (Gottfredson & Moriarty, 2006; Wiebush, 2000, 2002), but most jurisdictions have no choice but to begin with consensus-based assessments because they do not have the necessary historical data to develop actuarial instruments.

The actuarial approach to risk assessment is similar to that used by the automobile insurance industry to determine insurance rates. Insurance companies analyze historical data on driver characteristics and outcomes (accidents) to determine the set of driver characteristics most closely correlated with accidents. After those characteristics are identified, all new clients are assessed to determine the extent to which their characteristics are similar to those who have had low, medium, or high failure rates in the past.

(Continued)

(Continued)

In other words, the individual's future behavior is estimated based on the known outcomes of a group of individuals with similar characteristics (Wiebush, 2000, 2002).

Similarly, actuarial juvenile offender risk assessment instruments are based on the statistical relationship between youth characteristics (risk factors) and recidivism rates (for a discussion of the essential properties of assessment and classification systems, see Gottfredson & Moriarty, 2006; Wiebush, 2002; Wiebush, Baird, Krisberg, & Onek, 1995, pp. 181–183). These instruments are designed to estimate the likelihood of an individual's reoffending within a given time period, generally 18–24 months. Thus risk assessment instruments are used to separate offenders into risk levels, a practice sometimes called *risk level classification*. Ideally, offenders would be placed at various levels within a graduated sanction system based on their likelihood of recidivism.

A *valid* risk assessment instrument is one that does what it purports to do—that is, accurately distinguishes between subgroups of youth according to the probability that they will engage in delinquent behavior (Wiebush, 2002). A *reliable* instrument is one that successfully ensures that similar cases receive similar placements and similar recommendations for interventions and services. Research results supporting the validity of risk assessments have increased dramatically in recent years (Gottfredson & Moriarty, 2006). One reason is that, with the growth of automated court and correctional record systems, large databases are now available to researchers who want to conduct risk assessment studies.

Such risk assessment instruments have been validated on nearly a dozen state juvenile populations and in other studies (Wiebush, 2002). In addition, risk assessment instruments recently have been validated for several serious violent offender subgroups, including felony recidivists (Barnoski, 2004a), first-time referrals versus second- and third-time referrals (LeCroy, Krysik, & Palumbo, 1998), and potential chronic offenders among second-time offenders (Smith & Aloisi, 1999). Three risk assessment instruments have been validated for successful classification of offenders based on their likelihood of recidivating with violent offenses: in Maryland (Wiebush, Johnson, & Wagner, 1997), Missouri (Johnson, Wagner, & Matthews, 2001), and Virginia (Wiebush, Wagner, & Erlich, 1999). In Missouri, high-risk youth had a subsequent violent court referral rate that was six times greater than that of low-risk youth (Johnson et al., 2001).

A well-designed risk tool can identify a group of high-risk youth who are at least three times more likely to reoffend than youth who are classified as low risk (Wiebush, 2002). A total of 10 items make up the Model Risk Assessment Instrument recommended by the National Council of Juvenile and Family Court Judges and the National Council on Crime and

Delinquency (Appendix; Wiebush, 2002, p. 83). This instrument is a composite of several research-based risk tools that the NCCD has developed over the past 10 years. The risk factors from 13 different risk tools were compared, and the items that appeared repeatedly across jurisdictions were selected for inclusion in the model scale (Wiebush, 2002). Some items increase the classification power of the scales in some jurisdictions but not in others, according to NCCD validation studies in numerous states. This finding suggests that there are site-specific factors that influence either recidivism or the measurement of it. Therefore, it is essential that each jurisdiction validate its own risk assessment instrument.

Need and strength assessments are used to determine offenders' treatment needs and personal and family strengths. These are used in tandem with risk assessment to place offenders in different supervision levels, then in program interventions within various supervision levels, using a matrix that organizes sanctions and program interventions by risk level and offense severity. Use of these research-based tools will help communities design a system that is fair, just, and cost-effective. As an added benefit, risk assessment instruments based on objective criteria, instead of sole reliance on arrest records and court referrals in which they are unjustly overrepresented, will help reduce disproportionate minority representation in the juvenile justice, mental health, and child welfare systems.

A state or community cannot know for sure whether it is properly protecting the public from juvenile offenders and using its juvenile justice resources in the most cost-effective manner unless it performs formal risk assessments. In addition, without the information that such assessments provide, it has little chance of effectively targeting SVC delinquents. Better screening of court-referred youth to identify those with multiple risk factors for recidivism can provide a basis for early intervention, which can help to prevent their progression to more serious and violent behavior. Multiple-problem youth—those experiencing a combination of mental health and school problems along with drug use and victimization—are at greatest risk for continued and escalating offending (Huizinga & Jakob-Chien, 1998; Huizinga, Loeber, Thornberry, & Cothern, 2000; Loeber et al., 2008).

To be most effective, program or facility placements must match the developmental history of the delinquent career and the risk of recidivism. When offenders persist in serious and violent delinquency, their position in a graduated sanctions system should be advanced to protect the public (Figure 10.3). As offenders progress in the graduated sanction system, linked rehabilitation programs must become more structured and intensive, to effectively deal with the intractable problems that more dangerous offenders present while reserving secure confinement for the very small number of serious violent offenders.

The disposition or program placement matrix is a tool designed to structure decisions about the most appropriate level of supervision or custody for adjudicated offenders at the time of case disposition (Wiebush, 2002). It can be used in one of two ways: either as dispositional guidelines for the

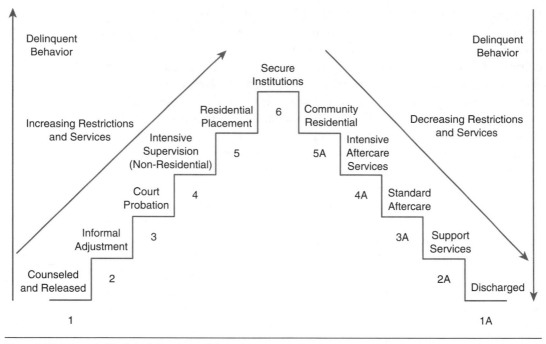

Figure 10.3 A Model of Graduated Sanctions

judiciary or as a way of structuring the recommendations made to judges by probation officers. The matrix serves a function that is critical to an effective system of graduated sanctions: linking each youth with the type of placement in the range of graduated sanctions that is most appropriate to his or her offense severity and level of risk. Respondents with the highest self-reported criminality (not lowest) tend to show the most responsiveness to the risk of sanctions (Schneider, 1990; Schneider & Ervin, 1990; Wright, Caspi, Moffitt, & Paternoster, 2004).

An excellent example of a state placement or disposition matrix is shown in Table 10.1. This is Missouri's Risk & Offense Case Classification Matrix, developed by the state's Office of State Courts Administrator. The complete Missouri Juvenile Offender Classification System includes the following:

- An *empirically validated risk assessment* for estimating a youthful offender's relative likelihood of future delinquency.
- The *classification matrix* (Table 10.1), which links the level of risk with offense severity to recommend graduated sanctions.
- A *need assessment* for identifying the underlying psychosocial needs of youth.
- A method for assessing juvenile offender adjustment to supervision through the use of a *supervision reassessment* form and a set of Web-based reports on the risk and need characteristics of youthful offenders. (Links are provided to each of these formal decision-making tools and written reports on system functions at the Missouri Office of State Courts Administrator: http://www.courts.mo.gov/page.asp?id=308.)

Table 10.1   Missouri Risk and Offense Case Classification Matrix

Offense severity	Group 1 offenses	Group 2 offenses	Group 3 offenses
Risk Level	*Status Offenses. Municipal Ordinances and Infractions*	*Class A, B.and C Misdemeanors and Class C and D Felonies*	*A* and B Felonies*
Low Risk	A) Warn and Counsel B) Restitution C) Community Service D) Court Fees and Assessments E) Supervision	A) Warn and Counsel B) Restitution C) Community Service D+) Court Fees and Assessments E) Supervision	B+) Restitution C+) Community Service D+) Court Fees and Assessments E) Supervision F) Day Treatment G) Intensive Supervision H) Court Residential Placement I) Commitment To DYS
Moderate Risk	A) Warn and Counsel B) Restitution C) Community Service D) Court Fees and Assessments E) Supervision	*A) Warn and Counsel* *B) Restitution* *C+) Community Service* *D+) Court Fees and Assessment* *E) Supervision* *F) Day Treatment*	B+) Restitution C+) Community Service D+) Court Fees and Assessments E) Supervision F) Day Treatment G) Intensive Supervision H) Court Residential Placement I) Commitment to DYS
High Risk	A) Warn and Counsel B) Restitution C) Community Service D) Court Fees and Assessments E) Supervision	B+) Restitution C+) Community Service D) Court Fees and Assessments E) Supervision F) Day Treatment G) Intensive Supervision H) Court Residential Placement I) Commitment to DYS	H) Court Residential Placement I) Commitment to DYS

NOTE: DYS = Division of Youth Services.

* Mandatory certification hearings are requred by statute for all Class A felonies. In the event that the juvenile is not certified, the juvenile officer should refer to this column of the matrix for classification purposes.

+ This symbol indicates options that should never be used as sole options for youths who score in that cell, but only in conjunction with other options.

This is a very user-friendly disposition matrix. It incorporates two dimensions, offense severity and risk level. The three groups of offenses are specified in Missouri's juvenile statutes. The risk levels are determined by offenders' scores on an empirically validated risk assessment instrument called a Risk Assessment Scale. In addition, a Needs Assessment Scale is used to match offenders with optional services in the intersecting boxes of the classification matrix. Notice how the schedules of disposition options form a natural continuum, moving from less restrictive alternatives for low-risk offenders adjudicated for group 1 offenses to secure confinement for high-risk offenders adjudicated for group 3 offenses.

Each city, county, or state that decides to implement a program placement matrix similar to this one would place its own current programs in sectors of the matrix that local professionals judge to be most appropriate. (The disposition options shown in the example in Table 10.1 are commonly used in a number of states.) This exercise often identifies gaps in the juvenile justice system continuum. Those gaps should be filled with evidence-based primary services for youth on probation and in juvenile correctional facilities (Tables 9.5, 9.7, and 9.8). The CS framework encourages a continuum-building approach to program improvements, and the program placement matrix encourages this.

In the remainder of this section, the graduated sanction component of the CS framework is illustrated. It consists of five levels of sanctions, moving from least to most restrictive:

1. Immediate intervention with first-time delinquent offenders (misdemeanors and nonviolent felonies) and nonserious repeat offenders

2. Intermediate sanctions for first-time serious or violent offenders, including intensive supervision for chronic and serious and violent offenders

3. Community confinement

4. Secure corrections for the most serious, violent, chronic offenders

5. Aftercare

These gradations—and the sublevels that can be created within them—form a continuum of intervention options that should be paralleled by a continuum of treatment options, which should include an array of referral and disposition resources for law enforcement, juvenile courts, and juvenile corrections officials.

Immediate Intervention

Early intervention services for disruptive children and child delinquents were reviewed in Chapter 9. Crisis services should be available in every community to help youth access needed services and to help families with short-term management of out-of-control adolescents. Yet few communities have family crisis centers or family stabilizing facilities; most have only crisis hotlines for adolescents, and these programs provide little parental support. Community assessment centers (for comprehensive assessments and service brokerage) are vitally important in performing screening and comprehensive assessments for delinquency, substance abuse, and mental health problems, and linking youth in need of services to agencies that provide these.

The Dawn Project in Indianapolis (Kamradt, 2000) is an excellent example of an immediate intervention that provides a wraparound framework; it incorporates New York City's Youth Emergency Service team concept of providing mobile, community-based services and crisis support around the clock. Among wraparound frameworks, the Connections wraparound program (Pullmann et al., 2006) appears to have the strongest empirical support to date; it has been recognized as a research-based program (http://guide.helpingamericasyouth.gov/).

The Annie E. Casey Foundation's Juvenile Detention Alternatives Initiative (JDAI) is viewed by many as the major juvenile justice reform event of the past decade (Box 10.6). Detention centers had become the dumping ground for high-need youth who should have been served in other systems but instead were referred to the juvenile court and detention centers. "School-based zero tolerance policies and practices [were] one of the primary forces driving these trends, with many jurisdictions now reporting that a sizable percentage—in some instances, a majority—of court referrals originated in schools, many for minor misbehaviors that previously were the responsibility of the education system" (Mendel, 2007, p. 13). Schools were not the only major contributors to overflowing detention centers. "The weaknesses of the nation's community mental health systems continued to propel many youth into detention even though meaningful treatment in these facilities remains but a sad illusion" (pp. 13–14).

IN FOCUS 10.6

The Annie E. Casey Foundation's Juvenile Detention Alternatives Initiative

Because of the overuse of detention and the unacceptable conditions in many detention centers, in 1992 the Annie E. Casey Foundation launched the JDAI, a multimillion-dollar 5-year, five-site experiment designed "to streamline and rationalize local juvenile detention systems" (Stanfield, 2000, p. 1). This very successful initiative provides a blueprint for detention reform that any jurisdiction experiencing common detention problems can follow.

(Continued)

(Continued)

Steinhart (2000) describes in detail the major milestones in a comprehensive juvenile detention planning strategy:

Stage 1: Document and describe the current juvenile detention system (Steinhart, 2000, pp. 20–36). Step 1 should consist of a quantitative analysis of current detention use and characteristics of detained youth. Step 2 is a system analysis, a review of detention policies and procedures. Step 3 is an analysis of the conditions of confinement (Burrell, 2000) to meet legal standards of care and to ensure the protection of children and staff. Step 4 is a cost analysis, including the cost per day per detention bed, alternative program cost per day, proposed cost of new facilities, case processing costs, and policy-related costs.

Stage 2: Identify local juvenile detention goals, which constitute the essential framework for local detention policy (Steinhart, 2000, pp. 37–39). Secure pretrial detention is justified by state and federal laws as a means to protect the public and ensure a minor's court appearance. The U.S. Constitution bars the use of pretrial detention for the purpose of punishment (Burrell, 2000).

Stage 3: Define the reformed system. Key reform strategies should include developing objective screening criteria and risk assessment instruments, addressing unnecessary case processing delays, developing alternatives to secure detention, dealing with minors in postdisposition detention, addressing conditions of confinement, dealing with disproportionate minority and female confinement, and deciding whether to build additional detention capacity (Steinhart, 2000, pp. 40–57).

Stage 4: Identify the cost of reforms, resources needed, and barriers to reform (Steinhart, 2000, pp. 58–62). These are important considerations in the development of a realistic plan.

Stage 5: Finalize and draft the action plan. The following are important considerations in setting priorities (Steinhart, 2000, pp. 63–67):

- Comprehensive reform is best.
- Front gate controls (objective risk screens) are a vital first step.
- Reduction of overcrowding must be a priority.
- Facility or program defects affecting the health and safety of children must be addressed.
- A continuum of alternatives to secure custody should be established (DeMuro, 2000).
- Priority should be assigned to reforms that are likely to address the problems causing the highest detention loads.
- Projections of future detention populations must be made.
- Management information system improvements are important, especially to increase accountability and improve operations.

Data have been gathered on the sites that successfully undertook major reforms of their detention systems using the JDAI framework, including restrictive admission criteria and development of viable, low-cost alternatives to detention. These data from selected JDAI sites show that reductions in detention do not lead to expected increases in delinquency; rather, detention reductions often lead to juvenile delinquency reductions and lower costs (Figure 10.4). In addition, reduced confinement in secure state correctional facilities has been a result of detention reductions in several sites (Figure 10.5), because detained youth are at an elevated risk of long-term secure incarceration.

Intermediate Sanctions

Intensive supervision has empirical support as a research-based program service for juveniles who have been adjudicated delinquent (Chapter 9, Table 9.5), and this is an excellent point from which offenders can be moved up and down in the graduated sanctions continuum (Figure 10.3). The primary services that have the strongest research support for probationers (Chapter 9, Table 9.5) are cognitive-behavioral therapy, group counseling, vocational training, and mentoring. The four most effective services form a nice continuum in terms of degree of control: vocational training, mentoring, group counseling, and cognitive–behavioral therapy. A search of the *Helping America's Youth Community Guide* reveals numerous effective pro - grams that use these services (http://guide.helpingamericasyouth.gov/). For aggressive youth, aggression replacement training, which uses cognitive–behavioral therapy in a group counseling format, is a low-cost option that

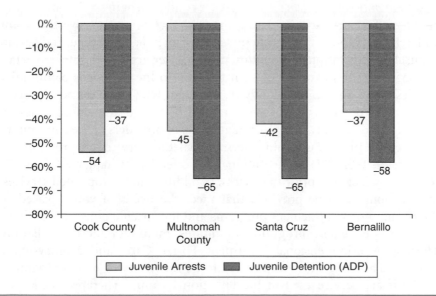

Figure 10.4   Impact of JDAI on Juvenile Delinquency and Detention Rates

NOTE: Figure shows juvenile crime reduced and detention reduced in JDAI model sites.

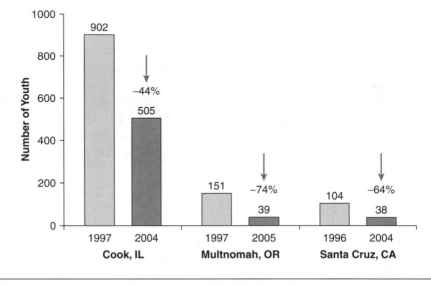

Figure 10.5   Impact of JDAI on Juvenile Offender Admissions to Secure Confinement

was cost-effective when used for probationers in the State of Washington (Barnoski, 2004b).

Community Confinement

Community confinement refers to secure confinement in small community-based, staff-secure facilities (group homes) that offer intensive treatment and rehabilitation services. These services include individual and group counseling, educational programs, medical services, and intensive staff supervision. The proximity of such facilities to the offender's community enables direct and regular family involvement with the treatment process and a phased reentry into the community that draws on community resources and services. The placement status of offenders in the community confinement programs would determine whether services for probationers (Chapter 9, Table 9.5) or institutionalized offenders (Chapter 9, Table 9.7) should be selected as priority services. In addition to the top-rated services, others should also be provided that meet the needs of youth placed in the community confinement programs and the specific objectives of those programs. Excellent program candidates include Functional Family Therapy, Multidimensional Treatment Foster Care, and Multisystemic Therapy. These are widely considered to be exemplary or model programs. The primary service used in the Functional Family Therapy and Multi-dimensional Treatment Foster care programs is family counseling. Cognitive–behavioral treatment is the primary service used in multisystemic therapy, and it also is considered to be a multimodal program in that the therapist works with the child, family, and peer groups simultaneously and in multiple environments.

Secure Corrections

The very few juveniles who cannot be confined safely in the community, who constitute an ongoing threat to community safety, or who have failed to respond to high-quality community-based correctional programs may need placement in training schools, camps, ranches, or other secure care options that are not community based. These facilities should offer comprehensive treatment programs for these youth that include evidence-based services, including behavior management, cognitive-behavioral therapy, job training, and interpersonal skill training (and other effective primary services shown in Table 9.8, Chapter 9).

In an ideal world, states would use only small facilities to confine their most dangerous juvenile offenders, because large congregate facilities have been shown to be ineffective in reducing recidivism with these offenders (Austin, Johnson, & Weitzer, 2005; Krisberg & Howell, 1998; Zavlek, 2005). Small correctional units and nonresidential programs with treatment orientations are more effective as well as more humane. Jurisdictions are advised to hold the maximum capacity of residential juvenile correctional facilities to approximately 50 beds (Zavlek, 2005). Most states are locked financially into the large juvenile correctional facilities they currently have and some have built larger ones recently. But a few states managed to maintain or create some small facilities or intensive treatment programs throughout the "get tough" movement, including Massachusetts, Missouri, Oregon, Pennsylvania, Washington, and Wisconsin. The State of North Carolina stands out for having *reduced* its reliance on large juvenile correctional facilities during this period. That accomplishment is detailed later in this chapter.

A new Wisconsin study shows that providing more treatment-focused services rather than harsher or more security-focused sanctions for serious and violent youth is cost-beneficial (Caldwell, Vitacco, & Van Rybroek, 2006). The Wisconsin program—the Mendota Juvenile Treatment Center (MJTC)—was created to provide mental health services to the most disturbed boys held in the state's secure correctional facilities. Youth were generally transferred to the MJTC because of their failure to adjust in the traditional correctional setting. The MJTC consisted of three units with 14 or 15 single-bed units, and the comparison group was in cottages of up to 50 double-bunked youth in the state's conventional juvenile correctional institutions (JCIs). The MJTC had more than twice the ratio of clinical staff to residents, compared with the JCIs, and a cognitive–behavioral treatment approach was used along with a variant of the "decompression" treatment model (which Caldwell developed) in the MJTC. Consequently, the daily bed cost in the intensive treatment program was more than twice that of the usual JCI program. However, the MJTC youths tended to stabilize and show behavioral improvements more quickly, and they had less than half the recidivism rates of the JCI comparison group. Consequently, the MJTC youths had significantly shorter overall periods of confinement.

The per-youth cost of the JCI comparison group was nearly $150,000. As a result of improving institutional adjustment and decreasing the length of stay of the MJTC youths, the mean marginal cost of treating them was approximately $7,000, an added cost of 4.5% over the mean cost for the JCI comparison group. The additional $7,000 investment per MJTC-treated youth generated mean marginal benefits (on recidivism costs avoided) of $50,000 per youth ($8,000 in avoided criminal justice processing costs plus $42,000 in avoided prison costs) over the 4.5-year follow-up period. This translates into a cost–benefit ratio of about 1 to 7; that is, the MJTC program produced benefits of $7.18 for every dollar of costs.

Aftercare

An estimated 200,000 juveniles and young adults ages 24 and younger leave secure juvenile correctional facilities or state and federal prisons and return home each year (Mears & Travis, 2004). Thus effective aftercare (or reentry, to use the currently popular term) is an important component of residential programs for juvenile offenders. Standard parole practices, particularly those that have a primary focus on social control, have not been effective in normalizing the behavior of high-risk juvenile parolees over the long term. Consequently, there is growing interest in intensive aftercare programs that provide high levels of social control and treatment services.

More and more, practitioners favor linking parole or aftercare with existing juvenile court programs, stepping offenders back down their continuum of graduated sanctions as recommended in the CS (see Figure 10.3). This is a sound approach because creating a separate aftercare track with the Intensive Aftercare Program (IAP) has not proved to be effective (Washington State Institute for Public Policy, 2002; Wiebush, Wagner, McNulty, et al., 2005), and postrelease supervision can best be met by giving court counselors responsibility for case management and supervising offenders. Put simply, postrelease supervision matters in terms of both frequency and duration (Chung, Schubert, & Mulvey, 2007). This two-site study, in Maricopa County (Phoenix), Arizona, and Philadelphia County, Pennsylvania, also found that court supervision—more so than community-based services—helped to promote successful community reintegration by connecting released offenders with schooling and work involvement.

Individualized services can also help facilitate a successful transition, such as Operation New Hope (http://guide.helpingamericasyouth.gov/). A developmental perspective is strongly recommended (Mears & Travis, 2004; Steinberg et al., 2004), buttressed by a supportive family and community network (see Box 10.7 and Roush, Moeser, & Walsh, 2005; Zimmerman, Hendrix, Moeser, & Roush, 2004).

IN FOCUS 10.7

Promising Approaches and Resources for Reentry Clients

A. Provide services and support for people who are or have been incarcerated:

1. For incarcerated people: Provide needed services and supports related to family, employment, mental and physical health, and spirituality, starting at the point of incarceration. Begin planning for release.

2. For those about to be released: Prepare a comprehensive discharge plan that includes living arrangements, medications, identification, transportation, emergency funds, escorts, and linkage to community or faith-based organizations and mentors.

3. For formerly incarcerated people: Make sure that individuals have access to supports and mentoring related to housing, substance abuse treatment, medicine and health care, education, job training, employment, child care, identification, transportation, and emergency funds.

B. Support children and families affected by incarceration: From incarceration through reentry, reach out to locate families of those in prison and assist them in maintaining ties, involve them in planning for release, and provide them with support. Make sure children are not blamed or penalized for their parents' circumstances or behavior.

C. Reduce legal and practical barriers to reintegration, including legal barriers to accessing employment, housing, and other benefits and services, as well as the loss of the right to vote.

D. Promote policies that support reentry of prisoners into communities. Criminal justice and sentencing, diversion, and release policies should reduce reliance on mass incarceration, maximize community-based sanctions and supervision, address the impact of sentencing on children and families, and reduce racial disparities.

In 2000, the State of Washington initiated a pilot rehabilitation program for juvenile offenders sentenced to state juvenile justice institutions (Washington State Institute for Public Policy, 2004). The program focuses on offenders with co-occurring substance abuse and mental health disorders. Offenders with both of these conditions are known to pose a high risk for committing new crimes upon reentry to the community. The legislation directed the Department of Social and Health Services' Juvenile

Rehabilitation Administration to develop the program. The specific approach adopted by Juvenile Rehabilitation Administration—the Family Integrated Transitions (FIT) program—was designed and implemented by program developers at the University of Washington. The FIT program uses a combination of evidence-based approaches tailored to the particular needs of these high-risk youth. It is an intensive treatment program that begins in the juvenile institution and continues for 4 to 6 months in the community. The FIT program was piloted in four Washington counties.

Researchers (Washington State Institute for Public Policy, 2004) found that without FIT, 41% of offenders were reconvicted for a new felony within 18 months of release from a Juvenile Rehabilitation Administration institution. For those who participated in FIT, the recidivism rate dropped to 27%, a statistically significant difference. This program should be replicated and researched elsewhere.

Mental Health Treatment

Provision of valid mental health problem assessment and effective treatment for serious emotionally disturbed youth in the juvenile justice and other child-serving systems is vitally important. The surgeon general's report (U.S. Department of Health and Human Services, 1999) called for nationwide attention to providing effective services to children, adolescents, and adults. More recent studies show that nearly three-fourths of detained female youth and two-thirds of detained male youth were assessed to have a psychiatric disorder, including minor ones (Teplin, Abram, McClelland, Dulcan, & Washburn, 2006). Assessments of juvenile offenders in secure, long-term correctional facilities also indicate serious mental health and substance abuse disorders (Wasserman, Ko, & McReynolds, 2004).

Progress has been made in providing effective services such as cognitive–behavioral treatment (Landenberger & Lipsey, 2005; Lipsey & Landenberger, 2006), and numerous other programs have demonstrated effectiveness, but delivering mental health services with fidelity remains a serious problem (Knitzer & Cooper, 2006). New technology makes mental health assessments of offenders in the juvenile justice system easier using the Voice DISC-IV (Wasserman, McReynolds, Lucas, Fisher, & Santos, 2002), and other unobtrusive mental health screening instruments are available (Grisso & Underwood, 2004; Grisso, Vincent, & Seagrave, 2005; Roberts & Bender, 2006). The voice format may be preferable to the paper format for screening juvenile justice system youth for mental health problems because it may reduce incomplete data, it may increase reporting of stigmatized behaviors, and it can automatically generate scored reports and aggregate data (Hayes, McReynolds, Wasserman, & Haxton, 2005). However, the overall protocol is as important as the mental health assessments themselves (Wasserman, Ko, & Jensen, 2002; Wasserman et al., 2004; Box 10.8). In addition, needed treatment can be more easily linked with evidence-based prevention and treatment services for children and adolescents with mental health problems (Wasserman, Ko, et al., 2002; Weisz, Sandler, Durlak, & Anton, 2005).

IN FOCUS 10.8
Best Practices for Clinical Assessment in Different Juvenile Justice Settings

Mental health assessments should be based on multiple methods of evaluation and on the input of multiple informants. A structured interview is one important component of a mental health assessment. Other important components include direct observation, a mental status examination, chart review, interviews with parents or caregivers, and a family psychiatric and psychosocial (psychological and social) history.

Assessments should be based on reliable and valid instruments. Use of a common assessment language eliminates uncertainty about the criteria used to determine diagnoses and enables comparison across studies and facilities.

Assessments should include parental input. Parental input is valuable in diagnosing certain disorders, particularly attention deficit hyperactivity disorder. Incorporating parental reports into mental health assessments of youth in the justice system is complicated by several factors, including parents' unavailability or reluctance to incriminate their children. The accuracy of parental reports may also be limited by parent–child separation. However, when parental and youth reports of attention deficit hyperactivity disorder symptoms are combined, increased rates of this disorder are detected (Loeber, Farrington, Stouthamer-Loeber, & Van Kammen, 1998).

Assessments should focus on recent symptoms in order to determine current treatment needs. Depending on the purpose of the assessment and the setting in which it takes place, the time frame for diagnostic status might vary from the past year to the past month. Assessments should be driven by practical decisions that take into consideration needs at various stages of justice system processing. For example, assessments might aim to accurately identify at least two groups of youth: those whose mental health needs should be met quickly, such as youth who recently have attempted suicide or who currently suffer from a panic disorder or substance dependence, and those who need close supervision and regular reassessment, such as youth with less severe disorders (e.g., depression or posttraumatic stress disorder) that may worsen under the stress of confinement.

Some youth should be reassessed periodically. Youth should be reassessed regularly when they are held in custody over an extended period of time, as symptom profiles may shift. Mood disorders and anxiety disorders, in particular, may wax and wane over time.

Comprehensive Strategy Implementation

Implementation of the CS is a deliberate process because it engages communities and states in a long-term system reform process. Complete implementation of the prevention, early intervention, and graduated sanction components may take 4–5 years because new system tools and infrastructures must be developed. Full implementation within the juvenile justice system should result in less use of secure confinement, freeing resources that can be allocated to prevention and front-end services. Accomplishing full cross-agency implementation involving child welfare, child protection, mental health, education, and juvenile justice agencies may take longer. States and communities that achieve this goal should realize reductions in a wide range of child and adolescent problem behaviors. However, full CS implementation is not needed for communities and states to realize tangible benefits. Indeed, most of them take an incremental approach, implementing parts of the CS framework in a planned sequence. Ongoing training and technical assistance are essential to successful implementation. Of course, incorporating the CS in statewide legislation greatly facilitates implementation and diffusion. North Carolina is a case in point.

In the mid-1990s, the juvenile justice system in North Carolina was experiencing the consequences of "get tough" policies. Some of the state's juvenile reformatories—called Youth Development Centers (YDCs)—were overcrowded and overpopulated with minor offenders. Admissions were increasing at a rate of approximately 10% per year (Lubitz, 2001). In 1996, only one-fifth of the juveniles confined in YDCs were violent felony offenders; the majority (nearly 60%) were moderately serious offenders (Lubitz, 2001), and about one-fifth were misdemeanants. The growth in admissions had been driven by the increased confinement of misdemeanants and moderately serious offenders, not by any increase in the numbers of violent offenders.

Influenced by the CS, North Carolina state officials and legislators saw a way to address two policy concerns. First, they wanted to increase public safety by targeting the most serious, violent, *and* chronic juvenile offenders for more restrictive sanctions, particularly confinement in the YDCs. Second, they wanted to preserve the futures of the state's young people by increasing early intervention efforts with community treatment programs. North Carolina's Juvenile Justice Reform Act of 1998 (S.L. 1998-202) incorporated the CS framework and addressed both of these policy goals by incorporating the graduated sanction scheme recommended in the CS. The Juvenile Justice Reform Act implemented the CS framework.

The 1998 Reform Act established Juvenile Crime Prevention Councils (JCPCs) in every county across the state to implement the prevention component of the CS. Each JCPC has a membership of not more than 25 people, all of whom are appointed by county boards of commissioners. The councils are made up of representatives of the full array of county government, social service, and education agencies, as well as youth representatives and representatives of the juvenile justice system, the faith community, and the business sector. The JCPCs are charged with developing comprehensive delinquency prevention plans; they also fund and monitor programs, ensuring that a wide variety of services and dispositional options are available. In sum, the JCPC programs in North Carolina may play a big role in the overall functioning of the state's juvenile justice system. These may keep youths out of the juvenile justice system by providing services to those who have elevated risk of delinquency involvement or minor delinquency.

The Department of Juvenile Justice and Delinquency Prevention has developed a Strategic Planning Tool that JCPCs use to map the flow of juveniles in each county's juvenile justice system. It is divided into sections that correspond to the dispositional levels in the juvenile justice system (e.g., juveniles at intake, diversion plans, approved for court, adjudicated, YDC commitments). Electronic client tracking data for prevention clients and tracking data for court-referred youth show offenders' levels of system penetration. The Strategic Planning Tool also enables the JCPCs to determine the number of youths who need services in each level of the system.

The act also mandated the use of the formal decision-making model recommended in the CS, consisting of risk and need assessments and an offender classification matrix to place offenders along a continuum of programs and sanctions. The North Carolina disposition matrix uses two factors to determine the placement of adjudicated juvenile offenders: current offense and risk level. A simple formula—factoring in chronic offending and whether the current offense was committed while the offender was on probation—guides determination of the risk level. The intersection of the risk level and current offense governs placement of an offender at Level 1, 2, or 3. For example, an offender with a serious and chronic offense history (i.e., high risk) who has been adjudicated for a violent offense would earn a Level 3 disposition, commitment to a YDC. Level 2 is an intermediate disposition, and Level 1 is a community disposition. Admissions to YDCs have been reduced by two-thirds (68%) in the 9 years since the department was created (Figure 10.6). In addition, the proportion of committed offenders with SVC offense histories has increased significantly.

The sharp reduction in confinement, coupled with physical deterioration in some of the existing secure confinement facilities, recently led the Department of Juvenile Justice and Delinquency Prevention to undertake additional major reforms in its correctional programming. In the spring of 2008, the Department of Juvenile Justice and Delinquency Prevention ceremoniously dedicated the first of four smaller, community-connected replacement YDCs to open across the state this year. A new program concept will be applied in each of these facilities. This treatment approach, a blended education–treatment Model of Care, features community-based programming that keeps committed offenders connected to their homes, families, and communities and the more effective court-based programs.

The Jackson Project is the first site to implement the Department of Juvenile Justice and Delinquency Prevention's new Model of Care. The project is located on the campus of Stonewall Jackson Youth Development

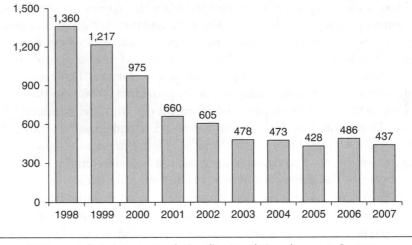

Figure 10.6   Admissions to North Carolina Youth Development Centers, 1998–2007

Center in Concord, North Carolina, within an existing housing unit, the Kirk Building. The Jackson Project serves a maximum of 16 students, randomly assigned from three North Carolina counties. Department of Juvenile Justice and Delinquency Prevention staff has been trained to use cognitive-behavioral skills that allow them to serve as key agents of change for the youth. The staff-to-youth ratio, which is critical to the success of programming, is one staff member per four youth. In addition, education is offered in small classes, with teachers assisting in behavior management and individualized instruction being conducted by youth counselors. As youth progress through the program, they are expected to spend more time in community-based activities, including vocational training, jobs, and educational pursuits. Family and community involvement in all treatment-related activities is also encouraged. Early outcomes of the Jackson Project are encouraging. Of the 18 youth released from the Jackson Project in 2007, only 33% (six) have subsequently been arrested for another criminal offense, compared with 45% of control group members (North Carolina Department of Juvenile Justice and Delinquency Prevention, 2008b).

Two other examples follow that demonstrate the utility of formal decision-making tools in conjunction with the CS framework. First, Orange County, California, probation officials targeted potential chronic and serious offenders among first-time court referrals, using an empirically based risk assessment instrument (Schumacher & Kurz, 2000). The nationally acclaimed 8% Early Intervention Program (also called "The 8% Solution," Schumacher & Kurz,, 2000) was developed for the highest-risk offenders (the 8% group), whereas the medium-risk group (22%) is assigned to the Intensive Intervention Program, and the remainder (70%) is assigned to the Immediate

Accountability Program, supervised by volunteer probation officers. This systematic way of managing offenders proved very helpful in developing a continuum of sanctions and matching youth with a parallel continuum of appropriate programs (Figure 10.7; Schumacher & Kurz, 2000).

The second example illustrates that juvenile courts can carry out risk-focused prevention by targeting the problem behaviors that are precursors to active delinquency involvement. Guided by the CS, San Diego County's strategic plan linked the prevention and graduated sanction components in a comprehensive "Breaking Cycles" program (Burke & Pennell, 2001). The prevention component targeted youth who had not yet entered the juvenile justice system but evidenced problem behaviors (chronic disobedience to parents, curfew violations, repeated truancy, running away from home, drug and alcohol use, or other serious behavior problems). An evaluation of the program showed that the prevention strategy dramatically reduced the number of at-risk youths entering the juvenile justice system and that the graduated sanction component was effective in deterring offenders from progressing to more serious delinquency (Burke & Pennell, 2001). This program reflects two key CS principles: the importance of prevention programs in reducing the number of juvenile justice system clients and in forestalling the development of more serious delinquent careers.

Each of these initiatives represents a different way of implementing a continuum of programming while planning strategically to strengthen the system as a whole. Such system reform is a key goal in using the CS framework as a guide. Another way of thinking about building such a continuum is to construct a series of programs that parallel the development of offender careers. The concept here is prevention and intervention windows of opportunity that are illustrated in Figure 10.8. This figure is another way of illustrating the general theory of delinquency and gang involvement that

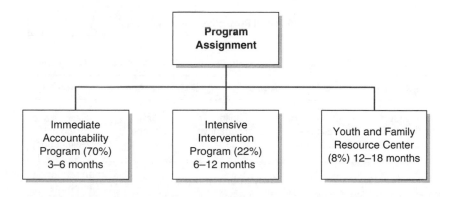

Figure 10.7   Orange County Model Juvenile Justice Continuum

I presented in Chapter 4. The figure is organized around age periods, from about age 3 into young adulthood. The top section of the figure shows the major protective and risk factor domains: family, school, peer group, individual, and community contexts. These domains are organized according to their approximate relationship to developmental aging of children and adolescents. The middle section of Figure 10.8 illustrates the faulty developmental process that leads to SVC delinquency if prevention and intervention efforts are not successful. The bottom section of the figure illustrates the parallel types of interventions that would be appropriate, given youngsters' progression along the gang involvement pathway and into progressively more serious delinquency involvement.

There is a large window of opportunity for intervention between the onset of delinquency and the point at which juvenile court intervention occurs. Stouthamer-Loeber and Loeber (2002) found that by the time a youngster got to court for an index offense in Pittsburgh, his or her parents probably had coped for several years with the child's problem behavior (see the onset age of violent behavior in the Pittsburgh study shown in Figure 5.5). "Almost half the boys who eventually became [self-reported] persistent serious delinquents had an onset of serious delinquency before age 12" (p. 79). Overall, two-thirds of the delinquents were not brought to juvenile court for at least 5 years, and 40% of the self-reported persistent serious delinquents did not have a court petition by age 18, which means that the juvenile court system cannot possibly intervene in their criminal careers except on an informal basis. Stouthamer-Loeber and Loeber identified three ways of reducing the obvious intervention gap shown in the Pittsburgh study data: make services more accessible to parents, implement school-based programs, and maintain interagency collaboration between the juvenile court and other child and family service agencies. In fact, such intervention lags are common in other key agencies (Burns et al., 2001).

Risk and Protective Factors				
Family	School	Peer Group	Individual Characteristics	Community
Age 3	**Age 6**	**Age 9**	**Age 12**	**Age 15**	**Age 18**
Conduct Problems	Elementary School Failure	Child Delinquency	Gang Member	Serious and Violent Delinquency
Prevention		**Early Intervention**		**Treatment and Sanctions**

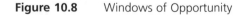

Figure 10.8   Windows of Opportunity

The aforementioned examples are but a few illustrations of CS implementation (see Howell, 2003b, pp. 278–304, for numerous others). A reasonable estimate is that juvenile justice policies and practices have been influenced by the CS in at least 20 states and up to 50 sites. Several states enacted legislation that promoted both graduated sanctions and individualized treatment, as recommended in the CS (Mears, 2002).

To increase community capacity for building such a continuum of programs and services, it is advisable to develop a well-organized interagency infrastructure to better integrate services in real time. The necessary components are shown in Box 10.9. Implementing the CS framework means integrating mental health, child welfare, education, substance abuse, and juvenile justice system services. To accomplish this, an infrastructure probably will be needed, consisting of information exchange, cross-agency client referrals, a networking protocol, interagency councils, and service integration models.

IN FOCUS 10.9

Necessary Components of an Interagency Infrastructure for Service Integration

- *Information exchange.* Exchange of information is important for coordination, control, planning, and client assessment purposes. Confidentiality of client records often deters collaboration; however, barriers to information sharing can be reduced through identification of legal and policy barriers and often removed, especially when youth and parents (or other caregivers) are actively involved in services planning (Mankey, Baca, Rondenell, Webb, & McHugh, 2006).
- *Cross-agency client referrals.* The key to successful cross-agency client referrals is each agency's need to see a return on interagency investments in the form of service resources for referred clients. The immediate targets for cross-agency referrals are youth in two or more systems. However, the primary clients should be all youth currently in or at risk of residential placement because of the associated high cost and lower effectiveness of this option.
- *Networking protocol.* This refers to negotiated agreements between agencies that outline information exchange and cross-agency client referral conditions and procedures. Such agreements stimulate growth in communication and increase client sharing.
- *Interagency councils.* Buttressed by information exchange and effective cross-agency client referrals, participation in interagency councils will lead to resource sharing and joint action to solve service issues and problems.

(Continued)

(Continued)

- *Integrated services.* Comprehensive and objective assessments of treatment needs provide the basis for development of client and family treatment plans involving multiple agencies and integrated services. The networking agreement should ensure that all youth and families receive the same assessment and case management protocols from the respective agencies at several locations. Information gathered by one service provider should be available to other service providers via an integrated management information system that links key agencies, including law enforcement, juvenile justice, education, mental health, substance abuse, and child welfare agencies.

Other Statewide Reforms

Other states have undertaken significant juvenile justice system reforms, including California, Illinois, Louisiana, Ohio, Pennsylvania, Washington, and Wisconsin. New initiatives in several of these states have shown that by changing how they fund their juvenile justice systems, states and localities can succeed in keeping more youth at home, reduce the number of youth incarcerated, and promote better outcomes for young people moving through these systems (Tyler, Ziedenberg, & Lotke, 2006, p. 1). Four of these states (Pennsylvania, Illinois, Louisiana, and Washington) received $10 million each from the John D. and Catherine T. MacArthur Foundation as centerpieces of its $100-million initiative to implement its "Models for Change." Each of these four states seeks to move toward a more rational, fair, effective, and developmentally appropriate juvenile justice system. Additional information is available at the MacArthur Foundation Web site: http://www.macfound.org/site/c.lkLXJ8MQKrH/b.943477/k.9538/Domestic_Grantmaking__Juvenile_Justice.htm. At the Georgetown University Public Policy Institute, the Center for Juvenile Justice Reform trains public agency leaders through a variety of activities. Additional information is available at http://cjjr.georgetown.edu/index.html.

Evaluation of Reforms

A method has not been developed to evaluate with quantitative methods the success of system reforms that are stimulated by a self-empowerment framework such as the CS. However, it is possible to evaluate programs within each continuum sector (e.g., prevention, graduated sanctions, and aftercare). The use of Lipsey's Standardized Program Evaluation Protocol should greatly facilitate this enterprise, and work is needed to integrate its use with risk and needs and strengths tools in case management of offenders.

The recommended evaluation design would incorporate a system flow perspective, using the CS framework that encompasses the entire juvenile justice system from primary prevention to discharge from postdispositional placement (Figure 10.9). In this design, developed by my colleague, Dr. Mark Lipsey, youths who enter the juvenile justice system are viewed as moving along alternative pathways of services and sanctions, during which they interact with juvenile justice service programs and supervision contexts. Each such pathway is associated with certain outcomes and costs, with the outcomes themselves entailing later costs or cost savings according to how positive they are. The key concept of the evaluation design is to use the automated state data systems to continuously monitor those outcomes and costs in a way that will allow periodic assessment of the effectiveness of the major pathways and, collectively, the overall juvenile justice system. The critical elements of this evaluation system are systematic identification of the relevant service and sanction pathways in the state or local data systems (as the case may be, wherever a continuum of program services is implemented), risk and need information for each juvenile at entry, recidivism outcomes after completion of a pathway, service and supervision costs, and expected costs associated with recidivism and reentry into the juvenile justice system.

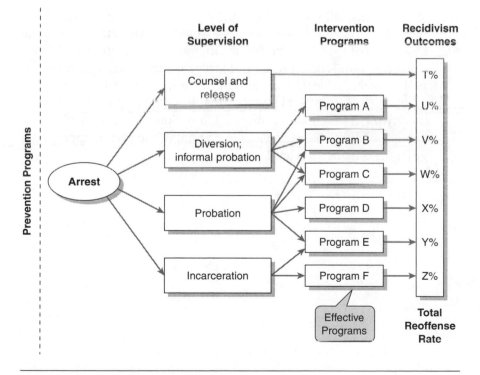

Figure 10.9 Comprehensive Strategy Evaluation Design

Some scholars have called for monitoring the overall performance of juvenile justice systems with objective criteria. The juvenile delinquency guidelines developed by the National Council of Juvenile and Family Court Judges (2005) provide a useful framework for this purpose. In addition, the September 2008 issue of *Criminal Justice Policy Review* is devoted to improving the capacity of juvenile justice systems to hold offenders accountable for their performance. Such reviews should encompass other child-serving systems and the criminal justice system as well.

Discussion Topics

1. How could the Comprehensive Strategy be applied to child and adolescent problems such as an epidemic of school suspensions?

2. How could the Comprehensive Strategy be applied to a youth gang problem?

3. How do formal decision-making tools help communities in strategic planning?

4. Take an example from the list of "Common Juvenile Justice System Conditions" (Box 10.3) and explain how the Comprehensive Strategy could be used to address them.

5. Working in small groups, construct a continuum of effective probation and correctional programs that would appropriately fit into the nine boxes of the Missouri Risk & Offense Case Classification Matrix using program services listed in Lipsey's evidence-based services for probationers (Table 9.5) and also those for institutionalized offenders (Table 9.8). Also, use blueprint programs (Table 9.1). Feel free to modify the arrangement of disposition options if you determine that another evidence-based service or program would also be appropriate given the classification level.

CHAPTER 11

What Doesn't Work in Preventing and Reducing Juvenile Delinquency

Thanks to the voluminous increase in the number of program evaluations in the past couple of decades, evidence is accumulating that some prevention and intervention strategies and programs simply do not work with juvenile offenders. I address many of the strategies and programs that do not work in the first main section of this chapter and then discuss the evidence to date on many others for which the research findings are unclear, contradictory, or nonexistent. I discuss a particularly ineffective strategy in some detail in the next chapter: the failed policy of transferring juveniles to the criminal justice system.

Ineffective Prevention Approaches

D.A.R.E.

I begin this section with a discussion of the delinquency prevention approach known as D.A.R.E. (Drug Abuse Resistance Education). My purpose is not to single out this well-intentioned program for criticism; rather, I believe that D.A.R.E provides an informative example of how some interventions have staying power despite their ineffectiveness.

D.A.R.E. is not effective (Rosenbaum, 2007); it is perhaps the most widely acclaimed "successful" intervention of all ineffective delinquency prevention programs. Launched in 1983 by the Los Angeles Police Department and the Los Angeles Unified School District, it enjoyed instant success because it fit with former First Lady Nancy Reagan's "Just Say No" to drugs campaign (Boyle, 2001). D.A.R.E. has grown into a $200-million-per-year enterprise that employs 50,000 police officers who teach the D.A.R.E. curriculum, lecturing against drug use in nearly half of the nation's elementary schools (Gottfredson & Gottfredson, 2002). Thus D.A.R.E. is the most frequently used substance abuse educational curriculum in the United States.

D.A.R.E. is one of the most poignant examples of a supposed panacea that continues to be used despite strong empirical evidence that it is not effective. More than 30 evaluations have been made of D.A.R.E. (Rosenbaum, 2007), and the findings can be summarized in this way (p. 816): First, the core D.A.R.E. curriculum has some immediate beneficial effects on student knowledge of drugs, attitudes about drug use, social skills, and attitudes toward the police; second, these positive effects dissipate quickly (typically within 1 to 2 years); and third, D.A.R.E.'s effects on drug use behaviors are extremely rare and very small, and these too dissipate quickly. Claims have been made that the revised D.A.R.E. curriculum is effective, presumably based on an evaluation sponsored by the Robert Wood Johnson Foundation, but the results have not been published in refereed journals according to Rosenbaum (2007). "In any event, D.A.R.E is alive and well. Rather than being shelved and replaced by other more effective programs, it has been rescued and rehabbed" (p. 820).

Zero Tolerance Policies

In Chapter 2, I show how misguided zero tolerance policies in schools can have devastating consequences on youths' futures. Zero tolerance policies are not effective because they call for immediate and severe punishment of every infraction of codes of conduct, school rules, and laws, and such an approach is not realistic. First, rules must be applied with some discretion. Second, every student rule violation is not brought to the attention of school authorities. Because the authorities are unable to enforce zero tolerance policies completely and consistently, children and adolescents come to see the authorities as arbitrary and capricious in their enforcement of the rules. The authorities lose credibility, and the validity of codes of conduct, school rules, and laws is undermined. This also weakens the bonding of students to the school and teachers and undermines healthy social development, and thus may contribute to delinquency involvement. Last, the central weapon school officials use in application of zero tolerance policies is punishment (Lyons & Drew, 2006). The next section explains why this is not effective.

There is another harmful effect of tolerance policies on youths, however. Schools may feed students into the school-to-prison pipeline by removing them from school altogether through zero tolerance and other harsh discipline policies. School suspension increases the likelihood of detention and involvement in gangs and of arrest and court referral, followed by a greater probability of secure confinement in a state juvenile correctional facility, and finally imprisonment; this sequence is called the school-to-prison pipeline (Christle, Jolivette, & Nelson, 2005). Minority youths, especially African Americans, are far more likely to have their life chances blocked off by discriminatory zero tolerance policies (National Association for the Advancement of Colored People, 2006).

Ineffective Juvenile Justice Programs and Strategies

Punishment for Juvenile Offenders

Punishment is not effective for juvenile offenders. The purposes of punishment should not be confused with rehabilitation, however. Punishment serves only the purpose of "justice," to exact a penalty from one who has wronged society. But the administration of more and more severe punishments for juvenile offenders has become common in the United States (Box 11.1). Surprisingly, neither the certainty nor the severity of punishment decreases recidivism among most juveniles (Schneider, 1990; Schneider & Ervin, 1990). In her evaluation of the Office of Juvenile Justice and Delinquency Prevention (OJJDP) national restitution program, Schneider (1990) found that adolescents who believed they were more likely to be caught committed more, rather than fewer, subsequent offenses. All of the youths had been convicted of offenses that would have been crimes if committed by adults, and many would be considered to fall into the category of serious and chronic offenders. Even those who believed they would be punished more severely if they were caught committed more, rather than fewer, subsequent offenses.

IN FOCUS 11.1

A Brief History of the U.S. Wars on Crime and Drugs

Legislators and policy makers in the United States tend to "declare war" on social problems, and their actions in response to such problems are often characterized by aggression (Zimring, 1998a). The "war on crime" begun by the Nixon administration and the "war on drugs" fought by the Reagan administration, the Clinton administration, and both Bush administrations are the results of events that made crime a prominent public policy issue.

Crime first became an important public policy issue in modern times when presidential candidate Barry Goldwater, looking for a message to grab the public's attention, made frightening pronouncements about crime and

(Continued)

(Continued)

demanded "law and order," so women and children would be safe on the streets (Chambliss, 1995). The media and the public responded with alarm, and a "moral panic" was created. Congress soon got on the bandwagon, passing the Omnibus Crime Control and Safe Streets Act of 1968, which legalized wiretapping and bugging by federal agents and local police without a court order. The act also authorized $3 billion for prison construction. In that same year, presidential candidate Richard Nixon was hammering away at the issue of law and order. By the time he was elected president, surveys showed that Americans placed "crime, lawlessness, looting and rioting" as their second main concern, behind the Vietnam War (Chambliss, 1995, p. 247). In 1970, President Nixon signed into law the Organized Crime Control Act, which contained "some revolutionary changes in the administration of criminal law" (Chambliss, 1995, p. 249). These included changes in evidence-gathering requirements, new federal sanctions and punishments, and the creation of a powerful investigative federal grand jury. In addition, the act allowed the courts to compel witnesses to testify if they were granted immunity and expanded conditions under which witnesses could be charged with perjury.

The New Right—a U.S. political movement formed in 1974 that melded extreme conservatism with the Religious Right—perfected "single-issue politics" (Reeves & Campbell, 1994), and there is no better example than the Reagan administration's war on drugs. Reeves and Campbell (1994) and Brownstein (1996) meticulously documented the role of the media, politicians, law enforcement representatives, and the U.S. government in the creation of a moral panic over crack cocaine that demonized poor, young black youth. Brownstein's work details how actions, decisions, interpretations, and interactions between criminal justice policy makers and analysts, law enforcement representatives, and news makers—all of whom acted as claim makers in the context of the evolving crack cocaine market to support their own interests—contributed to the construction of a violent crime wave, and young people, especially juveniles, were identified as the main perpetrators. The demonization of juveniles was so effective that homicides involving juvenile suspects still receive more extensive news coverage than the more prevalent murders by adults (Pizarrro, Chermak, & Gruenewald, 2007).

Reeves and Campbell's analysis of 270 television news reports broadcast between 1981 and 1988 (the Reagan years) "demonstrate how, in constructing and reaffirming cocaine as a moral disease and a criminal pathology, the network news also facilitated the staging and legitimating of Reagan's war on drugs as a major political spectacle" (p. 1). "Just say no" was the simple solution and slogan. At the height of this "war," 1986, Reagan announced his "urinary crusade," in which he asked members of his cabinet to voluntarily submit to drug testing. Unbelievably, this request deteriorated into "jar wars" (pp. 180–181) as political candidates challenged one another to pass the drug abstinence test.

Reagan appointed a "drug czar" to lead the "war on drugs," and his administration and the administrations of every president since that time have spent billions of dollars fighting the "war," yet there is no evidence that this spending has had any significant impact. The total cost of the U.S. war on drugs is about $45 billion per year (Executive Office of the President of the United States, 2005).

Asset forfeiture laws soon were made an instrument of the war on drugs. These laws allowed federal agents to seize and dispose of a person's car, house, or other property if there was probable cause that the property had been used in relation to drug trafficking—even if the owner was never arrested or convicted of any crime (Bovard, 1999). Without any due process of law, agents seized cars, boats, homes, and other properties presumably used in connection with criminal drug trafficking.

In one of the most notorious asset forfeiture cases, the U.S. Supreme Court upheld the constitutionality of these laws (Biskupic, 1996). The defendant, Guy Jerome Ursery, was arrested for growing marijuana on his land. Law enforcement agencies seized his home. He argued that this violated his constitutional protection against double jeopardy, contending that he was punished twice for the same offense by being arrested and losing his home. The Supreme Court ruled against him in a vote of eight to one. Speaking for the majority, Chief Justice William H. Rehnquist reasoned that the government did not violate Ursery's constitutional right against double jeopardy because the civil action was taken against his home, not against him. His house was deemed guilty.

In another case, Florida police seized the automobile of Tyvessel White, who was arrested for an offense unrelated to drug trafficking. However, police suspected that White had used his car to deliver illegal drugs, and they seized it under the state's asset forfeiture law. Although White was never charged with drug trafficking, the U.S. Supreme Court upheld the car seizure, simply on the grounds that the automobile was suspected of being involved in a crime (Bovard, 1999). More than $5.9 billion was deposited in the U.S. Justice Department's Asset Forfeiture Fund between 1985 (when federal authority to seize property was expanded) and 1999 (Fields, 1999). The Civil Asset Forfeiture Reform Act of 2000 amended the federal law to require that the government show a preponderance of the evidence, not just probable cause, in order to seize personal property; the new law also provides some recourse for falsely accused citizens. The new act was opposed by the Clinton administration, the U.S. Justice and Treasury departments, and law enforcement organizations, on the grounds that it would unreasonably restrict their use of the 1985 law (Fields, 1999). Nevertheless, the act was passed in Congress, and President Clinton signed it into law on August 23, 2000.

In recent years, the "war on crime" has taken on a new dimension inspired by the "broken windows" philosophy of policing (Kelling & Coles, 1996; Wilson & Kelling, 1982), which is based on the notion that small crimes lead

(Continued)

(Continued)

inevitably to bigger ones (but see Harcourt, 2001). The idea is that just as unrepaired broken windows on buildings in a neighborhood often lead to further deterioration of the area, ignored minor offenses and other public disorderly behavior frighten citizens and lead to more serious crimes (Greene, 1999). Beginning in 1993, New York City led the way in implementing a zero tolerance policing strategy based on this concept, strictly enforcing laws concerning disorderly behavior in public places. William Bratton, then the new commissioner of the New York Police Department, "took the handcuffs off" the police (Bratton, 1998). Patrol officers were "unleashed" and directed by Commissioner Bratton to "stop and search citizens who were violating the most minor laws on the books (e.g., drinking a beer or urinating in public), to run warrant checks on them, or just pull them in for questioning about criminal activity in their neighborhood" (Greene, 1999, p. 175).

Commissioner Bratton and New York's mayor, Rudy Giuliani, attributed a drop in serious and violent crime rates in the city to these zero tolerance policing strategies (Bratton, 1998). However, the connection was overstated (Harcourt & Ludwig, 2006), if not purely coincidental (Greene, 1999). In fact, certain forms of violence had been declining substantially in New York City for 8 years before the implementation of "broken windows" policing, and the declines could not plausibly be explained by these later events (Zimring & Fagan, 2000). As Sampson and Raudenbush (2001) observe, "It is the structural characteristics of neighborhoods, as well as neighborhood cohesion and informal social control—not levels of disorder—that most affect crime" (p. 4). Serious and violent crime rates were dropping sharply at the same time across the country in cities where no such strategies were implemented. Moreover, reports of police brutality increased in New York City during this period (Amnesty International, 1996, 1999). Nevertheless, other cities emulated New York's zero tolerance approach and, generally, more aggressive policing. Boston's Gun Project/Operation Ceasefire is a case in point (see Chapter 7). Richmond's Project Exile—based on zero tolerance for gun violations—served as another popular model that many other jurisdictions replicated (Ludwig, 2005). However, the legal changes giving police broader investigative and arrest authority probably had a far greater impact than widely publicized models of zero tolerance policing. Now, complaints of excessive use of force by police are common, with more than 26,000 filed in 2002, but few were substantiated by police investigations (Hickman, 2006). However, only 19% of large municipal police departments had a civilian complaint review board or agency in their jurisdictions. More independent oversight of police is needed (Greene, 2007). Police brutality charges continue to increase (Johnson, 2007).

Although scholars disagree over the developments that account for the onset of extremely punitive crime and delinquency philosophy and policies in the United States beginning in the 1970s (cf. Beckett & Sasson, 2003; Bishop, 2006; Cullen, 2005; Mears, 2006), there is no question that arrest, prosecution, and confinement rates were driven up drastically in the 1980s and 1990s by the four domestic U.S. "wars": the "war on crime," the "war on drugs," the "war on gangs," and the "war on juveniles" (Howell, 2003b). Undoubtedly, the centerpiece of the war on drugs was the battle against the so-called crack cocaine epidemic (Brownstein, 1996; Reeves & Campbell, 1994). The wars on juveniles and gangs followed, and the demonization of juveniles and other gang members, who were presumed to have played a central role in cocaine distribution, became a popular theme in broadcast media (Chapter 2) and for politicians (McCollum, 1997) in the 1990s.

The "politics of panic" began to dominate crime control policies (Beckett & Sasson, 2003) as "wars" on crime, drugs, gangs, and juveniles hyped crime issues. Soon, bringing juveniles into court in chains became common (M. T. Moore, 2007). A new breed of lobbyists emerged who promoted conservative punitive reforms such as "three strikes," "mandatory minimums," and "truth in sentencing" legislation. Ready-made bills were carried into lawmakers' offices, and print media promoted more conservative and punitive crime control measures (Beckett & Sasson, 2003; Brownstein, 1996; Reeves & Campbell, 1994). Punitive laws, policies, and practices had been institutionalized by systematic initiatives on the part of conservatives, but others also played a key role. The mass media, government, and law enforcement helped to construct an epidemic of violent crime related to crack cocaine and then used that epidemic to support a vast expansion in the criminal justice system (Brownstein, 1996). The growth of state prisons (Irwin, 2005; Mauer & Meda, 2003) and supermax prisons (Mears, 2005) should have been predicted.

The International Association of Chiefs of Police (2000) called on President George W. Bush to create a national commission, like the 1967 President's Commission on Law Enforcement and the Administration of Justice (called the Crime Commission, established in 1965), to examine the widespread and deeply rooted problems that already were evident in the U.S. criminal justice system at the beginning of the new millennium. Concerned in particular about police corruption, racial profiling, and criminal court proceedings (Fields, 2000), the association had hoped that a comprehensive review of law enforcement and the administration of justice in the United States would prompt changes in the system that would lead to more measured responses to crime. This request fell on deaf ears.

Collectively, the four domestic wars explain the unusual 40-year emphasis on punishment at the expense of rehabilitation, but the sheer growth and pervasiveness of the criminal justice system could not have been predicted. At the beginning of 2008, for the first time in our nation's history, one out of every 100 Americans is in prison (state or federal prisons and jails; Figure 11.3). In fact, the number of inmates confined in U.S. prisons exceeds the total in the 26 largest European inmate populations (Pew Charitable Trusts, 2008).

Schneider (1990, p. 109) wondered why juveniles who think they will be caught and who believe they will be punished commit more offenses, so she conducted analyses to examine several possible explanations. First, would the severity of punishment be important if the certainty of punishment was high enough? This explanation was not supported in the data. Second, would the certainty of punishment be important for people who believed they would be punished severely if they persisted in committing offenses? This explanation was not supported. Third, would the certainty and severity of punishment be important for very-high-rate offenders? This possibility was partially supported in the data. However, this principle applied only when juveniles had six or more prior offenses. Schneider states, "This suggests that there may be a point in a juvenile career where some of the youths recognize the severity of future actions and intentionally reduce their criminal activity" (p. 109). However, most do not. Shannon (1991) found no evidence of deterrence based on severity of sanctions but some evidence that future offense seriousness may be reduced by frequent interventions. Alternatively, we may overestimate the judgmental maturity of adolescents (Scott, 2000). They may not respond to punishment threats in the corrective manner that is often assumed. This may be attributable to the fact that they have no control over most of the risk factors that underlie their problem behaviors—especially their parents, schools, and communities.

Scared Straight Programs

Scared Straight programs are not effective. The Scared Straight approach was invented during the sixth moral panic over juvenile delinquency in the late 1970s (Finckenauer & Gavin, 1999), when a group of inmates at New Jersey's Rahway State Prison, known as the Lifers' Group, created what later became known around the world as the Scared Straight program. Also known as "juvenile awareness," the program brought boys and girls into the prison and subjected them to shock therapy consisting of threats, intimidation, emotional shock, loud and angry bullying, and persuasion. The idea was to literally scare them away from delinquency, to scare them straight. This presumed panacea was widely acclaimed and described as successful (Finckenauer & Gavin, 1999, pp. 29, 123–128). Many writers and producers for the print and broadcast media were enamored of it because of its simplicity and deterrent appeal. As many as 12,500 youths visited the Lifers each year.

However, as Finckenauer and Gavin (1999, pp. 85–93) report, empirical evidence of the effectiveness of the Rahway State Prison Scared Straight program was lacking from the beginning. Evaluations of other Scared Straight programs were mixed but generally showed negative results (pp. 129–139; see also Petrosino, Turpin-Petrosino, & Finckenauer, 2000). When Lipsey (1992) conducted a meta-analysis to examine the effectiveness of juvenile delinquency programs, his deterrence program category included several Scared Straight programs with other shock incarceration programs. Lipsey found that, on average, exposure to these programs increased recidivism about 12%. Remarkably, Scared Straight programs survived the negative evaluations, in part because they reinvented themselves by downplaying the scare tactics and emphasizing their shift in emphasis to the provision of education for youngsters about crime consequences (Finckenauer & Gavin, 1999, pp. 215–219).

Perhaps more important to the staying power of Scared Straight is the current political climate, which demands that something be done about the juvenile delinquency problem and that this something be "rough and tough." In addition, the current media climate promoting "get tough" measures—in which programs such as Scared Straight play well—helps to perpetuate the myth of their effectiveness. Various states and localities continue to replicate Scared Straight in one form or another (Finckenauer & Gavin, 1999, pp. 127–129). In 2001, middle school students in Washington, D.C., were taken on tours of the jail, where they were strip-searched; the ensuing public outcry resulted in the disciplining of several school employees (Blum, 2001).

Another version of Scared Straight in Jacksonville, Florida, is an unusually popular program that has received national attention for its "get tough" approach (Hunzeker, 1995). Developed by a prosecutor, Harry Shorstein, this program puts a slightly different twist on the original Scared Straight concept described here. It exposes young delinquents to the harsh realities of adult jail (shock incarceration) and uses them as examples of youngsters gone bad to scare others, in an attempt to generate a general deterrence effect. In this program, letters are sent to county students advising them that some of their peers are doing time in the county jail. The jailed youngsters also are paraded in chains and handcuffs in front of public school students as living testimony to how serious the state is about juvenile delinquency (Hunzeker, 1995). This program has not been evaluated, but programs sharing its characteristic features (shock incarceration and Scared Straight) have been shown typically to increase recidivism (Lipsey, 1992; Lipsey & Wilson, 1998).

Boot Camps

Neither juvenile nor adult boot camps have proven to be effective, according to a comprehensive meta-analysis (Wilson, MacKenzie, & Mitchell, 2005). The use of boot camps for juvenile offenders grew in popularity during the early years of the current moral panic over juvenile delinquency. About the only positive thing that can be said about boot camps is that the inmates in them view their environment as being more therapeutic than traditional juvenile reformatories (MacKenzie, Wilson, Armstrong, & Gover, 2001; see also Gover, MacKenzie, & Armstrong, 2000; Styve, MacKenzie, & Gover, 2000). However, this advantage appears to be offset by the potential in boot camps for psychological, emotional, and physical abuse of youngsters— particularly for children with histories of abuse and family violence

(MacKenzie et al., 2001). Staff abuses—even the deaths of several youngsters—have been reported in some juvenile boot camps (Blackwood, 2001; Goodnough, 2006; Krajicek, 2000). Maryland closed its boot camps after abuses were uncovered; Florida refused after the accused staff were exonerated. One state, Georgia, has abandoned boot camps in response to research evidence showing their ineffectiveness (Rubin, 2001). With these exceptions, the popularity of boot camps seems to continue to grow in the juvenile justice system nearly unabated. Authorities continue to find creative ways to implement the concept. One Texas county established a school-based boot camp program; it was not effective (Trulson, Triplett, & Snell, 2001).

Large Custodial Facilities

The "get tough on juveniles" trend appears to have worsened conditions of confinement, particularly overcrowding. "Crowding occurs when the number of residents occupying all or part of a facility exceeds some predetermined limit based on square footage, utility use, or even fire codes" (Snyder & Sickmund, 2006, p. 223). In 2002 (the most recent data), 36% of all correctional facilities holding juvenile offenders reported crowding. A direct correlation is seen between facility sizes and crowding, and most juvenile offenders held in confinement were in the larger facilities (pp. 222–223). More than 6 in 10 of the very large facilities (more than 200 juvenile residents) said they had locked gates in fences or walls with razor wire (p. 222).

Large, congregate, custodial juvenile corrections facilities are not effective in rehabilitating juvenile offenders. Studies have shown that in large, overcrowded correctional facilities, both treatment opportunities and effectiveness of service delivery are diminished and larger facilities are more likely than smaller ones to be crowded (Snyder & Sickmund, 2006, p. 223). Large facilities with little treatment programming in states such as California and Texas have produced very high recidivism rates, as expected (Blackburn, Mullings, Marquart, & Trulson, 2007; Ezelle, 2007; Lattimore, Macdonald, Piquero, Linster, & Visher, 2004; Trulson, Marquart, Mullings, & Caeti, 2007). Custodial concerns tend to override concerns about the delivery of treatment services in these settings, and program quality suffers (Roush & McMillen, 2000). However, abuses of children's rights can occur in any sized juvenile facilities. Since its enactment in 1980, the Civil Rights of Institutionalized Persons Act has allowed the Civil Rights Division of the U.S. Department of Justice to investigate possible civil rights violations pertaining to people in publicly operated institutions and to bring consequent legal actions against state or local governments (Blalock & Arthur, 2006). Since 2000, 20 Civil Rights of Institutionalized Persons Act investigations have been made of 23 juvenile justice facilities in more than a dozen states (U.S. Department of Justice, 2007).

Long Terms of Confinement

Sentencing juveniles to long terms of confinement is not cost-effective. Long periods of confinement do not reduce recidivism rates among juveniles, even though it might seem that they should. This is the simplistic notion behind deterrence philosophy: The longer punishment is administered, the lower the likelihood of subsequent criminality. Research has shown that this is not the case. The preponderance of evidence suggests that periods of confinement should be very brief, to minimize the negative influences of other antisocial youths in the facilities (Henggeler, Schoenwald, Borduin, Rowland, & Cunningham, 1998). These include the possibility of gang involvement (Howell, Curry, Pontius, & Roush, 2003) and the risk of violent victimization (Bishop & Frazier, 2000; Forst, Fagan, & Vivona, 1989; Parent et al., 1994). Juveniles should also be confined only briefly so that they can begin the process of community reintegration as early as possible (Krisberg, Neuenfeldt, Wiebush, & Rodriguez, 1994). In fact, Lipsey and Wilson's (1998) meta-analysis of institutional programs suggests that an optimal treatment program participation period is approximately 6 months; however, some confined youths view more intensive, long-term correctional programs favorably (Bishop & Frazier, 2000). In all likelihood, these youths have multiple serious problems that require long-term intensive services to ameliorate them.

Curfew Laws

Empirical research does not support the argument that curfew laws reduce juvenile crime and victimization (Adams, 2007). Adams's conclusion is based on at least a dozen scientific studies of them. For example, a national study (McDowall, Loftin, & Wiersema, 2000) examined the effects of new curfew laws in 57 large cities and found that the introduction of these laws was not followed by reductions in juvenile arrests in any serious crime category. The researchers note that "any impacts of the laws were small, and they applied only to a few offenses," such as burglary, larceny, and simple assault (pp. 88–89). These decreases occurred only for revised laws. Nighttime curfew laws appear to be no more effective than daytime laws. In a California study, Males and Macallair (1998) found that stricter curfew enforcement did not reduce juvenile crime rates. In some instances, serious crime increased at the very time officials were touting the crime reduction effects of strict curfew enforcement.

Curfew laws cannot reasonably be expected to reduce violent juvenile crimes significantly because, ironically, most of them are imposed at a time—late at night—when few juvenile violent offenses occur. Only about one in five violent juvenile crimes occurs during curfew hours, typically between 10:00 P.M. and 6:00 A.M. (Snyder & Sickmund, 1999, p. 65).

Out-of-Home Placements

The most restrictive out-of-home placements for mental health treatment, including psychiatric hospitalization, and placements in residential treatment centers are not effective for most child and adolescent offenders (Burns, Goldman, Faw, & Burchard, 1999; Knitzer & Cooper, 2006; U.S. Department of Health and Human Services, 2001). Inpatient hospitalization is the least effective of all (U.S. Department of Health and Human Services, 2001, p. 171); indeed, it may do more harm than good in many cases (Weithorn, 1988). In short, "bed-driven" treatment for mental health problems is not effective.

Disproportionate Minority Confinement

Reducing disproportionate minority confinement, also called disproportionate minority contact (both abbreviated DMC) of juveniles has been federal policy in the United States since 1992 (Box 11.2). The International Convention on the Elimination of All Forms of Racial Discrimination (no. 9464 in United Nations Treaty Series 660, no. 14 [July 3, 1966]: 211–318), to which the United States is a party, defines race discrimination as conduct that has the purpose or effect of restricting rights on the basis of race. Under the convention, governments may not engage in benign neglect; that is, they may not ignore the need to secure equal treatment of all racial and ethnic groups but rather must act affirmatively to prevent or end policies that have unjustified discriminatory effects.

Yet egregious DMC persists (Hawkins & Kempf-Leonard, 2005; McCord et al., 2001, pp. 228–260), and the actual differentials in minority–nonminority crime rates do not justify the large differentials in the two groups' representation in the juvenile and criminal justice systems (Snyder & Sickmund, 2006). In one of the most transparent disparities, blacks are disproportionately processed in the juvenile and criminal justice systems for drug offenses, yet their drug use rates are no higher than those of white youngsters (Centers for Disease Control and Prevention, 2006).

Aside from racism and prejudice, the large DMC discrepancies in both the juvenile and criminal justice systems appear to be attributable mainly to crime control policies and initiatives—particularly the U.S. domestic "wars" (Box 11.2)—and minorities were targeted in each one of these. Although inequitable juvenile justice policies and practices must be changed—and there is some evidence of improvement between 1992 and 2002 (see Figure 11.1 and Snyder & Sickmund, 2006, p. 211)—the reality is that the juvenile justice system is joined at the hip to the adult criminal justice system. The connection is evident in the dual adult and juvenile roles of police and prosecutors at the front end (via arrests) and at the back end (via transfers to the criminal justice system). Police in the adult criminal justice system are the major source of referrals to the juvenile system. More often than not, criminal system prosecutors decide who is to be charged, adjudicated, and transferred (Chapter 12).

The contribution of prosecutors to DMC in the juvenile justice system cries out for attention because of their key role as gatekeepers. They typically decide whether to petition youth for delinquent offenses and bring them into juvenile court. Their track record for fairness in the criminal justice system is not good. Discrimination based on defendants' race or ethnicity occurs at all stages of the criminal justice system: arrest, pretrial release, prosecutor decision making, sentencing, imprisonment, and prison release decision making (see Chapter 12). However, inequities in executions (compounded by wrongful ones) are the most egregious of all problems. In the criminal justice system, DMC can literally become a matter of life or death (Liebman, Fagan, & West, 2000).

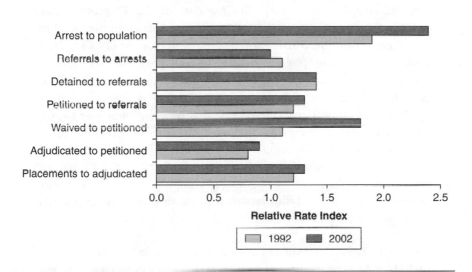

Figure 11.1   Relative Rates of Minority and Nonminority System Processing

NOTE: Numbers are per 100,000.

IN FOCUS 11.2

The Disproportionate Minority Confinement Initiative

The reduction of disproportionate minority confinement became official U.S. juvenile justice policy when the 1992 amendments to the Juvenile Justice and Delinquency Prevention (JJDP) Act of 1974 (P.L. 93-415) were enacted into law. The JJDP Act amendments (42 U.S.C. Sec. 5633[a][23])

(Continued)

(Continued)

required that states receiving JJDP Act formula grants provide assurances that they will develop and implement plans to reduce the overrepresentation of minorities in the juvenile justice system—that is, where the proportion of minority youth in confinement exceeds the proportion those minority groups represent in the general population. Congress incorporated a financial incentive to accelerate states' progress toward full compliance with the mandate by requiring that 25% of a state's annual formula grant allocation from the OJJDP be withheld for noncompliance. States that failed to make progress, or at least show a good-faith effort, would be required to allocate the remaining 75% of their formula grant funds toward achieving compliance. To meet the mandate of the Disproportionate Minority Confinement (DMC) Initiative, states must complete the three phases required in the OJJDP Formula Grants Regulation (28 CFR 31)— problem identification, problem assessment, and program intervention— within established time frames. The DMC Initiative was based on prior research on the issue of disproportionate minority confinement (Pope & Feyerherm, 1990, 1991) and the efforts of advocacy groups (see Howell, 1997, pp. 37–38).

Leiber (2002) recently completed a comprehensive assessment of the results of the DMC Initiative that focuses on the first two key components of the DMC mandate and states' efforts to comply: problem identification and problem assessment. Leiber reports the following key findings concerning the problem identification stage:

- Minority youth overrepresentation was evident in 32 states.
- Minority youth overrepresentation existed at all decision points.
- The decision point where minority youth overrepresentation was greatest varied from state to state.
- Where states differentiated between minority groups, overrepresentation existed for African Americans and Hispanics.

The problem assessment stage—that is, uncovering explanations for minority overrepresentation—proved to be very difficult for states to accomplish. Because the instructions OJJDP provided lacked specificity, Leiber (2002) notes, "states often did not understand how to do an assessment study and/or were not in position to conduct the kind of research needed to identify the causes of DMC" (p. 17). Thus, the sophistication of the assessment strategies used varied from state to state. Leiber reports, "OJJDP has begun to address these deficiencies, and these efforts may result in a greater number of states becoming more committed to DMC and [thus obtaining] information to better inform strategies to reduce the disproportionate representation of minority youth in our juvenile justice system" (p. 19). Because of the problems noted, the prospects for success of the DMC Initiative in the program intervention stage are uncertain at this time.

Latino and Latina youth appear to be reducing the gap relative to black youth as victims of disproportionate minority representation (Snyder & Sickmund, 2006, p. 211; Villarruel & Walker, 2002). Building Blocks for Youth has developed an "action packet" that includes suggested steps that youth advocates can take to eliminate the disparate treatment of Latino and Latina youth in the justice system and sample materials. The action packet is available on the Building Blocks for Youth Web site at http://www.building blocksforyouth.org/latino_rpt/act_pk_main.html.

General Deterrent Policies

Policies aimed at general deterrence are not effective in reducing crime rates. This conclusion has not changed since the 1970s (see Blumstein, Cohen, & Nagin, 1978; Zimring & Hawkins, 1973). As Tonry (1994b) asserts, "A fair-minded survey of existing knowledge provides no grounds for believing that the War on Drugs or the harsh policies exemplified by 'three strikes and you're out' laws and evidenced by a tripling in America's prison population since 1980 could achieve their ostensible purposes" (p. 479). "Three strikes" laws promoted in the "war on crime" (Box 11.1) do not deter crime (Kovandzic, Sloan, & Vieraitis, 2002; Shichor & Sechrest, 1996), imprisonment does not reduce recidivism (Spohn & Holleran, 2002), and there is compelling evidence that offenders sentenced to prison have higher rates of recidivism and recidivate more quickly than offenders placed on probation (Spohn & Holleran, 2002, p. 350). Moreover, the death penalty has no deterrent effect (Cheatwood, 1993; Harries & Cheatwood, 1997; Zimring, 1999).

Punishment in Adult Prisons and Parole Failure

Adult prisons are not effective for inmates of any age. Approximately two-thirds of inmates are rearrested within 3 years of release from adult prisons, and more than half of released prisoners are returned to prison (Langan & Levin, 2002). High prison recidivism rates are found in research dating back to the 19th century (Chambliss, 1995, p. 255). Yet

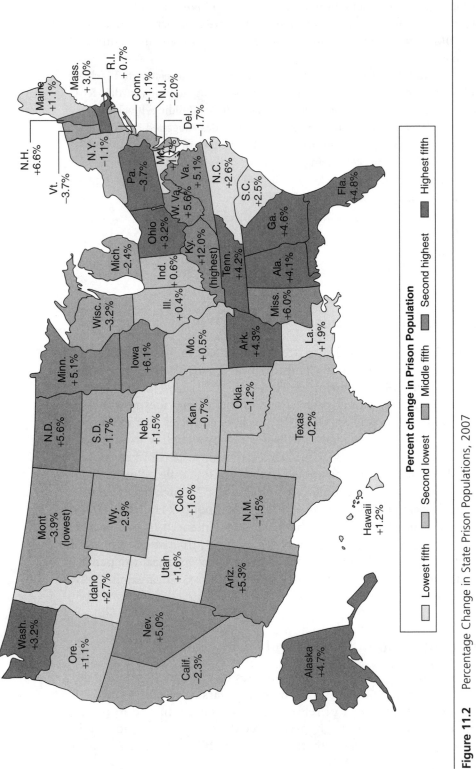

Percent change in Prison Population

☐ Lowest fifth   ☐ Second lowest   ■ Middle fifth   ■ Second highest   ■ Highest fifth

Figure 11.2   Percentage Change in State Prison Populations, 2007

NOTE: Figure shows percentage change in state prison populations by quintile from December 31, 2006, to January 1, 2008, unless otherwise noted in the appendix.

state prison systems have grown dramatically in the past two decades (Mears & Castro, 2006; for a history of the onset of the adult prison building boom, see Schlosser, 1998). In the past 25 years, the rate of imprisonment in the United States has more than tripled (Zimring, 2007; Figure 11.3). The number of prisoners held in conditions of extreme isolation in "supermax" prisons has grown to more than 20,000 (Amnesty International, 2002; Lovell, Johnson, & Cain, 2007; Mears & Castro, 2006). Between 1980 and 2005, the number of federal and state prisoners grew by more than 350% in the United States (Bureau of Justice Statistics, 2007; Harrison & Beck, 2006). The correctional system as a whole increased almost as dramatically as prisons did from 1980 to 2005 (Mears, 2008). "Including individuals on probation or parole or in jail or prison, it grew by over 280% from 1,842,100 to 7,056,000. Put differently, over 5 million more individuals were added to correctional systems over a 25-year period" (p. 150).

On any given day in the United States, 1 of every 32 adults (more than 7 million offenders) are under some form of correctional supervision (Bureau of Justice Statistics, 2007), with about one-third of them incarcerated and the remainder on probation or parole (Glaze & Bonczar, 2006). Of those incarcerated, nearly 700,000 return to the community each year (Sabol, Minton, & Harrison, 2007; see also Hughes & Wilson, 2002; Travis, 2005), yet neither short nor long terms in prison reduce their criminal activity (Lipsey & Cullen, 2007). Adult prisoners are not likely to receive rehabilitation services or job skill preparation while in prison; moreover, when released, they usually return to communities that are not well prepared to accept them (Petersilia, 2001, 2003; Travis & Petersilia, 2001).

As a general rule, "policies such as 'three strikes' laws and enhanced sentences, which bloat the prison population even more, as well as the policy of sticking a higher proportion of juvenile offenders into adult facilities have little to no appreciable impact on crime rates" (Pratt, 2008, p. 45). Pratt (2008, p. 43) suggests that sanctions tend to work best "when the goals of the sanction are modest." By this he means that, rather than attempting to write laws that exact punishments for given crimes, research suggests that particular types of sanction threats (e.g., the threat of incarceration) can bring about a particular type of prosocial behavior (e.g., paying fines) for a particular segment of the adult offender population (e.g., probationers).

But there is no standard sentencing approach. There was a standard approach 30 years ago, indeterminate sentencing, but this has given way to a wide variety of sentencing options, including mandatory minimum sentences, three-strikes laws (designed to increase prison terms for repeat offenders), and "truth in sentencing" laws (which require that offenders serve some specified proportion of their sentences). The result, as Travis and Petersilia (2001) put it, is "a national crazy quilt made up of piecemeal

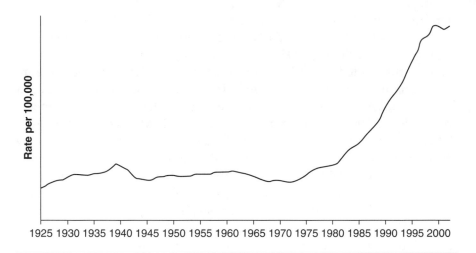

Figure 11.3   U.S. Imprisonment Rate, 1925–2002

sentencing reforms—without a public rationale that would explain the relationship between imprisonment and release" (p. 296).

Parole is no longer effective (Solomon, Kachnowski, & Bahati, 2005). More and more inmates are being released unconditionally, without formal supervision. Travis and Petersilia (2001) suggest that, "taken together, these three developments paint a picture of a system that has lost its way" (p. 299). Although the number of people reentering society has increased fourfold in the past 20 years, and spending on corrections has increased nearly sevenfold in the same period, they have been no better prepared to reintegrate upon their release, according to a recent report (Council of State Governments, 2005).

Disputed Program Interventions

There is conflicting evidence about the effectiveness of several popular program interventions. These include programs that provide therapy for antisocial adolescents in groups, detention, drug testing and drug courts, treatment for alcohol and drug abuse, electronic monitoring, sex offender treatment, wilderness challenge programs, police in schools, gang street sweeps, balanced and restorative justice, and motivational interviewing.

Programs Involving Older Groups of Antisocial Adolescents

This is a special case in which program-by-program reviews can produce a misleading conclusion. For more than a decade, we were led to believe that treatment services delivered to large groups of antisocial adolescents may not be effective. Just two or three studies were repeatedly cited as suggesting that programs that create intense group interactions between homogeneous groups of antisocial youths might actually increase the forms of behavior they are intended to prevent (see Dishion, McCord, & Poulin, 1999; Gottfredson, 1987). This is called the *iatrogenic effect,* meaning that the problem being addressed is inadvertently caused by the treatment procedure.

A recent study (Weiss et al., 2005) and Lipsey's meta-analyses refute the iatrogenic effect hypothesis. Tables 9.5 and 9.8 in Chapter 9 indicate that group counseling is effective for both juvenile probationers and institutionalized youth. In the latter setting, all therapy participants would be delinquents. Lipsey's findings strongly suggest that skilled therapists can manage groups of antisocial youth and effectively neutralize the negative reinforcements delinquents may give each other. He finds that group counseling can be quite effective for probationers when supplemented with interpersonal skill training, vocational education training, cognitive–behavioral treatment, or mentoring (Lipsey, 2007). The success of aggression replacement training is a case in point (Barnoski, 2004a). However, as Barnoski's study indicates, to achieve positive effects, aggression replacement training therapists must adhere closely to the treatment protocol.

Negative Effects of Detention

Nearly three-fourths of detained female youth and two-thirds of detained male youth have a psychiatric disorder (Teplin et al., 2006, p. 1591). This may help explain why lengthy periods of detention (more than 30 days) tended to wipe out the positive effects of court rehabilitation programs (Wooldredge, 1988). Other studies show that the detention of juveniles is associated with a number of negative outcomes, including an increased likelihood of subsequent delinquency and higher rates of future offending (Green, Carlson, & Colvin, 2001; Holman & Ziedenberg, 2006; Roy, 1995). On the other hand, detention is necessary to protect the public from dangerous juveniles, ensure that juveniles at high risk do not abscond, and ensure the safety of some offenders; most centers successfully achieve these objectives, and many of them have very innovative programming (National Council of Juvenile and Family Court Judges, 2005; Roush, 1996a).

Drug Testing and Specialized Drug Courts

Drug testing is widespread in the juvenile justice system, and although there is strong professional and public support for it, under the assumption that it has a deterrent value (Crowe, 1998), to date no research has found evidence that it is an effective strategy for reducing juvenile offending. Haapanen and Britton (2002) conducted a well-designed California study in which they randomly assigned juvenile parolees to different frequencies of drug testing; they found no reductions in arrests or improved adjustment on parole in the higher-frequency test groups or for particular offender types. In fact, counter to conventional wisdom, "there was a tendency for higher testing groups to do worse" on parole (p. 232). One potential value of drug testing is the use of positive tests as a predictor of recidivism, but it appears that a history of drug use serves this purpose equally well (p. 236).

Many practitioners consider drug courts to be the panacea for substance-using delinquents. However, evaluations of juvenile drug courts are sparse, mainly because of the short history of these specialized courts. These specialized courts suffer from the same limitation as programs such as D.A.R.E. and boot camps: failure to address the key determinants of delinquency. Illegal substance use is a risk factor for delinquency and recidivism, but drug courts tend to ignore other risk factors and are mainly punitive in their orientation. Drug courts rarely incorporate a treatment orientation, although some do. Based on a comprehensive review, the National Institute of Justice (2006) concludes that neither general treatment research nor drug court evaluations have produced definitive information on juveniles.

Treatment for Alcohol and Drug Abuse

The results of the few studies that have examined drug and alcohol treatment for juvenile offenders have been mixed (Baer, MacLean, & Marlatt, 1998). It also is unclear whether alcohol and drug abuse treatment programs reduce delinquency. Based on his meta-analyses, Lipsey (personal communication, July 16, 2007) assures us that sufficient high-quality studies supporting the effectiveness of drug treatment for juveniles are not available to develop evidence-based guidelines, but it may be useful to experiment further with the few research-supported models for probationers that do exist (see Table 9.5 in Chapter 9).

In some cases, ineffective aftercare (relapse prevention) may negate the small positive gains achieved in drug treatment programs (Sealock, Gottfredson, & Gallagher, 1997). Some programs (e.g., group therapy) may increase juveniles' associations with problem peers, negating any positive program effects (Henggeler, 1997, pp. 264–265). However, the main problem with alcohol and drug treatment programs seems to be their failure to address adequately the family, school, and community problems that are strongly associated with adolescent drug use. Many of these programs have a punitive orientation. As Henggeler (1997) observes, "It seems unrealistic to expect treatment programs (e.g., boot camps, wilderness training) that are not family- and community-based and do not address the multiple determinants of drug abuse, to be effective, and such a view is supported by the adult drug-abuse (Institute of Medicine, 1990) and delinquency (Henggeler & Schoenwald, 1994) treatment literatures" (p. 265). There are exceptions, of course, such as the use of Multisystemic Therapy for substance-abusing and substance-dependent delinquents (Henggeler, Pickrel, & Brondino, 1999).

Electronic Monitoring

The use of electronic monitoring (EM) technology for controlling offenders in North America and Europe is growing, and it is increasingly used with juvenile offenders. EM is often used in conjunction with home detention in monitoring an offender's whereabouts via an electronic device attached to the wrist or ankle and by random phone calls to his or her residence (Austin, Johnson, & Weitzer, 2005). The potential benefits of EM include reducing costs of supervision, reducing institutional populations, allowing the offender to remain in school while under supervision, improving compliance with conditions of probation such as curfew restrictions, and enhancing the potential for rehabilitation by keeping offenders at home and in close contact with family members (Austin et al., 2005; Wiebush, Wagner, Prestine, & Baird, 1992). Although its efficacy has not been tested in all of these environments, early studies suggest that the main value of EM would be for monitoring offenders rather than for rehabilitative purposes. Use of EM as an alternative to detention and to ensure participation in treatment programs is recommended by the National Council of Juvenile and Family Court Judges (2005) in its *Juvenile Delinquency Guidelines* (pp. 168, 171).

It is surprising that few published studies of EM are available even though such monitoring has been widely used for juveniles for nearly a decade (Cohn, Biondi, Flaim, Paskowski, & Cohn, 1997; Torbet, 1999). Vaughn (1989) reviewed eight electronic monitoring programs. Most were used as alternatives to prehearing detention, four were used to supplement probation, and three were used for offenders released early from an institution. Failure rates in the programs ranged from 5% to 30%, and most of the failures resulted from technical violations rather than new offenses. Enhancing program completion may be a key benefit of EM. A study of youth detained at home in Lake County, Indiana, reported that those assigned to electronic monitoring had a higher program completion rate (90% versus 75%) and a lower recidivism rate (17% versus 26%) than youth who were not monitored electronically (Roy & Brown, 1995). This study suggests that EM might increase treatment program completions. However, this and EM's potential negative psychological effects on young offenders must be researched (see Roy, 1995, 1997).

Sex Offender Treatment

Although some progress has been made in conducting research on their characteristics and on objective risk assessments of juvenile sex offenders (Righthand & Welch, 2001; Prentky & Righthand, 2003), progress has been slow in designing effective treatments for them, but some approaches look promising (Center for Sex Offender Management, 2006; Veneziano & Veneziano, 2002). Unfortunately, none of the approaches developed specifically for juvenile sex offenders to date has proved to be effective

(Harris, Rice, & Quinsey, 1998; Katner, 2002). As in the case of drug treatment, Lipsey informs us (personal communication, July 16, 2007) that sufficient high-quality studies supporting the effectiveness of sex offender treatment for juveniles are not available to permit him to develop evidence-based guidelines but that it may be useful to experiment further with the few research-supported models for probationers that do exist (see Box 11.3 and Table 9.5 in Chapter 9).

IN FOCUS 11.3
Sex Offender Treatment

Most sex offender treatment programs for children and adolescents use one of the following three treatment modalities in both residential facilities and outpatient programs:

- Psychological therapy, which includes sex education, victim empathy, group counseling, individual counseling, and accountability therapy
- Biological treatment, which includes the use of medication or drugs to suppress the male sex drive (known as chemical castration)
- Behavior modification, which includes social skill acquisition, modeling or role-playing therapy, individual behavioral therapy, and assertiveness training

---

Wilderness Challenge Programs

Wilderness challenge programs have long been promoted as a means of ameliorating delinquent behavior. As Wilson and Lipsey (2000, p. 1) note, these programs, which typically involve youth participation in a series of physically challenging activities such as rock climbing, are presumed to prevent or reduce delinquency through two interrelated dimensions of experiential learning. First, participants must master a series of incrementally challenging activities in which they come to realize skill mastery, which presumably builds confidence, self-esteem, and self-empowerment. Second, the group context in which the wilderness challenge program is implemented affords participants an opportunity to learn prosocial interpersonal skills that will transfer to situations outside the program.

Wilson and Lipsey (2000) found that wilderness challenge programs appear to be far less effective for serious and violent delinquents than for other delinquents. The researchers found that the key ingredients of more effective wilderness challenge programs appear to be inclusion of a therapeutic component and program formats of short duration. The programs they examined that had therapeutic components used a wide variety of techniques, including behavior management, family therapy, reality therapy, and cognitive-behavioral techniques. Wilson and Lipsey (2000) advise that because of the small number of studies conducted to date, it is not yet "possible to draw convincing conclusions about the effectiveness of wilderness programs and how best to optimize them for reducing antisocial and delinquent behavior" (p. 8).

Police in Schools

Although permanent placement of police in schools has become common, this practice has never been evaluated. This trend began with School Resource Officers (SROs), an idea that grew out of the police–school liaison concept. Early in their history, SROs functioned much like probation officers in schools except that, with the advent of the "war on drugs" and fear of school shootings, expectations of SROs vis-à-vis school safety grew. Many school systems dropped the original title (or renamed them something like School Safety Agents) and generally came to rely on them as police in schools. There is insufficient evidence to say whether SROs are effective (Gottfredson & Gottfredson, 2007). The same observation applies to security or surveillance procedures including metal detectors, closed-circuit monitoring, and limiting access by intruders (Gottfredson & Gottfredson, 2007).

The National Study of Delinquency Prevention in Schools (Gottfredson et al., 2000) found that 66% of middle schools and 57% of high schools use some form of security or surveillance strategy, including metal detectors; police or security personnel in schools; locker searches; and drug-, gun-, or bomb-sniffing dogs. Schools are "increasingly developing crisis prevention plans which often involve the use of S.W.A.T. teams on campus, evacuation readiness plans, and helicopters" (Gottfredson et al., 2002b).

The American Civil Liberties Union (2007) investigated the growth of school security forces in New York City schools and around the country. Their findings were astounding; the size of school security forces has skyrocketed in New York City and in many other urban school systems in the United States. "At the start of the 2005–2006 school year, the city employed a total of 4,625 School Safety Agents (SSAs) and at least 200 armed police officers assigned exclusively to schools. These numbers would make the NYPD's School Safety Division rank as the tenth largest police force in the country—larger than the police forces of Washington, D.C., Detroit, Boston, or Las Vegas" (p. 4). Abuses of students' rights and arrests of students for minor infractions have mushroomed at about the same pace, including the following:

- Intrusive searches
- Derogatory, abusive, and discriminatory comments and conduct
- Unauthorized confiscation of students' personal items
- Inappropriate sexual attention
- Physical abuse
- Arrest for minor noncriminal violations of school rules

The American Civil Liberties Union report (2007, p. 4) makes four simple recommendations for reforming New York City's school policing program, all of which can be accomplished without compromising school safety:

- Authority over school safety must be restored to school administrators.
- School safety personnel must be trained to function in accordance with sound educational practices and to respect the differences between street and school environments.
- The role of police personnel in schools must be limited to legitimate security concerns for children and educators.
- Students, families, and educators must be given meaningful mechanisms, including access to a civilian complaint review board, to report wrongdoing by school-based police personnel.

Gang Street Sweeps and Roundups

The Los Angeles Police Department (LAPD) has long been a leader in gang suppression tactics. The most notorious gang sweep, Operation Hammer, was an LAPD Community Resources Against Street Hoodlums (CRASH) unit operation (Klein, 1995, pp. 162–163). It was begun in south-central Los Angeles in 1988, when a force of a thousand police officers swept through the area on a Friday night and again on Saturday, arresting likely gang members on a wide variety of offenses, including existing warrants, new traffic citations, curfew violations, illegal gang-related behaviors, and observed criminal activities. All of the 1,453 people arrested were taken to a mobile booking operation adjacent to the Los Angeles Memorial Coliseum. Most of the arrested youths were released without charges. Slightly more than half were gang members. There were only 60 felony arrests, and charges were filed on only 32 of them. As Klein (1995) describes it, "This remarkably inefficient process was repeated many times, although with smaller forces— more typically one hundred or two hundred officers" (p. 162).

The LAPD Rampart Division's CRASH unit polices the Rampart area, a mostly poor and Hispanic district west of downtown Los Angeles and home to the 18th Street gang. Rafael Perez, an officer in the Rampart Division, was arrested in 1998 for stealing cocaine from a police warehouse. He implicated 70 CRASH antigang officers in a variety of illegal activities: planting evidence, intimidating witnesses, beating suspects, giving false testimony, selling drugs, and covering up unjustified shootings (see Leinwand, 2000). Incredibly, the Rampart CRASH officers, who were fiercely involved in fighting gangs, came to act like gang members themselves (Deutsch, 2000; Leinwand, 2000). The line between right and wrong became fuzzy for these officers as the us-against-them ethos apparently overcame them (Deutsch, 2000). CRASH officers wore special tattoos and pledged their loyalty to the antigang unit with a code of silence (Leinwand, 2000). They protected their turf by intimidating Rampart-area gang members with unprovoked beatings and threats. They arrested street gang members "by the carload" (Bandes, 2000, p. M6).

The use of singular suppression tactics in combating gangs and gun crime has earned only "a mixed report card" (Decker, 2003, p. 290; see also Bynum & Varano, 2003; Fagan, 2002; Ludwig, 2005). The positive effects of suppression tend to be short-lived (Klein, 1995; Papachristos, 2001). For example, serious gang problems returned after the successes attributed to the Boston Ceasefire project (Braga et al., 2001), dubbed the "Boston Miracle" (Kennedy, 2007), and homicides increased (Braga & Pierce, 2005). Remarkably, in Chicago efforts by federal law enforcement and prosecution succeeded in toppling a major organized criminal gang, the Gangster Disciples, but little difference was observable at the neighborhood level (Papachristos, 2001). The main differences locally were that the gang reverted to a collection of loosely organized groups that still dealt drugs and formed associations with other gangs; "they just joined a different gang" (Papachristos, 2001, p. 69).

But the Boston Ceasefire project did create a strong individual deterrence model that instituted a zero tolerance policy for any law-breaking activity on the part of identified individuals (Kennedy, 1999), and this has achieved broad appeal (Kennedy, 2007). High-rate violent offenders (identified through a review of police arrest records in a problem analysis) were rounded up and notified in a community meeting that they were subject to long prison sentences for any subsequent law, probation, or parole violations. Successful convictions that drew long federal sentences were widely publicized in the community to deter others.

Although other replication sites have not achieved the short-term homicide reductions seen in Boston (Chapter 7), the offender roundups (dubbed call-ins or offender notifications elsewhere) have remained popular. This zero tolerance procedure has raised due process issues in some places. If arrest records are used to generate a list of high-rate offenders, minorities are more likely to populate the list and be subjected to offender roundups because they are far more likely than whites to be arrested for the same offenses. Innocent people can be inadvertently snared in the gang sweeps (S. Moore, 2007), even if gang intelligence databases are used in identifying the targets (Wright, 2006).

It is not surprising that the zero tolerance roundups have not produced consistent noteworthy results. First, the cross-agency "problem analysis" approach used in Boston remains very difficult to implement anywhere, particularly in larger cities (Duane, 2006; Ludwig, 2005; Skogan & Steiner, 2004; Tita et al., 2003). Second, such a small subset of high-rate offenders typically is targeted that a large overall impact on city-wide crime rates is unrealistic. Third, in cities that have well-established gangs, these groups constantly regenerate themselves. Therefore, gang suppression tactics must be coupled with prevention and intervention measures to reduce the strength of gangs (Chapter 7). There is some evidence that a youth outreach (or social intervention) strategy may be more effective in reducing the violent behavior of the younger, less violent gang youth and that a combined youth outreach and police suppression strategy might be more effective with the older, more criminally active and violent gang youth, particularly with respect to drug-related crimes (Spergel, 2007).

Balanced and Restorative Justice

Curiously, implementation of the balanced and restorative justice (BARJ) approach has not produced recidivism reductions among juvenile offenders to date that equal its widespread intuitive and emotional appeal, in a variety of formats (Bradshaw & Roseborough, 2005; Nugent, Williams, & Umbreit, 2004; Turner, Schroeder, Lane, & Petersilia, 2001; Umbreit, Coates, & Vos, 2002). Two possible explanations come to mind. The first one is that BARJ does not place strong emphasis on providing rehabilitative services for offenders. Second, restitution is the main service used in BARJ, and though effective, restitution produces below-average recidivism reductions among court-referred juvenile offenders (based on Lipsey's meta-analyses; Chapter 9, Table 9.5), who typically are BARJ clients. Therefore, it appears that the recidivism reduction potential in BARJ applications could be increased by using more effective services in conjunction with restitution. Cognitive–behavioral therapy, group counseling, vocational training, and mentoring should be considered (Table 9.5). Other BARJ outcomes are good, such as client satisfaction, fairness, and diversion (Umbreit et al., 2002).

Motivational Interviewing

Motivational interviewing (MI) is widely promoted in some states as an effective method of counseling juvenile delinquent offenders. But this is not the main evidence base for MI (Rubak, Sandbaek, Lauritzen, & Christensen, 2005). MI is a client-centered, directive method for enhancing intrinsic motivation to change by exploring and resolving subjects' ambivalence or motivation to change (http://www.motivationalinterview.org/). "Motivational interviewing is a particular way of helping clients recognise and do something about their current or potential problems. It is viewed as being particularly useful for clients who are reluctant to change or who are ambivalent about changing their behavior" (Rubak et al., 2005, p. 305). According to this meta-analysis, MI is "broadly applicable in the management of diseases that to some extent are associated with behavior," and it "has been used and evaluated in relation to alcohol abuse, drug addiction, smoking cessation, weight loss, adherence to treatment and follow-up, increasing physical activity, and in the treatment of asthma and diabetes" (pp. 305–306). Some of the subjects in these studies were adolescents, although the overwhelming majority were adults. Nevertheless, the research suggests that MI may increase the effectiveness of therapy for adolescents' drug and alcohol abuse, particularly for the purpose of engaging subjects in therapy at the beginning of treatment. Reference was made to MI in Chapter 8: "Research strongly suggests that motivational interviewing techniques, rather than persuasion tactics, effectively enhance motivation for initiating and maintaining behavior changes" (Crime and Justice Institute, 2004, p. 4). However, MI has not been tested, nor is it recommended, specifically for juvenile offenders at the MI Web site or in the cited meta-analysis. However, Rubak et al. (2005) note that there "are no apparent harmful effects or adverse effects of motivational interviewing" (p. 310).

Discussion Topics

1. Why have Scared Straight programs had such staying power despite their ineffectiveness?

2. Which of the ineffective programs surprises you most?

3. Is it surprising to you that adult prisons are not effective? Why are more and more of them built if they are not effective? Are there alternatives?

4. Why are "bed-driven" treatment programs ineffective?

5. Why do you suppose the adoption of new treatment techniques such as motivational interviewing is rapid, when more effective research-based services often are adopted slowly?

CHAPTER 12

Transfer of Juveniles to the Criminal Justice System

I begin this chapter with a brief description of juvenile justice philosophy in the United States, followed by a discussion of the principal mechanisms used to remove juveniles from the juvenile justice system and turn them over to the criminal justice system. I use the special case of one particular 11-year-old boy charged with murder as a backdrop for considering the adequacy of the criminal justice system for handling juvenile offenders. The remainder of the chapter addresses the appropriateness of transferring juveniles to the criminal justice system.

Juvenile Justice Philosophy

Juvenile justice policy in the United States has long been grounded in three philosophical principles that govern how justice should be administered when the accused offenders are children and adolescents. These principles are tied to our society's views about childhood and adolescence as periods of maturation and social development. From the time juvenile courts were first established, they have recognized that "children are developmentally different from adults; they are developing emotionally and cognitively; they are impressionable; and they have different levels of understanding than adults" (National Council of Juvenile and Family Court Judges, 1998, p. 1). It has been understood that a separate court system is appropriate for children and adolescents because, by virtue of their age and immaturity, they are not fully responsible for their delinquent behavior, and if they receive treatment in rehabilitation programs, they can become productive members of society.

These views are based on three clusters of philosophical principles that are central to the administration of justice in the American juvenile justice system: diminished capacity, proportionality, and room to reform (Zimring, 1998b). Each of these principles is based in the understanding that children are not little adults, and they should not be treated as such. This view gave rise to the first juvenile court more than a century ago.

Issues grouped in the diminished capacity (or responsibility) category relate to the degree to which children and adolescents should be held responsible for their delinquent acts. Culpability is the key issue here: whether juvenile offenders can fully appreciate or control their actions (Grisso & Schwartz, 2000, p. 267). Although older adolescents may have adult-like capacities for reasoning, their ability to exercise sound judgment in ambiguous or stressful situations—especially in a peer group context—may be limited (Scott, 2000). In other words, they lack the experience that adults have accumulated, which provides the basis for making sound judgments about the potential consequences of their actions. It's not so much that punishment should fit the crime but that punishment should fit the level of maturity of the offender (Grisso et al., 2003). New research on adolescent brain development (which I will discuss at the end of this chapter) raises more questions about the mental capacity of juveniles.

The logic of proportionality is that "even after a youth passes the minimum threshold of competence that leads to finding capacity to commit crime, the barely competent youth is not as culpable and therefore not as deserving of a full measure of punishment as a fully qualified adult offender" (Zimring, 1998b, p. 486). Therefore, the punishments meted out to juveniles for crimes they have committed should be graduated (i.e., made increasingly more severe) and in proportion to the offenses. Because of the malleability of youngsters, adolescence has traditionally been recognized as "a stage of developmental immaturity that rendered youths' transgressions less blameworthy than those of adults and required a special legal response" (Grisso, 1996, p. 230). Mitigation of punishments for juveniles because of their lack of development of social and mental capacity is not something new or something that originated in the United States. This principle has its origins in ancient civilizations, including the Code of Hammurabi (written more than 4,000 years ago), the Twelve Tables of Roman law (about 450 BC), Saxon law (about 500–600 AD), and English common law (about the mid-1300s AD).

The third philosophical principle is room to reform. Policies based on this principle "are derived from legal policies toward young persons in the process of growing up. They are the same policies we apply to young drivers, teen pregnancy, and school dropouts" (Zimring, 1998b, p. 486). We do not ban juveniles from society for transgressions in these and other arenas. As Zimring (1998a) explains, "Room-to-reform policies address not so much the amount of punishment imposed as the kind of punishment and the kind of consequences that should be avoided" (p. 87). These policies are intended as safeguards, to reduce the permanent costs of adolescent mistakes and enable young offenders to make successful adolescence-to-adulthood transitions with their life chances intact.

These three philosophical underpinnings are the basis of the fundamental difference between the juvenile court and the adult criminal court: The juvenile court seeks to rehabilitate juvenile delinquents, thereby preventing future criminal behavior, whereas the adult criminal court seeks to induce law-abiding behavior by means of punishment for wrongdoing. Juvenile courts were created in part to implement these three philosophical principles.

Juvenile Justice Policies and Practices

Each state has its own laws governing how juvenile offenders are handled. Adjudication of their offenses originates exclusively in juvenile courts in every state (except in instances in which state law excludes classes of juvenile offenders from juvenile court jurisdiction). This practice resulted from the creation of a separate juvenile justice system in the United States in the late 19th and early 20th centuries. Because the state laws give juvenile courts exclusive jurisdiction over offenders below a specific age (typically 18), other laws must be used to transfer juveniles from the juvenile justice system to the criminal justice system. Four types of laws are used for this purpose (Box 12.1).

IN FOCUS 12.1

Mechanisms Used to Transfer Juveniles to the Criminal Justice System

Four primary mechanisms are used to transfer juveniles from the juvenile justice system to the criminal justice system. *Transfer* is the general term commonly used to describe this process. The term *waiver* is also used, but as a general descriptive term it can lead to some confusion because, technically speaking, *waiver* refers to the judicial form of transfer—that is, judicial waiver—which is only one of the four transfer mechanisms.

Judicial waiver: The juvenile court judge has the authority to waive juvenile court jurisdiction and transfer the case to criminal court. In some states this process is called *certification, remand,* or *binding over for criminal prosecution.* In other states, judges *transfer* or *decline* rather than waive jurisdiction.

Concurrent jurisdiction: Original jurisdiction for certain cases is shared by the criminal and juvenile courts, and the prosecutor has discretion to file

(Continued)

(Continued)

such cases in either court. Transfer under concurrent jurisdiction provisions is also known as *prosecutorial waiver* or *direct file.*

Statutory exclusion: Some state statutes exclude juveniles who are accused of certain offenses from juvenile court jurisdiction. Under statutory exclusion provisions, cases originate in criminal rather than juvenile court. Statutory exclusion is also known as *legislative exclusion, automatic transfer,* or *mandatory transfer.* These statutes typically exclude from juvenile court youths who are charged with particular offenses beyond a certain age (e.g., youths age 14 and older charged with violent crimes).

Blended sentencing: Some state statutes increase the sentencing options available in the juvenile court by linking juvenile and adult sentencing. The juvenile court in 15 of the blended sentencing states may impose a juvenile or adult sentence, impose both a juvenile and an adult sentence, or impose a sentence past the normal limit of juvenile court jurisdiction. In 17 blended sentencing states, the criminal court may conditionally return transferred juveniles to the juvenile system for their sentence. Blended sentencing is also known as *blended jurisdiction.*

Originally, juvenile court judges had exclusive authority to transfer juveniles to the criminal courts. (See Box 12.2 for a brief history of the American juvenile justice system.) The remaining three mechanisms (prosecutor discretion, statutory exclusion, and blended sentencing) have come into widespread use during the current moral panic over delinquency, in a wave of "get tough" juvenile legislation. More than half of the states now authorize others to make the transfer decision. Thus, the number of transferred cases has increased dramatically in the past 20 years.

IN FOCUS 12.2

The American Juvenile Justice System: A Brief History

Origins of the System

The philosophical foundations of the American system of juvenile justice are found in the concepts of childhood and adolescence developed by American social reformers. Before the time of the discovery of the New World, children often were discarded, ignored, and exploited. It was not uncommon in the ancient civilizations of the Middle East, Greece, Rome, and Europe for children to be thrown away. Infanticide appears to have been practiced as late as the

17th century in France and England. Thus the English and other Europeans who established the first colonies and formed the United States inherited a disregard for children from the practices of their homelands. The modern concepts of childhood and adolescence were not developed in the United States until after the colonial era.

To define the role of the state vis-à-vis children and adolescents, Americans adopted the English concept of *parens patriae* (Latin for "parent of his country"), or government as parent. The concept originated in medieval English doctrine, where it referred to the right of the king (the state) to provide protection for any people who did not possess full legal capacity, including insane and incompetent people and children. The right to intervene in family matters on behalf of children and to protect property rights of the young was bestowed on the crown. The jurisdiction of English chancery courts then was extended to abused, dependent, and neglected children. In the United States, the *parens patriae* concept was expanded to include delinquent children and provided the justification for treatment and incarceration of delinquents in the new juvenile justice system.

Formation of the System

The unique American system of juvenile justice was initially formed of two parts: correctional facilities for children and adolescents, and juvenile courts, but case processing actually involves several key options (Figure 12.1). The precedent for institutions for children originated in 16th-century European religious reform movements. These movements changed the public perception of children from "miniature adults" to immature people whose moral and mental capacities are not fully formed. Boarding schools were established for delinquent children to help develop their mental and moral capacities through strict daily regimens.

"Gentleman reformers" created the New York House of Refuge for delinquent children and adolescents in 1825. Because they believed that the unstable urban environment in East Coast cities was corrupting to children, these reformers felt that delinquents needed to be placed in a controlled environment, in a "refuge," where they could be inculcated with the "appropriate morality" and middle-class values (Finestone, 1976). Only the children the courts believed could still be rescued from delinquency were sent to the House of Refuge; these were children who were prematurely corrupted and corrupting. Older and more serious juvenile offenders were dealt with in the adult criminal system (Fox, 1970). The House of Refuge offered food, clothing, shelter, and education to homeless and destitute children (Fox, 1970) and encouraged their reformation through a complex system of rewards and punishments.

Other houses of refuge—the original American juvenile corrections facilities—soon were built in other East Coast cities, patterned after the English bridewells (institutions for youthful beggars and vagrants) and the Elmira Reformatory for adults. These institutions became family substitutes, "not only for the less serious juvenile [offenders], but for other children who were defined as a problem—the runaway, the disobedient or defiant child, or the vagrant who was in danger of falling prey to loose women, taverns, gambling halls, or theaters" (Empey, 1978, p. 82). Dependent, neglected, and delinquent children were housed together, a practice that still prevails in some juvenile detention facilities.

(Continued)

(Continued)

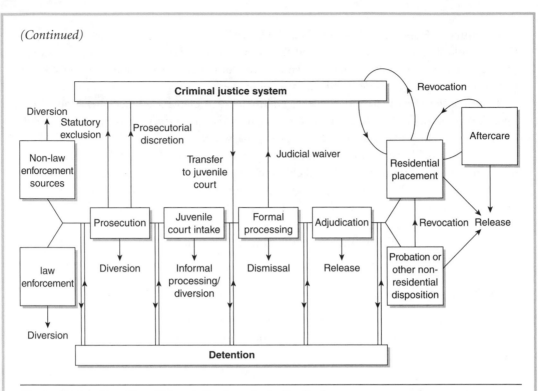

Figure 12.1   Case Flow Through the Juvenile Justice System

NOTE: This chart gives a simplified view of case flow through the juvenile justice system. Procedures vary between jurisdictions.

Invention of the Juvenile Court

Unlike juvenile correctional facilities, which preceded it by almost 75 years, the juvenile court is purely an American invention. In the late 1800s, the ladies of the Chicago Women's Club were finding that their efforts to improve the criminal justice system and the conditions in jails were inadequate, and they turned their reformist zeal to improving the conditions in which children were confined. They came up with the idea of establishing a special court and separate correctional procedures for children. The members of the club believed that a separate juvenile court could be an effective instrument for the advancement of youth welfare, that it could succeed where social institutions had failed. Thus they saw the juvenile court as "the cornerstone of a comprehensive child care system" (Finestone, 1976, p. 45).

The Juvenile Court Act was passed by the Illinois State Legislature in 1899. As envisaged in the statute, the first juvenile court was to represent a radical departure in the treatment of delinquents. The juvenile court would pay less attention to the offenses themselves (in contrast to the usual practice in adult criminal court) and more attention to the general circumstances underlying offenders' misconduct. The court was expected to protect youngsters from harmful influences and to rehabilitate them through the use of such mechanisms as probation, treatment, and incarceration, if necessary. In more serious cases, the juvenile court would rely on more restrictive measures to pursue the overall goal of remediating delinquent behavior. As Hutzler (1982) explains, "Whatever the conduct that brought the child to the court's attention, the juvenile court judge was to consider the broad range of social facts regarding the child and his family and to direct treatment 'in the child's best interests' and in accordance with his needs" (p. 27). By 1920, 46 of the 48 states had passed juvenile court laws (Tanenhaus, 2004, p. 128).

Every one of them had juvenile reformatories in one form or another; some of them were called industrial schools or training schools.

Differences Between Criminal Courts and Juvenile Courts

As in European courts, U.S. criminal court procedures were based on an accusatorial and adversarial model, in which charges are brought against the individual by the state and rebutted by the defendant's lawyer. People are tried in accordance with procedural rules and found guilty or innocent. Guilty people are sentenced to terms of community service, probation, jail, or prison, or their sentences can be conditionally set aside. The criminal courts are expected to ensure to defendants the basic protections set forth in the U.S. Constitution, including the right to an attorney, the right not to testify, the right to confront witnesses, and the right to a jury trial.

Juvenile courts, in contrast, are civil courts, and they do not follow criminal court procedures. They operate as nonadversarial, fact-finding courts. Juvenile courts consider extralegal factors that may be linked with the defendants' delinquency, especially family conditions, in deciding how to handle cases. Because these courts are designed to recognize the special needs and immature status of youngsters, they emphasize rehabilitation over punishment. Youngsters are adjudicated delinquent, not found guilty or innocent. Dispositions of cases are made instead of sentences. Socially minded judges preside over juvenile courts, hearing and adjudicating cases not according to rigid rules of law but according to the interests of society, the interests of the child, and child development principles. Juvenile courts have no juries; instead, court staffs include sociologists, psychologists, social workers, and child care specialists. Because juvenile courts are supposed to act in the best interests of the child, from the beginning they felt no need for the formulation of legal rules of defendant rights, due process, and constitutional safeguards that, presumably, mark the adult judicial process.

The seventh moral panic over delinquency and the related "superpredator" myth are major contributing factors to the large number of transfers. Another important factor is the erroneous view that offender rehabilitation programs in the juvenile justice system are not effective. For example, it has often been said that the juvenile justice system was not created to handle the "new breed" of juvenile offenders. This mistaken belief has given impetus to the movement to turn presumed juvenile justice system "failures" over to the criminal justice system.

The transformation of juvenile delinquents (in the public's mind) into adult-like hardened criminals is an important development. What previously were defined as "delinquent offenses" because of the juvenile age of the offenders came to be characterized as adult crimes. The age distinction was set aside. Images of "baby-faced criminals" stimulated legislatures to levy on juvenile offenders extremely punitive sanctions in the adult criminal justice system (Lyons, 1997). DiIulio and his colleagues (Bennett, DiIulio, & Walters, 1996) advocated incarcerating even preteen boys and other "superpredators" they characterized as savage, merciless killers. They argued that black inner-city boys, whom they said were products of moral poverty, should be removed from society, because they presumably were deranged. Unfortunately, the Psychopathy Checklist–Youth Version (PCL-YV) instrument—developed in a futile attempt to identify mentally deranged adolescents—is being marketed extensively in the United States for use in making transfer decisions on juveniles. This is inappropriate because use of this instrument is very likely to wrongly diagnose youngsters (Steinberg, 2002).

Transfer Trends and Policy Changes

Over the past 20 years, every state has made it easier to transfer adolescents from the juvenile justice system to the criminal justice system. Table 12.1 shows the expanded authority by which transfers can be ordered. As a result of the "get tough" movement, legislators enacted new laws that expanded the list of crimes for which juveniles could be transferred while excluding certain offenses from juvenile court jurisdiction and expanded the role of prosecutors in making the transfer decision. Many changes in the transfer of juveniles occurred in the 1990s, when all but six states enacted or expanded transfer provisions, mainly expanding the list of transferable offenses beyond serious violent crimes to include drug and property offenses and giving prosecutors more authority to make the transfer decision (Griffin, 2003).

Ironically, these changes resulted in the transfer of more *minor* juvenile offenders in the late 20th century. In the late 1980s, the most common judicially waived case was a person-related offense (Puzzanchera, Stahl, Finnegan, Tierney, & Snyder, 2003). By 1998, property offense cases were more likely than person offense cases to be judicially waived. Working in the juvenile justice field at that time has been described as being inside a walled village with a monster (the "get tough" movement) just outside the gates (Butts, 1999). Fearful villagers attempt to satisfy the hunger of the monster, first throwing over the wall the most violent youths in the village, and then younger youths, then kids charged with less serious offenses, and so on. But the monster's hunger is never abated. Some serious scholars felt as if they were witnessing a ritualized sacrifice of children to the criminal courts and prisons to ensure the well-being of the state, a form of restorative justice at the community level (Titus, 2005).

The black hole in the transfer picture has been expanded by two key actors: legislatures and prosecutors. Official statistics do not cover their

Table 12.1   Multiple Ways to Impose Adult Criminal Court Sanctions on Juveniles

State	Judicial waiver			Concurrent jurisdiction	Statutory exclusion	Reverse waiver	Once an adult always an adult	Blended sentencing	
	Discretionary	Presumptive	Mandatory					Juvenile	Criminal
Number of states	*45*	*15*	*15*	*15*	*29*	*25*	*34*	*15*	*17*
Alabama	■				■		■		
Alaska	■	■			■			■	
Arizona	■			■	■	■	■		
Arkansas	■			■		■		■	■
California	■	■		■	■	■	■		■
Colorado	■	■		■		■		■	■
Connecticut			■			■		■	
Delaware	■		■			■	■		
Dist. of Columbia	■	■		■			■		
Florida	■			■	■		■		■
Georgia	■		■	■	■	■			
Hawaii	■						■		
Idaho	■				■				■
Illinois	■	■	■		■	■	■	■	■
Indiana	■		■		■		■		
Iowa	■				■	■	■		■
Kansas	■	■					■	■	
Kentucky	■		■			■			■
Louisiana	■		■	■	■				
Maine	■	■					■		
Maryland	■				■	■	■		
Massachusetts					■			■	■
Michigan	■			■			■	■	■
Minnesota	■	■			■		■	■	
Mississippi	■				■	■	■		
Missouri	■						■		■
Montana				■	■	■		■	

(*Continued*)

Table 12.1 (Continued)

State	Judicial waiver			Concurrent jurisdiction	Statutory exclusion	Reverse waiver	Once an adult always an adult	Blended sentencing	
	Discretionary	Presumptive	Mandatory					Juvenile	Criminal
Number of states	45	15	15	15	20	25	34	15	17
Nebraska				■		■			■
Nevada	■	■			■	■	■		
New Hampshire	■	■					■		
New Jersey	■	■	■						
New Mexico					■			■	■
New York					■	■			
North Carolina	■		■				■		
North Dakota	■	■	■				■		
Ohio	■		■				■	■	
Oklahoma	■			■	■	■	■		■
Oregon	■				■	■	■		
Pennsylvania	■	■			■	■	■		
Rhode Island	■	■	■				■	■	
South Carolina	■		■		■				
South Dakota	■				■	■	■		
Tennessee	■					■	■		
Texas	■						■	■	
Utah	■				■		■		
Vermont	■			■	■	■		■	
Virginia	■		■	■		■	■		■
Washington	■					■	■		
West Virginia	■		■						■
Wisconsin	■				■	■	■		■
Wyoming	■			■		■			

NOTE: Table information is as of the end of the 2004 legislative session. In states with a combination of provisions for transferring juveniles to criminal court, the exclusion, mandatory waiver, or concurrent jurisdiction provisions generally target the oldest juveniles and those charged with the most serious offenses, whereas younger juveniles and those charged with less serious offenses may be eligible for discretionary waiver.

actions, creating a "dark figure of waiver" (Mears, 2003, p. 159). Twenty-five years ago, juvenile court judges transferred most juveniles to criminal court. Prosecutors now make most of the transfer decisions (45%), followed by state legislatures (40%) (Building Blocks for Youth, 2000).

Incredibly, the number of juveniles transferred to the criminal justice system each year is unknown. Criminal justice system authorities prefer not to maintain these data, despite the fact that the United States is the only developed nation that often tries its youngest offenders in the regular adult criminal courts (Zimring, 2002). Therefore, it is difficult to say with any certainty what the statistical trend may be. The best guess to date was made using 1996 data: approximately 220,000 law violations committed in that year by youths younger than 18 who were legally ineligible for juvenile court because of legislative age limits (Butts & Mitchell, 2000). "If only half of these cases actually went forward for criminal court processing, they would still far exceed the number of juveniles ending up in adult court by all other methods combined" (p. 186).

The research base on transfer practices points us to several general conclusions (Howell & Howell, 2007). First, there is a large amount of variation between the states in the use of transfer mechanisms, and this reflects their individual philosophies. Second, age is one of the most important factors in determining the likelihood for transfer. Third, for homicide offenders, the more risk factors youths have, the more likely they are to be transferred and to receive longer sentences than if retained in juvenile court. Fourth, legislatures and prosecutors are least adept at selecting the most dangerous candidates for transfer. Fifth, "juvenile status" is an extralegal factor that influences the length of sentence in adult court to the detriment of juveniles (Kurlychek & Johnson, 2004). This study and others show that juveniles are more likely than young adults (who are more dangerous offenders) to be incarcerated for similar crimes. In a report written for the federal Bureau of Justice Statistics, Brown and Langan (1998) show that transferred juveniles convicted of felonies were given longer prison sentences than adults. Transferred juveniles were sentenced to prison for a maximum of 9 years on average, compared with 7 years for under-18 adults (as defined by state statutes) and 5 years for adults 18 and older. These inequities demonstrate the inability of the criminal justice system to treat juvenile offenders fairly and apply a reasonable measure of proportionality to their cases.

Other issues have been raised concerning the role of prosecutors and legislatures. As Feld (1998b) notes, "Prosecutorial waiver suffers from all of the vagaries of individualized discretion and without even the redeeming virtues of formal criteria, written reasons, an evidentiary record, or appellate review. Legislative offense exclusion suffers from rigidity, over-inclusiveness, and politicians' demagogic tendency to get tough" (p. 244). In addition, prosecutors' actions and the conduct of criminal courts are disturbing to some observers (Center for Public Integrity, 2003; Liebman et al., 2000).

Transfer is further compounded by the fact that sentencing of juveniles and adults in criminal courts is grossly disproportionate. I noted the longer sentences for juveniles versus adults above. Later in this chapter, I'll discuss the criminal justice system's mishandling of juvenile offenders in the most important cases (for capital murder). Executions of juvenile offenders were permitted in the United States until this practice was finally prohibited in 2005 by the U.S. Supreme Court (*Roper v. Simmons*), thanks to the determined efforts of a large number of advocacy groups (Boyle, 2005). More juvenile offenders were executed in the United States in the 1990s than in all other countries combined.

In the following section, I examine the case of one 11-year-old murderer, Nathaniel Abraham. I discuss the premises on which the juvenile court judge based his decision about this youngster's fate at sentencing and then use the case as a backdrop against which to look at the relative merits of handling juveniles in the criminal justice system or the juvenile justice system.

The Nathaniel Abraham Case

Nathaniel Abraham is the youngest child offender in American history to face murder charges as an adult (*People v. Abraham*, 234 Mich. App. 640, 599 N.W.2d 736, 740, 1999). Nathaniel, age 11 (4 feet, 9 inches tall, weighing 65 pounds) at the time of the murder, admitted firing a shot that killed an 18-year-old youth outside a convenience store in Pontiac, Michigan. He had fired the shot, using a stolen .22 caliber rifle, from a considerable distance away from the store; he denied shooting *at* anyone (Moore, 2000). He was convicted at age 13 of second-degree murder in juvenile court, under an unusual Michigan law that allows juveniles to be tried as adults in juvenile court for certain charges, including murder.

Presiding Oakland County Juvenile Court Judge Moore had three options under the statute:

- To sentence Nathaniel as an adult, which, under the Michigan sentencing guidelines, would amount to 8 to 25 years in a state prison
- To apply a blended sentence, which would include a sentence as an adult with a delay in that sentence to follow a placement in the juvenile system, after which Nathaniel could be transferred to the adult correctional system if he were not already rehabilitated
- To sentence Nathaniel as a juvenile, which could include incarceration in a juvenile facility until his 21st birthday

Judge Moore weighed the evidence related to the three options, as required under Michigan law. He pondered several important considerations. Nathaniel was guilty of a very serious offense. However, his culpability in committing the offense was in question. Nathaniel's teacher said that he was functioning between the 6- and 8-year-old level in terms of emotional maturity, and he was unable to understand the difference between fantasy and reality. He had no prior record of delinquency, although it was noted that he had exhibited delinquent behavior for about 2 years before the offense. Nathaniel's mother had sought treatment for him through a community mental health agency, but he was placed on a waiting list for 6 months before any treatment was provided. He attended three treatment sessions before his mother discontinued treatment because she did not believe the therapist was helpful. Finally, Judge Moore considered the availability of future rehabilitation programs for Nathaniel in the two systems.

Facing enormous political pressure to adhere to the popular mantra of "Do adult crime, do adult time," Judge Moore made a courageous decision. On January 13, 2000, he chose the third option, to rehabilitate Nathaniel in the juvenile justice system while protecting the public by confining him in a secure juvenile facility for 8 years, until he reached age 21. In doing so, Judge Moore demonstrated confidence that the Michigan juvenile justice system could rehabilitate the youngster.

In rejecting the option of sentencing Nathaniel to an adult prison, Judge Moore said, "If we say 'yes,' even for this heinous crime, we have given up on the juvenile justice system" (p. 8). He also noted that Nathaniel "has not failed in our juvenile programs, but rather has not been given a chance to benefit from them" (p. 9). Prison, he argued, should be considered only as a last resort—only if the juvenile justice system has failed. Moreover, he asserted that the adult criminal justice system is "a failure" and expressed concern that Nathaniel might be brutalized in prison, which could destroy any hope for rehabilitation.

Does research support the premises on which Judge Moore based his decision to keep Nathaniel in the juvenile justice system? His decision turned on the failures of the criminal justice system in general, and in particular with juvenile offenders. Is the criminal justice system indeed a failure? The next section examines the evidence.

Is the Criminal Justice System Appropriate for Juvenile Offenders?

In this section I address the appropriateness of the use of the criminal justice system for handling juvenile offenders from several viewpoints, the first of which is a constitutional issue. I also consider the impact of transfer to the criminal justice system on the juveniles themselves, especially recidivism, and then examine some of the information available on the capacity of the criminal justice system to handle juvenile offenders appropriately. Each of these issues is addressed in far greater detail in Howell (2003b, pp. 158–172).

A Key Constitutional Issue

Under new transfer laws, youths as young as age 10 can be required to participate in criminal court trials that often require enormously important decisions by defendants, including pleading guilty to sentences that would extend well into their adult years and in some cases for the rest of their lives. Our legal system has long required that defendants be competent to stand trial—that is, to understand the trial process, assist counsel in their defense, and make important decisions about the waiver of constitutional rights that can be made only by the defendant. These are constitutional protections, under the general term "competence to stand trial." The largest group of exclusions is adults adjudged mentally ill or retarded.

In the first systematic, large-scale study to examine whether immaturity—rather than mental illness or mental retardation—can impair defendants' capacities to participate in their trials, researchers found that one in three 11- to 13-year-olds and one in five 14- to 15-year-olds performed at levels of understanding and reasoning about trial events that are comparable to those of mentally ill adults who have been found not competent to stand trial (Grisso et al., 2003). The competence-relevant capacities of 16- and 17-year-olds as a group did not differ significantly from those of young adults, aged 18–24. Children ages 11–13 were more than three times as likely as young adults to be found "seriously impaired" in evaluations of their abilities to understand the trial process and to contribute to their own defense. Young people in the 14–15 age range were twice as likely as young adults to be found "seriously impaired" and incompetent to stand trial. Therefore, the same due process constraints that prohibit the adjudication of mentally ill and mentally retarded defendants who do not understand the process they face or cannot assist their attorneys also apply to juveniles who are incompetent due to immaturity alone. From the standpoint of fairness and constitutionality, many young offenders—particularly those under the age of 16—may not be appropriate subjects for criminal adjudication.

By injecting common sense, laypersons often make points simply and clearly. This observation made by the Reverend Thomas Masters is a case in point: "There's no way in the world you can receive a fair trial in an adult arena where you're looked upon as an adult when you have the mind of a child" (quoted in Zaczor, 2002, p. 7A). There are other reasons that the criminal courts should not be entrusted with the adjudication of juvenile offenders (Geraghty, 1997; for a summary of Geraghty's points, see Howell, 2003b, pp. 162–164).

The Effects of Transfer on Recidivism

A review of 50 studies of juvenile transfers to the criminal justice system a decade ago has revealed that recidivism rates are higher among juveniles transferred to criminal court than among those retained in the juvenile justice system (Howell, 1996). That conclusion soon was updated with more recent studies suggesting that not only are transferred juveniles more likely to reoffend, but they have a higher likelihood of reoffending more quickly and at a higher rate and may commit more serious offenses after they are released from prison than juveniles retained in the juvenile justice system

(Bishop & Frazier, 2000). In addition, Bishop and Frazier note that juvenile transfers do not produce a general deterrent effect.

A Pennsylvania study (Myers, 2003) found that transfer approximately doubled the odds of subsequent arrest for a violent offense. Myers observed that legislative transfer laws "actually suggest a criminogenic effect—[that] these laws may serve to increase the frequency and seriousness of future offending by those youths who are excluded from the juvenile court" (p. 94). Another analysis in this study (Myers & Kiehl, 2001) uncovered an often unintended outcome of transfer. Unlike the juvenile justice system, in which offenders charged with a violent crime are held in a detention center, the transferred juveniles in Pennsylvania were more likely to be released on bail, giving them the opportunity to commit additional crimes *before* they went to trial.

A recent systematic review of transfer studies updates these prior findings. The current review was conducted by the federal Centers for Disease Control (McGowan et al., 2007), which for many years has sponsored a wide range of violence prevention initiatives in the United States. The review was overseen by an independent, nonfederal Task Force on Community Preventive Services (Task Force). It also manages the development of a *Guide to Community Preventive Services (Community Guide)*.

The Task Force review of published scientific evidence on the effectiveness of juvenile transfer laws and policies focused on preventing or reducing interpersonal violence among youth who experience the adult criminal system or among the juvenile population as a whole. The review team found that transferring juveniles to the adult justice system generally increases, rather than decreases, rates of violence among transferred youth—what is called an iatrogenic effect (Tonry, 2007). Evidence was insufficient for the Task Force to determine the effect of such laws and policies in reducing violent behavior in the overall juvenile population. Overall, the Task Force recommends against laws or policies facilitating the transfer of juveniles from the juvenile to the adult judicial system for the purpose of reducing violence. The Task Force (2007) found that transferred juveniles are 34% more likely to be rearrested for a violent or other crime than are juveniles retained in the juvenile justice system (McGowan et al., 2007, p. S14). In other words, "available evidence indicates that juveniles who experience the adult justice system, on average, commit more subsequent violent crime following release than juveniles retained in the juvenile justice system" (p. S5).

The Capacity of the Criminal Justice System to Handle Juvenile Offenders

Because of their youthfulness, juveniles are far more likely to be violently victimized in adult prisons than in juvenile correctional facilities. They are 8 times more likely to commit suicide, 500 times more likely to be sexually assaulted, and 200 times more likely to be beaten by staff than are juveniles in juvenile facilities (Beyer, 1997). It is difficult for juveniles to avoid being raped in prison, where at least 14% of inmates are raped (Beyer, 1997). Setting these terrible atrocities aside for the moment, are criminal courts and prisons effective in reducing repeat offending? This is their main objective. The evidence is overwhelming that they also fail on this measure.

Recidivism rates are very high among offenders whose cases are adjudicated in criminal courts. About two-thirds of adult probationers commit other crimes within 3 years of their sentences, and many of these crimes are serious (Manhattan Institute, 1999). Recidivism rates are similar for prisons. Approximately 67% of released prisoners are rearrested within 3 years, and more than half of released prisoners are returned to prison, like a revolving door (Langan & Levin, 2002). The failure of prisons is not a recent development. Similarly high prison recidivism rates are found in research dating back to the 19th century (Chambliss, 1995, p. 255).

Despite this dismal record, there is a widely held assumption that imprisonment policies and practices protect the public. Many policy makers, lawmakers, and adult corrections officials who embrace this assumption bristle at calls for the funding of prevention and treatment alternatives. Respected Senator Charles Grassley put it this way: "I support smart crime prevention programs. . . . However, it seems to me that many who blindly advocate prevention programs fail to understand that incarceration is the best form of crime prevention." His assumption is not supported by research, as seen in Chapter 9.

The main reason recidivism rates are so high in criminal courts is that, unlike the courts in other countries, U.S. criminal courts seldom use community corrections options and other advanced rehabilitation techniques (Tonry, 1999a, 1999c). Day fines, very popular in European countries for punishment of minor or moderate crimes, are seldom used in the United States. Prosecutorial fines are widely used in Germany and Holland but not in the United States. Many other countries use sentences of community service, scaled to the seriousness of the crime, as an alternative to incarceration; in the United States, only minor offenders are given such sentences. In contrast, sentencing guidelines, including mandatory minimums and "truth in sentencing" rules, are unique to the United States.

Other Evidence of a Flawed Criminal Justice System

The U.S. criminal justice system has many other flaws. Widespread problems render the system unsuitable for handling juvenile cases in a fair and just manner. In general, criminal justice system practices are discriminatory, arbitrary, and capricious (Liebman et al., 2000; Roberts & Stratton, 2000; Tonry, 1994a, 1994b, 1999b; Uviller, 1999).

Columbia University Law School researchers (Liebman et al., 2000) found that of the more than 4,500 U.S.-appealed state capital murder cases in the period 1973–1995, two-thirds of the convictions were overturned on appeal because they were flawed by serious, reversible error. The widely respected researchers characterize the criminal court process for handling capital murder cases as a "broken system." The criminal justice system does not appear to perform any better in handling juvenile capital murder cases (Cothern, 2000). Several studies have found that the majority of cases in which juvenile offenders were put to death had flaws in the criminal court procedures that resulted in the executions (see Amnesty International, 1998a, 1998b; Lewis et al., 1988; Robinson & Stephens, 1992). Now, wrongful convictions are a top priority on the public policy agenda (Zelman, 2006). Criminologists are calling for an immediate moratorium on executions (Acker, 2007).

These are not the only serious criminal justice system flaws. For example, discrimination based on defendants' race or ethnicity occurs at all stages of the criminal justice system: arrest (Mann, 1993; Sampson & Lauritsen, 1997), pretrial release (Bridges, 1997), federal pretrial release (bail) practices (Maxwell & Davis, 1999), prosecutor decision making (LaFree, 1980; Radelet, 1989; Spohn, Gruhl, & Welch, 1987; Uviller, 1999), sentencing (Mauer, 1997; McDonald & Carlson, 1992; Tonry, 1999b; Wooldredge, 1988), imprisonment (Austin, Marino, Carroll, McCall, & Richards, 2000; Chiricos & Crawford, 1995; Petersilia & Turner, 1985), and prison release decision making (Carroll & Mondrick, 1976; Petersilia, 1983). In addition, the poor and indigent are systematically discriminated against in criminal courts (Katz, 1970; Weston, 1969).

Research has also found that criminal justice system practices are unjustly inconsistent from one state or locality to the next. This is called justice by geography. This is most evident in arrests (Shannon, 1988; Smith, Visher, & Davidson, 1984), sentencing (Tonry, 1999c), imprisonment (Bridges, Crutchfield, & Simpson, 1987; Chiricos & Crawford, 1995; Crutchfield, Bridges, & Pitchford, 1994), and imposition of the death penalty (Willing & Fields, 1999). Imprisonment rates and the overrepresentation of minorities in prison also vary widely from state to state (Austin et al., 2000). Admissions of juveniles to adult prisons began declining in the mid-1990s, concurrent with the drop in juvenile violent crime rates (Snyder & Sickmund, 2006, p. 237).

Observers in other countries are somewhat baffled by U.S. crime control policies. In 1996, the *Economist* (a British journal) published a review of American crime and imprisonment trends titled "Violent and Irrational—and That's Just the Policy." As Weitekamp (2001), a German scholar, has noted, the United States

> has the highest incarceration rate in the Western industrialized world, applies . . . the most repressive criminal justice policies, still has the death penalty, executes record numbers, has almost more weapons in the streets than it has inhabitants, and fights "wars" against crime and drugs. (p. 314)

Sentences of Life Without Possibility of Parole

The Convention on the Rights of the Child (1989), Article 37(a), prohibits life imprisonment without the possibility of parole for offenses committed by people less than 18 years of age. The United States and Somalia are the only countries that have not ratified this convention (American Civil Liberties Union of Michigan, 2004). Only a handful of states have statutes that expressly prohibit sentences of life without parole (LWOP) for juveniles; the overwhelming majority of states appear to permit such sentences or make LWOP mandatory upon conviction in criminal court (Logan, 1998). Juveniles can be sentenced to LWOP in 41 states, 14 states allow a child of any age to be tried and punished as an adult and sentenced to life without parole, and three states (South Dakota, Vermont, and Wisconsin) allow children as young as age 10 to be tried and punished as adults and sentenced to life without parole (American Civil Liberties Union of Michigan, 2004). Human Rights Watch's (2005) study on LWOP sentences found 2,225 juveniles sitting in adult prisons, sentenced to LWOP. This astounding finding came from the study: In 11 out of 17 years (between 1985 and 2001), youth convicted of murder in the United States were *more* likely to enter prison with a LWOP sentence than adult murderers. Life sentences for juvenile offenders should be ended (see also Fagan, 2007).

Public Opinion on Transfers

Presumably because of the purported juvenile violence "epidemic," the actual increase in juvenile use of guns in homicides, and the "superpredator" myth, the general public came to favor transfer of some juveniles to the adult criminal justice system. Nevertheless, the public consistently favors rehabilitation of juvenile offenders (Cullen, 2006, 2007; Moon, Sundt, Cullen, & Wright, 2000; Nagin et al., 2006; Roberts, 1992). Only 3 out of 10 adults favored executing those who are juveniles at the time of their crime in a May 2002 Gallup poll (Death Penalty Information Center, 2003). When asked whether "the only way to protect society is to put the [most chronic] offenders in jail when they are young and throw away the key," nearly 8 out of 10 adults disagree (Moon et al., 2000). In this latter study, three-fourths of the respondents favored treatment for even juveniles who had been involved in a lot of crime in their lives. The public and a large number of police chiefs and other law enforcement officials also support delinquency prevention and early intervention (Cullen et al., 1998; Fight Crime: Invest in Kids, 2002; Soler, 2001).

Although a majority of surveyed Americans say they want some juveniles transferred to criminal courts, most also say they don't want juvenile prisoners mixed with adults (Cullen, Golden, & Cullen, 1983; Mears, 2000, 2001; Wu, 2000). It appears that people in general are unaware that most transferred juveniles are very likely to be mixed with adult criminals because, once transferred, they are transformed into "adults" under state laws and often incarcerated with even the worst adult criminals. Only six states absolutely prohibit this practice. At the same time, the public clearly favors "getting tough" with juvenile offenders, and the mistaken belief that sentencing people in criminal courts will deter others from committing crimes persists (see Bouley & Wells, 2001; Moon et al., 2000).

According to a recent poll by Zogby International, voters by a large majority oppose putting juveniles in adult prisons. Across lines of gender, economic class, ethnicity, and political and religious affiliation, approximately 7 in 10 think that putting youth under age 18 in adult correctional facilities makes them more likely to commit future crime. About the same percentage disagrees that treating youths as adults teaches them a lesson and serves as a deterrent. Of those polled, 72% of the public thinks that the decision to try a youth as an adult should be made by a judge. Only 9% think that decision should rest with a prosecutor, and 92% think that the decision to transfer a youth to adult court should be made on a case-by-case basis, not by a blanket policy. Surprisingly, given evidence of its effectiveness, only about one-third of the voting public believes that the juvenile justice system is doing an effective job in reducing either violent or nonviolent crime. Nevertheless, more than 9 out of 10 respondents said they believed that rehabilitative services and treatment will help reduce crime (Krisberg & Marchionna, 2007).

International Standards

As Human Rights Watch (1999) points out, international standards recognize that because children and adolescents are a particularly vulnerable group, they are entitled to special care and protection. They are still developing physically, emotionally, and mentally. With this reality in mind, international human rights documents strongly encourage countries to develop specialized laws, procedures, organizational authorities, and institutions for handling children and adolescents. This means that incarceration of juveniles in adult prisons is strongly discouraged, and United Nations Rules for the Protection of Children (Article 67) strictly prohibit "closed or solitary confinement or any other punishment that may compromise the physical or mental health of the juvenile concerned." Indeed, our own Supreme Court has recognized that youths deserve less punishment than adults because they may have less capacity to control their conduct and to think in long-range perspectives (*Eddings v. Oklahoma*, 455 U.S. 104, 115 n.11, 1982).

New Directions

This chapter examined the practice of transferring juveniles from the juvenile justice system to the criminal justice system. Before the juvenile justice system was created in the United States near the end of the 19th century, juveniles were handled in the criminal courts. With the creation of juvenile courts more than 100 years ago, Americans rejected the use of criminal courts and imprisonment to punish juveniles. For nearly a century,

Americans have accepted the juvenile justice system as society's treatment and control apparatus for nearly every juvenile offender. However, this acceptance has diminished with the recent moral panic over delinquency (Fagan & Zimring, 2000). Transfer of juveniles to the criminal justice system is now common in the United States.

In large part because of myths about a "new breed" of juvenile offenders and conjured-up projections that hundreds of thousands of them were soon emerging in America, policy makers and legislators moved away from the rehabilitation-oriented juvenile court and its individualized justice model for wayward people to embrace criminal court handling of juvenile offenses. This shift was not a minor one by any means. It meant giving up on rehabilitation and individualized treatment in favor of punishing specific offenses with blanket criteria. The new laws that excluded juveniles from the jurisdiction of juvenile courts included imposing automatic waivers, lowering the age of eligibility for transfer, and increasing the role of prosecutors in transfer decisions.

Treatment and control policies concerning juvenile offenders in the United States have thus come full circle, back to the practice of treating large numbers of juveniles as if they were adults. But the tide may well be turning. There is a groundswell of public opinion in opposition to the punitive ways in which children are currently handled by our trusted institutions, law enforcement, courts, and schools. As seen in Chapter 2, dissatisfaction is growing with school-based zero tolerance policies, especially when they make zero sense. Perhaps for some of the same reasons—and others as well—there is public disagreement with juvenile transfer policies.

A number of states have softened the impact of punitive reforms (Bishop, 2006). In her review of state juvenile code purpose clauses, Bishop found that 40 states identify treatment or rehabilitation as a goal, and 45 maintain allegiance to the juvenile court's traditional benevolent rehabilitation mission. Bishop also examined juvenile justice legislation enacted or introduced in the last 3 years (Box 12.3). She found that efforts are under way in a number of states to mitigate—and even abandon—punitive features of existing legislation and to address the treatment needs of most juvenile offenders, and at least 35 states have reorganized juvenile courts according to a family court model. Although there are variations between states, family courts typically hear all juvenile and family cases, including delinquency, child abuse and neglect, divorce, and domestic disputes. Only one study to date has examined the outcomes of such a unified court on delinquency outcomes (Gebo, 2005), and it found evidence of a more individualized approach to juvenile processing in the family court. It is also significant that juvenile courts waived 46% fewer cases to criminal courts in 2002 than in 1994 (Snyder & Sickmund, 2006, p. 186).

IN FOCUS 12.3

State Legislative Actions (enacted or introduced in 2002–2005) to Address the Treatment Needs of Juvenile Offenders

- Some legislation aims at improving individualized treatment for committed offenders (Mississippi, South Dakota, and Wyoming).
- Provision for mental health assessment and treatment was passed in four states (Idaho, Washington, Connecticut, and Virginia).
- Several states enacted laws to establish teen courts and other diversion programs.
- Four states (Michigan, Ohio, Colorado, and Indiana) passed legislation to provide drug treatment, and several others included drug treatment in other initiatives.
- The Mississippi legislature phased out its boot camps.
- Illinois established monetary incentives for counties to reduce commitments to state institutions.
- Colorado and South Dakota enacted measures to separate transferred offenders from incarcerated adults.
- Connecticut enacted a measure to raise (gradually) the age of juvenile court jurisdiction from 16 to 18 by 2010. (The North Carolina legislature also considered a similar measure.)
- Three states (Florida, Pennsylvania, and Washington) adopted evidence-based programming in juvenile corrections. (North Carolina, Tennessee, and Oregon legislatures have enacted a similar requirement.)

There now appears to be growing opposition to exposing adolescents to the harsh treatment that young offenders get in criminal courts and the stark realities of adult prisons (Irwin, 2005; Mauer & Meda, 2003). For example, in a feature article in *USA Today* M. T. Moore (2007) questions the practice of marching young offenders into criminal court in metal chains and shackles even though they have not been convicted of a crime and do not appear to be dangerous. What's at issue, Moore says, is whether children as young as 10 years of age need to be shackled for court security. Obviously not, but in more than half of the states (27), some juvenile courts require defendants to be handcuffed or shackled in courts (M. T. Moore, 2007).

The second source of change in public policy with respect to dispositions for juvenile offenders is a series of studies on adolescent brain development (Box 12.4). These studies appear to have been a major influence in the Supreme Court decision to outlaw the death penalty for juveniles who were under the age of 18 at the time of the crimes. The court said the executions violate the Eighth Amendment ban on cruel and unusual punishment. The majority opinion, written by Justice Anthony Kennedy, noted that age 18 is the point where society draws the line for many purposes between childhood and adulthood (Box 12.5). The majority of justices concluded that age 18 is the age at which the line for death eligibility ought to rest. It seemed that the Court may also have been persuaded that, in line with the recent brain development studies, adolescents may not have fully mature brains. Executions for those 15 and younger when they committed their crimes had already been outlawed, in 1988, in Thompson v. Oklahoma. This prohibition stands.

IN FOCUS 12.4
New Research on Adolescent Brain Development

Research now supports what parents of teenagers have known all along: that the teenager's brain is less mature than the adult brain. Researchers at the Harvard Medical School, the National Institute of Mental Health, the UCLA School of Medicine, and others have collaborated to map the development of the brain from childhood to adulthood and to examine its implications. Their research using magnetic resonance imaging has found that the teen brain is not a finished product but a work in progress. Until recently, most scientists believed that the essential "wiring" of the brain was completed at a very early age—perhaps by age 3—and that the brain matured fully in childhood. Psychologists assured us that adolescents had thinking ability comparable to that of adults by age 16.

With this new technology, neuroscientists have safely scanned children's and adolescents' brains into adulthood, tracking the development process. This has led them to discover that adolescents' brains are far less developed than previously believed and that the brain is still developing during the teen years. This lack of development affects higher-level or more complex cognitive functions such as planning, reasoning, judgment, and behavior control. This may help to explain certain teenage behavior that frustrates parents, such as recklessness and emotional outbursts.

One of the pioneering researchers, Dr. Jay Giedd of the National Institute of Mental Health, explains that the most surprising discovery is that there are two brain growth spurts. By age 6, the brain is already 95% of its adult size. Years ago, scientists thought that, for the most part, development of the brain was completed in the early years. Now, they have discovered a second growth spurt ("Inside the teenage brain," 2007).

The neuroscientists found that an interesting thing happens to the adolescent brain. During the teenage years, the brain overproduces gray matter, the tissue in which thinking takes place. We've heard the expression that teenagers seem to be in a fog. Well, they are. This thickening of the gray matter peaks at about age 11 in girls and age 12 in boys, roughly about the same time as puberty. After the overproduction of gray matter, the brain undergoes a process called pruning, much like pruning a tree of useless limbs, to allow the brain to grow with white matter, which insulates the brain's circuitry, making its operation more precise and efficient. Connections between neurons in the brain that are not used wither away, and those that are used stay—the "use it or lose it" principle. It is thought that this pruning process makes the brain more efficient by strengthening the connections that are used most often and eliminating the clutter of those that are not used at all. Researchers found that during this foggy period in the frontal lobe, adolescents often rely on parts of the brain that produce emotions, not evaluating the consequences of what they are doing. This may explain why teenagers are more likely to crash a car than at any other time of life and why they are more likely to engage in risky sex, drug abuse, or delinquency.

Dr. Giedd explains that the time from puberty and on into the adult years is a particularly critical time for the brain sculpting to take place. He likens the process to creating Michelangelo's *David*. The sculptor starts out with a huge block of granite, at the peak at the puberty years. Then pieces of the granite are removed to create the work of art, and that is the way the brain sculpts itself. Dr. Giedd and other neuroscientists agree that the brain does not cease to mature until the early 20s in the parts that govern impulsivity, judgment, planning for the future, foresight of consequences, and other characteristics that make people morally culpable.

IN FOCUS 12.5

Supreme Court Decision Outlawing Executions of Juveniles

The U.S. Supreme Court stated the following three reasons that make juveniles under 18 different from adults:

> First, as any parent knows and as the scientific and sociological studies tend to confirm, a lack of maturity and an underdeveloped sense of responsibility are found in youth more often than in adults and are more understandable among the youth. These qualities often result in impetuous and ill-considered actions and decisions. In recognition of the comparative immaturity and irresponsibility of juveniles, almost every State prohibits those under 18 years of age from voting, serving on juries, or marrying without parental consent.

(Continued)

(Continued)

*Second, juveniles are more vulnerable or susceptible to negative influ-
ences and outside pressures, including peer pressure. Youth is more
than a chronological fact. It is a time and condition of life when a person may be most susceptible to influence and to psychological damage.
This is explained in part by the prevailing circumstance that juveniles
have less control, or less experience with control, over their own environment. As legal minors, juveniles lack the freedom that adults have
to extricate themselves from a criminogenic setting.*

*Third, the character of a juvenile is not as well formed as that of an adult.
The personality traits of juveniles are more transitory, less fixed.*

A widely respected observer of how our youngest citizens are treated in
our juvenile and criminal justice systems, Bob Herbert (2007a), has called
attention to the mistake of making criminals out of kids, who are not hardened criminals in the same sense that life-course adults are. But overturn-
ing the current transfer laws, policies, and practices won't be easy. These
have the force of the influential National District Attorneys Association
(NDAA) behind them (Kupchik, 2006a, 2006b, pp. 313–314). According to
the NDAA *Resource Manual and Policy Positions on Juvenile Crime Issues*
(2000), "Transfer to the criminal court is necessary because the traditional
role of the juvenile justice system in seeking to place rehabilitation and the
interests of the child first should no longer be applicable in the case of serious, violent, or habitual offenders" (p. 7).

The NDAA *Resource Manual* also argues that transferring youth to the
criminal court will subject the "new breed of delinquents" to a more severe
sentencing framework than the juvenile court can provide. Using mantras
such as "old enough to do the crime, old enough to do the time," the NDAA
urges transfer policies with the stated goal of subjecting violent and chronic
adolescent offenders to different evaluative criteria than the juvenile court
administers (Kupchik, 2006b, p. 314). Others suggest that such policy positions amount to "dramatization of evil" (Titus, 2005), and "as in ancient
times, children subjected to juvenile waivers function as symbolic sacrificial
victims, [branded] as beyond the moral community although living within
it" (p. 123). In addition, our society is ambivalent and sometimes contradictory in making judgments about the competency of adolescents. "Are
there differences between adolescents and adults? I find it ironic that the
same Virginia legislative session that lowered the age of transfer to 14 also
passed a law that prohibited youth under the age of 18 from getting a tattoo
without their parents' permission because they were too immature to make
this decision on their own!" (Reppucci, 1999, p. 315).

My review of the evidence presented here confirms Judge Moore's judgment. Nathaniel Abraham served nearly 10 years in juvenile rehabilitation

and was released in January 2007. He earned a high school diploma in 2005 and has enrolled at Delta College. This happy outcome for Nathaniel probably would not have happened had Judge Moore sentenced him to a Michigan prison (Box 12.6).

IN FOCUS 12.6

Key Findings From a New National Study of Juvenile Transfers

National and state research and the experiences of young people, their parents, and their families give the Justice Policy Institute a concrete picture of how the laws governing the trying, sentencing, and incarceration of youth do not promote public safety. The following are more than a dozen key findings from this research.

1. The overwhelming majority of youth who enter the adult court are not there for serious, violent crimes.

2. Increasing numbers of young people have been placed in adult jails where they are at risk of assault, abuse, and death.

3. State laws may contradict core federal protections designed to prohibit confinement of juveniles with adults.

4. In contrast to growing numbers of youth incarcerated in adult jails, adult prisons' admissions of youth are declining.

5. The decision to send youth to adult court is most often not made by the one person best considered to judge the merits of the youth's case—the juvenile court judge.

6. Access to effective legal counsel is a deciding factor on whether a youth is prosecuted as an adult.

7. Youth of color are disproportionately affected by these policies.

8. Female youth are affected too, but little is known about them.

9. The consequences for prosecuting youth in adult court "aren't minor."

10. The research shows that these laws do not promote public safety.

11. These laws ignore the latest scientific evidence on the adolescent brain—the same evidence that informed the U.S. Supreme Court's decision to bar the juvenile death penalty.

12. Assessing the impact of youth incarceration is difficult because of a lack of available data.

13. The public should invest its dollars by strengthening the juvenile justice system.

The criminal justice system is the wrong place for any juvenile offender. It is a failure on many grounds: It is ineffective in rehabilitating offenders, is arbitrary and capricious, and discriminates against minorities. In addition, criminal justice court programs are largely ineffective, and the prison system operates like a revolving door. Both have all but abandoned rehabilitation in favor of punishment. The criminal justice system needs redirecting (Travis & Petersilia, 2001).

The criminal justice system that promised to protect the rights of juveniles (Ainsworth, 1991, 1995; Feld, 1998b, 1999) is like a fairy tale that never came true. Constitutional protections of individual rights for at least 9 out of 10 cases in criminal court are a myth because only about 5–10% of all criminal court cases go to trial, even though the Sixth Amendment to the U.S. Constitution guarantees all people the right to a speedy and public trial before an impartial jury. Thus important constitutional protections are available for only a small fraction of alleged offenders. In short, it appears that juveniles' constitutional rights are more likely to be violated in criminal courts than in juvenile courts. Justice is most likely to be served for juveniles in juvenile courts. Equally important, youngsters are far more likely to receive treatment and rehabilitation services in the juvenile justice system. Some critics of the juvenile justice system go so far as to call for the abolition of juvenile courts (Ainsworth, 1991, 1995; Feld, 1998a, Schwartz, 1999; Schwartz et al., 1998), but others have responded that this proposal amounts to "nonsense" (Arthur, 1998; Howell, 1998a; Rosenberg, 1993; Zimring, 2000, 2002).

Given the negative and unintended results of transfer laws, it appears that juvenile justice would be best served if juvenile courts were left alone. The criminal justice system lacks the capacity to handle juvenile cases effectively. Transferred juveniles are more likely to reoffend, and to do so more quickly and at higher rates, and perhaps to commit more serious offenses after they are released from prison than juveniles retained in the juvenile justice system. Therefore, juveniles should not be transferred to the criminal justice system.

State legislatures should act immediately on the recommendations of the Task Force on Community Preventive Services (2007) regarding transfer of juveniles (McGowan et al., 2007; Box 12.7):

- States that now set adult court jurisdiction at age 18 should keep it there, and other states should change their laws to restrict adult court jurisdiction to people 18 and older.
- All laws providing for automatic jurisdiction in the adult courts for young people under age 18 charged with designated serious crimes should be repealed.
- Laws permitting case-by-case transfers by prosecutors or criminal court judges should be reexamined to make sure that they permit transfers only in cases that are clearly not amenable to juvenile court handling (Tonry, 2007, p. 4).

Adopting these recommendations would bring the United States into compliance with international standards and also reduce delinquency. Ideally, all state policies that allow the transfer of juveniles to the criminal justice system for criminal conviction and adult punishment should be ended.

IN FOCUS 12.7

Task Force on Community Preventive Services, Finding and Recommendation

Finding:

Juvenile violence is a substantial public health problem in the United States. . . . Over the last 25 years, juveniles aged 10–17 years, who constitute less than 12% of the population, have been involved as offenders in approximately 25% of serious violent victimizations. The reduction of morbidity and mortality caused by violence is a major goal of public health. Similarly, the assurance of public safety and the reduction of violent crime are goals of the national system of justice. This report evaluates an approach to the prevention of violence by means of a legal policy that has expanded in recent decades in states across the nation in response to the perceived increase in juvenile violence and perceived challenges in the juvenile justice system in responding to juvenile violence. (Task Force on Community Preventive Services, 2007, p. 5)

Recommendation:

The Task Force evaluated the evidence on effectiveness of policies facilitating the transfer of juveniles from juvenile to adult justice systems to reduce violence. The Task Force found evidence of harm associated with strengthened juvenile transfer policies. Available evidence indicates that juveniles who experience the adult justice system, on average, commit more subsequent violent crime following release than juveniles retained in the juvenile justice system. Further, evidence that juveniles in the general population are deterred from violent crime by strengthened juvenile transfer policies is insufficient. As a means of reducing juvenile violence, strengthened juvenile transfer policies are counterproductive. The Task Force, therefore, recommends against policies facilitating the transfer of juveniles from juvenile to adult criminal justice systems for the purpose of reducing violence. (Task Force on Community Preventive Services, 2007, p. 5)

Discussion Topics

1. Why were juvenile offender transfer laws, policies, and practices ever entertained?

2. Is some amount of transfer of juvenile offenders necessary? Why or why not?

3. What are the major drawbacks to juvenile offender transfers?

4. Can these limitations be corrected?

5. Describe how juvenile correctional systems would operate if there were no transfers.

Concluding
Observations

We must get the right service to the right kid at the right time.

—John J. Wilson,
coauthor of the Comprehensive Strategy

The past 20 years have been a tumultuous period for the American juvenile justice system. Although many have claimed that a general "epidemic" of juvenile violence occurred in the United States from the mid-1980s through the early 1990s, research has shown that this did not actually happen—not an overall epidemic. To be sure, there were increases in violence in some areas, but not in others, and there was no large overall increase. The increase in homicide and suicide with guns was the high rate increase or "epidemic" component. The most recent moral panic over juvenile delinquency and the myths associated with it—such as that an epidemic of youth violence was taking place and that a new breed of juvenile superpredators was emerging—led to dramatic changes in juvenile justice policies and practices in the 1980s and 1990s, and their influence is still in evidence.

Significant changes have occurred in the boundaries of the juvenile justice system and in policies and procedures for handling juvenile offenders within it (Bishop, 2006; Fagan & Zimring, 2000). Large numbers of juvenile offenders have been removed from the juvenile justice system and placed in the criminal justice system. Blended sentence provisions have been enacted into law along with offense-based determinant and mandatory minimum sentences. Punitive measures are used more widely than ever before. New laws have designated more juveniles as serious offenders, brought more minor offenders into the system, and extended periods of confinement in juvenile correctional facilities. One comparison illustrates the overall trend. From 1990 through 1999, the total number of juvenile arrests for violent offenses *decreased* by 55%, and juvenile arrests for serious property offenses *decreased* by 23% (Snyder, 2000). Nevertheless, during approximately the same period, the total number of referrals to juvenile court *increased* by 44% (Stahl, 2001). Juvenile court intake and probation caseloads are overwhelming, and detention centers and juvenile reformatories have become and remain overcrowded, particularly with minor offenders. Minority youth, particularly black youngsters, are bearing the brunt of the punitive juvenile justice reforms that the panic over juvenile violence has wrought, although Latino and Latina youth are catching up (Villarruel & Walker, 2002). This is the general context in which juvenile justice systems across the United States currently operate. A growing number of state juvenile justice systems are now paying the price for violating the civil rights of confined people that are guaranteed under the Civil Rights of Institutionalized Persons Act. Since 2000, U.S. Department of Justice investigations have been made of 23 juvenile justice facilities in more than a dozen states (U.S. Department of Justice, 2007). Once again, juveniles are "victims of change" (Finestone, 1976).

In Chapter 10 of this book I described and illustrated a comprehensive framework for integrating the various segments of the juvenile delinquency prevention field and juvenile justice systems in a way that can restore balance to these systems and refocus them on their fundamental mission. Delinquency prevention, effective early intervention, and a continuum of graduated sanctions linked with rehabilitation programs in the juvenile justice system are the main components of the Comprehensive Strategy. In the first level, delinquency prevention and early intervention programs are promoted as the most cost-effective approaches to dealing with juvenile delinquency. Emphasis is placed on intervening early with disruptive children and their families, and immediately when delinquency first occurs, to prevent child delinquents from becoming serious, violent, and chronic offenders. When other institutions fail to prevent delinquency, the juvenile justice system intervenes, at the second level, working with other agencies to reduce delinquency. The juvenile justice system naturally takes a developmental perspective in interventions with children or adolescents and their families, schools, and delinquent peer groups.

The Comprehensive Strategy is a research-based framework that is grounded on information presented in Parts I and II of the book and on best practices and advanced management techniques that have been developed in the juvenile justice field over the past 25 years or more. I have used examples to illustrate the flexibility of the Comprehensive Strategy framework in several adaptations. Many more examples were documented in an earlier work (Howell, 2003b) that need not be repeated here.

The Comprehensive Strategy empowers local professionals and citizens to conduct an assessment of their community's delinquency problem, select solutions they want to implement to address identified problems, and integrate the selected programs in an overall continuum of prevention and rehabilitation programs and strategies. This research-based, data-driven, and outcome-focused strategy is more likely to be effective than piecemeal approaches. For one thing, this strategy brings multiple interventions into play that address risk factors (for prevention purposes) in each of the developmental domains: family, school, peer group, community, and individual characteristics. Similarly, programs address treatment needs in each of these developmental domains.

I described a continuum of effective prevention and early intervention programs in Chapter 9, and the principles behind them were presented in Chapter 8. I chose not to describe treatment programs in detail in Chapter 9 because such descriptions rapidly become outdated. Moreover, these are now online and stored in electronic databases of rated programs that are regularly updated as new studies are reported. In addition, Lipsey's pioneering meta-analyses have led to the development of a very practical method for assessing existing program interventions against evidence-based practices, which also provides guidelines for engaging service providers in improving current programs to emulate best practices.

Policy Change Proposals

Three recent and profound developments reported in this book have turned the juvenile justice ship back on course. The first of these is new research on development of the adolescent brain, leading to the discovery that adolescents' brains are far less developed than previously believed and that the brain is still developing during the teen years. This research reminds us of one of the key principles on which the juvenile justice system was founded: that children's developmental differences must be taken into account in how our society's institutions relate to them. The second profound development is the U.S. Supreme Court's 2005 decision (*Roper v. Simmons*) to prohibit executions of juvenile offenders. This decision realigns the United States with other developed countries that prohibit juvenile executions. Third, a systematic review of transfers of juveniles to the criminal justice system found that this policy does not pass the litmus test of reducing violence. Instead, "transferred juveniles are 34% more likely to be re-arrested for a violent or other crime than are juveniles retained" in the juvenile justice system (McGowan et al., 2007, p. S14).

Together, these three developments remind us why the juvenile justice system was created. A fresh view of its history is available that illuminates its philosophical principles (Tanenhaus, 2004). The creators of the first juvenile courts based them on accumulated wisdom at that time, that children must be diverted from jails and prisons (schools for crime) maintained by the criminal justice system, that communities must be mobilized to reclaim offenders and prevent delinquency, that root causes of delinquency must be identified, and, of course, that the developmental differences between children, adolescents, and adults must be honored. These principles and the recent history of the juvenile justice system suggest several policy changes that, if made, could improve system operations considerably.

Enormous amounts of juvenile justice system resources are wasted on the very large proportion of all juvenile offenders who will never become serious, violent, and chronic offenders. Lawmakers have gotten it backward in cracking down on first-time offenders, and this policy has overloaded juvenile courts, probation departments, and detention centers. We now know from several offender career studies that as many as two-thirds of all juvenile offenders will *never* become serious, violent, or chronic offenders. The necessary risk assessment technology is available today to sort these low-risk offenders out from the remainder so that they can receive the immediate sanctions and short-term program interventions that have proven effective with such juveniles.

More gender-specific programming is needed in the juvenile justice system. Although most girls who become juvenile offenders take pathways to serious and violent delinquency that are similar to those taken by boys, it appears that a small proportion of girls may take a unique pathway to serious, violent, and chronic offender careers that winds through the juvenile justice system (see Chapter 5). Even though programs for serious and violent juvenile offenders appear to be as effective for girls as for boys (Lipsey & Wilson, 1998, p. 332), girls can benefit from gender-specific programs such as the following:

- Programs that provide treatment for neglect and sexual and physical victimization
- Programs that provide medical care for pregnant teens
- Programs for unwed teenage mothers, including parent training and child care relief time
- Programs that build and preserve the teen mother–child bond
- Programs for sexually active females (and males)
- Programs that include peer mediation to deal with conflicts concerning boyfriends and peer status

Ideally, all state policies that allow the transfer of juveniles to the criminal justice system for criminal conviction and adult punishment should be ended. Aside from the fact that such policies are not the mark of a civilized society, the practice of exposing adolescents to adult courts and prisons is neither effective in reducing crime nor cost-effective. The criminal justice system does not have the capacity to treat or protect juveniles, and incarcerating juveniles in adult facilities is not effective in deterring crime.

Those who have criticized the juvenile justice system for its alleged lack of due process claim that juveniles' constitutional rights would be better protected in the criminal justice system (Feld, 1998a, 1999), but this has never proven to be true. Only about 5–10% of all criminal court cases proceed to trial, so only a small fraction of alleged offenders—less than 1 in 10—are afforded their constitutional process protections. Juveniles' constitutional rights are far more likely to be irrelevant in criminal courts than they are in juvenile courts. More than one-half of all cases referred to juvenile courts are adjudicated (Snyder & Sickmund, 2006, p. 171), at which point almost all constitutional protections afforded to adults apply to juveniles.

State legislatures should act immediately on the recommendations of the Task Force on Community Preventive Services (2007) regarding transfer of juveniles (see Box 12.2 in Chapter 12; also see Tonry, 2007, p. 4):

- States that now set adult court jurisdiction at age 18 should keep it there, and other states should change their laws to restrict adult court jurisdiction to people 18 and older.
- All laws providing for automatic jurisdiction in the adult courts for young people under age 18 charged with designated serious crimes should be repealed.
- Laws permitting case-by-case transfers by prosecutors or criminal court judges should also be repealed. Until these are eliminated, juvenile court judges should make all transfer decisions.

Adopting these recommendations would bring the United States into compliance with international standards and also reduce delinquency. Transferring juveniles from the juvenile justice system to the criminal justice system and confinement in prisons, where developmental and treatment programs are rare, drastically reduces their life chances, and this is simply morally wrong. By injecting common sense, laypersons often make points more simply and clearly than do academics. This observation made by the Reverend Thomas Masters is a case in point: "There's no way in the world you can receive a fair trial in an adult arena where you're looked upon as an adult when you have the mind of a child" (quoted in Zaczor, 2002, p. 7A).

Other ineffective programs and practices should be abandoned as well (see Chapter 11). The use of detention for punishment purposes is one of these. This practice accomplishes nothing positive (i.e., it does not motivate youths to receive treatment), and research suggests that excessive use of detention may wipe out the positive effects of treatment programs. Generally, punitive detention includes the broad category of "shock incarceration" and programs such as Scared Straight and boot camps, which do not have the intended deterrence effect and may actually *increase* recidivism.

Zero tolerance policies in schools are also ineffective and often make zero sense; for example, youths who are suspended or expelled from school for minor rule infractions often end up on the streets, where they may be exposed to harmful people and drawn into gangs. Large, congregate, custodial juvenile corrections facilities are not effective in rehabilitating juvenile offenders. Nor are long sentences effective. New research shows that curfew laws are not effective in reducing serious or violent juvenile crime. The hospitalization of youths with mental health problems is not effective.

In addition, there is conflicting evidence about the effectiveness of several popular program interventions. These include drug testing and drug courts, electronic monitoring, police in schools, balanced and restorative justice, and motivational interviewing. I discussed these and other disputed interventions in Chapter 11.

The criminal justice system has a dismal track record in that its three key components are largely ineffective, including sentencing, incarceration, and parole. Confinement does not reduce long-term crime, and executions have no deterrent effect. None of the widely used sentencing practices is effective, including mandatory minimum sentences, three-strikes laws, and "truth in sentencing" laws. The criminal justice system is described as "a system that has lost its way" (Travis & Petersilia, 2001, p. 299).

Unfortunately, some of the routine punitive practices of the criminal justice system have been brought into the juvenile justice system, where they are inappropriate. Shackling and handcuffing petitioned juvenile offenders when bringing them into court is a common example (M. T. Moore, 2007). Wherever it is not prohibited by state laws, the practice of shackling and handcuffing juvenile offenders for court appearances should be discontinued in the United States unless the presiding judge has ordered handcuffing or other necessary restraints for the juvenile for a particular court appearance based on a determination that the juvenile is a threat to the public safety based on prior court-related behavior. For juvenile offenders, this practice reinforces the myth that they are necessarily hardened criminals. With few exceptions, they are not, and shackling may also constitute cruel and unusual punishment, particularly for children and adolescents who have mental health problems. The Supreme Court has said that the practice of shackling defendants can prejudice a jury; therefore, adult criminal courts are prohibited from bringing adults in front of a jury in shackles (M. T. Moore, 2007).

Consideration should also be given to taking special precautions when placing juveniles in gang-related criminal intelligence databases. Constitutional due process issues come into play here because, across the United States, people identified in gang intelligence databases are more likely to be convicted and to receive sentence enhancements in states that have enacted such provisions. There should be a remedy to prevent erroneous identification as a gang member. One remedy is to provide for court hearings in which people could challenge the alleged gang status. Documenting a person as a gang member without such a hearing may well violate the due process requirements of the Constitution (Wright, 2006).

Another remedy is to ensure that the criminal intelligence database is managed properly. State and local agencies that receive federal funds to operate criminal intelligence systems must comply with specific regulations, including those in 28 CFR Part 23 (*Criminal Intelligence Systems Operating Policies*). Technical assistance reviews of criminal intelligence systems and their compliance with the regulation have been provided at no charge through funding from the U.S. Department of Justice, Bureau of Justice Assistance. In addition, such a review could address special procedures for handling criminal intelligence information on juveniles. One process for protecting juveniles is to firewall them in the criminal intelligence systems, restricting the dissemination of potentially incorrect information on their gang involvement. More frequent purging of the information on juveniles should also be considered, as suggested by research that shows that most adolescents who join a gang remain in it for less than 1 year (Chapter 7).

The United States must work to eliminate the disproportionate representation and confinement of minorities in the juvenile and criminal justice systems. The actual differences in minority and nonminority crime rates do not justify the large differences in the two groups' representation in the juvenile and criminal justice systems. The International Convention on the Elimination of All Forms of Racial Discrimination, to which the United States is a party, defines race discrimination as conduct that has the "purpose or effect" of restricting rights on the basis of race (Human Rights Watch, 2000). Under the convention, governments may not engage in "benign neglect"; that is, they may not ignore the need to secure equal treatment of all racial and ethnic groups but rather must act affirmatively to prevent or end policies that have unjustified discriminatory impacts. Although the United States has not undertaken a national initiative in the criminal justice system, it has made significant progress in the juvenile arena through the Office of Juvenile Justice and Delinquency Prevention's Disproportionate Minority Confinement Initiative. Nevertheless, greater effort must be exerted to achieve the overall goal. By using objective risk and need assessment instruments and placement instruments, communities can help greatly to reduce minority overrepresentation in the juvenile justice system.

Lerman, an expert on systems used for counting youths in all situations of confinement in the United States (in mental health, substance abuse, child welfare, juvenile corrections, and adult corrections facilities), last called attention to the need to improve them at the beginning of this decade (Lerman, 2002). Yet few improvements have been made. The data generated by existing information systems typically are 3 to 5 years behind current usage of the facilities and yield deficient resident and admission data. Admission data are not even collected for juvenile justice system detention and long-term correctional facilities, so system flows cannot be observed. Only a modest investment of fiscal resources would be needed to improve these systems so that they yield more timely reports, fuller coverage of facilities, improved demographic enumeration, and unduplicated counts of intersystem trends. It is shameful that we know so little about the numbers, characteristics, presenting problems, and outcomes of many of the children and adolescents in confinement in the United States today. Reliable data on admissions to each of these components of the U.S. child care apparatus would permit system flow analyses of the type described in Chapter 10, permitting researchers to evaluate the costs and benefits of service options across the entire array of interventions.

As a general observation, the spectrum of public sector services is overly reliant on institutional care. Service fragmentation is a main factor in the failure of child-serving systems to address the problems of youth. As Roush (1996a) sums it up, "Services fail because they are too crisis-oriented, too rigid in their classification of problems, too specialized, too isolated from other services, too inflexible to craft comprehensive solutions, too insufficiently funded, and they are mismanaged" (p. 29). By applying the principles and management tools of the Comprehensive Strategy, communities can resolve these problems. Orlando L. Martinez, commissioner of the Georgia Department of Juvenile Justice, eloquently stated, "The best way to predict a young person's future is to help create it" (quoted in Rubin, 2001, p. 15). As John Wilson (2000) has emphasized, preventing and reducing delinquency requires a coordinated effort at critical times in a child's life with a range of services, supports, and opportunities in a continuum of care.

Appendix

Two Model Assessment Instruments

Model Youth and Family Assessment of Needs and Strengths

Youth Name:_____ Case #: _____ Country: _____

DOB: ____/____/_____ Race: 1. African American 2. Caucasian 3. Hispanic 4. Other **Gender:** 1. Male 2. Female

Intake/Probation Officer:_____ Assessment Date: ____/____/_____ Type Assessment: 1. Initial 2. Reassessment

A. Family Needs and Strengths

_____ 1. *Substance Abuse*

    0 = No known current use or history of use by caregiver(s).

    1 = Uses but no dependence; occasional social use; relationships with family members not strained by use

    2 = Previous history of abuse but caregiver is currently in recovery after the completion of a treatment program and has had no relapse incidents.

    3 = Some disruption in functioning; use has negative impact on employment, family life, legal involvement, or other areas. May include caregiver in recovery who has had relapse incidents.

    5 = Major disruption in functioning resulting from frequent or chronic use of alcohol or illegal substances. Indicators may include loss of job, multiple arrests, chronic disruption of family life, or abusive destructive behavior due to substance abuse. Any admitted or clinically diagnosed dependency. Any previous or current referral for intensive outpatient/day treatment or inpatient treatment.

_____ 2. *Family Relationships* (Consider Parent-Parent, Parent-Child, Child-Child)

    −1 = Strong, supportive family relationships. While conflicts may occur, the home environment is very stable.

    1 = Parent-to-parent, parent-to-child verbal conflict is freqently disruptive but appears to have no long-term impact on family stability.

    2 = Family conflict or fights occur on a routine basis and create a highly unsettled or hostile family environment. Sporadic instances of physical assault may have occurred, but no serious injury has resulted. Conflict has a negative impact on family functioning according to family members or other reliable reporters. There is a probable need for outside intervention to address parent-parent or parent-child conflict.

    4 = Conflict in the home has resulted in repeated instances or a chronic condition of physical or emotional abuse, or any instance of physical abuse has resulted in injuries that necessitated medical attention.

_____ 3. *Living Situation and Finances*

    0 = Suitable living environment, and family has adequate resources to meet basic needs of children.

2 = Family has housing, but it does not meet the health and safety needs of the children due to such things as inadequate plumbing, heating, wiring, house-keeping, or size. Current financial stress that results in family confilct and need for outside assistance.

3 = Serious problems, including nomadic lifestyle or failure to provide meals or medical care to meet health and safety needs of the children. Family has eviction notice, house is condemned or uninhabitable, or family is homeless.

_____   4. *Parenting Skills*

−1 = Both caregivers or single caregiver display strong parenting practices that are age-appropriate for the children in areas of discipline, expectations, communications, protection, and nurturing.

1 = Some improvement of basic parenting skills is needed by one or more caregivers to effectively control or nurture children. Parents obviously care about children and make efforts to provide appropriate parenting, but there are shortcomings in discipline or extent of structure and supervision.

3 = Significant shortcomings in parenting skills as evidenced by constant conflict over discipline, children often left unsupervised, repeated instances of parent-child role reversal.

4 = Caregivers display destructive or abusive parenting. Parental discipline and control is almost nonnexistent. Parents contribute to child's delinquency or make excuses for it. Parents refuse responsibility for youth or abandon youth.

_____   5. *Disabilities of Caregivers*

0 = Caregiver has no known physical disabilities, mental illness, emotional problems, or cognitive disabilities, or, if present, that do not interefere with parenting.

1 = Emotional, physical, or cognitive disabilities that negatively affect family.

2 = Caregiver has ongoing need for formal mental health treatment or has a serious chronic health problem or cognitive disability that seriously impairs ability to provide for youth.

_____   6. *Intrafamilial Sexual Abuse*

0 = No known problems or reason to suspect intrafamilial sexual abuse.

2 = Intrafamilial sexual abuse has been alleged or substantiated. Includes child welfare reports, self-reports by youth, and abuse suspected by others.

_____   7. *Family Criminality*

0 = No caregiver or siblings have been convicted or adjudicated for criminal acts in last 3 years.

1 = Caregivers or siblings have record of convictions or adjudications within last 3 years.

2 = One or both caregivers or siblings are currently incarcerated or are on probation or parole.

B. Youth Needs and Strengths

_____ *1. Peer Relationships*

    −1 = Peers provide good support and influence. Friends not known to be delinquent or to have influenced involvement in delinquent behavior.

    0 = Youth is primarily a loner.

    1 = Youth sometimes associates with others who have been involved in delinquent or criminal activity, but this is not primary peer group.

    3 = Youth regularly associates with others who are involved in delinquent or criminal activity or drug or alcohol abuse. Youth usually is negatively influenced by peers, or youth usually provides a negative influence.

    4 = Youth is a gang member, or youth is a loner who commits serious solitary delinquent acts.

_____ *2. Adult Relationships*

    −1 = Youth has good relationship with parents and has strong relationships with several other prosocial adults in the community (e.g., teacher, coach, employer, neighbor).

    0 = Youth has poor relationship with parents (or parents a negative influence) but has strong relationships with several other prosocial adults in the community.

    1 = Youth has poor relationship with parents (or parents a negative influence) but has a strong relationship with a prosocial adult in the community.

    3 = Youth has no strong relationships with any prosocial adults at home or in the community.

_____ *3. School Functioning*

    −1 = Youth displays strong attachment or commitment to school as indicated by work effort, involvement in school activities, positive attitude toward school and teachers, and absence of behavioral or attendance problems.

    0 = No history of attendance or behavioral problems.

    1 = Occasional attendance or disciplinary problems that were handled at home or school.

    3 = Chronic truancy or severe school behavior problems that necessistated ouside intervention such as referral to the police or placement in an alternative educational program.

    4 = Youth is not attending school (dropped out or withdrawn) or has been expelled.

Is youth receiving, or diagnosed as needing, special education services?
_____ Yes   _____ No

_____ *4. Employment or Vocational Preparation*

0 = Youth does not attend school but is employed full time, or youth is in school full time.

1 = Youth is not in school and is not working, or is working less than 20 hours per week. Is motivated to work and has vocational interests but needs to receive additional training through vocational education, apprenticeship, or other employment-related program.

3 = Youth is not in school, is not employed, has few employment-related skills, and is not motivated to work or obtain training.

_____ *5. Substance Abuse*

−1 = No known current use or history of use.

1 = Occasional use but no dependence; satisfies curiosity or peer pressure; no pattern of strained relationship with parents concerning use.

3 = Some disruption in functioning; use has negative impact on scholastic achievement, attendance, employment, family life, legal involvement, or other areas. Any previous or current referral for outpatient substance abuse treatment. May include youth in recovery who has had relapse incidents.

5 = Major disruption in functioning resulting from frequent or chronic use of alcohol or illegal substances. Indicators may include drug- or alcohol-related chronic truancy or dropout, multiple school suspensions or expulsion, multiple sustance abuse–related arrests, chronic family conflict related to substance abuse, abusive or destructive behavior, or an admitted or clinically diagnosed dependency. Any previous or current referral for intensive outpatient/day treatment or inpatient substance abuse treatment.

_____ *6. Aggressive or Assaultive Behavior*

0 − Youth generally interacts with others in a positive way and resolves conflict without resorting to verbal threats, attempts to intimidate, or assaultive behavior.

2 = Occasionally provokes fights with peers or is sometimes threatening or verbally abusive to peers or adults. May have low tolerance for frustration or criticism and respond with angry outbursts.

4 = Frequently involved in threatening or assaultive behavior with peers and adults. Pervasive mood of anger and irritability. Uses anger, violence, or intimidation across situations and people. Any use of a weapon (knife, firearm) in threat or assault; or two or more arrests for a violent felony offense such as armed robbery, aggravated assault; or history of chronic or severe cruelty to animals.

_____ *7. Sexual Behavior*

0 = Youth appears to be sexually well-adjusted, and none of the following problems has been identified.

2 = May have sexual identity issues that result in conflict with self, family, or peers; or may be engaging in sexual practices that are potentially dangerous to health.

3 = Youth's sexual behavior inappropriate or disruptive of the youth's functioning. Excessive use of sexual language or references to sexual body parts; inappropriate touching of self or others; indecent exposure; invloved in prostitution, incestuous relationships, etc.

4 = Adjudicated for any sexual offense or uses sexual expression or behavior to attain power and control over others, harming or instilling fear in the victim.

_____ 8. *Emotional Stability* (mental health problems other than those described in items 6, 7, and 8)

0 = Appropriate adolescent response; no apparent dysfunction; or youth with conduct or substance abuse problems presenting with behavioral difficulties (not result of emotional instability).

3 = Periodic or sporadic responses that limit but do not prohibit adequate functioning. Has moderate levels of symptoms such as flashbacks to traumatic events, depression without suicidal gestures, disabling anxiety, or mood shifts. Any previous or current referral for outpatient mental health treatment.

5 = Responses that prohibit or severely limit adequate functioning. Current or prior symptoms may include hearing voices, delusions, confused thinking, dramatic mood swings; history of suicidal gestures or self-mutilation. May also have a previous or current diagnosis—by a licensed mental health provider—such as depression, anxiety, psychosis, suicidal or homicidal gestures. Any previous or current referral for inpatient mental health treatment. Or, youth may require psychotropic medication to aid in managing behavior.

_____ 9. *Attitudes and Values*

−1 = Expresses and generally abides by prosocial values and conventions; accepts responsibility for antisocial behavior and law violations. Usually takes responsibiltiy for feelings, attitudes, and behaviors.

2 = Expresses mixed values: some prosocial and some antisocial. May believe social norms and expectations don't always apply to him- or herself. Justifies, minimizes, denies, or blames others for involvement in delinquent activities. Often does not take responsibility for attitudes and behaviors.

4 = Consistently expresses negative, antisocial values; accepts or proud of delinquent activities; attitude reflects criminal thinking.

_____ 10. *History of Abuse or Neglect as a Victim*

0 = No history or indication of physical, sexual, or emotional abuse or neglect.

2 = One or two incidents (alleged or substantiated) of physical abuse or neglect.

4 = Chronic pattern (alleged or substantiated) of physical abuse or neglect, or any history of sexual abuse.

_____   *11. Parenting*

   0 = Youth is not a teen parent, or is a parent with adequate parenting skills.

   1 = Youth is a parent (or about to become one) and lacks some child-rearing skills; needs assistance or training to provide adequate care for the child.

   2 = Youth is a parent (or about to become one) and has minimal knowledge or skills for child rearing and nurturance, or has abdicated responsibility for the child, or has demonstrated abusive or neglectful parenting.

_____   *12. Physical Health and Hygiene*

   0 = No apparent problem.

   1 = Youth has medical, dental, or health education needs.

   2 = Youth has physical handicap or chronic illness that limits functioning or requires regular medication or occasional hospitalization.

_____   *13. Involvement in Structured Activities*

   −1 = In school and involved in one or more structured extracurricular activities such as athletics, clubs, employment.

   0 = In school and involved in unstructured activities or hobbies, or not in school but working full time.

   1 = Interested but not involved in any structured or unstructured activities.

   2 = Not involved and not interested in any structured or unstructured activities.

_____   *14. Total Family and Youth Score and Strengths and Needs Classification*

_____ −8 to 15, Low Needs _____ 16 to 35, Medium Needs _____ 36+ High Needs

Case Planning

List the three most serious problems to be addressed in the case plan:

Problem Area	Description
1.	
2.	
3.	

List the youth's major strengths that can be used in case planning:

Strength	Description
1.	
2.	
3.	

Specialized Assessments

Indicate areas where there may be a need for additional, specialized assessments to determine the full extent or nature of a problem. Items on which the family or youth has scored 2 or more points may require specialized assessments. Particular attention should be paid to family problems involving substance abuse, family conflict, and parenting skills and to youth problems involving school, substance abuse, assaultive behavior, sexual issues, and emotional stability.

Problem Area	Person Involved	Issue Needing Further Assessment

Model Risk Assessment Instrument

Youth's Name: _____ DOB: _____/_____/_____ ID#: _____

Race: 1. African American 2. Caucasian 3. Hispanic 4. Other: _____ Gender: 1. Male 2. Female

Officer Name: _____ Assessment Type: 1. Intake 2. Disposition   Date: ____/____/_____

Score

1. **Age at First Referral to Juvenile Court Intake**

    a. 16 or older . . . . −1

    b. 14 or 15 0

    c. 13 or younger 2   ____

2. **Total Number of Referrals to Intake** (count separate referral dates; enter actual number: ____)

    a. One . . . . −1

    b. Two or three 0

    c. Four or more 2   ____

3. **Total Referrals for Violent or Assaultive Offenses** (count separate referral dates; enter actual number:____)

    a. None 0

    b. One or more 1   ____

4. **Number of Prior Out-of-Home Placements**

    a. None 0

    b. One 1

    c. Two or more 2   ____

5. **School Discipline and Attendance in the Prior 12 Months**

    a. Enrolled, attending regularly, no suspensions; or graduated or GED . . . . −1

    b. Some truancy; suspended 1–2 times; considered somewhat disruptive 1

    c. Major truancy or dropped out; suspended 3+ times; considered seriously disruptive. 2   ____

6. **Substance Abuse**

    a. No problem, or experimentation only. 0

    b. Use sometimes interferes with functioning. 1

    c. Use frequently interferes with functioning; chronic abuse; dependency 2   ____

7. **Peer Relationships**

    a. Friends provide positive influence . . . . −1

    b. Some delinquent friends with negative influence. 0

    c. Most friends are delinquent; strong negative influence 2

    d. Gang membership or associate 3   ____

8. **Victim of Child Abuse or Neglect** (based on report to child welfare agency, substantiated or not)

   a. No 0

   b. Yes 1   ____

9. **Parental Supervision**

   a. Parental supervision and discipline usually effective; youth usually obeys rules; minor, sporadic conflict 0

   b. Parental supervision often ineffective or inconsistent; frequent parent-child conflict . . 1

   c. Little or no parental supervision or discipline; or constant conflict; youth usually disobeys 2   ____

10. **Parent or Sibling Criminality**

    a. No parents or guardians or siblings incarcerated or on probation in past 3 years 0

    b. Parent, guardian, or sibling incarcerated or on probation in past 3 years 1   ____

11. **Total Score**   ____

Scored Risk Level: _____ –4 to –1, Low Risk _____ 0 to 4, Medium Risk _____ 5 to 8, High Risk ___ 9+, Very High Risk

Mandatory Override: _____ None _____ Reason A _____ Reason B _____ Reason C

Discretionary Override: _____ No _____ Yes If yes, reason: _____

Final Risk Level: _____ Low Risk _____ Medium Risk _____ High Risk _____ Very High Risk

Credits and Sources

Chapter 1

Figure 1.1: "Serious, Violent, and Chronic Juvenile Offenders: An Assessment of the Extent of and Trends in Officially Recognized Serious Criminal Behavior in a Delinquent Population," by H. N. Snyder, in R. Loeber and D. P. Farrington (Eds.), *Serious and Violent Juvenile Offenders: Risk Factors and Successful Interventions* (p. 440), Thousand Oaks, CA: Sage. Copyright 1998 by Sage Publications, Inc. Reprinted with permission.

Chapter 2

Table 2.1: Snyder and Sickmund (2006, p. 70).

Figure 2.1: Skiba, R. J., and Peterson, R. (1999). The dark side of zero tolerance: Can punishment lead to safe schools? *Phi Delta Kappan, 80,* pp. 372–376. Reprinted by permission of the illustrator, Joe Lee.

Box 2.2: Education on Lockdown: The Schoolhouse to Jailhouse Track. Washington, DC: Advancement Project, 2005, pp. 16-17. Reprinted with permission.

Box 2.3: Dwyer and Osher (2000, p. 17).

Box 2.4: Dwyer and Osher (2000, p. 19).

Box 2.5: Dwyer and Osher (2000, p. 18).

Box 2.6: Arcia (2007).

Box 2.7: Center for the Prevention of School Violence (http://www.ncdjjdp.org/cpsv/toolkit/index.html).

Box 2.8: Keys to Reforming Zero Tolerance Policies: R. Skiba, C.R. Reynolds, S. Graham, P. Sheras et al., 2006. *Are zero tolerance policies effective in the schools? An evidentiary review and recommendations.* Washington, DC: American Psychological Association.

Box 2.9: Virginia Model for Student Threat Assessment reprinted with permission from Sopris West Educational Services. *Guidelines for responding to student threats of violence* by Dewey Cornell and Peter Sheras. Copyright © 2005.

Chapter 3

Box 3.1: Snyder and Sickmund (2006, pp. 122–124).

Figure 3.1: Juvenile Offenders and Victims: 2006 National Report by Howard N. Snyder and Melissa Sickmund. Washington, DC: U.S. Department of Justice, Office of Justice Programs, Office of Juvenile Justice and Delinquency Prevention. Copyright © 2006 by National Center for Juvenile Justice. p. 199.

Figure 3.2: J. A. Butts and H. N. Snyder, 2006, p. 5. *Too soon to tell: Deciphering recent trends in youth violence.* Issue Brief #110. Chicago, IL: Chapin Hall Center for Children. Reprinted with permission.

Fig 3.4: Centers for Disease Control and Prevention (2006)

Chapter 4

Table 4.1: "Common Risk and Protective Factors in Successful Prevention Programs," by J.A. Durlak, 1998, *American Journal of Orthopsychiatry, 68,* p. 514. Copyright © 1998 by American Journal of Orthopsychiatry. Washington, DC: American Psychological Association.

Table 4.2: "Common Risk and Protective Factors in Successful Prevention Programs," by J.A. Durlak, 1998, *American Journal of Orthopsychiatry, 68,* p. 516. Copyright © 1998 by American Journal of Orthopsychiatry. Washington, DC: American Psychological Association.

Table 4.3: Hawkins, Catalano, and Arthur (2002); Hawkins et al. (1998); Howell and Egley (2005b); Huizinga, Weiher, Espiritu, and Esbensen (2003); Lipsey and Derzon (1998); Loeber and Farrington (1998, 2001a); Loeber, Farrington, and Petechuk (2003); Loeber, Farrington, Stouthamer-Loeber, et al. (2003); Stouthamer-Loeber, Loeber, et al. (2002); Taylor (2008); Thornberry, Lizotte, Krohn, Smith, and Porter (2003).

Figure 4.1: "Moving risk factors into developmental theories of gang membership," by J. C. Howell & A. Egley, Jr. *Youth Violence and Juvenile Justice, 3,* p. 340. ©2005 by Sage Publications, Inc. Reprinted with permission.

Chapter 5

Figure 5.1: Thornberry, T. P. 2005, p. 164. "Explaining multiple patterns of offending across the life course and across generations." *The Annals of the American Academy of Political and Social Science,* 602, pp. 156-195. Thousand Oaks, CA: Sage Publications, Inc.

Figure 5.2: Thornberry, T. P. 2005, p. 165. "Explaining multiple patterns of offending across the life course and across generations." *The Annals of the American Academy of Political and Social Science,* 602, pp. 156-195. Thousand Oaks, CA: Sage Publications, Inc.

Box 5.2: Snyder and Sickmund (1999, pp. 80–81).

Figure 5.3: Modified from Figure A5 in Snyder, H.N., 1998, p. 440. "Serious, violent, and chronic juvenile offenders: An assessment of the extent of and trends in officially recognized serious criminal behavior in a delinquent population." In R. Loeber & D.P. Farrington (eds.), *Serious and violent juvenile offenders: Risk factors and successful interventions,* pp. 428-444. Thousand Oaks, CA: Sage Publications, Inc.

Figure 5.4: "Behavioral Antecedents to Serious and Violent Offending: Joint Analyses From the Denver Youth Survey, Pittsburgh Youth Study and the Rochester Youth Development Study," by R. Loeber, E. Wei, M. Stouthamer-Loeber, D. Huizinga, & T. P. Thornberry, 1999, *Studies on Crime and Crime Prevention,* 8, p. 247. Reprinted with permission.

Figure 5.5: Loeber, R., Farrington, D. P., Stouthamer-Loeber, M., & White, H. R. (2008). *Violence and serious theft: Development and prediction from childhood to adulthood* (Figure 4.10, p. 91). New York: Routledge.

Figure 5.6: Snyder, H. N., 2001, p. 45. "Epidemiology of official offending." In R. Loeber & D.P. Farrington (eds.) *Child delinquents: Development, intervention, and service needs,* pp. 24–46. Thousand Oaks, CA: Sage Publications, Inc.

Chapter 6

Figure 6.1: Egley, A.E. & O'Donnell, C.E., 2007. "The dark figure of officially-recorded gang crime." Paper presented at the annual meeting of the American Society of Criminology, Atlanta, GA. November.

Table 6.1: Egley, O'Donnell, and Curry (2007); special analysis, Curry and Howell (2007).

Table 6.2: National Youth Gang Survey data (Howell, 2006; Howell & Egley, 2005a).

Figure 6.2: National Youth Gang Center.

Table 6.3: Graffiti. Problem-Oriented Guides for Police. Problem-Specific Guides Series. Guide No. 9 (p. 9), by D. L. Weisel, 2004. Washington, DC: Office of Community Oriented Policing Services.

Box 6.4: Howell, J. C. (2007). Menacing or mimicking? Realities of youth gangs. *The Juvenile and Family Court Journal,* 58, 9–20.

Box 6.5: Quotes from Felson, M. (2006). The street gang strategy. In M. Felson, *Crime and nature* (pp. 305–324). Thousand Oaks, CA: Sage.

Figure 6.3: Egley, A. Jr., Howell, J. C., & Major, A. (2006). *National Youth Gang Survey: 1999–2001.* Washington, DC: U.S. Department of Justice, Office of Juvenile Justice and Delinquency Prevention, p. 24. Data are for 2000.

Figure 6.4: Egley, A. E., Howell, J. C., & Ritz, C. E. (2005, November). *Exploring gang migration and proliferation patterns in the National Youth Gang Survey.* Paper presented at the Annual Meeting of the American Society of Criminology, Toronto, Canada.

Figure 6.5: Bendixen, M., Endresen, I. M., & Olweus, D. (2006). Joining and leaving gangs: Selection and facilitation effects on self-reported antisocial behaviour in early adolescence. *European Journal of Criminology, 3,* 85–114.

Figure 6.6: Bendixen, M., Endresen, I. M., & Olweus, D. (2006). Joining and leaving gangs: Selection and facilitation effects on self-reported antisocial behaviour in early adolescence. *European Journal of Criminology, 3,* 85–114.

Chapter 7

Figure 7.1: Phoenix Police Department. (1981). *Hispanic gangs in Phoenix.* Phoenix, AZ: Author.

Figure 7.2: McGloin, J. M. (2005). Policy and intervention considerations of a network analysis of street gangs. *Criminology and Public Policy, 4,* 607–636.

Figure 7.3: Modified from Howell, J. C. (2003). *Preventing and reducing juvenile delinquency: A comprehensive framework.* Thousand Oaks, CA: Sage.

Figure 7.4: National Youth Gang Center. (2003). *OJJDP comprehensive gang model training.* Tallahassee, FL: Author.

Figure 7.5: National Youth Gang Center. (2003). *OJJDP comprehensive gang model training.* Tallahassee, FL: Author.

Chapter 8

Table 8.1: Cullen, F. T. (2005). The twelve people who saved rehabilitation: How the science of criminology made a difference. *Criminology, 43,* 1–42.

Figure 8.2: What 500 Intervention Studies Show About the Effects of Intervention on the Recidivism of Juvenile Offenders, p. 10. by M. W. Lipsey, 2000. Copyright © 2000 by Mark W. Lipsey. Reprinted by permission of Dr. Mark Lipsey.

Table 8.2: Lipsey, M. W. (1999). Can rehabilitative programs reduce the recidivism of juvenile offenders? An inquiry into the effectiveness of practical programs? *Virginia Journal of Social Policy and the Law, 6,* 611–641.

Table 8.3: M. W. Lipsey, 2006. *The Evidence Base for Effective Programs as a Source for Best Practice Guidelines.* Reprinted by permission of Dr. Mark Lipsey.

Box 8.3: Lipsey, M. W. (2002). Meta-analysis and program outcome evaluation. *Socialvetenskaplig Tidskrift, 9,* 194–208. Also Lipsey, M. W., & Wilson, D. B. (1993). The efficacy of psychological, educational, and behavioral treatment: Confirmation from meta-analysis. *American Psychologist, 48,* 1181 1209.

Chapter 9

Table 9.1: Elliott, D. S. (Ed.). (1998). *Blueprints for violence prevention.* Denver, CO: C&M. Also Mihalic, S., Irwin, K., Elliott, D., Fagan, A., and Hansen, D. (2001). Blueprints for violence prevention. *Juvenile Justice Bulletin.* Washington, DC. Office of Juvenile Justice and Delinquency Prevention.

Box 9.3: Lowenkamp, C. T., Latessa, E. J., & Smith, P. (2006). Does correctional program quality really matter? The impact of adhering to the principles of effective intervention. *Criminology and Public Policy, 5,* 575–594. Also Gendreau, P., & Andrews, D. (1996). *The correctional program assessment inventory* (6th ed.). Saint John: University of New Brunswick, and Gendreau, P., & Andrews, D. (2001). *The correctional program assessment inventory: 2000.* Saint John: University of New Brunswick.

Table 9.2: Personal communication, April 27, 2007.

Table 9.3: Adapted from "Effective Interventions With Serious Juvenile Offenders: A Synthesis of Research," by M. W. Lipsey and D. B. Wilson, in R. Loeber and D. P. Farrington (Eds.), *Serious and Violent Juvenile Offenders: Risk Factors and Successful Interventions* (p. 332), Thousand Oaks, CA: Sage. Copyright 1998 by Sage Publications, Inc. Adapted with permission.

Table 9.4: The evidence base for effective juvenile programs as a source for best practice guidelines, by M. W. Lipsey, 2007. Copyright © Mark W. Lipsey. Reprinted by permission of Dr. Mark Lipsey.

Table 9.5: The evidence base for effective juvenile programs as a source for best practice guidelines, by M. W. Lipsey, 2007. Copyright © Mark W. Lipsey. Reprinted by permission of Dr. Mark Lipsey.

Table 9.6: The evidence base for effective juvenile programs as a source for best practice guidelines, by M. W. Lipsey, 2007. Copyright © Mark W. Lipsey. Reprinted by permission of Dr. Mark Lipsey.

Table 9.7: What Works with Juvenile Offenders: Translating research into practice. Copyright ©2005 Mark W. Lipsey. Reprinted by permission of Dr. Mark Lipsey.

Table 9.8: Intervention Programs for Juvenile Offenders: "Best Practice" Guidelines from Meta-analysis. Copyright ©2005 Mark W. Lipsey. Reprinted by permission of Dr. Mark Lipsey.

Figure 9.1: R. Barnoski, 2004, p. 8. *Outcome Evaluation of Washington State's Research-Based Programs for Juvenile Offenders.* Olympia, WA: Washington State Institute for Public Policy.

Figure 9.2: The evidence base for effective juvenile programs as a source for best practice guidelines, by M. W. Lipsey, 2007. Copyright © Mark W. Lipsey. Reprinted by permission of Dr. Mark Lipsey.

Table 9.9: U.S. Office of Special Education Programs, Center on Positive Behavioral Interventions and Supports: http://www.pbis.org/main.htm.

Box 9.4: Beckett, M., Hawken, A., & Jacknowitz, A. (2001). *Accountability for after-school care: Devising standards and measuring adherence to them.* Santa Monica, CA: RAND.

Chapter 10

Box 10.1: Wilson, J. J., & Howell, J. C. (1993). *A comprehensive strategy for serious, violent and chronic juvenile offenders.* Washington, DC: Office of Juvenile Justice and Delinquency Prevention.

Box 10.2: Coolbaugh, K., & Hansel, C. J. (2000). The comprehensive strategy: Lessons learned from the pilot sites. *Juvenile Justice Bulletin.* Washington, DC: Office of Juvenile Justice and Delinquency Prevention. Also Howell, J. C. (Ed.). (1995). *Guide for implementing the Comprehensive Strategy for Serious, Violent, and Chronic Juvenile Offenders.* Washington, DC: Office of Juvenile Justice and Delinquency Prevention; Wiebush,

R. G. (Ed.). (2002). *Graduated sanctions for juvenile offenders: A program model and planning guide.* Oakland, CA: National Council on Crime and Delinquency and National Council of Juvenile and Family Court Judges; and Wilson, J. J., & Howell, J. C. (1993). *A comprehensive strategy for serious, violent and chronic juvenile offenders.* Washington, DC: Office of Juvenile Justice and Delinquency Prevention.

Figure 10.1: Wilson, J. J., & Howell, J. C. (1993). *A comprehensive strategy for serious, violent and chronic juvenile offenders.* Washington, DC: Office of Juvenile Justice and Delinquency Prevention.

Figure 10.2: U.S. Department of Justice, Office of Juvenile Justice and Delinquency Prevention, 2003.

Box 10.4: Wiebush, R. G. (Ed.). (2002). *Graduated sanctions for juvenile offenders: A program model and planning guide.* Oakland, CA: National Council on Crime and Delinquency and National Council of Juvenile and Family Court Judges.

Figure 10.3: Modified from Howell, J. C. (2003). *Preventing and reducing juvenile delinquency: A comprehensive framework.* Thousand Oaks, CA: Sage.

Table 10.1: Missouri Office of State Courts Administrator: http:// www.courts.mo.gov/file/Classification%20Matrix% 2012.20.00.pdf.

Figure 10.4: R. A. Mendel, 2007, p. 11. *Pathways to juvenile detention reform: Vol. 14. Beyond detention: System transformation through juvenile detention reform.* Baltimore, MD: Annie E. Casey Foundation. Reprinted with permission.

Figure 10.5: R. A. Mendel, 2007, p. 13. *Pathways to juvenile detention reform: Vol. 14. Beyond detention: System transformation through juvenile detention reform.* Baltimore, MD: Annie E. Casey Foundation. Reprinted with permission.

Box 10.7: Annie E. Casey Foundation (2006). *Reentry: Helping former prisoners return to communities, a guide to key ideas, effective approaches, and technical assistance resources for making connections.* Baltimore, MD: Annie E. Casey Foundation, p. 11. Reprinted with permission.

Box 10.8: G. A. Wasserman, S. J. Ko, and L. S. McReynolds, 2004, pp. 5-6. "Assessing the mental health status of youth in juvenile justice settings." *Juvenile Justice Bulletin.* Washington, DC: U.S. Department of Justice, Office of Juvenile Justice and Delinquency Prevention.

Figure 10.6: North Carolina Department of Juvenile Justice and Delinquency Prevention. (2008). *2007 annual report.* Raleigh: Author.

Figure 10.7: Adapted from Schumacher, M., & Kurz, G. (2000). *The 8% solution: Preventing serious, repeat juvenile crime.* Thousand Oaks, CA: Sage.

Figure 10.8: Modified from Howell, J. C. (2003). *Preventing and reducing juvenile delinquency: A comprehensive framework.* Thousand Oaks, CA: Sage.

Box 10.9: Howell, J. C., Kelly, M. R., Palmer, J., & Mangum, R. L. (2004). Integrating child welfare, juvenile justice and other agencies in a continuum of services for children, youth and families. *Child Welfare, 83,* 143–156.

Figure 10.9: The evidence base for effective juvenile programs as a source for best practice guidelines, by M. W. Lipsey, 2007. Copyright © Mark W. Lipsey. Reprinted by permission of Dr. Mark Lipsey.

Chapter 11

Figure 11.1: Snyder, H. N., & Sickmund, M. (2006). *Juvenile offenders and victims: 2006 national report.* Washington, DC: Office of Juvenile Justice and Delinquency Prevention.

Figure 11.2: F. E. Zimring, 2007, p. 882. "Protect individual punishment decisions from mandatory penalties." *Criminology and Public Policy, 6,* 881–886. Blackwell Publishing, Ltd.

Box 11.3: Katner, D. R. (2002). A defense perspective of treatment programs for juvenile sex offenders. *Juvenile Correctional Mental Health Report, 2*(2), 17–30.

Figure 11.3: F. E. Zimring, 2007, p. 882. "Protect individual punishment decisions from mandatory penalties." *Criminology and Public Policy, 6,* 881-886. Blackwell Publishing, Ltd.

Chapter 12

Box 12.1: Griffin, P. (2003). Trying and sentencing juveniles as adults: An analysis of state transfer and blended sentencing laws. *Special Project Bulletin.* Washington, DC: Office of Juvenile Justice and Delinquency Prevention. Also, Snyder, H. N., and Sickmund, M. (2006). *Juvenile offenders and victims: 2006 national report.* Washington, DC: Office of Juvenile Justice and Delinquency Prevention.

Box 12.2: Adapted from Howell, J. C. (2003). *Preventing and reducing juvenile delinquency: A comprehensive framework.* Thousand Oaks, CA: Sage.

Figure 12.1: Juvenile Offenders and Victims: 2006 National Report by Howard N. Snyder and Melissa Sickmund. Washington, DC: U.S. Department of Justice, Office of Justice Programs, Office of Juvenile Justice and Delinquency

Prevention. Copyright © 2006 by National Center for Juvenile Justice. p. 105.

Table 12.1: Juvenile Offenders and Victims: 2006 National Report by Howard N. Snyder and Melissa Sickmund. Washington, DC: U.S. Department of Justice, Office of Justice Programs, Office of Juvenile Justice and Delinquency Prevention. Copyright © 2006 by National Center for Juvenile Justice. p. 111. Also, Griffin, P. (2003). Trying and sentencing juveniles as adults: An analysis of state transfer and blended sentencing laws. *Special Project Bulletin*. Washington, DC: Office of Juvenile Justice and Delinquency Prevention.

Box 12.3: Adapted from Bishop, D. M. (2006). Public opinion and juvenile justice policy: Myths and misconceptions. *Criminology and Public Policy, 5*, 653–664.

Box 12.4: Giedd, J., Blumenthal, J., Jeffries, N., Castellanos, F., Liu, H., Zijdenbos, A., et al. (1999). Brain development during childhood and adolescence: A longitudinal MRI study. *Nature Neuroscience, 2*, 861–863. Also, Spinks, S. (Writer, Director, & Producer). (2002, January 31). Inside the teenage brain [televised interview with Jay Giedd]. In S. Tiller (Senior Producer), *Frontline*. Boston: WGBH Boston. Retrieved August 25, 2008, from http://www.pbs.org/ wgbh/pages/frontline/shows/teenbrain/; Fagan, J. (2005). Adolescents, maturity and the law. *The American Prospect. Special Report: Breaking Through*, pp. A5–A7; Fagan, J. (2007). End natural life sentences for juveniles. *Criminology*

and Public Policy, 6, 735–746; Juvenile Justice Center. (2004). *Adolescence, brain development, and legal culpability*. Washington, DC: Juvenile Justice Center, American Bar Association; and Waber, D. P., De Moor, C., Forbes, P. W., Almli, C. R., Botteron, K. N., Leonard, G., et al. (2007). The NIH MRI study of normal brain development: Performance of a population based sample of healthy children aged 6 to 18 years on a neuropsychological battery. *Journal of the International Neuropsychological Society, 13*, 1–18.

Box 12.5: National Council of Juvenile and Family Court Judges. (2005). *Juvenile delinquency guidelines*. Reno, NV: National Council of Juvenile and Family Court Judges, p. 21.

Box 12.6: Justice Policy Institute. (2007). *The consequences aren't minor: The impact of trying youth as adults and strategies for reform*. Washington, DC: Author.

Box 12.7: McGowan, A., Hahn, R., Liberman, A., Crosby, A., Fullilove, M., Johnson, R., et al. (2007). Effects on violence of laws and policies facilitating the transfer of juveniles from the juvenile justice system to the adult justice system: A systematic review. *American Journal of Preventive Medicine, 32*(4 Suppl. 1), 7–21. Also, Task Force on Community Preventive Services. (2007). Recommendation against policies facilitating the transfer of juveniles from juvenile to adult justice systems for the purpose of reducing violence. *American Journal of Preventive Medicine, 32*(4 Suppl. 1), 5–6.

Glossary

Adjudicated delinquent.   A youth who has been found by a judge in juvenile court to have committed a law violation, that is, a delinquent act.

Adjudicatory hearing.   The fact-finding (trial) phase of a juvenile case in which a judge receives and weighs evidence before deciding whether a delinquency or status offense has been proven beyond a reasonable doubt.

Aftercare.   Generally refers to the period of care after confinement in any setting, but the term is more specifically used in reference to "reintegrative" or "reentry" services that aim to link newly released incarcerated youths with their communities, families, schools, or jobs.

Age blocks.   Middle childhood, ages 7–9; late childhood, ages 10–12; early adolescence, ages 13–15; late adolescence, ages 16–19; early adulthood, ages 20–25 (Loeber et al., 2008).

Age cohort.   A group of people who are about the same age and who are followed up over time (Loeber et al., 2008).

Age–crime curve.   A universally observed curve showing that the prevalence of offenders is low in late childhood and early adolescence, peaks in middle to late adolescence, and decreases subsequently (Loeber et al., 2008).

Age of onset.   Youngest age at which offending is recorded through either self-reports or official records (Loeber et al., 2008).

Aggravating risk factors.   Factors that predict a high likelihood of later offending in the general population (Loeber et al., 2008).

Antisocial behavior.   Behaviors that inflict harm on others, including minor and moderate nondelinquent problem behaviors and delinquent offenses (Loeber et al., 2008).

Arrest.   Apprehension by the police and charging (booking) for an offense.

Best-practice program.   A program that is evidence based or research based (see *evidence-based program, research-based program,* and Chapter 8, Box 8.1).

Child delinquents.   Children (under age 13) who commit delinquent offenses.

Chronic juvenile offenders.   Those who commit four or more offenses of any type, including nonfelony offenses such as truancy and running away (Howell, 2003b).

Cohort.   All people who share a particular demographic characteristic; a birth cohort is all people born in a given year in a particular locality. See *age cohort.*

Conduct disorder.   Youth who persistently violate the rights of others and breach age-appropriate norms of society are classified by the American Psychiatric Association's *Diagnostic and Statistical Manual of Mental Disorders,* Fourth Edition (DSM-IV) as having conduct disorder (CD). The DSM-IV categorizes CD behaviors into four main groupings: aggression to people and animals, destruction of property, deceitfulness or theft, and serious violations of rules (American Psychiatric Association, 2000).

Conviction.   Sentencing in criminal court for committing a crime.

Crime Index.   Includes all eight crimes in the Violent Crime Index and Property Crime Index (Snyder & Sickmund, 2006, p. 122). See *Violent Crime Index* and *Property Crime Index.*

Cumulative onset.   The cumulative percentage of people starting to offend up to a certain age (Loeber et al., 2008).

Delinquent juvenile.   Any juvenile who, while less than 18 years of age but at least 6 years of age (which varies in state laws), commits a crime or infraction under state law or under an ordinance of local government, including a violation of motor vehicle laws.

Desistance.   Cessation of offending forever or for a long period of time (Loeber et al., 2008).

Developmental delinquency pathway.   Pattern of development in offending from less serious problem behaviors to more serious offenses (Loeber et al., 2008).

Developmental sequence.   Order of occurrence of different problem behaviors (Loeber et al., 2008).

Drug dealing.   Selling marijuana and other illegal drugs (Loeber et al., 2008).

Duration.   The number of years for which people offend (Loeber et al., 2008).

Escalation.   Increasing severity of offenses committed by a person over time (Loeber et al., 2008).

Evidence-based program.   A program or practice that meets the following requirements: (a) The program or practice is governed by a program manual or protocol that specifies the nature, quality, and amount of service that constitutes the program; and (b) scientific research using methods that meet high scientific standards for evaluating the effects of such programs must have demonstrated with two or more separate client samples that the program improves client outcomes central to the purpose of the program (Tennessee Code Annotated, Title 37, Chapter 5, Part 1, Section 1; see Chapter 8, Box 8.1).

Firearm.   A weapon (e.g., handgun, rifle, or shotgun) that propels a shot or bullet by gunpowder.

Gang.   A group that has three or more members, generally ages 12–24; shares some sense of identity, especially symbols and a name; views itself as a gang and is recognized by others as a gang; has some permanence and a degree of organization; uses verbal and nonverbal forms of communication; and is involved in an elevated level of criminal activity (Curry & Decker, 2003; Esbensen, Winfree, He, & Taylor, 2001; Klein, 1995).

Gang migration.   The movement of gang members from one geographic area to another (Maxson, 1998).

Hindering risk factors.   Factors that predict a low likelihood of desisting from offending among those who have previously offended (Loeber et al., 2008).

Hybrid gang culture.   Gang culture characterized by a mixture of graffiti and symbols (that are copied from other gangs); less concern over turf or territory; members of mixed race or ethnicity; members may belong to more than one gang; members may switch from one gang to another (Starbuck et al., 2001).

Indicated (or tertiary) prevention programs.   Programs provided to people who either have a particular problem (i.e., "indicated") or are predisposed to a given problem, such as delinquency.

Juvenile.   Generally considered adolescents, ages 13–19, but state statutes define juveniles as those who are under the original jurisdiction of juvenile courts, which can range from as young as age 6 (in North Carolina) through age 17 (Snyder & Sickmund, 2006, p. 103).

Meta-analysis.   A quantitative technique for coding, analyzing, and summarizing research evidence. Used for statistically representing and analyzing findings from a set of empirical research studies, typically a large ("meta" or more comprehensive) set of studies (Lipsey & Wilson, 2000).

Minor theft.   Stealing outside the home or shoplifting (Loeber et al., 2008).

Moderate theft.   Typically defined as stealing a bicycle or skateboard, stealing things worth more than $5, joyriding, purse snatching, dealing in stolen goods, or stealing from a car (Loeber et al., 2008).

Moderate violence.   Violent act such as gang fighting (Loeber et al., 2008).

Odds ratio.   A measure of the strength of a relationship between two variables (i.e., number of times more likely).

Offending frequency.   The annual rate of offending for those who are offenders (Loeber et al., 2008).

Offending or offenses.   Delinquent acts committed during the juvenile years (under age 18) and criminal acts committed during adulthood (from age 18 onward) (Loeber et al., 2008).

Official offending.   Offenses measured by means of information from the criminal court, juvenile court, or police arrest records.

Pathway.   A segment of a delinquent or criminal career trajectory; "the stages of behavior that unfold over time in a predictable order" (Loeber et al., 1997, p. 322). See *developmental delinquency pathway*.

Persistence.   The proportion of offenders who continue to offend over different age blocks (Loeber et al., 2008).

Prevalence.   The proportion of a population (expressed as a percentage) who engage in illegal offenses or other problem behaviors (Loeber et al., 2008).

Preventive promotive factors.   Factors that predict a low probability of offending in the general population (Loeber et al., 2008).

Primary (or universal) prevention programs.   Programs provided to a whole population group, such as all children through school-wide implementation.

Probability or forward probability.   The probability that a person will escalate over time from less serious to more serious forms of offending (Loeber et al., 2008).

Promotive factors. Factors that predict a low probability of serious offending either in the general population or among offenders (Loeber et al., 2008). See *preventive promotive factors* and *remedial promotive factors.*

Property Crime Index. Includes burglary, larceny–theft, motor vehicle theft, and arson (Snyder & Sickmund, 2006, p. 122).

Protective factors. Factors that predict a low probability of offending among youth exposed to risk factors (Loeber et al., 2008).

Psychopathology. Any sort of psychological disorder that causes distress, either for the individual or for those in the individual's life. Depression, schizophrenia, attention deficit hyperactivity disorder, alcohol dependency, conduct disorder, and bulimia are all forms of psychopathology (Steinberg, 2002, p. 36).

Psychopathy. A very specific and distinctive type of psychopathology, a type of personality disorder defined chiefly by a combination of manipulative, stimulation-seeking antisocial behavior, callousness, and emotional detachment (Steinberg, 2002, p. 37).

Public order offenses. Obstruction of justice, disorderly conduct, escapes from institutions, weapon offenses, and probation and parole violations (Snyder & Sickmund, 2006).

Remedial promotive factors. Factors that predict cessation of offending among those who have previously offended (Loeber et al., 2008).

Reported offending. Offending as measured by means of self-reports and reports by parents and teachers (Loeber et al., 2008).

Research-based program. A program or practice that has some research demonstrating effectiveness but that does not yet meet the standard of an evidence-based program (Tennessee Code Annotated, Title 37, Chapter 5, Part 1, Section 1; see Chapter 8, Box 8.1).

Resilience. The ability to survive adverse conditions or to achieve positive outcomes in the face of high risks (Tiet & Huizinga, 2002).

Risk factors. Factors that predict a high likelihood of offending either in the general population or among offenders (Loeber et al., 2008). See also *aggravating risk factors* and *hindering risk factors.*

Selective or secondary prevention programs. Programs that focus on at-risk populations.

Self-reported offending. Offending as measured by means of self-reports only (Loeber et al., 2008).

Serious juvenile offenders. Those who commit the following felony offenses: larceny or theft, burglary or breaking and entering, extortion, arson, and drug trafficking or other controlled dangerous substance violations (Federal Bureau of Investigation, 2006).

Serious theft. Breaking and entering or auto theft (Loeber et al., 2008).

Serious violence. Forcible robbery, attacking with intent to injure, sexual coercion, or rape.

Serious, violent, chronic juvenile offenders. Those who commit four or more serious or violent offenses (Howell, 2003b).

Specialization.   The tendency for people to commit some types of offenses disproportionately and repeatedly (Loeber et al., 2008).

Status offenses.   Noncriminal offenses that apply only to children and adolescents, such as being truant, running away from home, possessing alcohol or cigarettes, or disobeying.

Substance use.   Use of alcohol, tobacco, marijuana, or other psychoactive substances (Loeber et al., 2008).

System of care.   "A comprehensive spectrum of mental health and other necessary services which are organized into a coordinated network to meet the multiple and changing needs of severely emotionally disturbed children and adolescents" (Stroul & Friedman, 1986, p. iv).

Tertiary prevention programs.   See *indicated prevention programs.*

Theft.   See *minor theft, moderate theft,* and *serious theft.*

Trajectories.   Classification of individuals according to their pattern of offending over time (Loeber et al., 2008).

Transfer hearings.   At a probable cause hearing in juvenile court, a prosecutor or a judge may give notice that if probable cause is found, the juvenile may be transferred to the adult system for prosecution.

Transitions (within trajectories).   Short-term changes in social roles within long-term trajectories, such as dropping out of school, divorce, and desistance from delinquency.

Tyranny of small numbers.   The mathematical principle that, when translated into a percentage, a small increase in a small number will appear to be much larger than a nominal increase in a large number.

Universal prevention programs.   See *primary prevention programs.*

Violence.   See *moderate violence* and *serious violence.*

Violent Crime Index.   Includes murder and nonnegligent manslaughter, forcible rape, robbery, and aggravated assault (Snyder & Sickmund, 2006, p. 122).

References

Acker, J. A. (2007). Impose an immediate moratorium on executions. *Criminology and Public Policy, 6,* 641–650.

Acoca, L. (1998). Outside/inside: The violation of American girls at home, on the streets, and in the juvenile justice system. *Crime & Delinquency, 44,* 561–589.

Acoca, L. (1999). Investing in girls: A 21st-century strategy. *Juvenile Justice, 6*(1), 3–13.

Acoca, L., & Dedel, K. (1998). *No place to hide: Understanding and meeting the needs of girls in the California juvenile justice system.* San Francisco: National Council on Crime and Delinquency.

Adams, K. (2007). Abolish juvenile curfews. *Criminology and Public Policy, 6,* 663–671.

Advancement Project. (2005). *Education on lockdown: The schoolhouse to jailhouse track.* Washington, DC: Author.

Agnew, R. (2005). *Why do criminals offend? A general theory of crime and delinquency.* Los Angeles, CA: Roxbury.

Ainsworth, J. E. (1991). Re-imagining childhood and reconstructing the legal order: The case for abolishing the juvenile court. *North Carolina Law Review, 89,* 1083–1133.

Ainsworth, J. E. (1995). Youth justice in a unified court: Response to critics of juvenile court abolition. *Boston College Law Review, 36,* 927–951.

American Bar Association. (2001). *Zero tolerance report.* Chicago: Author.

American Bar Association & National Bar Association. (2001). *Justice by gender: The lack of appropriate prevention, diversion and treatment alternatives for girls in the juvenile justice system.* Washington, DC: Authors.

American Civil Liberties Union. (2007). *Criminalizing the classroom: The over-policing of New York City schools.* New York: American Civil Liberties Union, New York Civil Liberties Union.

American Civil Liberties Union of Michigan. (2004). *Second chances: Juveniles serving life without parole in Michigan.* Detroit: Author.

American Psychiatric Association. (2000). *Diagnostic and statistical manual of mental disorders* (4th ed., rev.). Washington, DC: Author.

Amnesty International. (1996). *United States of America: Use of electro-shock stun belts.* New York: Author.

Amnesty International. (1998a). *Betraying the young: Human rights violations against children in the US justice system.* New York: Author.

Amnesty International. (1998b). *On the wrong side of history: Children and the death penalty in the USA.* New York: Author.

Amnesty International. (1999). *Race, rights, and brutality: Portraits of abuse in the USA.* New York: Author.

Amnesty International. (2002). *Amnesty International report 2002.* New York: Author.

Andrews, D. A. (2006). Enhancing adherence to risk-need-responsivity. *Criminology and Public Policy, 5,* 595–602.

Andrews, D. A., & Bonta, J. (1998). *The psychology of criminal conduct* (2nd ed.). Cincinnati, OH: Anderson.

Andrews, D. A., & Bonta, J. (2006). *The psychology of criminal conduct* (4th ed.). Cincinnati, OH: Anderson/LexisNexis.

Andrews, D., Bonta, J., & Wormith, S. (2006). The recent past and near future of risk and/or need assessment. *Crime and Delinquency, 52,* 7–27.

Annie E. Casey Foundation. (2006). *Reentry: Helping former prisoners return to communities, a guide to key ideas, effective approaches, and technical assistance resources for making connections.* Baltimore, MD: Author.

Aos, S., Phipps, P., Barnoski, R., & Lieb, R. (2001). *The comparative costs and benefits of programs to reduce crime* (Version 4.0). Olympia: Washington State Institute for Public Policy. Retrieved June 6, 2002, from http://www.wsipp.wa.gov/crime/costben.html

Arbreton, A. J. A., & McClanahan, W. (2002). *Targeted outreach: Boys and Girls Clubs of America's approach to gang prevention and intervention.* Philadelphia: Public/Private Ventures.

Archbold, C. A., & Meyer, M. (2000). Anatomy of a gang suppression unit: The social construction of an organizational response to gang problems. *Police Quarterly, 2*(2), 201–224.

Arcia, E. (2007). A comparison of elementary/K–8 and middle schools' suspension rates. *Urban Education, 42,* 456–459.

Armstrong, M. L. (1998). *Adolescent pathways: Exploring the intersections between child welfare and juvenile justice, PINS, and mental health.* New York: Vera Institute of Justice.

Arthur, L. G. (1998). Abolish the juvenile court? *Juvenile and Family Court Journal, 49*(1), 51–58.

Associated Press. (1996, February 18). Expert warns of US "bloodbath" (AP wire story).

Augimeri, L. K., Jiang, D., Koegl, C., & Carey, J. (2006). *Differential effects of the SNAP™ Under 12 Outreach Project (SNAP™ ORP) associated with client risk and treatment intensity.* Retrieved August 11, 2008, from http://www.allacademic.com/meta/p_mla_apa_research_citation/2/0/1/5/6/p201560_index.html

Austin, J., Johnson, K. D., & Weitzer, R. (2005). Alternatives to the secure detention and confinement of juvenile offenders. *Juvenile Justice Bulletin.* Washington, DC: U.S. Department of Justice, Office of Justice Programs, Office of Juvenile Justice and Delinquency Prevention.

Austin, J., Marino, A. B., Carroll, L., McCall, P. L., & Richards, S. C. (2000, November). *The use of incarceration in the United States: National policy white paper for the American Society of Criminology, National Policy Committee.* Paper presented at the annual meeting of the American Society of Criminology, San Francisco.

Backer, T. E. (1993). Information alchemy: Transforming information through knowledge utilization. *Journal of the American Society for Information Science, 44,* 217–221.

Baer, J. S., MacLean, M. G., & Marlatt, G. A. (1998). Linking etiology and treatment for adolescent substance abuse: Toward a better match. In R. Jessor (Ed.), *New perspectives on adolescent risk behavior* (pp. 182–220). New York: Cambridge University Press.

Baldry, A. C., & Farrington, D. P. (2007). Effectiveness of programs to prevent school bullying. *Victims and Offenders, 2,* 183–204.

Ball, R. A., & Curry, G. D. (1995). The logic of definition in criminology: Purposes and methods for defining "gangs." *Criminology, 33,* 225–245.

Bandes, S. (2000, November 19). To reform the LAPD, more civilian pressure is necessary. *Los Angeles Times,* p. M6.

Barnoski, R. (2004a). *Assessing risk for re-offense: Validating the Washington State juvenile court assessment.* Olympia: Washington State Institute for Public Policy.

Barnoski, R. (2004b). *Outcome evaluation of Washington State's research-based programs for juvenile offenders.* Olympia: Washington State Institute for Public Policy.

Battin, S. R., Hill, K. G., Abbott, R. D., Catalano, R. F., & Hawkins, J. D. (1998). The contribution of gang membership to delinquency beyond delinquent friends. *Criminology, 36,* 93–115.

Baumeister, R. F., Smart, L., & Boden, J. W. (1996). Relation of threatened egotism to violence and aggression: The dark side of high self-esteem. *Psychological Review, 103,* 5–33.

Bazemore, G., & Umbreit, M. S. (1997). *Balanced and restorative justice: A framework for juvenile justice in the 21st century.* Washington, DC: U.S. Department of Justice, Office of Juvenile Justice and Delinquency Prevention.

Becker, H. (1963). *Outsiders: Studies in the sociology of deviance.* New York: Free Press.

Beckett, K., & Sasson, T. (2003). *The politics of injustice: Crime and punishment in America.* Thousand Oaks, CA: Sage.

Beckett, K., & Sasson, T. (2004). *The politics of injustice: Crime and punishment in America* (2nd ed.). Thousand Oaks, CA: Pine Forge.

Beckett, M., Hawken, A., & Jacknowitz, A. (2001). *Accountability for after-school care: Devising standards and measuring adherence to them.* Santa Monica, CA: RAND.

Bendixen, M., Endresen, I. M., & Olweus, D. (2006). Joining and leaving gangs: Selection and facilitation effects on self-reported antisocial behaviour in early adolescence. *European Journal of Criminology, 3,* 85–114.

Bennett, W. J., DiIulio, J. J. Jr., & Walters, J. P. (1996). *Body count: Moral poverty . . . and how to win America's war against crime and drugs.* New York: Simon & Schuster.

Bernard, T. J. (1992). *The cycle of juvenile justice.* New York: Oxford University Press.

Bernard, T., & Ritti, R. R. (1991). The Philadelphia Birth Cohort and selective incapacitation. *Journal of Research in Crime and Delinquency, 28,* 33–54.

Beyer, M. (1997). Experts for juveniles at risk of adult sentences. In P. Puritz, A. Capozello, & W. Shang (Eds.), *More than meets the eye: Rethinking assessment, competency and sentencing for a harsher era of juvenile justice* (pp. 1–22). Washington, DC: American Bar Association Juvenile Justice Center.

Bilchik, S. (1998). A juvenile justice system for the 21st century. *Juvenile Justice Bulletin.* Washington, DC: U.S. Department of Justice, Office of Juvenile Justice and Delinquency Prevention.

Bilukha, O., Hahn, R. A., Crosby, A., Fullilove, M. T., Liberman, A., et al. (2005). Effectiveness of early childhood home visitation in preventing violence: A systematic review. *American Journal of Preventive Medicine, 28*(2 Suppl. 1), 11–39.

Bingenheimer, J. B., Brennan, R. T., & Earls, F. J. (2005). Firearm violence exposure and serious violent behavior. *Science, 308,* 1323–1326.

Bishop, D. M. (2006). Public opinion and juvenile justice policy: Myths and misconceptions. *Criminology and Public Policy, 5,* 653–664.

Bishop, D. M., & Frazier, C. E. (2000). Consequences of transfer. In J. Fagan & F. E. Zimring (Eds.), *The changing borders of juvenile justice: Transfer of adolescents to the criminal court* (pp. 227–276). Chicago: University of Chicago Press.

Biskupic, J. (1996, June 25). Civil forfeiture in drug case upheld, 8 to 1. *USA Today,* pp. 1A–3A.

Bjerregaard, B. (2008). Gang membership and drug involvement: Untangling the complex relationship. *Crime and Delinquency.*

Blackburn, A. G., Mullings, J. L., Marquart, J. W., & Trulson, C. R. (2007). The next generation of prisoners: Toward an understanding of violent institutionalized delinquents. *Youth Violence and Juvenile Justice, 5,* 35–56.

Blackwood, A. (2001, July 8). Boy's death puts spotlight on boot camps. *News and Observer* (Raleigh, NC), p. 15A.

Blalock, B., & Arthur, P. (2006). Advocates needed to safe-guard rights of youth in DOJ conditions cases. *Youth Law News, 27*(4), 1–5.

Block, R., & Block, C. R. (1993). *Street gang crime in Chicago* (Research in Brief). Washington, DC: National Institute of Justice.

Bloom, B., Owen, B., Deschenes, E. P., & Rosenbaum, J. (2002). Improving juvenile justice for females: A state-wide assessment for California. *Crime and Delinquency, 48,* 526–552.

Blum, A. (2001, July 13). Vance punishes 8 after probe of student tours of D.C. jail. *Washington Post,* p. B4.

Blumstein, A. (1983). Selective incapacitation as a means of crime control. *American Behavioral Scientist, 27,* 87–108.

Blumstein, A. (1995a, August). Violence by young people: Why the deadly nexus? *National Institute of Justice Journal, 229,* 1–9.

Blumstein, A. (1995b). Youth violence, guns, and the illicit-drug industry. *Journal of Criminal Law and Criminology, 86,* 10–36.

Blumstein, A. (1996). *Youth violence, guns, and the illicit drug markets* (Research Preview). Washington, DC: National Institute of Justice.

Blumstein, A., Cohen, J., & Nagin, D. (Eds.). (1978). *Deterrence and incapacitation: Estimating the effects of criminal sanctions on crime rates.* Washington, DC: National Academy of Sciences.

Blumstein, A., Cohen, J., Roth, J. A., & Visher, C. A. (Eds.). (1986). *Criminal careers and career criminals.* Washington, DC: National Academy Press.

Blumstein, A., & Rosenfeld, R. (1999). Trends in rates of violence in the U.S.A. *Studies on Crime and Crime Prevention, 8,* 139–167.

Bonta, J. (1996). Risk-needs assessment and treatment. In A. T. Harland (Ed.), *Choosing correctional options that work* (pp. 10–32). Thousand Oaks, CA: Sage.

Bouley, E., & Wells, T. (2001). Attitudes of citizens in a south-ern rural county toward juvenile crime and justice issues. *Journal of Contemporary Criminal Justice, 17,* 60–70.

Bovard, J. (1999, May 27). Your car may be committing crimes. *USA Today,* p. 15A.

Boyle, P. (2001, April). A DAREing rescue. *Youth Today,* pp. 1, 16–19.

Boyle, P. (2005). Behind the death penalty ban. *Youth Today, 14*(1), 36–38.

Bradshaw, W., & Roseboro, D. (2005). An empirical review of family group conferencing in juvenile offenses. *Juvenile and Family Court Journal, 56,* 21–28.

Braga, A. A. (2004). *Gun violence among serious young offend-ers. Problem-oriented guides for police.* Problem-Specific Guides Series Guide No. 23. Washington, DC: Office of Community Oriented Policing Services.

Braga, A. A., Kennedy, D. M., & Tita, G. E. (2002). New approaches to the strategic prevention of gang and group-involved violence. In C. R. Huff (Ed.), *Gangs in America III* (pp. 271–285). Thousand Oaks, CA: Sage.

Braga, A. A., Kennedy, D. M., Waring, E. J., & Piehl, A. M. (2001). Problem-oriented policing, deterrence, and youth violence: An evaluation of Boston's Operation Ceasefire. *Journal of Research in Crime and Delinquency, 38,* 195–225.

Braga, A. A., & Pierce, G. L. (2005). Disrupting illegal firearms markets in Boston: The effects of Operation Ceasefire on the supply of new handguns to criminals. *Criminology and Public Policy, 4,* 717–748.

Brame, B., Nagin, D. S., & Tremblay, R. E. (2001). Developmental trajectories of physical aggression from school entry to late adolescence. *Journal of Child Psychology and Psychiatry and Allied Disciplines, 42,* 503–512.

Bratton, W. (1998). *Turnaround: How America's top cop reversed the crime epidemic.* New York: Random House.

Brendtro, L. K., & Ness, A. E. (1995). Fixing flaws or building strengths? *Reclaiming Children and Youth, 4,* 2–7.

Brent, D. A., & Birmaher, B. (2002). Adolescent depression. *New England Journal of Medicine, 347,* 667–671.

Brezina, T., Agnew, R., Cullen, F. T., & Wright, J. P. (2004). The code of the street: A quantitative assessment of Elijah Anderson's subculture of violence thesis and its contribution to youth violence research. *Youth Violence and Juvenile Justice, 2,* 303–328.

Bridges, G. S. (1997). *A study on racial and ethnic disparities in superior court bail and pre-trial detention practices in Washington.* Olympia: Washington State Minority and Justice Commission.

Bridges, G. S., Crutchfield, R. D., & Simpson, E. E. (1987). Crime, social structure and criminal punishment: White and nonwhite rates of imprisonment. *Social Problems, 34,* 345–361.

Broidy, L. M., Tremblay, R. E., Brame, B., Fergusson, D., Horwood, J. L., Laird, R., et al. (2003). Developmental trajectories of childhood disruptive behaviors and adolescent delinquency: A six-site, cross-national study. *Developmental Psychology, 39,* 222–245.

Bronfenbrenner, U. (1979). *The ecology of human develop-ment: Experiments by nature and design.* Cambridge, MA: Harvard University Press.

Brooks, K., Schiraldi, V., & Ziedenberg, J. (2001). *School house hype: Two years later.* Washington, DC: Justice Policy Institute, Center on Juvenile and Criminal Justice.

Brooks-Gunn, J., Graber, J. A., & Paikoff, R. L. (1994). Studying links between hormones and negative affect: Models and measures. *Journal of Research on Adol-escence, 4,* 469–486.

Brown, J. M., & Langan, P. A. (1998). *State court sentencing of convicted felons* (Bulletin). Washington, DC: Bureau of Justice Statistics.

Browning, K., & Huizinga, D. (1999). *Highlights of findings from the Denver Youth Survey.* Fact Sheet No. 1999-106. Washington, DC: Office of Juvenile Justice and Delinquency Prevention.

Brownstein, H. (1996). *The rise and fall of a violent crime wave: Crack cocaine and the social construction of a crime problem.* Guilderland, NY: Harrow and Heston.

Building Blocks for Youth. (2000). *Youth crime/adult time: Is justice served?* Washington, DC: Author.

Bureau of Alcohol, Tobacco and Firearms. (1999). *The Youth Crime Gun Interdiction Initiative performance report.* Washington, DC: Author.

Bureau of Justice Assistance. (1997). *Urban street gang enforcement*. Washington, DC: Author.

Bureau of Justice Statistics. (2007). *Key facts at a glance: Correctional populations*. Retrieved December 24, 2007, from http://www.ojp.gov/bjs/glance/tables/corr2tab.htm

Burke, C., & Pennell, S. (2001). *Breaking Cycles evaluation: A comprehensive approach to youthful offenders*. San Diego, CA: San Diego Association of Governments.

Burke, J. D., Loeber, R., & Birmaher, B. (2002). Oppositional defiant disorder and conduct disorder: A review of the past 10 years, Part II. *Journal of the American Academy of Child and Adolescent Psychiatry, 41,* 1275–1293.

Burns, B. J., Goldman, S. K., Faw, L., & Burchard, J. (1999). The wraparound evidence base. In B. J. Burns & S. K. Goldman (Eds.), *Promising practices in wraparound for children with serious emotional disturbances and their families: Systems of care* (pp. 77–100). Washington, DC: American Institutes for Research, Center for Effective Collaboration and Practice.

Burns, B. J., Landsverk, J., Kelleher, K., Faw, L., Hazen, A., & Keeler, G. (2001). Mental health, education, child welfare, and juvenile justice service use. In R. Loeber & D. P. Farrington (Eds.), *Child delinquents: Development, intervention, and service needs* (pp. 273–304). Thousand Oaks, CA: Sage.

Burrell, S. (2000). *Pathways to juvenile detention reform: Vol. 6. Improving conditions of confinement in secure detention facilities*. Baltimore, MD: Annie E. Casey Foundation.

Bursik, R. J. Jr., & Grasmick, H. G. (1993). *Neighborhoods and crime: The dimensions of effective community control*. New York: Lexington.

Bushway, S. D., Thornberry, T. P., & Krohn, M. D. (2003). Desistance as a developmental process: A comparison of static and dynamic approaches. *Journal of Quantitative Criminology, 19,* 129–153.

Butterfield, F. (1997, July 21). With juvenile courts in chaos, some propose scrapping them. *New York Times*, pp. A1, A13.

Butts, J. A. (1999, May). Feeding kids to the monster. *Youth Today*, p. 23.

Butts, J. A., Coggeshall, M., Gouvis, C., Mears, D., Travis, J., Waul, M., et al. (2002). *Youth, guns, and the juvenile justice system*. Washington, DC: The Urban Institute.

Butts, J. A., & Mitchell, O. (2000). Brick by brick: Dismantling the border between juvenile and adult justice. In C. M. Friel (Ed.), *Criminal justice 2000: Boundary changes in criminal justice* (Vol. II, pp. 167–213). Washington, DC: National Institute of Justice.

Butts, J. A., & Snyder, H. N. (1997). The youngest delinquents: Offenders under age 15. *Juvenile Justice Bulletin*. Washington, DC: Office of Juvenile Justice and Delinquency Prevention.

Butts, J. A., & Snyder, H. N. (2006). *Too soon to tell: Deciphering recent trends in youth violence*. Issue Brief #110. Chicago: Chapin Hall Center for Children.

Butts, J. A., & Snyder, H. N. (2007, Spring). Where are juvenile crime trends headed? *Juvenile and Family Justice Today*, pp. 16–20.

Butts, J. A., & Travis, J. (2002). *The rise and fall of American youth violence: 1980 to 2000*. Washington, DC: Urban Institute.

Bynum, T. S., & Varano, S. P. (2003). The anti-gang initiative in Detroit: An aggressive enforcement approach to gangs. In S. H. Decker (Ed.), *Policing gangs and youth violence* (pp. 214–238). Belmont, CA: Wadsworth/Thompson Learning.

Cairns, R. B., & Cairns, B. D. (1991). Social cognition and social networks: A developmental perspective. In D. J. Pepler & K. H. Rubin (Eds.), *The development and treatment of childhood aggression* (pp. 249–278). Hillsdale, NJ: Erlbaum.

Cairns, R. B., & Cairns, B. D. (1994). *Lifelines and risks: Pathways of youth in our time*. New York: Cambridge University Press.

Caldwell, M. F., Vitacco, M., & Van Rybroek, G. J. (2006). Are violent delinquents worth treating? A cost-benefit analysis. *Journal of Research in Crime and Delinquency, 43,* 148–168.

Caliber Associates. (2006). *National evaluation of the Title V Community Prevention Grants Program*. Washington, DC: U.S. Department of Justice, Office of Juvenile Justice and Delinquency Prevention.

Campbell, R., & Reeves, J. L. (1994). *Cracked coverage: Television news, the anti-cocaine crusade, and the Reagan legacy*. Durham, NC: Duke University Press.

Carroll, L., & Mondrick, M. E. (1976). Racial bias in the decision to grant parole. *Law and Society Review, 11*(1), 93–107.

Catalano, R. F., & Hawkins, J. D. (1996). The social development model: A theory of antisocial behavior. In J. D. Hawkins (Ed.), *Delinquency and crime: Current theories* (pp. 149–197). New York: Cambridge University Press.

Cauffman, E. (2004). A statewide screening of mental health symptoms among juvenile offenders in detention. *Journal of the American Academy of Child and Adolescent Psychiatry, 43,* 430–439.

Center for Public Integrity. (2003). *Harmful error: Investigating America's local prosecutors*. Washington, DC: Center for Public Integrity.

Center for Sex Offender Management. (2006). *Understanding treatment for adults and juveniles who have committed sex offenses*. Silver Spring, MD: Center for Sex Offender Management.

Centers for Disease Control and Prevention. (1994, March 4). Health risk behaviors among adolescents who do and do not attend school: United States, 1992. *Prevention Morbidity and Mortality Weekly Report, 43*(8), 129–132.

Centers for Disease Control and Prevention. (2006). Youth risk behavior surveillance: United States, 2005. *Prevention Morbidity and Mortality Weekly Report, 55*(SS-5), 1–108.

Chaiken, M. R. (2000). Violent neighborhoods, violent kids. *Juvenile Justice Bulletin*. Washington, DC: Office of Juvenile Justice and Delinquency Prevention.

Chambliss, W. J. (1995). Crime control and ethnic minorities: Legitimizing racial oppression by creating moral panics. In D. F. Hawkins (Ed.), *Ethnicity, race, and crime: Perspectives across time and place* (pp. 235–258). Albany: State University of New York Press.

Chandler, K. A., Chapman, C. D., Rand, M. R., & Taylor, B. M. (1998). *Students' reports of school crime: 1989 and 1995.* Washington, DC: Bureau of Justice Statistics and National Center for Education Statistics.

Chard-Wierschem, D. (1998). *In pursuit of the "true" relationship: A longitudinal study of the effects of religiosity on delinquency and substance abuse.* Unpublished doctoral dissertation, University at Albany, State University of New York.

Cheatwood, D. (1993). Capital punishment and the deterrence of violent crime in comparable counties. *Criminal Justice Review, 18,* 165–181.

Chesney-Lind, M. (1997). *The female offender: Girls, women, and crime.* Thousand Oaks, CA: Sage.

Chesney-Lind, M., & Brown, M. (1999). Girls and violence. In D. J. Flannery & C. R. Huff (Eds.), *Youth violence: Prevention, intervention, and social policy* (pp. 171–199). Washington, DC: American Psychiatric Press.

Chesney-Lind, M., & Sheldon, R. (1998). *Girls, delinquency, and juvenile justice.* Belmont, CA: West/Wadsworth.

Chicago Police Department, Gang Crime Section. (1992). *Street gangs.* Chicago: Author.

Chiricos, T. G., & Crawford, C. (1995). Race and imprisonment: A contextual assessment of the evidence. In D. F. Hawkins (Ed.), *Ethnicity, race, and crime. Perspectives across time and place* (pp. 281–309). Albany: State University of New York Press.

Christle, C. A., Jolivette, K., & Nelson, C. M. (2005). Breaking the school to prison pipeline: Identifying school risk and protective factors for youth delinquency. *Exceptionality, 13,* 69–88.

Chung, H. L., Schubert, C. A., & Mulvey, E. P. (2007). An empirical portrait of community reentry among serious juvenile offenders in two metropolitan cities. *Criminal Justice and Behavior, 34,* 1402–1426.

Coalition for Evidence-Based Policy. (2003). *Bringing evidence-driven progress to crime and substance-abuse policy: A recommended federal strategy.* Washington, DC: Coalition for Evidence-Based Policy.

Cohen, M. (1998). The monetary value of saving a high-risk youth. *Journal of Quantitative Criminology, 14,* 5–33.

Cohen, S. (1980). *Folk devils and moral panics: The creation of the mods and rockers.* New York: Basil Blackwell.

Cohn, A., Biondi, L., Flaim, L. C., Paskowski, M., & Cohn, S. (1997). Evaluating electronic monitoring programs. *Alternatives to Incarceration, 3,* 16–24.

Coie, J. D., & Dodge, K. A. (1998). The development of aggression and antisocial behavior. In N. Eisenberg (Ed.), *Handbook of child psychology: Vol. 3. Social, emotional, and personality development* (5th ed., pp. 779–861). New York: Wiley.

Coie, J. D., & Miller-Johnson, S. (2001). Peer factors and interventions. In R. Loeber & D. P. Farrington (Eds.), *Child delinquents: Development, intervention, and service needs* (pp. 191–209). Thousand Oaks, CA: Sage.

Coleman, J. S. (1988). Social capital in the creation of human capital. *American Journal of Sociology, 94*(Suppl.), 95–120.

Coleman, J. S. (1990). *Foundations of social theory.* Cambridge, MA: Harvard University Press.

Columbia University Department of Child and Adolescent Psychiatry. (2003). *Columbia University guidelines for child and adolescent mental health referral.* New York: Department of Child and Adolescent Psychiatry, Columbia University.

Convention on the Rights of the Child. (1989). Article 37(a), G.A. res. 44/25, annex, 44 U.N. GAOR Supp. (No. 49) at 167, U.N. Doc.A/44/49, entered into force September 2, 1990.

Cook, P. J., & Laub, J. H. (1998). The unprecedented epidemic of youth violence. In M. Tonry & M. H. Moore (Eds.), *Youth violence* (pp. 27–64). Chicago: University of Chicago Press.

Cook, P. J., & Ludwig, J. (2001, June 10). Protecting the public in presidential style. *News and Observer* (Raleigh, NC), p. A31.

Cook, P. J., & Ludwig, J. (2006). The social costs of gun ownership. *Journal of Public Economics, 90,* 379–391.

Coolbaugh, K., & Hansel, C. J. (2000). The comprehensive strategy: Lessons learned from the pilot sites. *Juvenile Justice Bulletin.* Washington, DC: Office of Juvenile Justice and Delinquency Prevention.

Cornell, D., & Sheras, P. (2006). *Guidelines for responding to student threats of violence.* Longmont, CO: Sopris West.

Cothern, L. (2000). Juveniles and the death penalty: A report of the federal Coordinating Council on Juvenile Justice and Delinquency Prevention. *Juvenile Justice Bulletin.* Washington, DC: Office of Juvenile Justice and Delinquency Prevention.

Coughlin, B. C., & Venkatesh, S. A. (2003). The urban street gang after 1970. *Annual Review of Sociology, 29,* 41–64.

Council of State Governments. (2005). *Report of the Re-Entry Policy Council.* Lexington, KY: Author.

Craig, W. M., Vitaro, C. G., & Tremblay, R. E. (2002). The road to gang membership. Characteristics of male gang and non-gang members from ages 10 to 14. *Social Development, 11,* 53–68.

Crick, N. R., & Grotpeter, J. K. (1995). Relational aggression, gender, and psychological adjustment. *Child Development, 66,* 710–722.

Crime and Justice Institute. (2004). *Implementing evidence-based practices in community corrections: The principles of effective intervention.* Boston: Author.

Crowe, A. H. (1998). *Drug identification and testing in the juvenile justice system.* Washington, DC: Office of Juvenile Justice and Delinquency Prevention.

Crowley, M. (2007, May). No mercy, kid! *Reader's Digest,* pp. 35–36.

Crutchfield, R. D., Bridges, G. S., & Pitchford, S. R. (1994). Analytical and aggregation biases in analyses of imprisonment: Reconciling discrepancies in studies of racial disparity. *Journal of Research in Crime and Delinquency, 31,* 166–182.

Cullen, F. T. (2005). The twelve people who saved rehabilitation: How the science of criminology made a difference. *Criminology, 43,* 1–42.

Cullen, F. T. (2006). It's time to reaffirm rehabilitation. *Criminology and Public Policy, 5,* 665–672.

Cullen, F. T. (2007). Make rehabilitation corrections' guiding paradigm. *Criminology and Public Policy, 6,* 717–728.

Cullen, F. T., Bose, B. A., Jonson, C. N. L., & Unnever, J. D. (2007). Public support for early intervention: Is child saving a "habit of the heart"? *Victims and Offenders, 2,* 109–124.

Cullen, F. T., & Gendreau, P. (2000). Assessing correctional rehabilitation: Policy, practice, and prospects. In J. Horney (Ed.), *Criminal justice 2000: Vol. 3. Policies, processes, and decisions of the criminal justice system* (pp. 109–175). Washington, DC: National Institute of Justice.

Cullen, F. T., Golden, K. M., & Cullen, J. B. (1983). Is child saving dead? Attitudes toward juvenile rehabilitation in Illinois. *Journal of Criminal Justice, 11,* 1–13.

Cullen, F. T., Wright, J. P., & Blevins, K. R. (2006). *Taking stock: The status of criminological theory.* New Brunswick, NJ: Transaction Press.

Cullen, F. T., Wright, J. P., Brown, S., Moon, M. M., Blankenship, M. B., & Applegate, B. K. (1998). Public support for early intervention programs: Implications for a progressive policy agenda. *Crime and Delinquency, 44,* 187–204.

Curry, G. D. (1998). Responding to female gang involvement. In J. Hagedorn & M. Chesney-Lind (Eds.), *Female gangs in America* (pp. 133–143). Chicago: Lakeview.

Curry, G. D. (2000). Self-reported gang involvement and officially recorded delinquency. *Criminology, 38,* 1253–1274.

Curry, G. D., & Decker, S. H. (2000). *Referrals and the referral process in the St. Louis family court.* St. Louis: Missouri Department of Criminology and Criminal Justice.

Curry, G. D., & Decker, S. H. (2003). *Confronting gangs: Crime and community* (2nd ed.). Los Angeles: Roxbury.

Curry, G. D., Decker, S. H., & Egley, A. Jr. (2002). Gang involvement and delinquency in a middle school population. *Justice Quarterly, 19,* 275–292.

Curry, G. D., Egley, A., & Howell, J. C. (2004, November). *Youth gang homicide trends in the National Youth Gang Survey: 1999–2003.* Paper presented at the annual meeting of the American Society of Criminology, Nashville, TN.

Curry, G. D., & Howell, J. C. (2007, April 18). *National Youth Gang Center.* Unpublished document, Tallahassee, FL.

Curry, G. D., & Spergel, I. A. (1988). Gang homicide, delinquency and community. *Criminology, 26,* 381–405.

Dahmann, J. (1983). *Prosecutorial response to violent gang criminality: An evaluation of Operation Hardcore.* Washington, DC: National Institute of Justice.

Death Penalty Information Center. (2003, January 7). *Facts about the death penalty.* Washington, DC: Author.

Decker, S. H. (1996). Collective and normative features of gang violence. *Justice Quarterly, 13,* 243–264.

Decker, S. H. (2003). Policing gangs and youth violence: Where do we stand, where do we go from here? In S. H. Decker (Ed.), *Policing gangs and youth violence* (pp. 287–293). Belmont, CA: Wadsworth/Thompson Learning.

Decker, S. H. (2007). Youth gangs and violent behavior. In D. J. Flannery, A. T. Vazsonyi, & I. D. Waldman (Eds.), *The Cambridge handbook of violent behavior and aggression* (pp. 388–402). Cambridge: Cambridge University Press.

Decker, S. H., Bynum, T., & Weisel, D. (1998). A tale of two cities: Gangs as organized crime groups. *Justice Quarterly, 15,* 395–423.

Decker, S. H., & Curry, G. D. (2000). Addressing key features of gang membership: Measuring the involvement of young members. *Journal of Criminal Justice, 28,* 473–482.

Decker, S., & Curry, G. D. (2002). "I'm down for my organization": The rationality of responses to delinquency, youth crime and gangs. In A. R. Piquero & S. G. Tibbits (Eds.), *Rational choice and criminal behavior* (pp. 197–218). New York: Routledge.

Decker, S. H., & Curry, G. D. (2003). Suppression without prevention, prevention without suppression. In S. H. Decker (Ed.), *Policing gangs and youth violence* (pp. 191–213). Belmont, CA: Wadsworth/Thompson Learning.

Decker, S. H., Katz, C. M., & Webb, V. J. (2008). Understanding the black box of gang organization: Implications for involvement in violent crime, drug sales, and violent victimization. *Crime & Delinquency, 54,* 153–172.

Decker, S. H., & Van Winkle, B. (1996). *Life in the gang: Family, friends, and violence.* New York: Cambridge University Press.

DeComo, R. E. (1998). Estimating the prevalence of juvenile custody by race and gender. *Crime & Delinquency, 44,* 489–506.

DeComo, R. E., & Wiebush, R. (Eds.). (2005). *Graduated sanctions for juvenile offenders: A program model and planning guide. Vol. II: Dispositional court hearing to case closure.* Reno, NV: National Council of Juvenile and Family Court Judges.

Degnan, W. (1994). *Lifeskills post-parole treatment program.* Sanger, CA: Operation New Hope.

Degnan, W., & Degnan, A. (1993). *Lifestyle changes: One step at a time.* Sanger, CA: Operation New Hope.

DeMuro, P. (2000). *Pathways to juvenile detention reform: Vol. 4. Consider the alternatives.* Baltimore, MD: Annie E. Casey Foundation.

Deutsch, L. (2000, February 26). Los Angeles police officer gets five years. *USA Today,* p. 6A.

DiIulio, J. J. Jr. (1995a). Arresting ideas. *Policy Review, 74,* 12–16.

DiIulio, J. J. Jr. (1995b, November 27). The coming of the super-predators. *Weekly Standard,* pp. 23–28.

DiIulio, J. J. Jr. (1996a). *How to stop the coming crime wave.* New York: Manhattan Institute.

DiIulio, J. J. Jr. (1996b, Spring). They're coming: Florida's youth crime bomb. *Impact,* pp. 25–27.

Dinkes, R., Cataldi, E. F., Kena, G., & Baum, K. (2006). *Indicators of school crime and safety, 2006.* Washington, DC: U.S. Department of Justice, National Center for Education Statistics, Bureau of Justice Statistics.

Dishion, T. J., McCord, J., & Poulin, F. (1999). When interventions harm: Peer groups and problem behavior. *American Psychologist, 54,* 755–764.

Donohue, E., Schiraldi, V., & Ziedenberg, J. (1999). *School house hype: School shootings and the real risks students face in America.* Washington, DC: Justice Policy Institute, Center on Juvenile and Criminal Justice.

Dorfman, L., & Schiraldi, V. (2001). *Off balance: Youth, race and crime in the news.* Washington, DC: Building Blocks for Youth.

Duane, D. (2006, January-February). Straight outta Boston. *Mother Jones*, pp. 61–80.

Dunford, F. W., & Elliott, D. S. (1984). Identifying career offenders using self-reported data. *Journal of Research on Crime and Delinquency, 21*, 57–86.

Durlak, J. A. (1998). Common risk and protective factors in successful prevention programs. *American Journal of Orthopsychiatry, 68*, 512–520.

Durlak, J. A., & Lipsey, M. W. (1991). A practitioner's guide to meta-analysis. *American Journal of Community Psychology, 19*, 291–332.

Dwyer, K., & Osher, D. (2000). *Safeguarding our children: An action guide.* Washington, DC: U.S. Departments of Education and Justice, American Institutes for Research.

Eber, L., Sugai, G., Smith, C. R., & Scott, T. M. (2002). Wraparound and positive behavioral interventions and supports in schools. *Journal of Emotional and Behavioral Disorders, 10*, 171–180.

Eddy, P., Sabogal, H., & Walden, S. (1988). *The cocaine wars.* New York: W.W. Norton.

Egley, A. Jr. (2005). *Highlights of the 2002–2003 National Youth Gang Surveys.* OJJDP Fact Sheet (June 2005-01). Washington, DC: U.S. Department of Justice, Office of Juvenile Justice and Delinquency Prevention.

Egley, A. Jr., Howell, J. C., & Major, A. K. (2004). Recent patterns of gang problems in the United States: Results from the 1996–2002 National Youth Gang Survey. In F. A. Esbensen, L. Gaines, & S. G. Tibbetts (Eds.), *American youth gangs at the millennium* (pp. 90–108) Prospect Heights, IL: Waveland.

Egley, A. Jr., Howell, J. C., & Major, A. (2006). *National Youth Gang Survey: 1999–2001.* Washington, DC: U.S. Department of Justice, Office of Juvenile Justice and Delinquency Prevention.

Egley, A. E., Howell, J. C., & Ritz, C. E. (2005, November). *Exploring gang migration and proliferation patterns in the National Youth Gang Survey.* Paper presented at the Annual Meeting of the American Society of Criminology, Toronto, Canada.

Egley, A. Jr., & Major, A. K. (2004). *Highlights of the 2002 National Youth Gang Survey.* OJJDP Fact Sheet (# 2004-01). Washington, DC: U.S. Department of Justice, Office of Juvenile Justice and Delinquency Prevention.

Egley, A. E., & O'Donnell, C. E. (2007, November). *The dark figure of officially-recorded gang crime.* Paper presented at the annual meeting of the American Society of Criminology, Atlanta, GA.

Egley, A. Jr., & O'Donnell, C. E. (2008). *Highlights of the 2007 National Youth Gang Survey: Preliminary findings.* Tallahassee, FL: National Youth Gang Center.

Egley, A. Jr., O'Donnell, C. E., & Curry, G. D. (2007). *Highlights of the 2005 National Youth Gang Survey: Preliminary findings.* Tallahassee, FL: National Youth Gang Center.

Egley, A. Jr., & Ritz, C. E. (2006). *Highlights of the 2004 National Youth Gang Survey.* OJJDP Fact Sheet #2006-01. Washington, DC: U.S. Department of Justice, Office of Juvenile Justice and Delinquency Prevention.

Eitle, D., Gunkel, S., & Gundy, K. V. (2004). Cumulative exposure to stressful life events and male gang membership. *Journal of Criminal Justice, 32*, 95–111.

Eitle, D., & Turner, R. J. (2002). Exposure to community violence and young adult crime: The effects of witnessing violence, traumatic victimization, and other stressful life events. *Journal of Research in Crime and Delinquency, 39*, 214–237.

Elder, G. H. Jr. (Ed.). (1985a). *Life course dynamics: Trajectories and transitions, 1968–1980.* Ithaca, NY: Cornell University Press.

Elder, G. H. Jr. (1985b). Perspectives on the life course. In G. H. Elder Jr. (Ed.), *Life course dynamics: Trajectories and transitions, 1968–1980* (pp. 23–49). Ithaca, NY: Cornell University Press.

Elliott, D. S. (1994a). Serious violent offenders: Onset, developmental course, and termination. *Criminology, 32*, 1–21.

Elliott, D. S. (1994b). *Youth violence: An overview.* Boulder, CO: Center for the Study and Prevention of Violence.

Elliott, D. S. (1995, November). *Lies, damn lies and arrest statistics.* Paper presented at the annual meeting of the American Society of Criminology, Boston.

Elliott, D. S. (Ed.). (1998). *Blueprints for violence prevention.* Denver, CO: C&M.

Elliott, D. S. (2000). Violent offending over the life course: A sociological perspective. In N. A. Krasnegor, N. B. Anderson, & D. R. Bynum (Eds.), *Health and behavior* (Vol. 1, pp. 189–204). Rockville, MD: National Institutes of Health.

Elliott, D. S., Huizinga, D., & Menard, S. (1989). *Multiple problem youth: Delinquency, substance abuse and mental health problems.* New York: Springer-Verlag.

Elliott, D. S., Huizinga, D., & Morse, B. (1986). Self-reported violent offending. *Journal of Interpersonal Violence, 1*, 472–514.

Elliott, D. S., & Mihalic, S. (2004). Issues in disseminating and replicating effective prevention programs. *Prevention Science, 5*, 47–53.

Ely, J. W., Osheroff, J. A., Ebell, M. H., Chambliss, M. L., Vinson, D. C., Stevermer, J. J., et al. (2002). Obstacles to answering doctors' questions about patient care with evidence: Qualitative study. *British Medical Journal, 324*, 710–718.

Empey, L. T. (1978). *American delinquency: Its meaning and construction.* Homewood, IL: Dorsey.

Esbensen, F., Deschenes, E. P., & Winfree, L. T. (1999). Differences between gang girls and gang boys: Results from a multi-site survey. *Youth and Society, 31*, 27–53.

Esbensen, F., & Huizinga, D. (1993). Gangs, drugs, and delinquency in a survey of urban youth. *Criminology, 31*, 565–589.

Esbensen, F., Huizinga, D., & Menard, S. (1999). Family context and criminal victimization in adolescence. *Youth & Society, 31*, 168–198.

Esbensen, F., Huizinga, D., & Weiher, A. W. (1993). Gang and non-gang youth: Differences in explanatory variables. *Journal of Contemporary Criminal Justice, 9,* 94–116.

Esbensen, F., Osgood, D. W., Taylor, T. J., Peterson, D., & Freng, A. (2001). How great is G.R.E.A.T.? Results from a longitudinal quasi-experimental design. *Criminology and Public Policy, 1,* 87–117.

Esbensen, F., & Tusinski, K. (2007). Youth gangs in the print media. *Journal of Criminal Justice and Popular Culture, 14,* 21–38.

Esbensen, F., Winfree, L. T., He, N., & Taylor, T. J. (2001). Youth gangs and definitional issues: When is a gang a gang, and why does it matter? *Crime & Delinquency, 47,* 105–130.

Espelage, D. L., Wasserman, S., & Fleisher, M. S. (2007). Social networks and violent behavior. In D. J. Flannery, A. T. Vazsonyi, & I. D. Waldman (Eds.), *The Cambridge handbook of violent behavior and aggression* (pp. 450–464). Cambridge: Cambridge University Press.

Espiritu, R. C., Huizinga, D., Crawford, A. M., & Loeber, R. (2001). Epidemiology of self-reported delinquency. In R. Loeber & D. P. Farrington (Eds.), *Child delinquents: Development, intervention, and service needs* (pp. 47–66). Thousand Oaks, CA: Sage.

Executive Office of the President of the United States. (2005). *National drug control strategy: FY 2006 budget summary.* Washington, DC: The White House.

Ezelle, M. E. (2007). Examining the overall and offense-specific criminal career lengths of a sample of serious offenders. *Crime and Delinquency, 53,* 3–37.

Fagan, J. (2002). Policing guns and youth violence. *The Future of Children, 12,* 133–151.

Fagan, J. (2005). Adolescents, maturity and the law. *The American Prospect. Special Report: Breaking Through,* pp. A5–A7.

Fagan, J. (2007). End natural life sentences for juveniles. *Criminology and Public Policy, 6,* 735–746.

Fagan, J., & Zimring, F. E. (Eds.). (2000). *The changing borders of juvenile justice: Transfer of adolescents to the criminal court.* Chicago: University of Chicago Press.

Farabee, D. (2005). *Rethinking rehabilitation: Why can't we reform our criminals?* Washington, DC: American Enterprise Institute for Public Policy Research.

Farrington, D. P. (1986). Age and crime. In M. Tonry & N. Morris (Eds.), *Crime and justice: An annual review of research* (Vol. 7, pp. 189–250). Chicago: University of Chicago Press.

Farrington, D. P. (2005). *Integrated developmental and life-course theories of offending.* New Brunswick, NJ: Transaction.

Farrington, D. P. (2007). Origin of violent behavior over the life span. In D. J. Flannery, A. T. Vazsonyi, & I. D. Waldman (Eds.), *The Cambridge handbook of violent behavior and aggression* (pp. 19–48). Cambridge: Cambridge University Press.

Farrington, D. P., Jolliffe, D., Loeber, R., & Homish, D. L. (2007). How many offenses are really committed per juvenile court offender? *Victims and Offenders, 2,* 227–249.

Farrington, D. P., & Welsh, B. C. (2007). *Saving children from a life of crime: Early risk factors and effective interventions.* New York: Oxford University Press.

Federal Bureau of Investigation. (2006). *Uniform crime report, 2005.* Washington, DC: Author.

Feld, B. C. (1993). Criminalizing the American juvenile court. In M. Tonry (Ed.), *Crime and justice: An annual review of research* (Vol. 17, pp. 197–280). Chicago: University of Chicago Press.

Feld, B. C. (1998a). Abolish the juvenile court: Youthfulness, criminal responsibility, and sentencing policy. *Journal of Criminal Law and Criminology, 88,* 68–136.

Feld, B. C. (1998b). Juvenile and criminal justice systems' responses to youth. In M. Tonry & M. H. Moore (Eds.), *Youth violence* (pp. 189–262). Chicago: University of Chicago Press.

Feld, B. C. (1999). The honest politician's guide to juvenile justice policy in the twenty-first century. *Annals of the American Academy of Political and Social Science, 564,* 10–27.

Feld, B. C. (2003). Competence, culpability, and punishment: Implications of Atkins for executing and sentencing adolescents. *Hofstra Law Review, 32,* 463–552.

Felson, M. (2006). The street gang strategy. In M. Felson, *Crime and nature* (pp. 305–324). Thousand Oaks, CA: Sage.

Ferguson, C. J., Miguel, C. S., Kilburn, J. C., & Sanchez, P. (2007). The effectiveness of school-based anti-bullying programs: A meta-analytic review. *Criminal Justice Review, 32,* 401–414.

Fessenden, F. (2000, April 8). Rampage killers: A statistical portrait. *New York Times.* Retrieved December 16, 2000, from http://www.nytimes.com/library/national/040900rampage-killers.html

Fields, G. (1999, July 21). Senate hearing takes up debate over police seizures of property. *USA Today,* p. 6A.

Fields, G. (2000, April 18). Police group wants national study of justice system. *USA Today,* p. 7A.

Fight Crime: Invest in Kids. (2002). *A school and youth violence prevention plan.* Washington, DC: Author. Retrieved August 20, 2002, from http://www.fight crime.org

Fight Crime: Invest in Kids. (2004). *Caught in the crossfire: Arresting gang violence by investing in kids.* Washington, DC: Author.

Finckenauer, J. O., & Gavin, P. W. (1999). *Scared Straight: The panacea phenomenon revisited.* Prospect Heights, IL: Waveland.

Finestone, H. (1976). *Victims of change.* Westport, CT: Greenwood.

Finkelhor, D., & Dziuba-Leatherman, J. (1994). Victimization of children. *American Psychologist, 49,* 173–183.

Fishman, M. (1978). Crime waves as ideology. *Social Problems, 25,* 531–543.

Flannery, D. J., Singer, M. I., van Dulmen, M., Kretschmar, J. M., & Belliston, L. M. (2007). Exposure to violence, mental health, and violent behavior. In D. Flannery, A. Vazonsyi, & I. Waldman (Eds.), *Cambridge handbook of violent behavior* (pp. 306–321). Cambridge: Cambridge University Press.

Flannery, D. J., Vazsonyi, A. T., & Waldman, I. D. (2007). *Cambridge handbook of violent behavior.* Cambridge: Cambridge University Press.

Fleisher, M. S. (1998). *Dead end kids: Gang girls and the boys they know.* Madison: University of Wisconsin Press.

Flores, A. W., Travis, L. F., & Latessa, E. (2003). *Case classification for juvenile corrections: An assessment of the Youth Level of Service/Case Management Inventory.* Cincinnati, OH: Center for Criminal Justice Research, University of Cincinnati.

Forst, M., Fagan, J., & Vivona, T. S. (1989). Youth in prisons and training schools: Perceptions and consequences of the treatment–custody dichotomy. *Juvenile and Family Court Journal, 39*(1), 1–14.

Fox, J. A. (1996a, October 10). The calm before the crime wave storm. *Los Angeles Times,* p. B9.

Fox, J. A. (1996b). *Trends in juvenile violence: A report to the United States attorney general on current and future rates of juvenile offending.* Washington, DC: Bureau of Justice Statistics.

Fox, S. J. (1970). Juvenile justice reform: A historical perspective. *Stanford Law Review, 22,* 1187–1239.

Freeman, R., Eber, L., Anderson, C., Irvin, L., Horner, R., Bounds, M., et al. (2006). Building inclusive school cultures using school-wide PBS: Designing effective individual support systems for students with significant disabilities. *Research and Practice for Persons With Severe Disabilities, 31,* 4–17.

Fritsch, E. J., Caeti, T. J., & Taylor, R. W. (2003). Gang suppression through saturation patrol and aggressive curfew and truancy enforcement: A quasi-experimental test of the Dallas Anti-Gang Initiative. In S. H. Decker (Ed.), *Policing gangs and youth violence* (pp. 267–284). Belmont, CA: Wadsworth/Thompson Learning.

Gambrill, E. (2006). Evidence based practice and policy: Choices ahead. *Research on Social Work Practice, 16,* 338–357.

Garascia, J. A. (2005). The price we are willing to pay for punitive justice in the juvenile detention system. *Indiana Law Journal, 80,* 489–515.

Gatti, U., Tremblay, R. E., Vitaro, F., & McDuff, P. (2005). Youth gangs, delinquency and drug use: A test of selection, facilitation, and enhancement hypotheses. *Journal of Child Psychology and Psychiatry, 46,* 1178–1190.

Gebo, E. (2005). Do family courts administer individualized justice in delinquency cases? *Criminal Justice Policy Review, 16,* 190–210.

Gendreau, P., & Andrews, D. (1996). *The correctional program assessment inventory* (6th ed.). Saint John: University of New Brunswick.

Gendreau, P., & Andrews, D. (2001). *The correctional program assessment inventory: 2000.* Saint John: University of New Brunswick.

Gendreau, P., Goggin, C., & Smith, P. (2001). Implementation guidelines for correctional programs in the "real world." In G. A. Bernfeld, D. P. Farrington, & A. W. Leschied (Eds.), *Offender rehabilitation in practice* (pp. 247–268). West Sussex, England: Wiley.

Gendreau, P., Smith, P., & French, S. A. (2006). The theory of effective correctional intervention with offenders: Empirical status and future directions. In F. T. Cullen, J. P. Wright, & K. R. Blevins (Eds.), *Taking stock: The status of criminological theory* (pp. 419–446). New Brunswick, NJ: Transaction.

Geraghty, T. F. (1997). Justice for children: How do we get there? *Journal of Criminal Law and Criminology, 88,* 190–241.

Gest, T., & Pope, V. (1996, March 25). Crime time bomb. *U.S. News & World Report,* pp. 29–36.

Giedd, J., Blumenthal, J., Jeffries, N., Castellanos, F., Liu, H., Zijdenbos, A., et al. (1999). Brain development during childhood and adolescence: A longitudinal MRI study. *Nature Neuroscience, 2,* 861–863.

Gilliam, W. S. (2005). *Prekindergarteners left behind: Expulsion rates in state prekindergartener programs.* New York: Foundation for Child Development.

Glass, G. V. (1976). Primary, secondary, and meta-analysis of research. *Educational Researcher, 5,* 3–8.

Glass, G. V., McGaw, B., & Smith, M. L. (1981). *Meta-analysis in social research.* Beverly Hills, CA: Sage.

Glaze, L. E., & Bonczar, T. P. (2006). *Probation and parole in the United States, 2005* (NCJ 215091). Washington, DC: U.S. Department of Justice, Bureau of Justice Statistics.

Goldstein, A. P., Glick, B., & Gibbs, J. C. (1998) *Aggression replacement training: A comprehensive intervention for aggressive youth* (Rev. ed.). Champaign, IL: Research Press.

Goldstein, H. (1979). Improving policing: A problem-oriented approach. *Crime and Delinquency, 25,* 236–258.

Gonzales, A. R. (2007, May 15). Prepared remarks of Attorney General Alberto R. Gonzales at the National Press Club on "Safer neighborhoods: A plan for partnership." Washington, DC: U.S. Department of Justice.

Goode, E., & Ben-Yehuda, N. (1994). *Moral panics: The social construction of deviance.* Cambridge, MA: Blackwell.

Goodnough, A. (2006, March 18). 2nd autopsy in youth boot camp death fails to end questions. *The New York Times.*

Gordon, R. A., Lahey, B. B., Kawai, E., Loeber, R., Stouthamer-Loeber, M., & Farrington, D. P. (2004). Antisocial behavior and youth gang membership: Selection and socialization. *Criminology, 42,* 55–88.

Gorman-Smith, D., & Loeber, R. (2005). Are developmental pathways in disruptive behaviors the same for girls and boys? *Journal of Child and Family Studies, 14,* 15–27.

Gottfredson, D. C. (2001). *Schools and delinquency.* New York: Cambridge University Press.

Gottfredson, D. C., Cross, A., & Soule, D. A. (2007). Distinguishing characteristics of effective and ineffective after-school programs to prevent delinquency and victimization. *Criminology and Public Policy, 6,* 289–318.

Gottfredson, D. C., Gerstenblith, S. A., Soule, D. A., Womer, S. C., & Lu, S. (2004). Do after school programs reduce delinquency? *Prevention Science, 5,* 253–266.

Gottfredson, D. C., & Gottfredson, G. D. (2002). Quality of school-based prevention programs. *Journal of Research in Crime and Delinquency, 39,* 3–35.

Gottfredson, D. C., & Soule, D. A. (2005). The timing of property crime, violent crime, and substance use among juveniles. *Journal of Research in Crime and Delinquency, 42,* 110–120.

Gottfredson, D. C., & Wilson, D. B. (2003). Characteristics of effective school-based substance abuse prevention. *Prevention Science, 4,* 27–38.

Gottfredson, D. C., Wilson, D. B., & Najaka, S. S. (2002a). School-based crime prevention. In L. W. Sherman, D. P. Farrington, B. C. Welsh, & D. L. MacKenzie (Eds.), *Evidence-based crime prevention* (pp. 56–164). London: Routledge.

Gottfredson, D. C., Wilson, D. B., & Najaka, S. S. (2002b). The schools. In J. Q. Wilson & J. Petersilia (Eds.), *Crime: Public policies for crime control* (pp. 149–189). Oakland, CA: Institute for Contemporary Studies Press.

Gottfredson, G. D. (1987). Peer group interventions to reduce the risk of delinquent behavior: A selective review and a new evaluation. *Criminology, 25,* 671–714.

Gottfredson, G. D., & Gottfredson, D. C. (2001). *Gang problems and gang programs in a national sample of schools.* Ellicott City, MD: Gottfredson Associates.

Gottfredson, G. D., & Gottfredson, D. C. (2007). School violence. In D. Flannery, A. Vazonsyi, & I. Waldman (Eds.), *Cambridge handbook of violent behavior* (pp. 344–358). Cambridge: Cambridge University Press.

Gottfredson, G. D., Gottfredson, D. C., Payne, A. A., & Gottfredson, N. C. (2005). School climate predictors of disorder: Results from a national study of delinquency prevention in schools. *Journal of Research in Crime and Delinquency, 42,* 412–444.

Gottfredson, M. R., & Hirschi, T. (1990). *A general theory of crime.* Stanford, CA: Stanford University.

Gottfredson, S. D., & Moriarty, L. J. (2006). Statistical risk assessment: Old problems and new applications. *Crime and Delinquency, 52,* 178–200.

Gover, A. R., MacKenzie, D. L., & Armstrong, G. S. (2000). Importation and deprivation explanations of juveniles' adjustment to correctional facilities. *International Journal of Offender Therapy and Comparative Criminology, 44,* 450–467.

Green, G. S., Carlson, P. M., & Colvin, R. E. (2004). Juvenile accountability and the specific deterrent effects of short-term confinement. *Juvenile and Family Court Journal, 55*(1), 63–69.

Greene, J. A. (1999). Zero tolerance: A case study of police policies and practices in New York City. *Crime and Delinquency, 45,* 171–187.

Greene, J. R. (2007). Make police oversight independent and transparent. *Criminology and Public Policy, 6,* 747–754.

Griffin, P. (2003). Trying and sentencing juveniles as adults: An analysis of state transfer and blended sentencing laws. *Special Project Bulletin.* Washington, DC: Office of Juvenile Justice and Delinquency Prevention.

Grisso, T. (1996). Society's retributive response to juvenile violence: A developmental perspective. *Law and Human Behavior, 20,* 229–247.

Grisso, T., & Schwartz, R. G. (Eds.). (2000). *Youth on trial: A developmental perspective on juvenile justice.* Chicago: University of Chicago Press.

Grisso, T., Steinberg, L., Woolard, J., Cauffman, E., Scott, E., Graham, S., et al. (2003). Juveniles' competence to stand trial: A comparison of adolescents' and adults' capacities as trial defendants. *Law and Human Behavior, 27,* 333–363.

Grisso, T., & Underwood, L. A. (2004). *Screening and assessing mental health and substance use disorders among youth in the juvenile justice system: A resource guide for practitioners.* Delmar, NY: National Center for Mental Health and Juvenile Justice, Policy Research Associates, Inc.

Grisso, T., Vincent, G., & Seagrave, D. (2005). *Mental health screening and assessment in juvenile justice.* New York: Guilford.

Grossman, D. C., Mueller, B. A., Riedy, C., Dowd, M. D., Villaveces, A., Prodzinski, J., et al. (2005). Gun storage practices and risk of youth suicide and unintentional firearm injuries. *Journal of the American Medical Association, 293,* 707–714.

Grossman, J. B., Price, M. L., Fellerath, V., Jucovy, L. Z., Kutloff, L. J., Raley, R., et al. (2002). *Multiple choices after school: Findings from the Extended-Service Schools Initiative.* New York: Wallace–Reader's Digest Fund.

Grove, W. M., Eckert, E. D., Heston, L., Bouchard, T. J., Segal, N., & Lykken, D. T. (1990). *Clinical vs. mechanical prediction: A meta-analysis.* Unpublished manuscript, University of Minnesota, Department of Psychology.

Grove, W. M., & Meehl, P. E. (1996). Comparative efficiency of informal (subjective, impressionistic) and formal (mechanical, algorithmic) prediction procedures: The clinical–statistical controversy. *Psychology, Public Policy, and Law, 2,* 293–323.

Gugliotta, G., & Leen, J. (1989). *Kings of cocaine.* New York: Simon & Schuster.

Haapanen, R. A., & Britton, L. (2002). Drug testing for youthful offenders on parole: An experimental evaluation. *Criminology and Public Policy, 1,* 217–243.

Hagan, J., & Foster, H. (2000). Making corporate and criminal America less violent: Public norms and structural reforms. *Contemporary Sociology, 29*(1), 44–53.

Hagan, J., & McCarthy, B. (1997). *Mean streets: Youth crime and homelessness.* Cambridge: Cambridge University Press.

Hahn, R. A., Bilukha, O., Crosby, A., Fullilove, M. T., Liberman, A., Moscicki, E., et al. (2005). Firearm laws and the reduction of violence. *American Journal of Preventive Medicine, 28,* 40–71.

Hahn, R. A., Fuqua-Whitley, D., Wethington, H., et al. (2007). Effectiveness of universal school based programs to prevent violent and aggressive behavior: A systematic review. *American Journal of Preventive Medicine, 33*(Supplement), S114–S129.

Hall, G. P., Thornberry, T. P., & Lizotte, A. J. (2006). The gang facilitation effect and neighborhood risk: Do gangs have a stronger influence on delinquency in disadvantaged areas? In J. F. Short & L. A. Hughes (Eds.), *Studying youth gangs* (pp. 47–62). Lanham, MD: AltaMira.

Hallfors, D. D., Cho, H., Sanchez, V., Khatapoush, S., Kim, H. M., & Bauer, D. (2006). Efficacy vs. effectiveness trial, results of an indicated "model" substance abuse program: Implications for public health. *American Journal of Public Health, 96,* 2254–2259.

Hallfors, D., & Godette, D. (2002). Will the "Principles of Effectiveness" improve prevention practice? Early findings from a diffusion study. *Health Education Research, 17,* 461–470.

Hammer, H., Finkelhor, D., & Sedlak, A. (2002). *Runaway/thrownaway children: National estimates and characteristics.* Washington, DC: Office of Juvenile Justice and Delinquency Prevention.

Hamparian, D. M., Schuster, R., Dinitz, S., & Conrad, J. P. (1978). *The violent few: A study of dangerous juvenile offenders.* Lexington, MA: Lexington.

Harcourt, B. E. (2001). *Illusion of order: The false promise of broken window policing.* Cambridge, MA: Harvard University Press.

Harcourt, B. E., & Ludwig, J. (2006). Broken windows: New evidence from New York City and a five-city social experiment. *University of Chicago Law Review, 73,* 271–320.

Harris, K., & Cheatwood, D. (1997). *The geography of execution: The capital punishment quagmire in America.* Lanham, MD: Rowman & Littlefield

Harris, G. T., Rice, M. E., & Quinsey, V. L. (1998). Appraisal and management of risk in sexual aggressors: Implications for criminal justice policy. *Psychology, Public Policy, and Law, 4,* 73–115.

Harrison, P. M., & Beck, A. J. (2006). *Prisoners in 2005. Bulletin.* Washington, DC: U.S. Department of Justice, Bureau of Justice Statistics.

Hartman, D. A., & Golub, A. (1999). The social construction of the crack epidemic in the print media. *Journal of Psychoactive Drugs, 31,* 423–433.

Hawkins, D. F., & Kempf-Leonard, K. E. (2005). *Our children, their children: Confronting racial and ethnic differences in American juvenile justice.* Chicago: University of Chicago Press.

Hawkins, J. D. (1999). Preventing crime and violence through Communities That Care. *European Journal on Crime Policy and Research, 7,* 443–458.

Hawkins, J. D., Catalano, R. F., & Arthur, M. W. (2002). Promoting science-based prevention in communities. *Addictive Behaviors, 27,* 951–976.

Hawkins, J. D., Herrenkohl, T. I., Farrington, D. P., Brewer, D. D., Catalano, R. F., & Harachi, T. W. (1998). A review of predictors of youth violence. In R. Loeber & D. P. Farrington (Eds.), *Serious and violent juvenile offenders: Risk factors and successful interventions* (pp. 106–146). Thousand Oaks, CA: Sage.

Hawkins, J. D., & Weis, J. G. (1985). The social development model: An integrated approach to delinquency prevention. *Journal of Primary Prevention, 6,* 73–97.

Hayes, M., McReynolds, L. S., Wasserman, G. A., & Haxton, W. (2005). Comparison of the MAYSI-2's Paper and Voice Formats. *Assessment, 12,* 395–403.

Henggeler, S. W. (1997). The development of effective drug abuse services for youth. In J. A. Egertson, D. M. Fox, &

A. I. Leshner (Eds.), *Treating drug abusers effectively* (pp. 253–279). New York: Basil Blackwell.

Henggeler, S. W., Pickrel, S. G., & Brondino, M. J. (1999). Multisystemic treatment of substance abusing and dependent delinquents: Outcomes, treatment fidelity, and transportability. *Mental Health Services Research, 1,* 171–184.

Henggeler, S. W., & Schoenwald, S. K. (1994). Boot camps for juvenile offenders: Just say "no." *Journal of Child and Family Studies, 3,* 243–248.

Henggeler, S. W., Schoenwald, S. K., Borduin, C. M., Rowland, M. D., & Cunningham, P. B. (1998). *Multisystemic treatment of antisocial behavior in children and adolescents.* New York: Guilford.

Henggeler, S. W., Schoenwald, S. K., Borduin, C. M., & Swenson, C. C. (2006). Methodological critique and meta-analysis as Trojan horse. *Children and Youth Services Review, 28,* 447–457.

Henry, R. (2007, June 17). Critics: Zero tolerance makes zero sense. *The News & Observer,* p. 11A.

Herbert, B. (2007a, April 9). 6-year-olds under arrest. *New York Times.* Retrieved January 13, 2008, from http://select.nytimes.com/2007/04/09/opinion/09herbert.html

Herbert, B. (2007b, June 9). School to prison pipeline. *New York Times.* Retrieved January 13, 2008, from http://select.nytimes.com/2007/06/09/opinion/09herbert.html

Hickman, M. J. (2006). *Citizen complaints about police use of force. Special report.* Washington, DC: Bureau of Justice Statistics.

Hill, K. G., Howell, J. C., Hawkins, J. D., & Battin-Pearson, S. R. (1999). Childhood risk factors for adolescent gang membership: Results from the Seattle Social Development Project. *Journal of Research in Crime and Delinquency, 36,* 300–322.

Hill, K. G., Lui, C., & Hawkins, J. D. (2001). Early precursors of gang membership: A study of Seattle youth. *Juvenile Justice Bulletin.* Washington, DC: U.S. Department of Justice, Office of Juvenile Justice and Delinquency Prevention.

Hindelang, M. J., Hirschi, T., & Weis, J. (1981). *Measuring delinquency.* Beverly Hills, CA: Sage.

Hipwell, A. E., Loeber, R., Stouthamer-Loeber, M., Keenan, K., White, H. R., & Kroneman, L. (2002). Characteristics of girls with early onset of disruptive and antisocial behavior. *Criminal Behavior and Mental Health, 12,* 99–118.

Hipwell, A. E., Pardini, D. A., Loeber, R., Sembower, M. A., Keenan, K., & Stouthamer-Loeber, M. (2007). Callous–unemotional behaviors in young girls: Shared and unique effects relative to conduct problems. *Journal of Clinical Child and Adolescent Psychology, 36,* 293–304.

Hipwell, A. E., White, H. R., Loeber, R., Stouthamer-Loeber, M., Chung, T., & Sembower, M. A. (2005). Young girls' expectancies about the effects of alcohol, future intentions and patterns of use. *Journal of Studies on Alcohol, 66,* 630–639.

Holman, B., & Ziedenberg, J. (2006). *The dangers of detention: The impact of incarcerating youth in detention and other secure facilities.* Washington, DC: Justice Policy Institute.

Howell, J. C. (Ed.). (1995). *Guide for implementing the Comprehensive Strategy for Serious, Violent, and Chronic Juvenile Offenders.* Washington, DC: Office of Juvenile Justice and Delinquency Prevention.

Howell, J. C. (1996). Juvenile transfers to the criminal justice system: State-of-the-art. *Law and Policy, 18,* 17–60.

Howell, J. C. (1997). *Juvenile justice and youth violence.* Thousand Oaks, CA: Sage.

Howell, J. C. (1998a, February–March). Abolish the juvenile court? Nonsense! *Juvenile Justice Update,* pp. 1–2, 10–13.

Howell, J. C. (1998b). Promising programs for youth gang violence prevention and intervention. In R. Loeber & D. P. Farrington (Eds.), *Serious and violent juvenile offenders: Risk factors and successful interventions* (pp. 284–312). Thousand Oaks, CA: Sage.

Howell, J. C. (1998c, March-April). Superpredators and the prophets of doom. *Youth Today,* p. 50.

Howell, J. C. (1998d). Youth gangs: An overview. *Juvenile Justice Bulletin,* Youth Gang Series. Washington, DC: Office of Juvenile Justice and Delinquency Prevention.

Howell, J. C. (1999). Youth gang homicides: A literature review. *Crime & Delinquency, 45,* 208–241.

Howell, J. C. (2000). *Youth gang programs and strategies.* Washington, DC: Office of Juvenile Justice and Delinquency Prevention.

Howell, J. C. (2003a). Diffusing research into practice using the Comprehensive Strategy for Serious, Violent, and Chronic Juvenile Offenders. *Youth Violence and Juvenile Justice: An Interdisciplinary Journal, 1,* 219–245.

Howell, J. C. (2003b). *Preventing and reducing juvenile delinquency: A comprehensive framework.* Thousand Oaks, CA: Sage.

Howell, J. C. (2006). *The impact of gangs on communities.* NYGC Bulletin No. 2. Tallahassee, FL: National Youth Gang Center.

Howell, J. C. (2007). Menacing or mimicking? Realities of youth gangs. *The Juvenile and Family Court Journal, 58,* 9–20.

Howell, J. C., & Curry, G. D. (2005). *Mobilizing communities to address gang problems.* Tallahassee, FL: National Youth Gang Center.

Howell, J. C., Curry, G. D., Pontius, M., & Roush, D. W. (2003). *National survey of youth gang problems in juvenile detention facilities.* East Lansing: Michigan State University, National Juvenile Detention Association, Center for Research and Professional Development.

Howell, J. C., & Decker, S. H. (1999). The youth gangs, drugs, and violence connection. *Juvenile Justice Bulletin,* Youth Gang Series. Washington, DC: Office of Juvenile Justice and Delinquency Prevention.

Howell, J. C., & Egley, A. Jr. (2005a). *Gangs in small towns and rural counties.* NYGC Bulletin No. 1. Tallahassee, FL: National Youth Gang Center.

Howell, J. C., & Egley, A. Jr. (2005b). Moving risk factors into developmental theories of gang membership. *Youth Violence and Juvenile Justice, 3,* 334–354.

Howell, J. C., Egley, A. Jr., & Gleason, D. K. (2000, November). *Youth gangs: Definitions and the age-old issue.* Paper presented at the annual meeting of the American Society of Criminology, San Francisco.

Howell, J. C., Egley, A. Jr., & Gleason, D. K. (2002). Modern day youth gangs. *Juvenile Justice Bulletin,* Youth Gang Series. Washington, DC: Office of Juvenile Justice and Delinquency Prevention.

Howell, J. C., & Gleason, D. K. (1999). Youth gang drug trafficking. *Juvenile Justice Bulletin,* Youth Gang Series. Washington, DC: Office of Juvenile Justice and Delinquency Prevention.

Howell, J. C., & Howell, M. Q. (2007). Violent juvenile delinquency: Changes, consequences, and implications. In D. Flannery, A. Vazonsyi, & I. Waldman (Eds.), *Cambridge handbook of violent behavior* (pp. 501–518). Cambridge: Cambridge University Press.

Howell, J. C., Kelly, M. R., Palmer, J., & Mangum, R. L. (2004). Integrating child welfare, juvenile justice and other agencies in a continuum of services for children, youth and families. *Child Welfare, 83,* 143–156.

Howell, J. C., & Lipsey, M. W. (2004a). A practical approach to evaluating and improving juvenile justice programs. *Juvenile and Family Court Journal, 55,* 35–48.

Howell, J. C., & Lipsey, M. W. (2004b). A practical approach to linking graduated sanctions with a continuum of effective programs. *Juvenile Sanctions Center Training and Technical Assistance Program Bulletin, 2*(1), 1–10. Reno, NV: National Council of Juvenile and Family Court Judges.

Howell, J. C., & Lynch, J. (2000). Youth gangs in schools. *Juvenile Justice Bulletin,* Youth Gang Series. Washington, DC: Office of Juvenile Justice and Delinquency Prevention.

Howell, J. C., Moore, J. P., & Egley, A. Jr. (2002). The changing boundaries of youth gangs. In C. R. Huff (Ed.), *Gangs in America* (3rd ed., pp. 3–18). Thousand Oaks, CA: Sage.

Hoyt, D. R., Ryan, K. D., & Cauce, A. M. (1999). Personal victimization in a high-risk environment: Homeless and runaway adolescents. *Journal of Research in Crime and Delinquency, 36,* 371–392.

Hsia, H. M., & Beyer, M. (2000). System change through state challenge activities: Approaches and products. *Juvenile Justice Bulletin.* Washington, DC: Office of Juvenile Justice and Delinquency Prevention.

Hughes, T., & Wilson, D. J. 2002. *Reentry trends in the United States.* Washington, DC: Bureau of Justice Statistics, U.S. Department of Justice.

Huizinga, D., Esbensen, F., & Weiher, A. W. (1996). The impact of arrest on subsequent delinquent behavior. In R. Loeber, D. Huizinga, & T. P. Thornberry (Eds.), *Program of Research on the Causes and Correlates of Delinquency: Annual report 1995–1996* (pp. 82–101). Washington, DC: Office of Juvenile Justice and Delinquency Prevention.

Huizinga, D., & Jakob-Chien, C. (1998). The contemporaneous co-occurrence of serious and violent offending and other problem behavior. In R. Loeber & D. P. Farrington (Eds.), *Serious and violent juvenile offenders: Risk factors and successful interventions* (pp. 46–67). Thousand Oaks, CA: Sage.

Huizinga, D., Loeber, R., & Thornberry, T. P. (1994). *Urban delinquency and substance abuse: Initial findings report.*

Washington, DC: Office of Juvenile Justice and Delinquency Prevention.

Huizinga, D., Loeber, R., & Thornberry, T. P. (1995). *Recent findings from the Program of Research on Causes and Correlates of Delinquency.* Washington, DC: Office of Juvenile Justice and Delinquency Prevention.

Huizinga, D., Loeber, R., Thornberry, T. P., & Cothern, L. (2000). Co-occurrence of delinquency and other problem behaviors. *Juvenile Justice Bulletin.* Washington, DC: Office of Juvenile Justice and Delinquency Prevention.

Huizinga, D., & Schumann, K. F. (2001). Gang membership in Bremen and Denver: Comparative longitudinal data. In M. W. Klein, H.-J. Kerner, C. L. Maxson, & E. G. M. Weitekamp (Eds.), *The Eurogang paradox: Street gangs and youth groups in the U.S. and Europe* (pp. 231–246). Amsterdam: Kluwer.

Huizinga, D., Weiher, A. W., Espiritu, R., & Esbensen, F. (2003). Delinquency and crime: Some highlights from the Denver Youth Survey. In T. P. Thornberry & M. D. Krohn (Eds.), *Taking stock of delinquency: An overview of findings from contemporary longitudinal studies* (pp. 47–91). New York: Kluwer Academic/ Plenum.

Human Rights Watch. (1999). *No minor matter: Children in Maryland's jails.* New York: Author.

Human Rights Watch. (2000). *United States—Punishment and prejudice: Racial disparities in the war on drugs.* New York: Author.

Human Rights Watch. (2005). *The rest of their lives: Life without parole for child offenders in the United States.* New York: Human Rights Watch/Amnesty International.

Hunzeker, D. (1995, May). Juvenile crime, grown up time. *State Legislatures,* pp. 15–19.

Hutson, H. R., Anglin, D., & Mallon, W. (1992). Injuries and deaths from gang violence: They are preventable. *Annals of Emergency Medicine, 21,* 1234–1236.

Hutzler, J. (1982). Cannon to the left, cannon to the right: Can the juvenile court survive? *Today's Delinquent, 1,* 25–38.

Hyman, I. A. & Perone, D. C. (1998). The other side of school violence: Educator policies and practices that may contribute to student misbehavior. *Journal of School Psychology, 30,* 7–27.

Hyman, I. A., & Snook, P. A. (1999). *Dangerous schools: What we can do about the physical and emotional abuse of our children.* Indianapolis: Jossey-Bass.

Institute of Medicine. (1990). *A study of the evolution, effectiveness, and financing of public and private drug treatment systems.* Washington, DC: National Academy Press.

Institute of Medicine. (1994). *Reducing risks for mental disorders: Frontier for preventive intervention research.* Washington, DC: National Academy Press.

International Association of Chiefs of Police. (2000). *A measured response to crime: IACP's call for a national commission.* Alexandria, VA: Author.

Ireland, T. O., Smith, C. A., & Thornberry, T. P. (2002). Developmental issues in the impact of child maltreatment on later delinquency and drug use. *Criminology, 40,* 359–400.

Irwin, J. (2005). *The warehouse prison: Disposal of the new dangerous class.* Los Angeles: Roxbury.

Irwin, K. (2004). The violence of adolescent life: Experiencing and managing everyday threats. *Youth and Society, 35,* 452–479.

Jackson, P. G., & Rudman, C. (1993). Moral panic and the response to gangs in California. In S. Cummings & D. J. Monti (Eds.), *Gangs: The origins and impact of contemporary youth gangs in the United States* (pp. 257–275). Albany: State University of New York Press.

Jang, S. J., & Johnson, B. R. (2001). Neighborhood disorder, individual religiosity, and adolescent use of illicit drugs: A test of multilevel hypotheses. *Criminology, 39,* 109–144.

Jessor, R., Donovan, J. E., & Costa, F. M. (1991). *Beyond adolescence: Problem behavior and young adult development.* Cambridge: Cambridge University Press.

Johnson, B. R., Li, S. D., Larson, D. B., & McCullough, M. (2000). A systematic review of the religiosity and delinquency literature. *Journal of Contemporary Criminal Justice, 16,* 32–52.

Johnson, K. (2006a, July 13). Cities grapple with crime by kids: Offenders as young as 10 showing up; special units targeting juveniles. *USA Today,* p. A3.

Johnson, K. (2006b, July 13). Police tie jump in crime to juveniles: Gangs, guns, add up to increased violence. *USA Today,* p. A1.

Johnson, K. (2007, December 18). Police brutality cases up 25%. *USA Today,* p. A1.

Johnson, K. (2008, January 8). Murder down 6.5% in big cities. *USA Today,* p. A1.

Johnson, K., Wagner, D., & Matthews, T. (2001). *Missouri juvenile risk assessment re-validation report.* Madison, WI: National Council on Crime and Delinquency.

Johnson, S. C. (2005, April 29). *North American youth gangs: Patterns and remedies.* Testimony before the U.S. House of Representatives, Subcommittee on the Western Hemisphere. Washington, DC: Heritage Foundation.

Johnston, L. D., Bachman, J. G., & O'Malley, P. M. (1995). *Monitoring the future.* Ann Arbor: University of Michigan, Institute for Social Research.

Johnston, L. D., O'Malley, P. M., Bachman, J. G., & Schulenberg, J. E. (2006). *Monitoring the future: National survey results on drug use, 1975–2005: Volume I, Secondary school students.* (NIH Publication No. 06-5883). Bethesda, MD: National Institute on Drug Abuse.

Jones, P. R., & Wyant, B. R. (2007). Target juvenile needs to reduce delinquency. *Criminology and Public Policy, 6,* 763–772.

Josi, D., & Sechrest, D. K. (1999). A pragmatic approach to parole aftercare: Evaluation of a community reintegration program for high-risk youthful offenders. *Justice Quarterly, 16,* 51–80.

Justice Policy Institute. (2007). *The consequences aren't minor: The impact of trying youth as adults and strategies for reform.* Washington, DC: Author.

Juvenile Justice Center. (2004). *Adolescence, brain development, and legal culpability.* Washington, DC: Juvenile Justice Center, American Bar Association.

Kalb, L. M., Farrington, D. P., & Loeber, R. (2001). Leading longitudinal studies on delinquency, substance use, sexual behavior, and mental health problems with childhood samples. In R. Loeber & D. P. Farrington (Eds.), *Child delinquents: Development, intervention, and service needs* (pp. 415–423). Thousand Oaks, CA: Sage.

Kalb, L. M., & Loeber, R. (2003). Child disobedience and noncompliance: A review. *Pediatrics, 111,* 641.

Kamradt, B. (2000). Wraparound Milwaukee: Aiding youth with mental health needs. *Juvenile Justice, 7*(1), 14–23.

Katner, D. R. (2002). A defense perspective of treatment programs for juvenile sex offenders. *Juvenile Correctional Mental Health Report, 2*(2), 17–30.

Katz, C. M., Webb, V. J., & Schaefer, D. R. (2000). The validity of police gang intelligence lists: Examining differences in delinquency between documented gang members and nondocumented delinquent youth. *Police Quarterly, 3*(4), 413–437.

Katz, J., & Jackson-Jacobs, C. (2004). The criminologists' gang. In C. Sumner (Ed.), *The Blackwell companion to criminology* (pp. 91–124). Malden, MA: Blackwell.

Katz, L. R. (1970). Gideon's trumpet: Mournful and muffled. *Criminal Law Bulletin, 6,* 529–576.

Kaufman, J. G., & Widom, C. S. (1999). Childhood victimization, running away, and delinquency. *Journal of Research in Crime and Delinquency, 36,* 347–370.

Keenan, K. (2001). Uncovering preschool precursor problem behaviors. In R. Loeber & D. P. Farrington (Eds.), *Child delinquents: Development, intervention, and service needs* (pp. 117–134). Thousand Oaks, CA: Sage.

Kelley, B. T., Huizinga, D., Thornberry, T. P., & Loeber, R. (1997). Epidemiology of serious violence. *Juvenile Justice Bulletin.* Washington, DC: Office of Juvenile Justice and Delinquency Prevention.

Kelling, G. L., & Coles, C. M. (1996). *Fixing broken windows: Restoring order and reducing crime in our communities.* New York: Free Press.

Kempf-Leonard, K., & Johansson, P. (2007). Gender and runaways: Risk factors, delinquency, and juvenile justice experiences. *Youth Violence and Juvenile Justice, 5,* 308–327.

Kempf-Leonard, K., & Tracy, P. E. (2000). The gender effect among serious, violent, and chronic offenders: A difference in degree rather than kind. In R. Muraskin (Ed.), *It's a crime: Women and justice* (pp. 453–478). Upper Saddle River, NJ: Prentice Hall.

Kempf-Leonard, K., Tracy, P. E., & Howell, J. C. (2001). Serious, violent, and chronic juvenile offenders: The relationship of delinquency career types to adult criminality. *Justice Quarterly, 18,* 449–478.

Kennedy, D. M. (1999, July). Pulling levers: Getting deterrence right. *National Institute of Justice Journal, 236,* 2–8.

Kennedy, D. M. (2007). *Going to scale: A national structure for building on proved approaches to preventing gang violence. A discussion document.* New York: Center for Crime Prevention and Control, John Jay College of Criminal Justice.

Kennedy, D. M., Piehl, A. M., & Braga, A. A. (1996). Youth violence in Boston: Gun markets, serious youth offenders, and a use-reduction strategy. *Law and Contemporary Problems, 59,* 147–196.

Kent, D. R., Donaldson, S. I., Wyrick, P. A., & Smith, P. J. (2000). Evaluating criminal justice programs designed to reduce crime by targeting repeat gang offenders. *Evaluation and Program Planning, 23,* 115–124.

Klein, M. W. (1971). *Street gangs and street workers.* Englewood Cliffs, NJ: Prentice Hall.

Klein, M. W. (1995). *The American street gang.* New York: Oxford University Press.

Klein, M. W. (2004). *Gang cop: The words and ways of office Paco Domingo.* Walnut Creek, CA: Alta Mira.

Klein, M. W., & Maxson, C. L. (1989). Street gang violence. In M. E. Wolfgang & N. A. Weiner (Eds.), *Violent crime, violent criminals* (pp. 198–234). Newbury Park, CA: Sage.

Klein, M. W., & Maxson, C. L. (2006). *Street gang patterns and policies.* New York: Oxford University Press.

Knitzer, J. (1982). *Unclaimed children: The failure of public responsibility to children and adolescents in need of mental health services.* Washington, DC: The Children's Defense Fund.

Knitzer, J., & Cooper, J.. (2006). Beyond integration: Challenges for children's mental health. *Health Affairs, 25,* 670–679.

Kortenkamp, K., & Ehrle, J. (2002). The well-being of children involved with the child welfare system: A national overview. *Juvenile and Family Justice Today, 11*(2), 20–25.

Kovacs, M. (1996). Presentation and course of major depressive disorder during childhood and later years of the life span. *Journal of the American Academy of Child and Adolescent Psychiatry, 35,* 705–715.

Kovandzic, T. V., Sloan, J. J., & Vieraitis, L. M. (2002). Unintended consequences of politically popular sentencing policy: The homicide-promoting effects of "three strikes" in U.S. cities (1980–1999). *Criminology and Public Policy, 1,* 399–424.

Krajicek, D. J. (2000, February). Boot camps get a kick in the head. *Youth Today,* p. A2.

Krisberg, B., Currie, E., Onek, D., & Wiebush, R. G. (1995). Graduated sanctions for serious, violent, and chronic juvenile offenders. In J. C. Howell, B. Krisberg, J. D. Hawkins, & J. J. Wilson (Eds.), *A sourcebook: Serious, violent, and chronic juvenile offenders* (pp. 142–170). Thousand Oaks, CA: Sage.

Krisberg, B., & Howell, J. C. (1998). The impact of the juvenile justice system and prospects for graduated sanctions in a comprehensive strategy. In R. Loeber & D. P. Farrington (Eds.), *Serious and violent juvenile offenders: Risk factors and successful interventions* (pp. 346–366). Thousand Oaks, CA: Sage.

Krisberg, B., & Marchionna, S. (2007, February). Attitudes of US voters toward youth crime and the justice system. *Focus: Views from the National Council of Crime and Delinquency.* Retrieved July 19, 2008, from the NCCD Web site: http://www.nccd-crc.org/nccd/pubs/zogby_feb07.pdf

Krisberg, B., Neuenfeldt, D., Wiebush, R. G., & Rodriguez, O. (1994). *Juvenile intensive supervision: Planning guide.* Washington, DC: Office of Juvenile Justice and Delinquency Prevention.

Krohn, M. D., Lizotte, A. J., Thornberry, T. P., Smith, C. A., & McDowall, D. (1996). Reciprocal causal relationships among drug use, peers, and beliefs: A five-wave panel model. *Journal of Drug Issues, 26,* 405–428.

Krohn, M. D., Thornberry, T. P., Rivera, C., & Le Blanc, M. (2001). Later careers of very young offenders. In R. Loeber & D. P. Farrington (Eds.), *Child delinquents: Development, intervention, and service needs* (pp. 67–94). Thousand Oaks, CA: Sage.

Krug, E. G., Dahlberg, L. L., Mercy, J. A., Zwi, A. B., & Lozano, R. (2002). *World report on violence and health.* Geneva, Switzerland: World Health Organization.

Kupchik, A. (2006a). *Judging juveniles: Prosecuting adolescents in adult and juvenile courts.* New York: New York University Press.

Kupchik, A. (2006b). The decision to incarcerate in juvenile and criminal courts. *Criminal Justice Review, 31,* 309–336.

Kurlychek, M. C., & Johnson, B. D. (2004). The juvenile penalty: A comparison of juvenile and young adult sentencing outcomes in criminal court. *Criminology, 42,* 485–517.

Kutash, K., Duchnowski, A. J., & Lynn, N. (2006). *School-based mental health: An empirical guide for decision-makers.* Tampa: University of South Florida, the Louis de la Parte Florida Mental Health Institute, Department of Child & Family Studies, Research and Training Center for Children's Mental Health.

Lacourse, E., Nagin, D. S., Vitaro, F., Cote, S., Arseneault, L., & Tremblay, R. E. (2006). Prediction of early-onset deviant peer group affiliation. *Archives of General Psychiatry, 63,* 562–568.

LaFree, G. D. (1980). The effect of sexual stratification by race on official reactions to rape. *American Sociological Review, 45,* 842–854.

Lahey, B. B., Gordon, R. A., Loeber, R., Stouthamer Loeber, M., & Farrington, D. P. (1999). Boys who join gangs: A prospective study of predictors of first gang entry. *Journal of Abnormal Child Psychology, 27,* 261–276.

Landenberger, N., & Lipsey, M. W. (2005). The positive effects of cognitive–behavioral programs or offenders: A meta-analysis of factors associated with effective treatment. *Journal of Experimental Criminology, 1,* 451–476.

Lane, J., & Meeker, J. W. (2000). Subcultural diversity and the fear of crime and gangs. *Crime & Delinquency, 46,* 497–521.

Langan, P. A., & Levin, D. J. (2002). *Recidivism of prisoners released in 1994* (Special Report). Washington, DC: Bureau of Justice Statistics.

Lattimore, P. K., Macdonald, J. M., Piquero, A. R., Linster, R. L., & Visher, C. A. (2004). Studying the characteristics of arrest frequency among paroled youthful offenders. *Journal of Research in Crime and Delinquency, 41,* 37–57.

Laub, J. H., & Lauritsen, J. L. (1998). The interdependence of school violence with neighborhood and family conditions. In D. S. Elliott, B. A. Hamburg, & K. R. Williams (Eds.), *Violence in American schools: A new perspective* (pp. 127–155). Cambridge: Cambridge University Press.

Lauritsen, J. L. (2003). How families and communities influence youth victimization. *Juvenile Justice Bulletin.* Washington, DC: U.S. Department of Justice, Office of Juvenile Justice and Delinquency Prevention.

Lauritsen, J. L., & Quinet, K. F. D. (1995). Repeat victimization among adolescents and young adults. *Journal of Quantitative Criminology, 11,* 143–166.

Lauritsen, J. L., & White, N. A. (2001). Putting violence in its place: The influence of ethnicity, gender, and place on the risk for violence. *Criminology and Public Policy, 1,* 37–60.

Lawrence, R., & Mueller, D. (2003). School shootings and the man-bites-dog criterion of newsworthiness. *Youth Violence and Juvenile Justice, 1,* 330–345.

Leahy, J. (2007). HPD's missing weapons tally is now 35: It's almost twice what was reported in April review of property room. *Houston Chronicle,* June 23, B3.

Le Blanc, M. (1998). Serious, violent, and chronic juvenile offenders: Identification, classification, and prediction. In R. Loeber & D. P. Farrington (Eds.), *Serious and violent juvenile offenders: Risk factors and successful interventions* (pp. 167–193). Thousand Oaks, CA: Sage.

Le Blanc, M., & Loeber, R. (1993). Precursors, causes and the development of criminal offending. In D. F. Hay & A. Angold (Eds.), *Precursors and causes in development and psychopathology* (pp. 233–263). New York: Wiley.

Le Blanc, M., & Loeber, R. (1998). Developmental criminology updated. In M. Tonry (Ed.), *Crime and justice: An annual review of research* (Vol. 23, pp. 115–198). Chicago: University of Chicago Press.

LeCroy, C. W., Krysik, J., & Palumbo, D. (1998). *Empirical validation of the Arizona Risk/Needs Instrument and assessment process.* Tucson: LeCroy & Milligan Associates.

Leffert, N., Saito, R. N., Blyth, D. A., & Kroenke, C. H. (1996). *Making the case: Measuring the impact of youth development programs.* Minneapolis: Search Institute.

Leiber, M. J. (2002). Disproportionate minority confinement (DMC) of youth: An analysis of state and federal efforts to address the issue. *Crime & Delinquency, 48,* 3–45.

Leinwand, D. (2000, February 25). LAPD, neighborhood shaken. *USA Today,* p. 3A.

Lemert, E. M. (1951). *Social pathology: Human deviance, social problems, and social control.* New York: McGraw-Hill.

Lerman, P. (2002). Twentieth-century developments in America's institutional systems for youth in trouble. In M. K. Rosenheim, F. E. Zimring, D. S. Tanenhaus, & B. Dohrn (Eds.), *A century of juvenile justice* (pp. 4–109). Chicago: University of Chicago Press.

Lerman, P., & Pottick, K. J. (1995). *The parents' perspective: Delinquency, aggression, and mental health.* Chur, Switzerland: Harwood.

Lewis, D. O., Pincus, J. H., Bard, B., Richardson, E., Prichep, L. S., Feldman, M., et al. (1988). Neuropsychiatric, psychoeducational, and family characteristics of 14 juveniles condemned to death in the United States. *American Journal of Psychiatry, 145,* 585–589.

Liebman, J. S., Fagan, J., & West, V. (2000). *A broken system: Error rates in capital cases, 1973–1995.* New York: Columbia University, School of Law.

Lien, I.-J. (2005). The role of crime acts in constituting the gang's mentality. In S. H. Decker & F. M. Weerman (Eds.), *European street gangs and troublesome youth groups* (pp. 105–125). Lanham, MD: AltaMira.

Lipsey, M. W. (1992). Juvenile delinquency treatment: A meta-analytic inquiry into the variability of effects. In T. D. Cook, H. Cooper, D. S. Cordray, H. Hartman, L. V. Hedges, R. J. Light, et al. (Eds.), *Meta-analysis for explanation* (pp. 83–127). New York: Russell Sage Foundation.

Lipsey, M. W. (1995). What do we learn from 400 research studies on the effectiveness of treatment with juvenile delinquents? In J. McGuire (Ed.), *What works: Reducing reoffending* (pp. 63–78). New York: Wiley.

Lipsey, M. W. (1999a). Can intervention rehabilitate serious delinquents? *Annals of the American Academy of Political and Social Science, 564,* 142–166.

Lipsey, M. W. (1999b). Can rehabilitative programs reduce the recidivism of juvenile offenders? An inquiry into the effectiveness of practical programs. *Virginia Journal of Social Policy and the Law, 6,* 611–641.

Lipsey, M. W. (2000a). Meta-analysis and the learning curve in evaluation practice. *American Journal of Evaluation, 21,* 207–212.

Lipsey, M. W. (2000b, July). *What 500 intervention studies show about the effects of intervention on the recidivism of juvenile offenders.* Paper presented at the Annual Conference on Criminal Justice Research and Evaluation, Washington, DC.

Lipsey, M. W. (2002). Meta-analysis and program outcome evaluation. *Socialvetenskaplig Tidskrift, 9,* 194–208.

Lipsey, M. W. (2005). The challenges of interpreting research for use by practitioners: Comments on the latest products from the Task Force on Community Preventive Services. *American Journal of Preventive Medicine, 28*(2S1), 1–3.

Lipsey, M. W. (2006). *The evidence base for effective juvenile programs as a source for best practice guidelines.* Nashville, TN: Vanderbilt University, Center for Evaluation Research and Methodology.

Lipsey, M. W. (2007). *A standardized program evaluation protocol for programs serving juvenile probationers.* Nashville, TN: Vanderbilt University, Center for Evaluation Research and Methodology.

Lipsey, M. W. (2008). *The Arizona Standardized Program Evaluation Protocol (SPEP) for assessing the effectiveness of programs for juvenile probationers: SPEP ratings and relative recidivism reduction for the initial SPEP sample.* Nashville, TN: Vanderbilt University, Center for Evaluation Research and Methodology.

Lipsey, M. W., & Cullen, F. T. (2007). The effectiveness of correctional rehabilitation: A review of systematic reviews. *Annual Review of Law and Social Science, 3,* 297–320.

Lipsey, M. W., & Derzon, J. H. (1998). Predictors of violent or serious delinquency in adolescence and early adulthood: A synthesis of longitudinal research. In R. Loeber & D. P. Farrington (Eds.), *Serious and violent juvenile offenders: Risk factors and successful interventions* (pp. 86–105). Thousand Oaks, CA: Sage.

Lipsey, M. W., Howell, J. C., & Tidd, S. T. (2003). *A standardized program evaluation protocol for North Carolina's juvenile justice system programs.* Nashville, TN: Vanderbilt University, Center for Evaluation Research and Methodology.

Lipsey, M. W., Howell, J. C., & Tidd, S. T. (2007a). *A practical approach to evaluating and improving juvenile justice programs utilizing the Standardized Program Evaluation Protocol (SPEP): An interim report.* Nashville, TN: Vanderbilt University, Center for Evaluation Research and Methodology.

Lipsey, M. W., Howell, J. C., & Tidd, S. T. (2007b). *The Standardized Program Evaluation Protocol (SPEP): A practical approach to evaluating and improving juvenile justice programs in North Carolina.* Final Evaluation Report. Nashville, TN: Vanderbilt University, Center for Evaluation Research and Methodology.

Lipsey, M. W., & Landenberger, N. A. (2006). Cognitive–behavioral interventions. In B. C. Welsh & D. P. Farrington (Eds.), *Preventing crime: What works for children, offenders, victims, and places* (pp. 57–71). Belmont, CA: Wadsworth.

Lipsey, M. W., & Wilson, D. B. (1993). The efficacy of psychological, educational, and behavioral treatment: Confirmation from meta-analysis. *American Psychologist, 48,* 1181–1209.

Lipsey, M. W., & Wilson, D. B. (1998). Effective interventions with serious juvenile offenders: A synthesis of research. In R. Loeber & D. P. Farrington (Eds.), *Serious and violent juvenile offenders: Risk factors and successful interventions* (pp. 313–345). Thousand Oaks, CA: Sage.

Lipsey, M. W., & Wilson, D. B. (2000). *Practical meta-analysis.* Thousand Oaks, CA: Sage.

Lipsey, M. W., & Wilson, D. B. (2001). The way in which intervention studies have "personality" and why it is important to meta-analysis. *Evaluation and the Health Professions, 24,* 236–254.

Lipsey, M. W., Wilson, D. B., & Cothern, L. (2000). Effective interventions for serious and violent juvenile offenders. *Juvenile Justice Bulletin.* Washington, DC: Office of Juvenile Justice and Delinquency Prevention.

Lipton, D., Martinson, R., & Wilks, J. (1975). *The effectiveness of correctional treatment: A survey of treatment evaluation studies.* New York: Praeger.

Littell, J. H. (2006). The case for multisystemic therapy: Evidence or orthodoxy? *Children and Youth Services Review, 28,* 459–472.

Lizotte, A. J., Krohn, M. D., Howell, J. C., Tobin, K., & Howard, G. J. (2000). Factors influencing gun carrying among young urban males over the adolescent–young adult life course. *Criminology, 38,* 811–834.

Loeber, R. (1988). Natural histories of juvenile conduct problems, delinquency, and associated substance abuse: Evidence for developmental progressions. In B. B. Lahey & A. E. Kazdin (Eds.), *Advances in clinical child psychology* (Vol. 11, pp. 73–124). New York: Plenum.

Loeber, R. (1990). Development and risk factors of juvenile antisocial behavior and delinquency. *Clinical Psychology Review, 10,* 1–41.

Loeber, R., Burke, J. D., Lahey, B. B., Winters, A., & Zera, M. (2000). Oppositional defiant and conduct disorder: A review of the past 10 years, part I. *Journal of the American Academy of Child and Adolescent Psychiatry, 39,* 1–17.

Loeber, R., DeLamatre, M., Tita, G., Stouthamer-Loeber, M., & Farrington, D. P. (1999). Gun injury and mortality: The delinquent backgrounds of juvenile victims. *Violence and Victims, 14,* 339–352.

Loeber, R., & Farrington, D. P. (Eds.). (1998). *Serious and violent juvenile offenders: Risk factors and successful interventions.* Thousand Oaks, CA: Sage.

Loeber, R., & Farrington, D. P. (2000). Young children who commit crime: Epidemiology, developmental origins, risk factors, early interventions, and policy implications. *Development and Psychopathology, 12,* 737–762.

Loeber, R., & Farrington, D. P. (Eds.). (2001a). *Child delinquents: Development, intervention, and service needs.* Thousand Oaks, CA: Sage.

Loeber, R., & Farrington, D. P. (2001b). Executive summary. In R. Loeber & D. P. Farrington (Eds.), *Child delinquents: Development, intervention, and service needs* (pp. xix–xxxi). Thousand Oaks, CA: Sage.

Loeber, R., & Farrington, D. P. (2001c). The significance of child delinquency. In R. Loeber & D. P. Farrington (Eds.), *Child delinquents: Development, intervention, and service needs* (pp. 1–22). Thousand Oaks, CA: Sage.

Loeber, R., Farrington, D. P., & Petechuk, D. (2003). Child delinquency: Early intervention and prevention. *Juvenile Justice Bulletin.* Washington, DC: U.S. Department of Justice, Office of Juvenile Justice and Delinquency Prevention.

Loeber, R., Farrington, D. P., Stouthamer-Loeber, M., Moffitt, T. E., Caspi, A., White, H. R., et al. (2003). The development of male offending: Key findings from fourteen years of the Pittsburgh Youth Study. In T. P. Thornberry & M. D. Krohn (Eds.), *Taking stock of delinquency: An overview of findings from contemporary longitudinal studies* (pp. 93–136). New York: Kluwer Academic/Plenum.

Loeber, R., Farrington, D. P., Stouthamer-Loeber, M., & Van Kammen, W. B. (1998). *Antisocial behavior and mental health problems.* Mahwah, NJ: Erlbaum.

Loeber, R., Farrington, D. P., Stouthamer-Loeber, M., & White, H. R. (2008). *Violence and serious theft: Development and prediction from childhood to adulthood.* New York: Routledge.

Loeber, R., & Hay, D. F. (1997). Key issues in the development of aggression and violence from childhood to early adulthood. *Annual Review of Psychology, 48,* 371–410.

Loeber, R., Kalb, L., & Huizinga, D. (2001). Juvenile delinquency and serious injury victimization. *Juvenile Justice Bulletin.* Washington, DC: Office of Juvenile Justice and Delinquency Prevention.

Loeber, R., Keenan, K., & Zhang, Q. (1997). Boys' experimentation and persistence in developmental pathways toward serious delinquency. *Journal of Child and Family Studies, 6,* 321–357.

Loeber, R., & Le Blanc, M. (1990). Toward a developmental criminology. In M. Tonry & N. Morris (Eds.), *Crime and justice: An annual review of research* (Vol. 12, pp. 375–473). Chicago: University of Chicago Press.

Loeber, R., Slot, W., & Stouthamer-Loeber, M. (2007). A cumulative, three-dimensional, development model of serious delinquency. In P.-O. Wikstrom & R. Sampson (Eds.), *The explanation of crime: Context, mechanisms and development series* (pp. 153–194). Cambridge: Cambridge University Press.

Loeber, R., & Stouthamer-Loeber, M. (1996). The development of offending. *Criminal Justice and Behavior, 23,* 12–24.

Loeber, R., Wei, E., Stouthamer-Loeber, M., Huizinga, D., & Thornberry, T. P. (1999). Behavioral antecedents to serious and violent offending: Joint analyses from the Denver Youth Survey, Pittsburgh Youth Study and the Rochester Youth Development Study. *Studies on Crime and Crime Prevention, 8,* 245–263.

Loeber, R., Wung, P., Keenan, K., Giroux, B., Stouthamer-Loeber, M., Van Kammen, W. B., et al. (1993). Developmental pathways in disruptive child behavior. *Development and Psychopathology, 5,* 103–133.

Logan, W. A. (1998). Proportionality and punishment: Imposing life without parole on juveniles. *Wake Forest Law Review, 33,* 681–725.

Lovell, D., Johnson, L. C., & Cain, K. C. (2007). Recidivism of supermax prisoners in Washington State. *Crime & Delinquency, 53,* 633–656.

Lowenkamp, C. T., Latessa, E. J., & Smith, P. (2006). Does correctional program quality really matter? The impact of adhering to the principles of effective intervention. *Criminology and Public Policy, 5,* 575–594.

Lubitz, R. (2001). *Strategies to reduce commitments to youth development centers.* Raleigh: North Carolina Department of Juvenile Justice and Delinquency Prevention.

Ludwig, J. (2005). Better gun enforcement, less crime. *Criminology and Public Policy, 4,* 677–716.

Lynch, J. P. (2002). *Trends in juvenile violent offending: An analysis of victim survey data.* Washington, DC: Office of Juvenile Justice and Delinquency Prevention.

Lynch, J. P., & Sabol, W. J. (1997). *Did getting tough on crime pay?* Washington, DC: Urban Institute.

Lyons, D. (1997, May). Juvenile justice comes of age. *State Legislatures,* pp. 12–18.

Lyons, W., & Drew, J. (2006). *Punishing schools: Fear and citizenship in American public education.* Ann Arbor: University of Michigan Press.

MacDonald, J. M., & Gover, A. R. (2005). Concentrated disadvantage and youth-on-youth homicide. *Homicide Studies, 9,* 30–54.

MacKenzie, D. L. (2006). *What works in corrections: Reducing the criminal activities of offenders and delinquents.* New York: Cambridge University Press.

MacKenzie, D. L., Wilson, D. B., Armstrong, G. S., & Gover, A. R. (2001). The impact of boot camps and traditional institutions on juvenile residents: Perceptions, adjustment, and changes in social bonds, impulsivity, and antisocial attitudes. *Journal of Research in Crime and Delinquency, 38,* 279–313.

Maguire, K., & Pastore, A. L. (Eds.). (1995). *Sourcebook of criminal justice statistics: 1994.* Washington, DC: Bureau of Justice Statistics.

Malcolm, J. L. (2002). *Guns and violence: The English experience.* Cambridge, MA: Harvard University Press.

Males, M. A. (1996). *The scapegoat generation: America's war on adolescents.* Monroe, ME: Common Courage.

Males, M. A., & Macallair, D. (1998). *The impact of juvenile curfew laws in California.* San Francisco: Justice Policy Institute, Center on Juvenile and Criminal Justice.

Manhattan Institute, Center for Civic Innovation. (1999). *"Broken windows" probation: The next step in fighting crime.* New York: Author.

Mankey, J., Baca, P., Rondenell, B. S., Webb, M., & McHugh, D. (2006). *Guidelines for juvenile information sharing.* Washington, DC: U.S. Department of Justice, Office of Juvenile Justice and Delinquency Prevention.

Mann, C. R. (1993). *Unequal justice: A question of color.* Bloomington: Indiana University Press.

Manning, P. K. (2003). *Policing contingencies.* Chicago: University of Chicago Press.

Manning, P. K. (2005). Problem-oriented policing: Editorial introduction. *Criminology & Public Policy, 4,* 149–154.

Martin, J., Nada-Raja, S., Langley, J., Freehan, M., McGee, R., Clarke, J., et al. (1998). Physical assault in New Zealand: The experience of 21 year old men and women in a community sample. *New Zealand Medical Journal, 111,* 158–160.

Martinson, R. (1974). What works? Questions and answers about prison reform. *Public Interest, 35,* 22–54.

Matthews, B., Hubbard, D. J., & Latessa, E. (2001). Making the next step: Using evaluability assessment to improve correctional programming. *Prison Journal, 8,* 454–472.

Mauer, M. (1997). *Intended and unintended consequences: State racial disparities in imprisonment.* Washington, DC: Sentencing Project.

Mauer, M., & Meda, C. E. (2003). *Invisible punishment: The collateral consequences of mass imprisonment.* New York: The New Press.

Maxson, C. L. (1998). Gang members on the move. *Juvenile Justice Bulletin,* Youth Gang Series. Washington, DC: Office of Juvenile Justice and Delinquency Prevention.

Maxson, C. L., Curry, G. D., & Howell, J. C. (2002). Youth gang homicides in the United States in the 1990s. In S. Decker & W. Reed (Eds.), *Responses to gangs: Evaluation and research* (pp. 111–137). Washington, DC: National Institute of Justice.

Maxson, C. L., Whitlock, M. L., & Klein, M. W. (1998). Vulnerability to street gang membership: Implications for prevention. *Social Service Review, 72,* 70–91.

Maxwell, S. R., & Davis, J. S. (1999). The salience of race and gender in pretrial release decisions: A comparison across multiple jurisdictions. *Criminal Justice Policy Review, 10,* 491–501.

McBride, A. G., Scott, R., Schlesinger, S. R., Dillingham, S. D., & Buckman, R. B. (1992). *Combatting violent crime: 24 recommendations to strengthen criminal justice.* Washington, DC: Office of the Attorney General, U.S. Department of Justice.

McCollum, B. (1997, March 20). *Statement by Crime Subcommittee chairman Bill McCollum for hearing on reforming juvenile justice in America.* Washington, DC: U.S. Government Printing Office.

McCord, J., & Conway, P. K. (2005). *Co-offending and patterns of juvenile crime.* (Research in Brief). Washington, DC: National Institute of Justice, U.S. Department of Justice.

McCord, J., Widom, C. S., & Crowell, N. A. (Eds.). (2001). *Juvenile crime, juvenile justice.* Washington, DC: National Academy Press.

McCorkle, R. C., & Miethe, T. D. (2002). *Panic: The social construction of the street gang problem.* Upper Saddle River, NJ: Prentice Hall.

McDonald, D. C., & Carlson, K. E. (1992). *Federal sentencing in transition, 1986–90.* Washington, DC: Bureau of Justice Statistics.

McDowall, D., Loftin, C., & Wiersema, B. (2000). The impact of youth curfew laws on juvenile crime rates. *Crime and Delinquency, 46,* 76–91.

McGarvey, E. L., & Waite, D. (2000). *Profiles of incarcerated adolescents in Virginia correctional facilities: Fiscal years 1993–1998.* Richmond: Virginia Department of Criminal Justice Services.

McGloin, J. M. (2005). Policy and intervention considerations of a network analysis of street gangs. *Criminology and Public Policy, 4,* 607–636.

McGowan, A., Hahn, R., Liberman, A., Crosby, A., Fullilove, M., Johnson, R., et al. (2007). Effects on violence of laws and policies facilitating the transfer of juveniles from the juvenile justice system to the adult justice system: A systematic review. *American Journal of Preventive Medicine, 32*(4 Suppl. 1), 7–21.

McGuire, C. (2007). *Working paper on Central American youth gangs in the Washington D.C. area.* Washington, DC: Washington Office on Latin America.

McGuire, J. (2002). Integrating findings from research reviews. In J. McGuire (Ed.), *Offender rehabilitation and treatment: Effective programmes and policies to reduce offending.* West Sussex, UK: Wiley.

McReynolds, L. S., Wasserman, G. A., DeComo, R. E., John, R., Keating, J. M., & Nolen, S. (2008). Psychiatric disorder in a juvenile assessment center. *Crime and Delinquency, 54,* 313–334.

Mears, D. P. (2000). Assessing the effectiveness of juvenile justice reforms: A closer look at the criteria and the impacts on various stakeholders. *Law and Policy, 22,* 175–202.

Mears, D. P. (2001). Getting tough with juvenile offenders: Explaining support for sanctioning juveniles as adults. *Criminal Justice and Behavior, 28,* 206–226.

Mears, D. P. (2002). Sentencing guidelines and the transformation of juvenile justice in the 21st century. *Journal of Contemporary Criminal Justice, 18,* 6–19.

Mears, D. P. (2003). A critique of waiver research: Critical next steps in assessing the impacts of laws for transferring juveniles to the criminal justice system. *Youth Violence and Juvenile Justice, 1,* 156–172.

Mears, D. P. (2005). A critical look at supermax prisons. *Corrections Compendium, 30,* 6–7, 45–49.

Mears, D. P. (2006). Exploring state-level variation in juvenile incarceration rates: Symbolic threats and competing explanations. *The Prison Journal, 86,* 470–490.

Mears, D. P. (2008). Accountability, efficiency, and effectiveness in corrections: Shining a light on the black box of prison systems. *Criminology and Public Policy, 7*, 143–152.

Mears, D. P., & Castro, J. L. (2006). Wardens' views on the wisdom of supermax prisons. *Crime and Delinquency, 52*, 398–431.

Mears, D. P., & Travis, J. (2004). Youth development and reentry. *Youth Violence and Juvenile Justice, 2*, 3–20.

Menard, S. (2002). Short- and long-term consequences of adolescent victimization. *Youth Violence Research Bulletin.* Washington, DC: Office of Juvenile Justice and Delinquency Prevention and Centers for Disease Control and Prevention.

Mendel, R. A. (2007). *Pathways to juvenile detention reform: Vol. 14. Beyond detention: System transformation through juvenile detention reform.* Baltimore, MD: Annie E. Casey Foundation.

Mihalic, S., & Irwin, K. (2003). Blueprints for violence prevention: From research to real-world settings: Factors influencing the successful replication of model programs. *Youth Violence and Juvenile Justice, 1*, 307–329.

Mihalic, S., Irwin, K., Elliott, D., Fagan, A., & Hansen, D. (2001). Blueprints for violence prevention. *Juvenile Justice Bulletin.* Washington, DC: Office of Juvenile Justice and Delinquency Prevention.

Miller, J. A. (2001). *One of the guys: Girls, gangs and gender.* New York: Oxford University Press.

Miller, J., Ross, T., & Sturgis, C. (2005). *Beyond the tunnel problem: Addressing cross-cutting issues that impact vulnerable youth. Briefing paper #2. Redirecting youth from the school-to-prison pipeline.* Baltimore, MD: Youth Transition Funders Group and the Annie E. Casey Foundation.

Miller, W. B. (1992). *Crime by youth gangs and groups in the United States.* Washington, DC: Office of Juvenile Justice and Delinquency Prevention.

Miller, W. B. (2001). *The growth of youth gang problems in the United States: 1970–1998.* Washington, DC: Office of Juvenile Justice and Delinquency Prevention.

Moffitt, T. E. (1993). Adolescence-limited and life-course–persistent antisocial behavior: A developmental taxonomy. *Psychological Review, 100*, 674–701.

Moffitt, T. E. (2007). A review of research on the taxonomy of life-course–persistent versus adolescent-limited antisocial behavior. In D. Flannery, A. Vazonsyi, & I. Waldman (Eds.), *Cambridge handbook of violent behavior* (pp. 49–74). Cambridge: Cambridge University Press.

Moffitt, T. E., Caspi, A., Rutter, M., & Silva, P. A. (2001). *Sex differences in antisocial behavior: Conduct disorder, delinquency, and violence in the Dunedin longitudinal study.* New York: Cambridge University Press.

Moon, M. M., Sundt, J. L., Cullen, F. T., & Wright, J. P. (2000). Is child saving dead? Public support for juvenile rehabilitation. *Crime & Delinquency, 46*, 38–60.

Moone, J. (1994). *Juvenile victimization: 1987–1992* (Fact Sheet No. 1994-17). Washington, DC: Office of Juvenile Justice and Delinquency Prevention.

Moore, E. A. (2000). Sentencing opinion: *People of the State of Michigan v. Nathaniel Abraham. Juvenile and Family Court Journal, 51*(2), 1–11.

Moore, J. W. (1978). *Homeboys: Gangs, drugs and prison in the barrios of Los Angeles.* Philadelphia: Temple University Press.

Moore, J. W. (1991). *Going down to the barrio: Homeboys and homegirls in change.* Philadelphia: Temple University Press.

Moore, J. W. (1998). Understanding youth street gangs: Economic restructuring and the urban underclass. In M. W. Watts (Ed.), *Cross-cultural perspectives on youth and violence* (pp. 65–78). Stamford, CT: JAI.

Moore, J. W., & Hagedorn, J. M. (2001). Female gangs. *Juvenile Justice Bulletin,* Youth Gang Series. Washington, DC: Office of Juvenile Justice and Delinquency Prevention.

Moore, M. T. (2005). Murders on rise in Philadelphia. *USA Today,* p. 3A.

Moore, M. T. (2007, June 18). Should kids go to court in chains? *USA Today,* pp. A1–2.

Moore, S. (2007, September 30). Reporting while black. *New York Times,* p. WK 4.

Morash, M. (1983). Gangs, groups, and delinquency. *British Journal of Criminology, 23*, 309–335.

Morenoff, J. D., Sampson, R. J., & Raudenbush, S. W. (2001). Neighborhood inequality, collective efficacy, and the spatial dynamics of urban violence. *Criminology, 39*, 517–559.

Myers, D. L. (2003). The recidivism of violent youths in juvenile and adult court. *Youth Violence and Juvenile Justice, 1*, 79–101.

Myers, D. L., & Kiehl, K. (2001). The predispositional status of violent youthful offenders: Is there a "custody gap" in adult criminal court? *Justice Research and Policy, 3*, 115–143.

Naber, P. A., May, D. C., Decker, S. H., Minor, K. I., & Wells, J. B. (2006). Are there gangs in schools? Depends on whom you ask. *Journal of School Violence, 5*, 53–72.

Nagin, D. S., & Land, K. C. (1993). Age, criminal careers, and population heterogeneity: Specification and estimation of nonparametric, mixed Poisson model. *Criminology, 31*, 327–362.

Nagin, D. S., Piquero, A. R., Scott, E. S., & Steinberg, L. (2006). Public preferences for rehabilitation versus incarceration of juvenile offenders: Evidence from a contingent valuation study. *Criminology and Public Policy, 5*, 627–652.

National Association for the Advancement of Colored People, Legal Defense and Educational Fund. (2006). *The school-to-prison pipeline: Racial segregation.* Baltimore, MD: Author.

National Center for Education Statistics. (1997). *Principal/school disciplinarian survey on school violence, Fast Response Survey System* (FRSS No. 63). Washington, DC: Author.

National Center for Education Statistics. (2007). *Indicators of school crime and safety: 2007.* Washington, DC: Author.

National Council of Juvenile and Family Court Judges. (1998). *The Janiculum Project: Structural, procedural and programmatic recommendations for the future juvenile court.* Reno, NV: Author.

National Council of Juvenile and Family Court Judges. (2005). *Juvenile delinquency guidelines.* Reno, NV: Author.

National District Attorneys Association. (2000). *Resource manual and policy positions on juvenile crime issues.* Alexandria, VA: Author.

National Institute of Justice. (2006). *Drug courts: The second decade.* Washington, DC: Author.

National Research Council & Institute of Medicine. (2002). *Community programs to promote youth development.* Washington, DC: National Academy Press.

National Youth Gang Center. (2002a). *A guide to assessing your community's youth gang problem.* Tallahassee, FL: Author.

National Youth Gang Center. (2002b). *Planning for implementation.* Tallahassee, FL: Author.

North Carolina Child Advocacy Institute. (2005). *One out of ten: The growing suspension crisis in North Carolina.* Raleigh: Author.

North Carolina Department of Juvenile Justice and Delinquency Prevention. (2008a). *2007 annual report.* Raleigh: Author.

North Carolina Department of Juvenile Justice and Delinquency Prevention. (2008b). *Report on the treatment staffing model at youth development centers.* Raleigh: Author.

Nugent, W., Williams, M., & Umbreit, M. (2004). Participation in victim–offender mediation and the prevalence of subsequent delinquent behavior: A meta-analysis. *Research on Social Work Practice, 14,* 408–416.

Obeidallah, D. A., & Earls, F. J. (1999). *Adolescent girls: The role of depression in the development of delinquency* (Research Preview). Washington, DC: National Institute of Justice.

Office of Special Education Programs Center on Positive Behavioral Interventions and Supports. (2004). *School-wide positive behavior support: Implementers' blueprint and self-assessment.* Eugene: Center on Positive Behavioral Interventions and Supports, University of Oregon.

Olson, D. E., & Dooley, B. (2006). Gang membership and community corrections populations: Characteristics and recidivism rates relative to other offenders. In J. F. Short & L. A. Hughes (Eds.), *Studying youth gangs* (pp. 193–202). Lanham, MD: AltaMira.

Olweus, D. (1991). Bully/victim problems among schoolchildren: Basic facts and effects of a school based intervention. In D. J. Pepler & K. H. Rubin (Eds.), *The development and treatment of childhood aggression* (pp. 441–448). Hillsdale, NJ: Erlbaum.

Osgood, D. W., & Anderson, A. L. (2004). Unstructured socializing and rates of delinquency. *Criminology, 42,* 519–550.

Osher, D., Dwyer, K., & Jackson, S. (2004). *Safe, supportive and successful schools: Step by step.* Longmont, CO: Sopris West.

Palmer, T. (1992). *The re-emergence of correctional intervention.* Newbury Park, CA: Sage.

Papachristos, A. V. (2001). *A.D., after the Disciples: The neighborhood impact of federal gang prosecution.* Peotone, IL: New Chicago Schools Press.

Papachristos, A. V., Meares, T., & Fagan, J. (2005). *Attention felons: Evaluating Project Safe Neighborhoods in Chicago.* Chicago: The Law School, University of Chicago.

Parent, D., Leiter, V., Livens, L., Wentworth, D., & Stephen, K. (1994). *Conditions of confinement: Juvenile detention and corrections facilities.* Washington, DC: Office of Juvenile Justice and Delinquency Prevention.

Patterson, G. R., Capaldi, D., & Bank, L. (1991). An early starter model for predicting delinquency. In D. J. Pepler & K. H. Rubin (Eds.), *The development and treatment of childhood aggression* (pp. 139–168). Hillsdale, NJ: Erlbaum.

Payne, A. A., Gottfredson, D. C., & Gottfredson, G. D. (2003). Schools as communities: The relationships among communal school organization, student bonding and school disorder. *Criminology, 41,* 749–778.

Petersilia, J. (1983). *Racial disparities in the criminal justice system* (Paper prepared for the National Institute of Corrections). Santa Monica, CA: RAND.

Petersilia, J. (2001). When prisoners return to communities: Political, economic, and social consequences. *Federal Probation, 65*(1), 3–8.

Petersilia, J. (2003). *When prisoners come home: Parole and prisoner reentry.* New York: Oxford University Press.

Petersilia, J., & Turner, S. (1985). *Guidelines-based justice: The implications for racial minorities.* Santa Monica, CA: RAND.

Peterson, D., Miller, J., & Esbensen, F. (2001). The impact of sex composition on gangs and gang delinquency. *Criminology, 39,* 411–439.

Peterson, D., Taylor, T. J., & Esbensen, F. (2004). Gang membership and violent victimization. *Justice Quarterly, 21*(4), 793–815.

Petrosino, A. (2005). From Martinson to meta-analysis: Research reviews and the U.S. offender treatment debate. *Evaluation and Policy, 1,* 149–171.

Petrosino, A., & Soydan, H. (2005). The impact of program developers as evaluators on criminal recidivism: Results from meta-analyses of experimental and quasi-experimental research. *Journal of Experimental Criminology, 1,* 435–450.

Petrosino, A., Turpin-Petrosino, C., & Finckenauer, J. (2000). Well-meaning programs can have harmful effects! Lessons from experiments of programs such as Scared Straight. *Crime and Delinquency, 46,* 354–379.

Pew Charitable Trusts. (2008). *One in 100: Behind bars in America 2008.* Washington, DC: Author.

Phoenix Police Department. (1981). *Hispanic gangs in Phoenix.* Phoenix: Author.

Pindur, W., & Elliker, J. (1999). *Norfolk Juvenile Justice Recidivism Evaluation Project.* Norfolk, VA: Old Dominion University.

Pizarrro, J. M., Chermak, S. M., & Gruenewald, J. A. (2007). Juvenile "super-predators" in the news: A comparison of adult and juvenile homicides. *Journal of Criminal Justice and Popular Culture, 14*, 84–111.

Pogarsky, G., Lizotte, A. J., & Thornberry, T. P. (2003). The delinquency of children born to young mothers: Results from the Rochester Youth Development Study. *Criminology, 41*(4), 1249–1286.

Police Executive Research Forum. (2006). *Chief concerns: A gathering storm—Violent crime in America.* Washington, DC: Author.

Police Executive Research Forum. (2007). *Violent crime in America: 24 months of alarming trends.* Washington, DC: Author.

Pope, C. E., & Feyerherm, W. H. (1990). Minority status and juvenile justice processing (2 parts). *Criminal Justice Abstracts, 22*, 327–336, 527–542.

Pope, C. E., & Feyerherm, W. H. (1991). *Minorities in the juvenile justice system.* Washington, DC: Office of Juvenile Justice and Delinquency Prevention.

Pratt, T. C. (2008). Rational choice theory, crime control pol icy, and criminological relevance. *Criminology and Public Policy, 7*, 43–52.

Prentky, R., & Righthand, S. (2003). *Juvenile Sex Offender Assessment Protocol II (J-SOAP-II) manual.* Washington, DC: U.S. Department of Justice, Office of Juvenile Justice and Delinquency Prevention.

Pullmann, M. D., Kerbs, J., Koroloff, N., Veach-White, E., Gaylor, R., & Sieler, D. (2006). Juvenile offenders with mental health needs: Reducing recidivism using wraparound. *Crime and Delinquency, 52*, 375–397.

Puritz, P., & Scali, M. A. (1998). *Beyond the walls: Improving conditions of confinement for youth in custody.* Washington, DC: U.S. Department of Justice, Office of Juvenile Justice and Delinquency Prevention.

Puzzanchera, C., Stahl, A. L., Finnegan, T. A., Tierney, N., & Snyder, H. N. (2003). *Juvenile court statistics: 1998.* Washington, DC: U.S. Department of Justice, Office of Juvenile Justice and Delinquency Prevention.

Radelet, M. L. (1989). Executions of whites for crimes against blacks: Exceptions to the rule? *Sociological Quarterly, 30*, 529–544.

Redondo, S., Sanchez-Meca, J., & Garrido, V. (1999). The influence of treatment programmes on the recidivism of juvenile and adult offenders: A European meta-analytic review. *Psychology, Crime, and Law, 5*, 251–278.

Re-Entry Policy Council. (2005). *Report of the Re-Entry Policy Council.* Lexington, KY: Council of State Governments.

Reeves, J. L., & Campbell, R. (1994). *Cracked coverage: Television news, the anti-cocaine crusade, and the Reagan legacy.* Durham, NC: Duke University Press.

Regnery, A. S. (1986). A federal perspective on juvenile justice reform. *Crime & Delinquency, 32*, 39–51.

Reich, K., Culross, P. L., & Behrman, R. E. (2002). Children, youth and gun violence: Analysis and recommendations. *Future of Children, 12*(2), 5–19.

Reiss, A. J. Jr. (1988). Co-offending and criminal careers. In M. Tonry & N. Morris (Eds.), *Crime and justice: An annual review of research* (Vol. 10, pp. 117–170). Chicago: University of Chicago Press.

Renouf, A. G., & Harter, S. (1990). Low self-worth and anger as components of the depressive experience in young adolescents. *Development and Psychopathology, 2*, 293–310.

Reppucci, N. D. (1999). Adolescent development and juvenile justice. *American Journal of Community Psychology, 27*, 307–326.

Resnick, M. D., Ireland, M., & Borowsky, I. (2004). Youth violence perpetration: What protects? What predicts? Findings from the National Longitudinal Study of Adolescent Health. *Journal of Adolescent Health, 35*, 424.e1–424.e10.

Ribando, C. (2005). *Gangs in Central America.* Washington, DC: Congressional Research Service, Library of Congress.

Richart, D., Brooks, K., & Soler, M. (2003). *Unintended consequences: The impact of "zero tolerance" and other exclusionary policies on Kentucky students.* Washington, DC: Building Blocks for Youth.

Rigby, K. (2004). Addressing bullying in schools. *School Psychology International, 25*, 287–300.

Righthand, S., & Welch, C. (2001). *Juveniles who have sexually offended. A review of the professional literature.* Washington, DC: U.S. Department of Justice, Office of Juvenile Justice and Delinquency Prevention.

Roberts, A., & Bender, K. (2006). Overcoming Sisyphus: Effective prediction of mental health disorders and recidivism among delinquents. *Federal Probation, Special Issue: Risk Assessment, 70*(September), 19–28.

Roberts, J. V. (1992). Public opinion, crime, and criminal justice. In M. H. Tonry (Ed.), *Crime and justice: A review of research* (Vol. 16, pp. 99–180). Chicago: University of Chicago Press.

Roberts, P. G., & Stratton, L. M. (2000). *The tyranny of good intentions: How prosecutors and bureaucrats are trampling the Constitution in the name of justice.* Roseville, CA: Forum.

Robinson, D. A., & Stephens, O. H. (1992). Patterns of mitigating factors in juvenile death penalty cases. *Criminal Law Bulletin, 28*, 246–275.

Romano, E., Tremblay, R. E., Vitaro, F., Zoccolillo, M., & Pagani, L. (2001). Prevalence of psychiatric diagnoses and the role of perceived impairment: Findings from an adolescent community sample. *Journal of Child Psychology and Psychiatry, 42*, 451–461.

Rosenbaum, D. P. (2007). Just say no to D.A.R.E. *Criminology and Public Policy, 6*, 815–824.

Rosenberg, I. M. (1993). Leaving bad enough alone: A response to the juvenile court abolitionists. *Wisconsin Law Review, 1993*(1), 163–185.

Rosenfeld, R., Fornango, R., & Baumer, E. (2005). Did Ceasefire, Compstat, and Exile reduce homicide? *Criminology and Public Policy, 4*, 419–449.

Roush, D. W. (1996a). *Desktop guide to good juvenile detention practice.* Washington, DC: U.S. Department of

Justice, Office of Juvenile Justice and Delinquency Prevention.

Roush, D. W. (1996b). A juvenile justice perspective. In C. M. Nelson, R. B. Rutherford, & B. I. Wolford (Eds.), *Comprehensive and collaborative systems that work for troubled youth: A national agenda* (pp. 29–60). Richmond, KY: National Juvenile Detention Association.

Roush, D. W., & McMillen, M. (2000). Construction, operations, and staff training for juvenile confinement facilities. *Juvenile Accountability Incentive Block Grants Program Bulletin*. Washington, DC: Office of Juvenile Justice and Delinquency Prevention.

Roush, D. W., Miesner, L. D., & Winslow, C. M. (2002). *Managing youth gang members in juvenile detention facilities*. East Lansing: Center for Research and Professional Development, National Juvenile Detention Association, School of Criminal Justice, Michigan State University.

Roush, D. W., Moeser, J., & Walsh, T. (2005). Reentry and removal: Implications for juvenile confinement facilities. *Juvenile and Family Court Journal, 56*, 1–23.

Roy, S. (1995). Juvenile offenders in an electronic home detention program: A study on factors related to failure. *Journal of Offender Monitoring, 8*, 9–17.

Roy, S. (1997). Five years of electronic monitoring of adults and juveniles in Lake County, Indiana. *Journal of Crime and Justice, 20*, 141–160.

Roy, S., & Brown, M. 1995. Juvenile electronic monitoring program in Lake County, Indiana: An evaluation. In J. Smykla & W. Selke (Eds.), *Intermediate sanctions: Sentencing in the 1990s* (pp. 21–35). Cincinnati, OH: Anderson.

Rubak, S., Sandbaek, A., Lauritzen, T., & Christensen, B. (2005). Motivational interviewing: A systematic review and meta-analysis. *British Journal of General Practice, 55*, 305–312.

Rubin, H. T. (2000). Teen Quest: Female-specific program services for Colorado's delinquent girls. *Juvenile Justice Update, 6*(3), 1–16.

Rubin, H. T. (2001, December–January). Georgia Department of Juvenile Justice moves forward by moving back to the community. *Juvenile Justice Update*, pp. 1–2, 14–16.

Rutter, M., Giller, H., & Hagell, A. (1998). *Antisocial behavior by young people*. New York: Cambridge University Press.

Sabol, W. J., Minton, T. D., & Harrison, P. M. (2007). *Prison and jail inmates at midyear 2006*. Bulletin. Washington, DC: U.S. Department of Justice, Bureau of Justice Statistics.

Sampson, R. J. (2002). The community. In J. Petersilia & J. Q. Wilson (Eds.), *Crime: Public policies for crime control* (pp. 225–252). Oakland, CA: Institute for Contemporary Studies Press.

Sampson, R. J., & Groves, W. B. (1989). Community structure and crime: Testing social-disorganization theory. *American Journal of Sociology, 94*, 774–802.

Sampson, R. J., & Laub, J. H. (1993). *Crime in the making: Pathways and turning points through life*. Cambridge, MA: Harvard University Press.

Sampson, R. J., & Laub, J. H. (1997). A life-course theory of cumulative disadvantage and the stability of delinquency. In T. P. Thornberry (Ed.), *Developmental theories of crime and delinquency* (Vol. 7). New Brunswick, NJ: Transaction.

Sampson, R. J., & Lauritsen, J. L. (1997). Racial and ethnic disparities in crime and criminal justice in the United States. In M. Tonry (Ed.), *Ethnicity, crime, and immigration: Comparative and cross-national perspectives* (pp. 311–374). Chicago: University of Chicago Press.

Sampson, R. J., & Raudenbush, S. W. (2001). *Disorder in urban neighborhoods: Does it lead to crime?* Washington, DC: National Institute of Justice.

Sampson, R. J., Raudenbush, S. W., & Earls, F. (1997). Neighborhoods and violent crime: A multilevel study of collective efficacy. *Science, 277*, 918–924.

Sanday, P. R. (1990). *Fraternity gang rape: Sex, brotherhood, and privilege on campus*. New York: New York University Press.

Sarri, R., Shook, J. J., Ward, G., Creekmore, M., Albertson, C., Goodkind, S., et al. (2001). *Decision making in the juvenile justice system: A comparative study in four states*. Washington, DC: National Institute of Justice.

Schlosser, E. (1998, December). The prison-industrial complex. *Atlantic Monthly, 282*, 51–77.

Schmidt, F. L. (1992). What do data really mean? Research findings, meta-analysis, and cumulative knowledge in psychology. *American Psychologist, 47*, 1173–1179.

Schneider, A. L. (1990). *Deterrence and juvenile crime: Results from a national policy experiment*. New York: Springer-Verlag.

Schneider, A. L., & Ervin, L. (1990). Specific deterrence, rational choice, and decision heuristics: Applications in juvenile justice. *Social Science Quarterly, 71*, 585–601.

Schram, P. J., & Gaines, L. K. (2005). Examining delinquent nongang members and delinquent gang members: A comparison of juvenile probationers at intake and outcomes. *Youth Violence and Juvenile Justice, 3*(2), 99–115.

Schumacher, M., & Kurz, G. (2000). *The 8% solution: Preventing serious, repeat juvenile crime*. Thousand Oaks, CA: Sage.

Schwartz, I. M. (1999). Will the juvenile court system survive? *Annals of the American Academy of Political and Social Science, 564*, 8–184.

Schwartz, I. M., Weiner, N. A., & Enosh, G. (1998). Nine lives and then some: Why the juvenile court will not roll over and die. *Wake Forest Law Review, 33*, 533–552.

Scott, E. S. (2000). Criminal responsibility in adolescence: Lessons from developmental psychology. In T. Grisso & R. G. Schwartz (Eds.), *Youth on trial: A developmental perspective on juvenile justice* (pp. 291–324). Chicago: University of Chicago Press.

Sealock, M. D., Gottfredson, D. C., & Gallagher, C. (1997). Drug treatment for juvenile offenders: Some good and bad news. *Journal of Research in Crime and Delinquency, 34*, 210–236.

Shaffer, J. N., & Ruback, R. B. (2002). Violent victimization as a risk factor for violent offending among juveniles.

Juvenile Justice Bulletin. Washington, DC: U.S. Department of Justice, Office of Juvenile Justice and Delinquency Prevention.

Shannon, L. W. (1968). *Juvenile delinquency in Madison and Racine.* Iowa City: University of Iowa.

Shannon, L. W. (1988). *Criminal career continuity: Its social context.* New York: Human Sciences Press.

Shannon, L. W. (1991). *Changing patterns of delinquency and crime: A longitudinal study in Racine.* Boulder, CO: Westview.

Sharpe, D. (1997). Of apples and oranges, file drawers and garbage: Why validity issues in meta-analysis will not go away. *Clinical Psychology Review, 17,* 881–901.

Sherman, L. W., Farrington, D. P., MacKenzie, D. L., & Welsh, B. C. (2006). *Evidence based crime prevention* (Rev. ed.). New York: Routledge.

Shichor, D., & Sechrest, D. K. (Eds.). (1996). *Three strikes and you're out: Vengeance as public policy.* Thousand Oaks, CA: Sage.

Sickmund, M., Sladkey, T., & Kang, W. (2004). *Census of juveniles in residential placement databook.* Washington, DC: U.S. Department of Justice, Office of Juvenile Justice and Delinquency Prevention.

Simpson, D. D. (2002). A conceptual framework for transferring research to practice. *Journal of Substance Abuse Treatment, 22,* 171–182.

Skiba, R. J., & Knesting, K. (2001). Zero tolerance, zero evidence: An analysis of school disciplinary practice. In R. J. Skiba & G. G. Noam (Eds.), *Zero tolerance: Can suspension and expulsion keep schools safe? New directions for youth development* (pp. 17–43). San Francisco: Jossey-Bass.

Skiba, R. J., & Noam, G. G. (2001). *Zero tolerance: Can suspension and expulsion keep schools safe? New directions for youth development.* San Francisco: Jossey-Bass.

Skiba, R. J., & Peterson, R. (1999). The dark side of zero tolerance: Can punishment lead to safe schools? *Phi Delta Kappan, 80,* 372–376.

Skiba, R., Reynolds, C. R., Graham, S., Sheras, P., Conoley, C., & Garcia-Vazquez, E. (2006). *Are zero tolerance policies effective in the schools? An evidentiary review and recommendations.* Washington, DC: American Psychological Association.

Skogan, W. G., & Hartnett, S. M. (1997). *Community policing, Chicago style.* New York: Oxford University Press.

Skogan, W. G., Hartnett, S. M., Bump, N., & Dubois, J. (2008). *Evaluation of CeaseFire-Chicago: Executive summary.* Chicago: Northwestern University.

Skogan, W. G., & Steiner, L. (2004). *CAPS at ten: Community policing in Chicago.* Chicago: Illinois Criminal Justice Information Authority.

Skowyra, K., & Cocozza, J. J. (2006). *A blueprint for change: A comprehensive model for the identification and treatment of youth with mental health needs in contact with the juvenile justice system.* Delmar, NY: National Center for Mental Health and Juvenile Justice.

Smith, C. A., Krohn, M. D., Lizotte, A. J., McCluskey, C. P., Stouthamer-Loeber, M., & Weiher, A. W. (2000). The effect of early delinquency and substance use on precocious transitions to adulthood among adolescent males. In G. L. Fox & M. L. Benson (Eds.), *Families, crime and criminal justice* (Vol. 2, pp. 233–253). Amsterdam: JAI.

Smith, C. A., Lizotte, A. J., Thornberry, T. P., & Krohn, M. D. (1995). Resilient youth: Identifying factors that prevent high-risk youth from engaging in delinquency and drug use. In J. Hagan (Ed.), *Delinquency in the life course* (pp. 217–247). Greenwich, CT: JAI.

Smith, C. A., & Thornberry, T. P. (1995). The relationship between childhood maltreatment and adolescent involvement in delinquency. *Criminology, 33,* 451–477.

Smith, D. A., Visher, C. A., & Davidson, L. A. (1984). Equity and discretionary justice: The influence of race on police arrest decisions. *Journal of Criminal Law and Criminology, 75,* 234–249.

Smith, W. R., & Aloisi, M. F. (1999). Prediction of recidivism among "second timers" in the juvenile justice system: Efficiency in screening chronic offenders. *American Journal of Criminal Justice, 23,* 201–222.

Snyder, H. N. (1988). *Court careers of juvenile offenders.* Washington, DC: Office of Juvenile Justice and Delinquency Prevention.

Snyder, H. N. (1998). Serious, violent, and chronic juvenile offenders: An assessment of the extent of and trends in officially recognized serious criminal behavior in a delinquent population. In R. Loeber & D. P. Farrington (Eds.), *Serious and violent juvenile offenders: Risk factors and successful interventions* (pp. 428–444). Thousand Oaks, CA: Sage.

Snyder, H. N. (2000). Juvenile arrests 1999. *Juvenile Justice Bulletin.* Washington, DC: Office of Juvenile Justice and Delinquency Prevention.

Snyder, H. N. (2001). Epidemiology of official offending. In R. Loeber & D. P. Farrington (Eds.), *Child delinquents: Development, intervention, and service needs* (pp. 25–46). Thousand Oaks, CA: Sage.

Snyder, H. N. (2006). Juvenile arrests 2004. *Juvenile Justice Bulletin.* Washington, DC: U.S. Department of Justice, Office of Juvenile Justice and Delinquency Prevention.

Snyder, H. N., & Sickmund, M. (1995). *Juvenile offenders and victims: A national report.* Washington, DC: Office of Juvenile Justice and Delinquency Prevention.

Snyder, H. N., & Sickmund, M. (1999). *Juvenile offenders and victims: 1999 national report.* Washington, DC: Office of Juvenile Justice and Delinquency Prevention.

Snyder, H. N., & Sickmund, M. (2000). Challenging the myths. *Juvenile Justice Bulletin,* 1999 National Report Series. Washington, DC: Office of Juvenile Justice and Delinquency Prevention.

Snyder, H. N., & Sickmund, M. (2006). *Juvenile offenders and victims: 2006 national report.* Washington, DC: Office of Juvenile Justice and Delinquency Prevention.

Snyder, H. N., Sickmund, M., & Poe-Yamagata, E. (1996). *Juvenile offenders and victims: 1996 update on violence.* Washington, DC: Office of Juvenile Justice and Delinquency Prevention.

Snyder, H. N., & Swahn, M. H. (2004). Juvenile suicides: 1981–1998. *Youth Violence Research Bulletin.* Washington, DC: U.S. Department of Justice, Office of Juvenile Justice and Delinquency Prevention.

Soler, M. (2001). *Public opinion on youth, crime, and race: A guide for advocates.* Washington, DC: Building Blocks for Youth. Retrieved January 16, 2002, from http://www.buildingblocksforyouth.org/advocacyguide.html

Solis, A., Schwartz, W., & Hinton, T. (2003). *Gang Resistance Is Paramount (GRIP) program evaluation: Final report October 1, 2003.* Los Angeles: University of Southern California, USC Center for Economic Development.

Solomon, A. L., Kachnowski, V., & Bahati, A. (2005). *Does parole work? Analyzing the impact of postprison supervision on rearrest outcomes.* Washington, DC: The Urban Institute.

Song, D. H., Naude, G. P., Gilmore, D. A., & Mongard, F. (1996). Gang warfare: The medical repercussions. *Journal of Trauma, 40,* 810–815.

Spergel, I. A. (1995). *The youth gang problem.* New York: Oxford University Press.

Spergel, I. A. (2007). *Reducing youth gang violence: The Little Village Gang Project in Chicago.* Lanham, MD: AltaMira.

Spergel, I. A., & Curry, G. D. (1990). Strategies and perceived agency effectiveness in dealing with the youth gang problem. In C. R. Huff (Ed.), *Gangs in America* (pp. 288–309). Newbury Park, CA: Sage.

Spergel, I. A., & Curry, G. D. (1993). The National Youth Gang Survey: A research and development process. In A. Goldstein & C. R. Huff (Eds.), *The gang intervention handbook* (pp. 359–400). Champaign, IL: Research Press.

Spergel, I. A., Wa, K. M., & Sosa, R. V. (2006). The comprehensive, community-wide, gang program model: Success and failure. In J. F. Short & L. A. Hughes (Eds.), *Studying youth gangs* (pp. 203–224). Lanham, MD: AltaMira.

Spohn, C., Gruhl, J., & Welch, S. (1987). The impact of the ethnicity and gender of defendants on the decision to reject or dismiss felony charges. *Criminology, 25,* 175–191.

Spohn, C., & Holleran, D. (2002). The effect of imprisonment on recidivism rates of felony offenders: A focus on drug offenders. *Criminology, 40,* 329–357.

Stahl, A. L. (2001). *Delinquency cases in juvenile court, 1998.* Fact Sheet #2001-31. Washington, DC: U.S. Department of Justice, Office of Juvenile Justice and Delinquency Prevention.

Stahl, A. L., Puzzanchera, C., Livsey, S., Sladky, A., Finnegan, T. A., Tierney, N., et al. (2007). *Juvenile court statistics: 2003–2004.* Pittsburgh: National Center for Juvenile Justice.

Stanfield, R. (2000). *Pathways to juvenile detention reform: Overview. The JDAI story: Building a better detention system.* Baltimore, MD: Annie E. Casey Foundation.

Starbuck, D., Howell, J. C., & Lindquist, D. J. (2001). Hybrid and other modern gangs *Juvenile Justice Bulletin,* Youth Gang Series. Washington, DC: Office of Juvenile Justice and Delinquency Prevention.

Stattin, H., & Magnusson, D. (1991). Stability and change in criminal behaviour up to age 30. *British Journal of Criminology, 31,* 327–346.

Steffensmeier, D., Schwartz, J., Zhong, H., & Ackerman, J. (2005). An assessment of recent trends in girls' violence using diverse longitudinal sources: Is the gender gap closing? *Criminology, 43,* 355–405.

Steinberg, L. (2002). The juvenile psychopath: Fads, fiction, and facts. In National Institute of Justice, *Perspectives on crime and justice: 2000–2001 lecture series* (Vol. V). Washington, DC: U.S. Department of Justice, National Institute of Justice.

Steinberg, L., Chung, H. L., & Little, M. (2004). Reentry of young offenders from the justice system: A developmental perspective. *Youth Violence and Juvenile Justice, 2,* 21–38.

Steinhart, D. (2000). *Pathways to juvenile detention reform: Vol. 1. Planning for juvenile detention reforms.* Baltimore, MD: Annie E. Casey Foundation.

Stephens, R. L., Holden, E. W., & Hernandez, M. (2004). System-of-care practice review scores as predictors of behavioral symptomatology and functional impairment. *Journal of Child and Family Studies, 13,* 179–191.

Stouthamer-Loeber, M., & Loeber, R. (2002). Lost opportunities for intervention: Undetected markers for the development of serious juvenile delinquency. *Criminal Behavior and Mental Health, 12,* 69–82.

Stouthamer-Loeber, M., Loeber, R., Farrington, D. P., Zhang, Q., Van Kammen, W. B., & Maguin, E. (1993). The double edge of protective and risk factors for delinquency: Interactions and developmental patterns. *Development and Psychopathology, 5,* 683–701.

Stouthamer-Loeber, M., Loeber, R., Stallings, R., & Lacourse, E. (2008). Desistance from and persistence in offending. In R. Loeber, D. P. Farrington, M. Stouthamer-Loeber, & H. R. White (Eds.), *Violence and serious theft: Development and prediction from childhood to adulthood* (pp. 269–306). New York: Routledge.

Stouthamer-Loeber, M., Loeber, R., Van Kammen, W. B., & Zhang, Q. (1995). Uninterrupted delinquent careers: The timing of parental help-seeking and juvenile court contact. *Studies on Crime and Crime Prevention, 4,* 236–251.

Stouthamer-Loeber, M., Loeber, R., Wei, E., Farrington, D. P., & Wikstrom, P. H. (2002). Risk and promotive effects in the explanation of persistent serious delinquency in boys. *Journal of Consulting and Clinical Psychology, 70,* 111–123.

Stretesky, P. B., & Pogrebin, M. R. (2007). Gang-related gun violence: Socialization, identity, and self. *Journal of Contemporary Ethnography, 36,* 85–114.

Stroul, B. A., & Friedman, R. (1986). *A system of care for severely emotionally disturbed youth.* Washington, DC: Georgetown University, Child and Adolescent Service System Program Technical Assistance Center.

Styve, G. J., MacKenzie, D. L., & Gover, A. R. (2000). Perceived conditions of confinement: A national evaluation of juvenile boot camps and traditional facilities. *Law and Human Behavior, 24,* 297–308.

Tanenhaus, D. S. (2004). *Juvenile justice in the making.* New York: Oxford University Press.

Task Force on Community Preventive Services. (2007). Recommendation against policies facilitating the transfer of juveniles from juvenile to adult justice systems for the purpose of reducing violence. *American Journal of Preventive Medicine, 32*(4 Suppl. 1), 5–6.

Taylor, T. J. (2008). The boulevard ain't safe for your kids: Youth gang membership and violent victimization. *Journal of Contemporary Criminal Justice, 24*(2), 125–136.

Teplin, L. A., Abram, K. M., McClelland, G. M., Dulcan, M. K., & Washburn, J. J. (2006). Psychiatric disorders of youth in detention. *Juvenile Justice Bulletin.* Washington, DC: Office of Juvenile Justice and Delinquency Prevention.

Thaker, S., Steckler, A., Sanchez, V., Khatapoush, S., Rose, J., & Hallfors, D. D. (2007, July 16). Program characteristics and organizational factors affecting the implementation of a school-based indicated prevention program. *Health Education Research.*

Thompkins, D. E. (2000). School violence: Gangs and a culture of fear. *The Annals of the American Academy of Political and Social Science, 567,* 54–71.

Thornberry, T. P. (1998). Membership in youth gangs and involvement in serious and violent offending. In R. Loeber & D. P. Farrington (Eds.), *Serious and violent juvenile offenders: Risk factors and successful interventions* (pp. 147–166). Thousand Oaks, CA: Sage.

Thornberry, T. P. (2005). Explaining multiple patterns of offending across the life course and across generations. *The Annals of the American Academy of Political and Social Science, 602,* 156–195.

Thornberry, T. P., Huizinga, D., & Loeber, R. (1995). The prevention of serious delinquency and violence: Implications from the Program of Research on the Causes and Correlates of Delinquency. In J. C. Howell, B. Krisberg, J. D. Hawkins, & J. J. Wilson (Eds.), *A sourcebook: Serious, violent, and chronic juvenile offenders* (pp. 213–237). Thousand Oaks, CA: Sage.

Thornberry, T. P., Huizinga, D., & Loeber, R. (2004). The causes and correlates studies: Findings and policy implications. *Juvenile Justice, 10*(1), 3–19.

Thornberry, T. P., & Krohn, M. D. (2000). The self-report method for measuring delinquency and crime. In D. Duffee (Ed.), *Criminal justice 2000* (pp. 33–84). Washington, DC: U.S. Department of Justice, the National Institute of Justice.

Thornberry, T. P., & Krohn, M. D. (2001). The development of delinquency: An interactional perspective. In S. O. White (Ed.), *Handbook of youth and justice* (pp. 289–305). New York: Plenum.

Thornberry, T. P., & Krohn, M. D. (2003). *Taking stock of delinquency: An overview of findings from contemporary longitudinal studies.* New York: Kluwer Academic/ Plenum.

Thornberry, T. P., & Krohn, M. D. (2005). Applying interactional theory to the explanation of continuity and change in antisocial behavior. In D. P. Farrington (Ed.), *Integrated developmental and life-course theories of offending* (pp. 183–210). New Brunswick, NJ: Transaction.

Thornberry, T. P., Krohn, M. D., Lizotte, A. J., & Chard-Wierschem, D. (1993). The role of juvenile gangs in facilitating delinquent behavior. *Journal of Research in Crime and Delinquency, 30,* 55–87.

Thornberry, T. P., Krohn, M. D., Lizotte, A. J., Smith, C. A., & Tobin, K. (2003). *Gangs and delinquency in developmental perspective.* New York: Cambridge University Press.

Thornberry, T. P., Lizotte, A. J., Krohn, M. D., Farnworth, M., & Jang, S. J. (1994). Delinquent peers, beliefs, and delinquent behavior: A longitudinal test of interactional theory. *Criminology, 32,* 601–637.

Thornberry, T. P., Lizotte, A. J., Krohn, M. D., Smith, C. A., & Porter, P. K. (2003). Causes and consequences of delinquency: Findings from the Rochester Youth Development Study. In T. P. Thornberry & M. D. Krohn (Eds.), *Taking stock of delinquency: An overview of findings from contemporary longitudinal studies* (pp. 11–46). New York: Kluwer Academic/Plenum.

Thornberry, T. P., & Porter, P. K. (2001). Advantages of longitudinal research designs in studying gang behavior. In M. W. Klein, H.-J. Kerner, C. L. Maxson, & E. G. M. Weitekamp (Eds.), *The Eurogang paradox: Street gangs and youth groups in the U.S. and Europe* (pp. 59–78). Amsterdam: Kluwer.

Thornberry, T. P., Smith, C. A., Rivera, C., Huizinga, D., & Stouthamer-Loeber, M. (1999). Family disruption and delinquency. *Juvenile Justice Bulletin.* Washington, DC: U.S. Department of Justice, Office of Juvenile Justice and Delinquency Prevention.

Thornburgh, N. (2006, April 17). Dropout nation. *Time,* pp. 31–40.

Thrasher, F. M. (1927). *The gang: A study of 1,313 gangs in Chicago.* Chicago: University of Chicago Press.

Thrasher, F. M. (1936). The boys' club and juvenile delinquency. *American Journal of Sociology, 41,* 66–80.

Tiet, Q. Q., & Huizinga, D. (2002). Dimensions of the construct of resilience and adaptation among inner-city youth. *Journal of Adolescent Research, 17,* 260–276.

Tiet, Q. Q., Wasserman, G. A., Loeber, R., McReynolds, L. S., & Miller, L. S. (2001). Developmental and sex differences in types of conduct problems. *Journal of Child and Family Studies, 10,* 181–197.

Tita, G., Riley, K. J., & Greenwood, P. (2003). From Boston to Boyle Heights: The process and prospects of a "pulling levers" strategy in a Los Angeles barrio. In S. H. Decker (Ed.), *Policing gangs and youth violence* (pp. 102–130). Belmont, CA: Wadsworth/Thompson Learning.

Titus, J. J. (2005). Juvenile transfers as ritual sacrifice: Legally constructing the child scapegoat. *Youth Violence and Juvenile Justice, 3,* 116–132.

Toch, H. (2007). Sequestering gang members, burning witches, and subverting due process. *Criminal Justice and Behavior, 32,* 274–288.

Tolan, P. H., & Gorman-Smith, D. (1998). Development of serious and violent offending careers. In R. Loeber & D. P. Farrington (Eds.), *Serious and violent juvenile offenders: Risk factors and successful interventions* (pp. 68–85). Thousand Oaks, CA: Sage.

Tolan, P. H., Gorman-Smith, D., & Loeber, R. (2000). Developmental timing of onsets of disruptive behaviors and later delinquency of inner-city youth. *Journal of Child and Family Studies, 9,* 203–330.

Tonry, M. (1994a). *Malign neglect: Race, crime, and punishment in America.* New York: Oxford University Press.

Tonry, M. (1994b). Racial politics, racial disparities, and the war on crime. *Crime & Delinquency, 40,* 475–494.

Tonry, M. (1999a). Community penalties in the United States. *European Journal on Criminal Policy and Research, 7*(1), 5–22.

Tonry, M. (1999b). *The fragmentation of sentencing and corrections in America: Sentencing and corrections issues for the 21st century* (Research in Brief, Papers from the Executive Sessions on Sentencing and Corrections). Washington, DC: National Institute of Justice.

Tonry, M. (1999c). Parochialism in U.S. sentencing policy. *Crime & Delinquency, 45,* 48–65.

Tonry, M. (2007). Treating juveniles as adult criminals: An iatrogenic violence prevention strategy if ever there was one. *American Journal of Preventive Medicine, 32*(4 Suppl. 1), 3–4.

Torbet, P. M. (1999). *Holding juvenile offenders accountable: Programming needs of juvenile probation departments.* Pittsburgh: National Center for Juvenile Justice.

Torbet, P. M., & Szymanski, L. (1998). State legislative responses to violent juvenile crime: 1996–1997 update. *Juvenile Justice Bulletin.* Washington, DC: Office of Juvenile Justice and Delinquency Prevention.

Tracy, P. E., & Kempf-Leonard, K. (1998). Sanctioning serious juvenile offenders: A review of alternative models. In W. Laufer & F. Adler (Eds.), *Advances in criminological theory* (pp. 135–171). New Brunswick, NJ: Transaction.

Travis, J. (2005). *But they all come back: Facing the problem of prisoner reentry.* Washington, DC: The Urban Institute Press.

Travis, J., & Petersilia, J. (2001). Reentry reconsidered: A new look at an old question. *Crime & Delinquency, 47,* 291–313.

Tremblay, R. E. (2003). Why socialization fails: The case of chronic physical aggression. In B. B. Lahey, T. E. Moffitt, & A. Caspi (Eds.), *Causes of conduct disorder and juvenile delinquency* (pp. 182–224). New York: Guilford.

Tremblay, R. E., Masse, L., Pagani, L., & Vitaro, F. (1996). From childhood physical aggression to adolescent maladjustment: The Montreal Prevention Experiment. In R. D. Peters & R. J. McMahon (Eds.), *Preventing childhood disorders, substance abuse, and delinquency* (pp. 268–298). Thousand Oaks, CA: Sage.

Triplett, W. (2004). Gang crisis. *The Congressional Quarterly Researcher, 14*(18), 421–444.

Trulson, C. R., Marquart, J. W., Mullings, J. L., & Caeti, T. J. (2007). In between adolescence and adulthood: Recidivism outcomes for a cohort of state delinquents. *Youth Violence and Juvenile Justice, 3,* 355–377.

Trulson, C., Triplett, R., & Snell, C. (2001). Social control in a school setting: Evaluating a school-based boot camp. *Crime and Delinquency, 47*(4), 573–609.

Turner, S., Schroeder, A., Lane, J., & Petersilia, J. R. (2001). *Evaluation of the South Oxnard Challenge Project, 1997–2001.* Santa Monica, CA: RAND.

Tyler, J. L., Ziedenberg, J., & Lotke, E. (2006). *Cost effective corrections: The fiscal architecture of rational juvenile justice systems.* Washington, DC: The Justice Policy Institute.

Tyler, K. A., & Bersani, B. E. (2008). A longitudinal study of early adolescent precursors to running away. *Journal of Early Adolescence, 28,* 230–251.

Tyler, K. A., Hoyt, D. R., & Whitbeck, L. B. (2000). The effects of early sexual abuse on later sexual victimization among female homeless and runaway adolescents. *Journal of Interpersonal Violence, 15,* 235–250.

Umbreit, M. S., Coates, R., & Vos, B. (2002). *The impact of restorative justice conferencing: A review of 63 empirical studies in 5 countries.* St. Paul, MN: Center for Restorative Justice & Peacemaking.

U.S. Department of Education. (2003). *Office of Civil Rights elementary and secondary survey: 2000.* Washington, DC: U.S. Department of Education, Office of Civil Rights.

U.S. Department of Health and Human Services. (1999). *Mental health: A report of the surgeon general.* Rockville, MD: Author.

U.S. Department of Health and Human Services. (2001). *Youth violence: A report of the surgeon general.* Rockville, MD: Author.

U.S. Department of Justice. (2007). *Department of Justice activities under the Civil Rights of Institutionalized Persons Act: Fiscal year 2006.* Washington, DC: Office of the Attorney General, U.S. Department of Justice.

U.S. General Accounting Office. (2002). *Gun control: Opportunities to close loopholes in the national instant criminal background check system.* Washington, DC: U.S. Government Printing Office.

U.S. General Accounting Office. (2005). *Gun control and terrorism: FBI could better manage firearm-related background checks involving terrorist watch list records.* Washington, DC: U.S. Government Printing Office.

Uviller, H. R. (1999). *The tilted playing field: Is criminal justice unfair?* New Haven, CT: Yale University Press.

Valdez, A. (2000). *Mara Salvatrucha: A South American import.* Yaphank, NY: National Alliance of Gang Investigators' Associations. http://www.nagia.org/Gang%20Articles/Mara%20Salvatrucha.htm

Valdez, A. (2007). *Gangs: A guide to understanding street gangs* (5th ed.). San Clemente, CA: LawTech.

Vaughn, J. (1989). A survey of juvenile electronic monitoring and home confinement programs. *Juvenile and Family Court Journal, 40*(4), 1–36.

Venkatesh, S. A. (1996). The gang and the community. In C. R. Huff (Ed.), *Gangs in America* (2nd ed., pp. 241–256). Thousand Oaks, CA: Sage.

Veneziano, C., & Veneziano, L. (2002). Adolescent sex offenders: A review of the literature. *Trauma, Violence, and Abuse, 3,* 247–260.

Vigil, J. D. (2002). *A rainbow of gangs: Street cultures in the mega-city.* Austin: University of Texas Press.

Villalva, M. (2000, February 8). Parental survey reveals "clear" fear: Violence against, or by, their child. *USA Today,* pp. 8D, 10D.

Villarruel, F. A., & Walker, N. E. (2002). *Donde esta la justicia? A call to action on behalf of Latino and Latina youth in the U.S. justice system.* Washington, DC: Building Blocks for Youth.

Violence Policy Center. (2007). *Drive-by America.* Washington, DC: Author.

Violent and irrational—and that's just the policy. (1996, June 8). *Economist,* pp. 23–25.

Virginia Department of Juvenile Justice. (2005). Juvenile recidivism in Virginia. *Department of Juvenile Justice Research Quarterly, III,* 1–12.

Waber, D. P., De Moor, C., Forbes, P. W., Almli, C. R., Botteron, K. N., Leonard, G., et al. (2007). The NIH MRI study of normal brain development: Performance of a population based sample of healthy children aged 6 to 18 years on a neuropsychological battery. *Journal of the International Neuropsychological Society, 13,* 1–18.

Warr, M. (2002). *Companions in crime: The social aspects of criminal conduct.* New York: Cambridge University Press.

Washington State Institute for Public Policy. (2002). *Washington State's implementation of aggression replacement training for juvenile offenders: Preliminary findings.* Olympia: Author.

Washington State Institute for Public Policy. (2004). *Washington State's family integrated transitions program for juvenile offenders: Outcome evaluation and benefit-cost analysis.* Olympia: Author.

Wasserman, G. A., Ko, S. J., & Jensen, P. (2002). *Guidelines for child and adolescent mental health referral.* New York: Columbia University Center for the Promotion of Mental Health in Juvenile Justice. Retrieved May 6, 2002, from http://www.promotementalhealth.org

Wasserman, G. A., Ko, S. J., & McReynolds, L. S. (2004). Assessing the mental health status of youth in juvenile justice settings. *Juvenile Justice Bulletin.* Washington, DC: U.S. Department of Justice, Office of Juvenile Justice and Delinquency Prevention.

Wasserman, G. A., McReynolds, L. S., Lucas, C., Fisher, P., & Santos, L. (2002). The Voice DISC-IV with incarcerated youth: Prevalence of disorder. *Journal of the American Academy of Child and Adolescent Psychiatry, 41,* 314–321.

Wasserman, G. A., & Seracini, A. M. (2001). Risk factors and interventions. In R. Loeber & D. P. Farrington (Eds.), *Child delinquents: Development, intervention, and service needs* (pp. 165–190). Thousand Oaks, CA: Sage.

Weisel, D. L. (2002). The evolution of street gangs: An examination of form and variation. In W. Reed & S. Decker (Eds.), *Responding to gangs: Evaluation and research* (pp. 25–65). Washington, DC: National Institute of Justice.

Weisel, D. L. (2004). *Graffiti. Problem-oriented guides for police.* Problem-Specific Guides Series. Guide No. 9. Washington, DC: Office of Community Oriented Policing Services.

Weisel, D. L., & Howell, J. C. (2007). *Comprehensive gang assessment: A report to the Durham Police Department and Durham County Sheriff's Office.* Durham, NC: Durham Police Department.

Weiss, B., Caron, A., Ball, S., Tapp, J., Johnson, M., & Weisz, J. R. (2005). Iatrogenic effects of group treatment for antisocial youth. *Journal of Consulting and Clinical Psychology, 73,* 1036–1044.

Weisz, J., Sandler, I., Durlak, J., & Anton, B. (2005). Promoting and protecting youth mental health through evidence-based prevention and treatment. *American Psychologist, 60,* 628–648.

Weitekamp, E. G. M. (2001). Gangs in Europe: Assessments at the millennium. In M. W. Klein, H.-J. Kerner, C. L. Maxson, & E. G. M. Weitekamp (Eds.), *The Eurogang paradox: Street gangs and youth groups in the U.S. and Europe* (pp. 309–324). Amsterdam: Kluwer.

Weitekamp, E. G. M., Kerner, H.-J., Schindler, V., & Schubert, A. (1995). On the "dangerousness" of chronic/habitual offenders: A re-analysis of the 1945 Philadelphia birth cohort data. *Studies on Crime and Crime Prevention, 4,* 159–175.

Weithorn, L. A. (1988). Mental hospitalization of troublesome youth: An analysis of skyrocketing admission rates. *Stanford Law Review, 40,* 773–838.

Wellford, C., Pepper, J. V., & Petrie, C. (2005). *Firearms and violence: A critical review.* Washington, DC: National Academies Press.

Welsh, B. C., & Farrington, D. P. (2006). Evidence-based crime prevention. In B. C. Welsh & D. P. Farrington (Eds.), *Preventing crime: What works for children, offenders, victims, and places* (pp. 1–17). Dordrecht, The Netherlands: Springer.

Welsh, B. C., & Farrington, D. P. (2007). Save children from a life of crime. *Criminology and Public Policy, 6,* 871–880.

Weston, D. A. (1969). Fines, imprisonment, and the poor. Thirty dollars or thirty days. *California Law Review, 57,* 778–821.

Whitbeck, L. B., Hoyt, D. R., & Yoder, K. A. (1999). A risk-amplification model of victimization and depressive symptoms among runaway and homeless adolescents. *American Journal of Community Psychology, 27,* 273–296.

Widom, C. S., & Maxfield, M. G. (2001). *An update on the "cycle of violence"* (Research in Brief). Washington, DC: National Institute of Justice.

Wiebe, D. J., Meeker, J. W., & Vila, B. (1999). *Hourly trends of gang crime incidents, 1995–1998.* Irvine: University of California, Focused Research Group on Gangs.

Wiebush, R. G. (2000). *Risk assessment and classification for serious, violent, and chronic juvenile offenders.* Madison, WI: National Council on Crime and Delinquency.

Wiebush, R. G. (Ed.). (2002). *Graduated sanctions for juvenile offenders: A program model and planning guide.* Oakland, CA: National Council on Crime and Delinquency and National Council of Juvenile and Family Court Judges.

Wiebush, R. G., Baird, C., Krisberg, B., & Onek, D. (1995). Risk assessment and classification for serious, violent, and chronic juvenile offenders. In J. C. Howell, B. Krisberg, J. D. Hawkins, & J. J. Wilson (Eds.), *A sourcebook: Serious, violent, and chronic juvenile offenders* (pp. 171–212). Thousand Oaks, CA: Sage.

Wiebush, R. G., Johnson, K., & Wagner, D. (1997). *Development of an empirically-based risk assessment instrument and placement recommendation matrix for the Maryland Department of Juvenile Justice.* Madison, WI: National Council on Crime and Delinquency.

Wiebush, R. G., Wagner, D., & Erlich, J. (1999). *Development of an empirically-based assessment instrument for the Virginia Department of Juvenile Justice.* Madison, WI: National Council on Crime and Delinquency.

Wiebush, R. G., Wagner, D., McNulty, B., Wang, Y., & Le, T. N. (2005). *Implementation and outcome of evaluation of the intensive aftercare program. Final Report.* Washington, DC: U.S. Department of Justice, Office of Juvenile Justice and Delinquency Prevention.

Wiebush, R. G., Wagner, D., Prestine, R., & Baird, C. (1992). *The impact of electronic monitoring on juvenile recidivism: Results of an experimental test in the Cuyahoga County Juvenile Court.* Madison, WI: National Council on Crime and Delinquency.

Williams, K., Curry, G. D., & Cohen, M. (2002). Gang prevention programs for female adolescents: An evaluation. In W. L. Reed & S. H. Decker (Eds.), *Responding to gangs: Evaluation and research* (pp. 225–263). Washington, DC: U.S. Department of Justice, National Institute of Justice.

Willing, R., & Fields, G. (1999, December 20). Geography of the death penalty. *USA Today*, pp. 1A, 6A.

Wilson, D. B., Gottfredson, D. C., & Najaka, S. S. (2001). School-based prevention of problem behaviors: A meta-analysis. *Journal of Quantitative Criminology, 17,* 247–272.

Wilson, D. B., MacKenzie, D. L., & Mitchell, F. N. (2005). *Effects of correctional boot camps on offending.* A Campbell Collaboration systematic review, available at http://www.campbellcollaboration.org/frontend2.asp?ID=34

Wilson, J. J. (2000, July 14). Remarks made at BARJ Special Emphasis States Roundtable, San Diego, CA.

Wilson, J. J., & Howell, J. C. (1993). *A comprehensive strategy for serious, violent and chronic juvenile offenders.* Washington, DC: Office of Juvenile Justice and Delinquency Prevention.

Wilson, J. Q. (1995). Crime and public policy. In J. Q. Wilson & J. Petersilia (Eds.), *Crime* (pp. 489–507). San Francisco: Institute for Contemporary Studies.

Wilson, J. Q., & Kelling, G. L. (1982, March). Broken windows. *Atlantic Monthly, 249,* 29–38.

Wilson, S. J., & Lipsey, M. W. (2000). Wilderness challenge programs for delinquent youth: A meta-analysis of outcome evaluations. *Evaluation and Program Planning, 23,* 1–12.

Wilson, S. J., & Lipsey, M. W. (2007). School-based interventions for aggressive and disruptive behavior: Update of a meta-analysis. *American Journal of Preventive Medicine, 33*(Supplement), S130–S143.

Wilson, S. J., Lipsey, M. W., & Derzon, J. H. (2003). The effects of school-based intervention programs on aggressive behavior: A meta-analysis. *Journal of Consulting and Clinical Psychology, 71,* 136–149.

Wilson, S. J., Lipsey, M. W., & Soydan, H. (2003). Are mainstream programs for juvenile delinquency less effective with minority youth than majority youth? A meta-analysis of outcomes. *Research on Social Work Practice, 13,* 3–20.

Wolfgang, M. E., Figlio, R. M., & Sellin, T. (1972). *Delinquency in a birth cohort.* Chicago: University of Chicago Press.

Woodward, L. J., & Fergusson, D. M. (2000). Childhood and adolescent predictors of physical assault: A prospective longitudinal study. *Criminology, 38,* 233–262.

Wooldredge, J. D. (1988). Differentiating the effects of juvenile court sentences on eliminating recidivism. *Journal of Research in Crime and Delinquency, 25,* 264–300.

Wright, J. D. (2006). The constitutional failure of gang databases. *Stanford Journal of Civil Rights and Civil Liberties, 2,* 115–142.

Wright, B. R. E., Caspi, A., Moffitt, T. E., & Paternoster, R. (2004). Does the perceived risk of punishment deter criminally prone individuals? Rational choice, self-control, and crime. *Journal of Research in Crime and Delinquency, 41,* 180–213.

Wu, B. (2000). Determinants of public opinion toward juvenile waiver decisions. *Juvenile and Family Court Journal, 51*(1), 9–20.

Wyrick, P. (2006). Gang prevention: How to make the "front end" of your anti-gang effort work. *United States Attorneys' Bulletin, 54,* 52–60.

Wyrick, P. A., & Howell, J. C. (2004). Strategic risk-based response to youth gangs. *Juvenile Justice, 10,* 20–29.

Young, D., Moline, K., Farrell, J., & Bierie, D. (2006). Best implementation practices: Disseminating new assessment technologies in a juvenile justice agency. *Crime and Delinquency, 52,* 135–158.

Zaczor, B. (2002, September 8). Boys' case revives Fla. trial law debate. *News and Observer* (Raleigh, NC), p. 7A.

Zahn, M. (2007). *Girls study group.* Presentation at the 12th National Workshop on Adult and Juvenile Female Offenders, Baltimore, MD, October 23.

Zatz, M. S. (1987). Chicano youth gangs and crime: The creation of moral panic. *Contemporary Crises, 11,* 129–158.

Zavlek, S. (2005). Planning community-based facilities for violent juvenile offenders as part of a system of graduated sanctions. *Juvenile Justice Bulletin.* Washington, DC: U.S. Department of Justice, Office of Juvenile Justice and Delinquency Prevention.

Zelman, M. (2006). Criminal justice system reform and wrongful conviction: A research agenda. *Criminal Justice Policy Review, 17,* 468–492.

Zimmerman, C. R., Hendrix, G., Moeser, J., & Roush, D. W. (2004). *Desktop guide to reentry for juvenile confinement facilities.* Washington, DC: U.S. Department of Justice, Office of Juvenile Justice and Delinquency Prevention.

Zimring, F. E. (1996, August 19). Crying wolf over teen demons. *Los Angeles Times*, p. B5.

Zimring, F. E. (1998a). *American youth violence*. New York: Oxford University Press.

Zimring, F. E. (1998b). Toward a jurisprudence of youth violence. In M. Tonry & M. H. Moore (Eds.), *Youth violence* (pp. 477–501). Chicago: University of Chicago Press.

Zimring, F. E. (1999). The executioner's dissonant song: On capital punishment and American legal values. In A. Sarat (Ed.), *The killing state: Capital punishment in law, politics, and culture* (pp. 137–147). New York: Oxford University Press.

Zimring, F. E. (2000). The punitive necessity of waiver. In J. Fagan & F. E. Zimring (Eds.), *The changing borders of juvenile justice: Transfer of adolescents to the criminal court* (pp. 207–226). Chicago: University of Chicago.

Zimring, F. E. (2002). The common thread: Diversion in the jurisprudence of juvenile courts. In M. K. Rosenheim, F. E. Zimring, D. S. Tanenhaus, & B. Dohrn (Eds.), *A century of juvenile justice* (pp. 142–157). Chicago: University of Chicago Press.

Zimring, F. E. (2007). Protect individual punishment decisions from mandatory penalties. *Criminology and Public Policy*, 6, 881–886.

Zimring, F. E., & Fagan, J. (2000). The search for causes in an era of crime declines: Some lessons from the study of New York City homicide. *Crime & Delinquency*, 46, 446–456.

Zimring, F. E., & Hawkins, G. J. (1973). *Deterrence*. Chicago: University of Chicago Press.

Index

About the Author

James C. (Buddy) Howell, PhD, worked at the federal Office of Juvenile Justice and Delinquency Prevention (OJJDP) in the U.S. Department of Justice for 21 years, mostly as director of research and program development. He was also director of the National Institute of Juvenile Justice and Delinquency Prevention and deputy administrator of OJJDP. He currently is senior research associate with the National Youth Gang Center in Tallahassee, Florida, and special advisor to the Life History Research Program at the University of Pittsburgh. He is an associate editor of the journal *Youth Violence and Juvenile Justice,* author of the book *Juvenile Justice and Youth Violence* (Sage), and lead editor of *A Sourcebook: Serious, Violent, and Chronic Juvenile Offenders* (Sage). Some of his more than 70 published works have appeared in *Crime & Delinquency, Criminology,* the *Journal of Research in Crime and Delinquency,* and *Youth Violence and Juvenile Justice.* Dr. Howell is very active in helping states and localities reform their juvenile justice systems and use evidence-based programs and in working with these entities to address youth gang problems in a balanced approach.